In Jesus' Name

In Jesus' Name

Evangelicals and Military Chaplaincy

JOHN D. LAING

RESOURCE *Publications* · Eugene, Oregon

IN JESUS' NAME
Evangelicals and Military Chaplaincy

Resource Publications
An Imprint of Wipf and Stock Publishers
199 W. 8th Ave., Suite 3
Eugene, OR 97401
www.wipfandstock.com

ISBN 13: 978-1-60608-798-5

Manufactured in the U.S.A.

To the Lord Jesus Christ
and to
the men and women
who have sacrificed
for the freedom to worship

Contents

Preface

INTEREST IN NON-TRADITIONAL MINISTRY appears to be on the rise. A growing numbers of seminaries and divinity schools are offering courses of study in chaplaincy ministry, and growing numbers of believers are leaving traditional church settings for less traditional places and formats for worship. As a professor of theology and philosophy who happens to be a military chaplain, I never thought I would write a book of this sort. I envisioned writing texts on Divine Providence, Christology, or God and Time, but circumstances conspired to make me set those things aside for a time, and think more deeply about the issues addressed in this book. I was asked by some students and my Dean to teach a course in chaplaincy ministry. While looking for textbooks, I discovered that most books on chaplaincy are of three forms: historical/biographical, practical ministry, or devotional. That is, the books I found were historical accounts of chaplains involved in particular wars or armies, or were biographies of specific chaplains, or they were sort-of "how-to" books on chaplaincy, or they were reflections by chaplains serving in war zones. Most included very little theological reflection on the issues chaplains face, and those that did were almost never written from an evangelical point of view. Thus, I found that, while the different kinds of books were informative and helpful for an aspect of the course I was asked to teach, they did not address all of the issues that I felt are most important for would-be chaplains to think about in the context of the seminary classroom.

In addition to this deficiency, I also discovered that many Christian laypersons with a heart for the military are interested in how military chaplaincy works. Specifically, I became aware of the fact that many persons in the churches are concerned that chaplains are not, or cannot, preach the Gospel. I wanted to address this important issue, for I believe that the support of persons in the local church is imperative for the success of chaplaincy ministry. I also think that addressing this issue can help alleviate some concerns of those who have loved ones serving in the military, for they can rest assured that chaplains can (and often do) provide the kind of spiritual care they desire.

Similarly, I felt that this book could serve as an aid to those already serving in the military. It can be useful to chaplains in a variety of ways. For non-evangelical chaplains, it can help in their understanding of those evangelicals with whom they work, both within the chaplaincy and within the units they serve. For evangelical chaplains, it can help in their own working through the issues related to this important ministry to which God has called them. For line officers who are current or future commanders, it can help in their understanding of the needs and commitments of evangelical Christians within the unit and who may serve their commands as chaplains.

One difficulty in writing a book of this sort is space constraints. Many of the chapters could be books in themselves and so, some readers may find the treatment of some material to be too brief, vague, cursory, or generalized. For that, I can only apologize. I have, however, attempted to introduce the reader to the most relevant topics associated with chaplaincy in the twenty-first century, and to point him to further reading, if he so desires.

1

"For God and Country"

The Role of the Military Chaplain

The blessing and protection of Heaven are at all times necessary, but especially so in times of public distress and danger.

—General George Washington, requesting a chaplain for each regiment in the Continental Army

INTRODUCTION

The U. S. Army uses several slogans to describe the nature of the work and ministry of the Army chaplain. Perhaps the best-known is the official motto of the Army chaplaincy, *Pro Deo et Patria*, the Latin of "For God and Country." These four words are meant to summarize the dual role of the chaplain as one who ministers in the context of service to country. It has often been pointed out that "God" comes first in the slogan, and that this indicates our primary mission and loyalty (i.e., to God), though unfortunately this is not always the case with all chaplains. Nevertheless, the point is meant to embody the values and goals of the military chaplaincy as a whole—to serve God by ministering to those who dedicate their lives to protect the freedoms and interests of our country.

Chaplaincy is a unique form of ministry. When seminary students or interested parishioners have asked me about my duties or functions as a military chaplain, I have often playfully described it as part pastor, part

psychologist, part traveling evangelist, part teacher/professor, part cheer-
leader, part political strategist/advisor, and part marriage counselor. This,
of course, is something of an overstatement as there are competencies in
the aforementioned list in which few chaplains have expertise (e.g., most
chaplains engage in pastoral counseling, but not psychotherapy), but it
does hint at the multi-faceted work involved in the chaplain ministry. In
this way, then, it is to be distinguished from pastoral ministry in a local
church. As diverse as chaplaincy work can be, even within a particular
form of chaplaincy, perhaps its most unique aspect has to do with the
context within which that work is conducted. That is, while chaplains
certainly are first and foremost ministers or clergy, they nevertheless
serve secular institutions with secular purposes.

One of the issues that has proven somewhat controversial in my own
denomination in recent years has been the question of the relationship
between chaplain ministry and pastoral ministry. The North American
Mission Board, the endorsing agency of the Southern Baptist Convention's
chaplains, has determined that it will no longer endorse women to chaplain ministry in the military, as this has been deemed too close to pastoral
ministry about which the denomination as a whole has agreed should
only be conducted by men.[1] As noted above, chaplaincy certainly involves
work that is similar at times to that of the local pastor, yet it is also clearly
distinct at times. In setting forth the difference between chaplains and
local pastors, Paget and McCormack note the unique locus of authority
and the unique clients of chaplains:

> Community clergy usually minister to a group of people who
> have like or similar religious beliefs and who share many common
> cultural identities—language, geographic location, socioeconomic
> status, or ethnic identity. Chaplains, on the other hand, usually
> minister to a group of people of many different religious beliefs
> or no beliefs at all. These people usually represent diverse cultural
> identities, including those of education, profession, and political
> persuasion. Community clergy are given authority by a congrega-

1. See, for example, the Baptist Faith and Message (2000) statement on The Church.
The North American Mission Board, the endorsing agency of the SBC for chaplains, has
actually determined that the exclusion will be based on ordination. If a particular chaplaincy position requires ordination, then it will not endorse a woman to that position.
If it does not require ordination (and the woman is not ordained), then it may endorse
her for that position. While such a rule is not perfect, it serves to fulfill the intent of the
prohibition against women serving in pastoral positions.

tion or ecclesiastical body, whereas chaplains are given authority
by the institution that *employs* them in addition to the ecclesiastical
body that *endorses* them. And community clergy usually minister
in a house of worship while the chaplain usually ministers in the
marketplace—venues not usually considered 'religious.'[2]

While there surely are differences between parish ministry and
chaplaincy, and while it must be admitted that the Bible refers primarily
to pastors when it discusses clerical qualifications and responsibilities,
there is nevertheless a biblical basis for chaplain ministry. It is to this that
we now turn.

BIBLICAL BASIS FOR CHAPLAINCY

It would be the height of hubris to suggest that one could, even in a book-
length treatment, offer a complete biblical basis for chaplaincy. However,
there are some themes and specific texts found in the Bible which are
particularly relevant for addressing those issues unique to chaplaincy
ministry. Taking ministry outside the walls of the church is certainly
biblical—many prison and hospital chaplains have heard the call of God
on their lives in the words of Jesus regarding the separation of the sheep
and the goats and the rewards for those who took ministry to the needy
(with whom Jesus personally identified): "For I was hungry and you gave
Me something to eat; I was thirsty and you gave Me something to drink; I
was a stranger and you took Me in; I was naked and you clothed Me; I was
sick and you took care of Me; I was in prison and you visited Me" (Matt
25:35–36, HCSB). The guiding principle for chaplains here is the two-fold
belief that what we do for others we do for Christ, and that we must be
proactive in taking God's Word, grace and love to the very persons we
may be inclined to overlook or who may not come (for whatever reason)
to a local church worship service.

In addition to this teaching, though, is the very ministry of Christ
himself, which (at least in the gospel accounts) was characterized by his
active seeking out of persons in need of ministry. Even though Jesus spoke
in the synagogues on occasion (Matt 4:23; Luke 13:10), he primarily conducted his ministry out among the people, preaching on hillsides (Matt
5:1f.) and plains (Luke 6:17f.); from a boat on the Sea (Luke 5:1f.) and
in the Judean wilderness. He went "into the trenches" with his ministry,

2. Paget and McCormack, *Work of the Chaplain*, iv.

choosing to focus on those who might not regularly attend synagogue and read Torah, even drawing criticism/censure for eating with tax collectors and sinners (Mark 2:16; cf. Luke 5:29–30; Matt 9:10–11) and allowing women of questionable character to touch him (Luke 7:39). As Jesus noted, he came not to call the righteous, but the unrighteous (Mark 2:17; cf. Matt 9:12; Luke 5:31), and he focused his time and energy in that effort. So Jesus' teaching and example point to a principle of taking ministry to the people, and this is the primary thrust behind chaplaincy ministry. But the connection to military ministry is admittedly vague at best. There are other examples of ministry in the Bible that lend themselves better to military chaplaincy.

The two roles/functions of ministers in the Bible that seem to most closely approximate chaplaincy ministry are the Levites who carried the Ark of the Covenant and accompanied the Israelite army into battle, and the court prophets. Each of these groups had its successes and failures; its unique opportunities for spiritual leadership and its dangers for falling into false belief.

The story of the Israelite conquest of the Canaanite city of Jericho is perhaps the best known in which the Levites' activity with the army is highlighted (Josh 2). Children in churches have learned the story from their earliest years through songs like, "Joshua fought the battle of Jericho" and even videos in which French-speaking English peas hurl grape slushies upon the unsuspecting Israelite gourds, asparagus, and cucumbers. The biblical account is more serious, but still includes some unorthodox military maneuvers.

The inhabitants of Jericho had heard of the Israelite escape from Egypt and the subsequent destruction of Pharaoh's army in the Red Sea, in addition to the victories of the Israelites over the Amorites on the West bank of the Jordan (2:9–11). As a result, they were afraid, were on high alert, and took additional defensive measures by closing the city to all traffic (6:1; cf. 2:2–3). The Bible makes it clear that the city was a formidable stronghold, and archaeological evidence suggests that the walls of the city stood as high as 30 feet.[3] The time and expense required to attack

---

3. There has been much discussion about the walls of Jericho and their destruction, mostly surrounding the dating and cause of their fall. The most widely accepted date among Old Testament scholars comes from Kathleen Kenyon, around 1550 BC. In her many writings about excavations at Jericho, she attributed their fall to an earthquake. Her dates, however, called into question the biblical account, which suggest a date of

such a fortress was often prohibitive, and the potential for loss of life in a siege was great. In fact, there are cases of sieges in the Ancient world taking years, since armies frequently had to withdraw in order to plant and harvest crops. Thus, the conquest of Jericho was a daunting task for the largely nomadic Israelite people.

However, God had a plan to expedite the conquest by removing the walls without the use of battering rams or siege works. Instead, the soldiers and priests were commanded to march around the city blowing trumpets and carrying the Ark of the Covenant. Specifically, a contingent of at least eleven priests (a minimum of four to carry the Ark and seven to walk in front of it blowing trumpets), along with both forward and rear details of soldiers, were to march around the city once a day for six days (6:8–9). On the seventh day, they were to march around the city seven times and the priests were to give a prolonged blast on the trumpets. At that time, Joshua would command the people to shout, and the city walls would collapse. The soldiers would then enter the city and kill all the inhabitants (except Rahab and her family). This, we are told, is exactly what happened (6:11–21).

This story is sometimes highlighted in discussions of the biblical basis for military chaplaincy, presumably due to the prominent role of the priests in the battle; but it is a mistake to view the Leverite role here as normative. Some military commanders have viewed the placement of priests at the front of the Army as a paradigm for eliciting God's favor in war. The Nazi military leadership used this supposed divine obligation and the concomitant effect of the chaplain's presence on morale at the front lines as the justification for what has come to be known as "Uriah's law," which ordered German chaplains to the places with the most ferocious and fierce fighting.[4] With the chaplain at the front, God would protect the soldiers and the soldiers would be encouraged to drive forward with the attack. However, the practice of viewing the chaplain as a holy

---

ca. 1400 BC. Garstang originally proposed this date. See Garstand and Garstang, *Story of Jericho.* It has recently been defended by Wood. Wood, "Did the Israelites Conquer Jericho?"44–58.

4. Bergen notes that many German chaplains saw these orders not as what they were—an attempt to undermine Christianity by the German high command—but as an opportunity to prove their manhood to the soldiers they so desperately wanted to connect with. Bergen, "German Military Chaplains."

accompaniment, similar to the role of the Ark at Jericho, does have some potential pitfalls. Two in particular come to mind.

First, those whom the chaplain serves can come to see him as a sort of good-luck charm. In my years as a chaplain, I have had many soldiers and officers joke about wanting to be close to me when the "balloon goes up." While most are half-joking, it is clear that there is a prevalent view among the populace that God will somehow show me (and those in close proximity) special favor for protection in times of conflict. In fact, one commander made it clear to me that he literally wanted me by his side at all times in the combat zone. When comments of this sort are made, I have found it helpful to remind folks that God can provide protection to a singular individual while withholding protection (or worse—executing judgment; He can make lightning strike with pinpoint accuracy) from those in the same locale, and that many godly people, more godly than myself, have died at the hands of evil men. After all, one need only consider the crucifixion of Jesus to recognize that godliness does not ensure divine protection from evil and suffering. In addition to being in error, this view (of the chaplain as holy amulet) opens the door to two spiritual problems.

One of the dangers of this line of thinking, whether on the part of the command or the lowest ranking soldier, is that it can sometimes lead to reckless activity on the mistaken assumption that God will supernaturally protect our soldiers because of the chaplain's presence.[5] Commanders may be inclined to choose the more dangerous course of action, or soldiers on the front lines may take greater risks in the face of enemy fire. But the more common, and arguably more dangerous, aspect of this error is the spiritual problems it may elicit. It may detract from devotion to God. Paradoxically, as reverence of God's minister increases, reverence for God can diminish as individuals begin to focus on man rather than the Lord. Holiness, which can only properly be ascribed to God (and then derivatively to things/persons associated with or connected to Him) begins to be ascribed to a man. As this shift subtly takes place in the minds of the people (in this case, soldiers), devotion to God is displaced. The chaplain

---

5. Of course, God *could* choose to supernaturally protect our soldiers, and there is good reason to think that He has done so on occasion. There are published accounts of soldiers miraculously escaping attacks that should have left them maimed or dead from virtually every was in U.S. history. A very popular account of such events from the recent Iraq war is Chaplain Carey Cash's account of the Marines' 1st Battalion, 5th Regiment's battle in Baghdad, in which the marines faced ambush after ambush while losing only one soldier, when literally hundreds could have been lost. Cash, *Table in the Presence*.

may find that the soldiers he ministers to place their faith in an object (i.e., him) instead of the Lord. This is exactly what happened with the Israelites and the bronze serpent after God delivered them from snakes (compare Num 21:6–9; 2 Kgs 18:4).

Second, a related problem can arise in the mind of the chaplain as he is constantly identified (more often by others) with God, holiness and truth. He can develop a sort of spiritual arrogance as others continually show deference to him because of his supposed holiness. As the chaplain is revered as the "man of God," he can begin to see himself as set apart, not for service, but for recognition or honor. Such an attitude, of course, can lead to tragic consequences. One only need consider the story of the Levite Uzzah, whose job was to carry the Ark. When one of the oxen pulling the cart (on which the Ark sat) slipped, Uzzah reached out to stabilize the Ark and grabbed it. He was instantly struck down. David was angry with God for killing Uzzah, but we are told the reason for Uzzah's death: irreverence (2 Sam 6:7).[6] It is clear, then, that Uzzah began to see his own

---

6. The reasons for Uzzah's death are many, but at the root seems to be a spiritual arrogance on his part. He and his fellow Kohathites (a clan within the Levitical tribe) failed to follow the LORD's explicit instructions to carry the Ark on their shoulders using the gold-covered poles specifically designed for the task (Exod 37:3–5) and instead placed it on a cart drawn by oxen (1 Chr 15:13–15). This was in direct violation of Moses' intent in the distribution of oxen to the Levites, where the Kohathites were specifically excluded because they had no need for oxen or carts (Num 7:6–9). In addition, the Kohathites were specifically told to avoid touching the holy items of the tabernacle; only Aaron and his descendants were to do so, covering them with leather bags and cloths before anyone else moved them (Num 4:5, 15, 19). In fact, the Kohathites were told that they should not even go near or look at the holy items, on pain of death (Num 1:52; 4:51, 20), yet Uzzah touched the Ark, arguably the most holy item since it functioned as God's footstool and the mercy seat. So there are two clear instances here where Uzzah ignored the command of God regarding proper activity. While the seriousness of defying explicit commands of God should not be downplayed, it does appear that the sin here was particularly pernicious due to the persons involved and the nature of the sin. Uzzah's whole function within the Israelite community was to properly handle the Tabernacle items—to do so was to communicate the holiness, majesty, splendor, and power of God to God's people first, and the nations second. To improperly handle the items was to detract from the LORD's holiness, majesty, splendor and power in the sight of His people and in the sight of the nations. This, then, undermines the very existence of Israel as a nation set apart unto God, for its purpose was to be a light to the nations so that all people would come to know that the LORD is God over all peoples and the cosmos itself. Thus, Uzzah's failure here was far more serious than merely touching an object he had been forbidden to touch for no other reason than a capricious decision by a fickle deity. Quite the contrary, his impetuous and unthinking act symbolically called into question the lordship of Yahweh, the value of the covenant community, and the purpose of God's plan for the created order!

role as equal in importance to the Ark, perhaps more important. While the Ark itself held no special powers, it was Uzzah's attitude toward the things of God that endangered him—he saw his own role as vital to God's program, but this is simply not the case. God is able to accomplish His goals with or without our help. It is vitally important that we chaplains resist the temptation to see ourselves as necessary to God's work or as needed by God, and to instead maintain a sense of humility and awe at the prospect of serving the Lord in the ministries for which He has called and equipped us.

In addition to the potential for spiritual problems engendered by this use of the story of Jericho, it should be noted that the identification (or even comparison) of the Levites' work in the Israelite army with the modern military chaplaincy is specious at best. It is true that the Levites carried the Ark and led the Israelite army into battle on some occasions, and that the Ark seemed to have served as a sort of rallying mark for the nation (Josh 3:3). However, it is important to note that these activities were not the norm for the Israelite army or even the conquest of Canaan. In fact, it seems that the activities at Jericho were unique for religious reasons.

Jericho was the first city attacked in Canaan. As such, it served as a symbol of God's determination to give the land to the Israelites and of the Israelite faith to follow God into the land. The activities of the Levites and the army at Jericho also had a cultic function. The marching around the city by the Levites obviously marks the city as belonging to God. The Ark contained the stone tablets on which Torah was inscribed, and therefore symbolized the covenant God had made with the people as mediated by Moses. One of the features of that covenant was God's promise to give the Israelites the land of Canaan, and so carrying the Ark around Jericho symbolized the beginning of the fulfillment of His covenant promises to this generation of Israelites. The blowing of the trumpets symbolized victory for God's army. Thus, from the very first day of the seven-day siege, the Israelites had proclaimed victory for God's army and in so doing, the fulfillment of His covenant promises. The number seven is widely known to be a number of fulfillment as well as a symbol of divine completion. In

---

Because Uzzah was a priest, his action carried more weight than the actions of someone from other tribes. This same line of reasoning can help explain the wrath of God poured out as a result of Korah's rebellion in the wilderness—it was a rebellion of the spiritual leadership of Israel. When the spiritual leaders fail, so do the people. If the people fail, then the covenant seemingly fails as well.

the creation account, God is said to have rested on the seventh day, thus completing His creative work (Gen 2:1–3). The writer of Hebrews uses the imagery of the Sabbath day to refer to the culmination of God's plan for the ages; for the eschatological completion of the created order and the salvation of mankind (Heb 4). In the conquest of Jericho, the seventh day served as the culmination of God's plan for the battle, while heralding the beginning of His plan for the people of Israel in the land (if they remain faithful).

Thus, it is important to note that the Levites were not leading into battle so that God might bless the activities their governmental leaders had already purposed. Instead, they were leading the Israelite nation into the Promised Land, to take possession of the land Yahweh had promised as part of His covenants with Moses and Abraham. The leading of the Israelite people by the priests should not be seen as a norm for ancient Israeli battle tactics, but should be seen as a special instance in which the people were appropriating the blessings of God's covenantal promises. The taking of the Promised Land cannot be separated from God's covenants with Abraham and Moses. The story of the crossing of the Jordan River prior to the battle of Jericho, and the Levitical role in that event make this clear.

Joshua records that, just prior to breaking camp, the people were instructed to consecrate themselves because the LORD would do mighty works. After this, Joshua sent the priests ahead of the people (Josh 3:5–6). The purpose was that they would "know that the living God is among" them and that God will remove the current inhabitants from the land (Josh 3:10). Thus, a miraculous sign accompanied the movement into the East bank. When the feet of the priests touched the Jordan River, the water stopped flowing so that the people could cross on dry land even though the river was at flood stage (Josh 3:15–17).

The priests stood with the Ark in the middle of the dry river bed until all of the Israelites (except the women and children from Reuben, Gad and the half-tribe of Mannasseh; Josh 1:12–15), had crossed (Josh 4:10). This event is no doubt meant to mimic the crossing of the Red Sea in addition to its more utilitarian purpose of an expeditious crossing. The generation that had witnessed the deliverance from the hand of Pharaoh in Egypt and from the Egyptian army at the Red Sea had passed away, and now a new generation of the faithful was poised to attain the blessings of a covenantal relationship with the LORD (which the previous generation had missed (Josh 4:23–24)). After all the people had reached the far bank, Joshua ordered one man from each tribe to go back and take a stone from the middle of the river, to stack these stones on the East bank of the Jordan as a sign of God's covenant, and to do the same in the middle of the river bed (Josh 4:1–9). This sign-making activity unites the special work of the Levites in the initial stages of the conquest with the LORD's covenant faithfulness; it highlights the religious component of the taking of the land with the battle of Jericho as the initial step in the overall divine conquest of Palestine, and it shows that the Levitical activity at Jericho was not meant to serve as a paradigm for priestly functions in the army and therefore, it should not be used as a basis for military chaplaincy.

However, to say that the Levitical activity at Jericho is not a paradigm for military chaplaincy is not to say that the concept of priests traveling with the army cannot be drawn from the Levite activities during the conquest of Canaan; just the opposite. It is clear from other texts that the Levites did participate in the military activities of ancient Israel, and it seems that their function was primarily to provide spiritual support to the military members. So caution should be exercised when attempting to draw out specific chaplaincy roles or activities from the Leverite ministry with the Israelite army. However, that work can lead us to the general principle that God desires ministry to soldiers, and it is in this general principle that military chaplaincy is grounded.

A second group of persons in ancient Israel who functioned similarly to modern chaplains were the court prophets. The relationship between political and religious leaders in the Ancient Near East is not completely clear. While the Israelite monarchy seems to have had some form of religious advisement position (either official or unofficial) from its inception (e.g., Saul had Samuel and Ahijah, then a group of unnamed prophets and then evidently, none or ineffectual ministers, since he had to consult a spiritist (1Sam 28:6–7), David had Nathan, Abiathar, and Zadok), it is far from clear that all countries in the region had such a close connection between the two. For example, Wilson suggests that the *apilu* ("answerers") only played a peripheral role within the social structure of Mari and that the king did not seem to take their messages seriously.[7] Still, there were times when leaders would consult with their respective gods regarding legislation and, more commonly, battle plans. The court prophets in

7. Wilson, *Prophecy and Society*, 100–102.

Israel seemed to have been employed by the court and therefore, often felt indebted to the king and his wishes.

The minister who serves at the pleasure of a secular authority will always experience temptation and pressure to approve of the ruler's [or commander's] desires and even clothe it with divine sanction. Bergen tells of an Uraguayan Navy Captain who was complicit with the murder of several political subversives in the late 1970s. When he spoke with his chaplain about his feelings of guilt, he was told that he should not feel guilty because "war is war" and he had afforded the individuals a quick and relatively painless death.[8] Cox has famously argued that the structure of the military chaplaincy serves as an impediment to the chaplain's prophetic voice: "How does a chaplain proclaim a prophetic gospel when he is wearing the uniform of the military, is paid by the state, and furthermore is dependent on his superior officers for advancement?"[9] Cox does not see the problem as unique to the military chaplaincy or to chaplains in general, but rather as one which constrains all clergy. He argues that pastors cannot have a prophetic voice as long as the churches they serve remain beholden to the state (in the form of the non-profit tax exemption): "Substantively, this tax relief amounts to a grant—and like all grants it *never* comes without certain strings attached (as some churches have learned when their tax-exempt status was threatened for this or that controversial activity)."[10] So Cox uses the military chaplaincy to point out a more general problem with the muting of prophetic activity in American culture.[11] While it should be noted that Cox's position was largely formed in response to the War in Vietnam; despite his own frustration at the fact that many churches did, at least initially, support the war, he still has a point to make about allegiances which chaplains would do well to acknowledge.

Taking ministry outside the walls of the church and into the workplace, hospital, prison, school, and even onto the battlefield offers opportunities

8. Bergen, "Introduction," 21.

9. Cox, "Introduction," x.

10. Ibid., xi.

11. Cox writes, "The question of how one speaks truth to power is not a question that chaplains alone must grapple with. In a sense their difficult situation has the merit of being at least a *clearly* difficult one. Its limitations and constrictions are out in the open. But these difficulties really amount to a more severe case of what in some way infects us all." Ibid., xi.

for ministry that may not otherwise have arisen. It is clear that military chaplains, for instance, are afforded the chance to minister to persons in the throes of death and despair that no local pastor would gain, simply due to his proximity to the injured/dying. Yet in order to do this, chaplains have found that they need to work with the institutions within which they minister. This aspect of chaplaincy can offer some unique challenges.

Having a secular employer generally and a supervisor with the potential for outright hostility to religion specifically can cause some unique challenges. Most chaplains serve as the director of spiritual care for the institution within which they work, but also hold position/rank within the organization. For example, military chaplains hold commissions in the officer corps. This dual role can lead to some difficulty in performing the tasks of ministry because of the perceptions of those to whom the chaplain seeks to minister. Bergen notes the difficulty here. She writes, "Military chaplains operate in a peculiar sphere between religious and military worlds. As a result, they face suspicion and criticism from all sides. Have chaplains typically served secular instead of spiritual authorities or advanced the cause of victory above the needs of the soldiers in their care?"[12] The pull of competing allegiances and responsibilities is not unique to military chaplaincy. Holst describes the dual role of the hospital chaplain in similar terms:

> The hospital chaplain walks between two worlds: religion and medicine. To put it in more political language, between two monolithic structures: the church and the hospital. . . .The chaplain has allegiance to both worlds and both worlds have an allegiance to the chaplain. By training, history, and ordination, the chaplain feels a deep kinship to the church; but the chaplain's daily interactions are in the hospital, as well as are the chaplain's accountability to and salary from the hospital.[13]

The chaplain, as Holst notes, has obligations and commitments to the two worlds—to clerical ministry and to the success of the institution—but in some ways, is in tension with both. In fact, Holst points out that chaplains often receive criticism from those in each world: "Chaplains are an enigma to both worlds: medicine does not consider them 'medical enough' and questions their relevance; the church often does not consider them 'pastoral

12. Bergen, "Introduction," 16.
13. Holst, "The Hospital Chaplain: Between Worlds," 12.

enough' and questions their identity."[14] What is key for the chaplain's success is to ensure that those worlds do not come into conflict, but when they do, to make a sound judgment regarding which is to take precedent.

WORKING FOR A SECULAR EMPLOYER

In his discussion of the development of military chaplaincy in eighteenth and nineteenth-century Prussia, Lehmann notes that the success of the chaplaincy became intertwined with the popularity of the crown. When William Fredrick I, King of Prussia, first spoke with August Franke, the leader of the strongly conservative and evangelistic Christian Pietist movement in Halle, about using Halle-trained ministers for the military chaplaincy, he had a secular aim for the corps, despite Franke's desire to see all peoples to come to a saving knowledge of Jesus Christ. The king wanted to build a strong standing army of disciplined, loyal, and professional soldiers, and he believed that strong religious belief would aid in that goal. As Lehmann writes, "In short, with the help of Halle-trained military chaplains, the king hoped to lower the number of desertions, raise ethical standards, and improve the performance of his army."[15] This goal, in and of itself, is harmless enough, but it belies a secular use of chaplains which can prove disastrous if not kept in check. In the German army of the twentieth century, what began as an innocent, mutually beneficial agreement developed into a one-sided affair in which the chaplaincy seemingly lost its soul.

Lehmann argues that the transformation of the German chaplaincy from Pietist soldiers of Christ to nationalistic soldiers of Nazism really began with the rise of Napoleon Bonaparte and his threat to Prussia. Napoleon had become emperor after the failure of the revolutionary governments, but he retained much of the ideology of the French Revolution, which had at its core a program to dechristianize the nation and cut its historic ties to Roman Catholicism. The culmination of this effort is described by Noll:

> On November 10, 1793, France's greatest church, the Cathedral of Notre Dame, witnessed an unprecedented spectacle. For over six hundred years, from the time this magnificent gothic structure began to be constructed in the mid-twelfth century, it had served

14. Ibid., 26.
15. Lehmann, "In Service of Two Kings," 125–40.

as a symbol for the Christian identity of the nation. But now in the enthusiasm of revolution the cathedral had been renamed the Temple of Reason. A papier-mâché mountain with Greco-Roman motifs stood in the nave. Historian Simon Schama describes what happened next: 'Liberty (played by a singer from the Opéra), dressed in white, wearing the Phrygian bonnet and holding a pike, bowed to the flame of Reason and seated herself on a bank of flowers and plants.' This inverted 'worship service' was a high point in the French Revolution's program of dechristianization, whereby leaders of the Revolution attempted to throw off what they felt to be the heavy, dead hand of the church. In Paris, the revolutionaries renamed 1,400 streets in order to eliminate reference to saints as well as monarchs. Priests, bishops, and other religious were forced to leave their posts.[16]

Napoleon's conquest of Europe was seen as an attempt to bring the secular ideology of the French Revolution to the rest of the Continent. In reaction to Napoleon's secularism and conquest of Europe, Prussian ministers began to see the work of their king in battle against the French as the work of God. When the Prussians and others in coalition defeated Napoleon, most Prussian clergy saw it as a sign of God's hand: "The two kings, the Prussian sovereign and the God of the Bible, had joined hands in this victory, so the Prussian Protestant clergy believed, and military chaplains had no difficulties in explaining that soldiers' lives lost in the war against Napoleon had been sacrificed in a holy cause."[17] A new wave of spiritual awakening mixed with eschatological expectation swept over Prussia, but it was mixed with nationalistic pride. The Prussian preachers began to identify the German peoples (*Volksgemeinschaft*) with God's children and saw the French as their arch enemies: "In 1870–71 the newly discovered notion of *Volksgemeinschaft* did a great deal to shape the way the Old Testament legacy was interpreted. Prussian Protestant pastors did not search for specific lessons in the Hebrew Bible; rather, they projected nationalistic, and in some cases even chauvinistic, militaristic, and racist, notions into the story of God's relationship with the people of the covenant. In short, nationalistic rhetoric had defeated theological reflection."[18] Lehmann continues:

16. Noll, *Turning Points*, 246.

17. Lehmann, 130.

18. Ibid., 131

. . . the story of Prussian military chaplains shows that as they got involved in politics, they began to neglect their pastoral and spiritual responsibilities. At first, it seemed that by preaching nationalism, military chaplains would gain new authority and their message take on additional meaning. Such was the case in the Franco-Prussian War of 1870–71, when military chaplains appealed to German nationalism and to the Germans as a "chosen people," and when national rhetoric dominated most of their sermons. But already in 1870–71, many military chaplains had crossed a crucial line: rather than consoling those whose lives were endangered, and caring for those in agony and pain, they attempted to inspire the soldiers to fight. They thereby became agents of political propaganda. The chaplains transformed their role into that of missionaries of another faith, namely, the belief in the special role of the German *Volk*. This kind of nationalistic evangelization had far-reaching consequences.[19]

The danger of one's allegiance to the institution overwhelming his allegiance to the faith is constant. Sometimes it comes from one's own affection for the institution and what it stands for, but sometimes it is explicitly fostered by the institutional hierarchy. I once had a commander who sat down with me and the Judge Advocate General (JAG; military lawyer) to talk about our duties as his special advisors during the mission. The commander told the JAG that his job was to tell him how he can do what he wants to do without violating the law, and he told me that my job was to tell him how he can do what he wants to do without violating morals or humanity. We responded that it is our job to advise him of the legal, ethical, and religious issues involved in any given specific operation and to tell him how to avoid problems and/or pitfalls, but it may include advisement to abandon a particular course of action. Our duties to him were not as *"YES"-men*, but rather as protectors of his integrity and command. He agreed and clarified that he was not seeking divine or legal sanction for immoral acts. Unfortunately, though, this is not always the case.

The story of the Hebrew prophet Micaiah can serve to warn chaplains against being seduced by an overdeveloped sense of duty to their employers' wishes. The tale of the alliance of Jehoshaphat and Ahab against Ramoth-gilead and Ahab's subsequent death is well known. Jehoshaphat, king of Judah, was visiting his brother-in-law, Ahab, the wicked king of Israel. Ahab asked Jehoshaphat if he would support him in

19. Ibid., 134–35.

a military campaign against the Aramean inhabitants of Ramoth-gilead. Even though he agreed to an alliance, Jehoshaphat suggested they ask God if they should proceed with the plans to attack. Ahab agreed that this was a good idea and summoned his court prophets—approximately 400 men—to the city gate where he and Jehoshaphat sat on their thrones. The prophets unanimously supported Ahab's plans, but Jehoshaphat was not convinced. He asked a keenly insightful question: "Isn't there a prophet of Yahweh here anymore?" (2 Chr 18:6; 1 Kgs 22:7, HCSB). Jehoshaphat had enough spiritual insight to see the hypocrisy and cow-towing of the court prophets. Ahab admitted that there was one more prophet, but this one, Micaiah, never prophesied well for him. Jehoshaphat asked to hear from him, so Ahab had him brought before them.

When Micaiah appeared before the kings, he initially followed the advice of the official who brought him there and supported the kings' plans, though it seems that he did so in such a way that they knew he was not serious. When pressed by the kings to speak God's Word truthfully, he told them that Israel was like "sheep without a shepherd," and that Ahab would die if they marched into battle. Ahab was understandably upset with this proclamation, as were his court prophets. One of them, Zedekiah, even assaulted Micaiah, and acused him of being a false prophet. Ahab then had Micaiah imprisoned. Micaiah responded that everyone will know that he is a true prophet when both Zedekiah and Ahab are dead. The kings went off to battle, and a randomly shot arrow pierced Ahab's armor in between the links. He died after withdrawing from the front lines. The story is particularly relevant for chaplains because of the way Micaiah responded in the face of both pressure and persecution.

Micaiah purposed to speak God's Word (2 Chr 18:12–13; 1 Kgs 22:12–14). The official sent to get Micaiah "instructed" him that all of the court prophets were supporting the king's plans and that his words should be the same. There is nothing particularly noteworthy about the terminology here, though it appears that the official may have threatened Micaiah.[20] Micaiah responded that he would only speak God's Word; that he would only say what God wanted him to say. There are two important

---

20. The Hebrew term translated "instructed" here is really a generic term for speaking (*dbr*). It is used thousands of times in the Old Testament in verbal and noun forms. While it can mean, admonish, and there is some evidence that the *dbr*-root is associated with subjugation, persecution, and perhaps intimidation, no conclusive evidence has linked its use for speech with these negative meanings.

points here for chaplaincy. First, Micaiah was committed to God's Word, and he saw his ministry as grounded in that Word. Evangelical Christians must remain committed to biblical preaching and teaching. Exposition of the Bible should be the primary goal of sermons, and the chaplain's life should be grounded in God's Word. While some evangelicals have begun to move away from exegesis and Bible-based sermons in favor of culturally relevant *sharing*, the heart of authentic ministry must be found in God's Word. Some of these issues will be addressed in chapter five. Second, Micaiah had made a conscious decision to speak God's Word, to speak the truth, prior to being put in a situation where there was pressure to compromise. He had even earned a reputation whereby, while Ahab hated him, he was known as a person who will "tell it like it is," even if unpopular (2 Chr 18:7; 1 Kgs 22:8). Chaplains and those contemplating chaplaincy ministry should decide ahead of time to stand up for the truth, so that when a situation arises where there is a temptation to compromise, that temptation will be minimized and hopefully, overcome.

Micaiah confronted the king with the truth (vv. 14–24). When he went before the king, Micaiah shared God's Word despite the enormous amount of pressure to conform.[21] Instead of *rubber-stamping* the king's desires and falling in line with the other prophets summoned, he warned the king of defeat and accused the court prophets of being under the influence of an evil spirit and offering false prophecies. His warning to the king was meant for his good and the good of the nation. If it had been

---

21. There has been some debate over the nature of Micaiah's initial response to Ahab's query, in which Micaiah told him to go into battle and gain victory. Chisolm suggests that Micaiah spoke a lie because that was God's word. As evidence, he points to Micaiah's answer to the official (that he would only speak God's word) and notes that Micaiah "did not necessarily vow to tell the truth, but only the word of the Lord, which in this case was a false oracle of victory." Chisolm, "Does God Deceive?" 15. Chisolm also suggests that Zedekiah, the leading court prophet, correctly stated that the Spirit of the Lord was in him and speaking through him. Ibid., 16. This, though, is doubtful, for two reasons. First, Jehoshaphat's question which led to Micaiah being summoned indicates that he did not believe the court prophets were speaking for Yahweh. Second, Micaiah's answer to Zedekiah about the Spirit's movement from him to Micaiah also indicates that the Spirit was never with Zedekiah. Micaiah responded that the true locus of the Spirit will be seen when Zedekiah hides in fear (i.e., dies; 1 Kgs 22:28). Chisolm argues that Micaiah only gave the truth because Ahab insisted on it, but it seems that Ahab would not have done so if Micaiah's initial answer were not clearly sarcastic or provocative. Some scholars have suggested that God's activity here was permissive; He permitted Ahab to be deceived. See, for example, Mayhue, "False Prophets," 135–63; Kaiser, *Toward Old Testament Ethics*, 256.

heeded, it would have almost certainly preserved the lives of many of God's people.[22] Chaplains have an obligation to share with commanders truths gleaned from God's Word which are applicable to the situations their employers (commanders) face. We have a divine mandate to share with those secular employers the convictions we hold as an overflow of our walks with the Lord. This is why chaplains are there; when we fail to share the truth out of fear of reprisal, we cease to function as chaplains and become a waste of resources.

Micaiah suffered as a result of his faithfulness to God (2 Chr 18:25–27; 1 Kgs 22:26–28). Ahab did not really want to hear the truth, as his response to Micaiah's prophecy indicates. He ordered Micaiah thrown in prison with minimal rations (bread and water) until he returned. It seems that Ahab interpreted Micaiah's prophecy of doom as treasonous. He may have wished to execute Micaiah on the spot, but fear of the people, of the status of his alliance with Jehoshaphat, or perhaps even of God seems to have prevented it. Micaiah understood this, and staked his life on the trustworthiness of the word he shared. He appealed to all the people at the city gate as witnesses to his prophecy, for good or ill. If Ahab did return, he would be shown a false prophet, the people would serve as witnesses against him, and even Jehoshaphat would approve his execution. If Ahab did not return, presumably Micaiah would go free. While Ahab's son, Joash (1 Chr 18:25; 1 Kgs 22:26) had control over Micaiah and he may have desired to execute Micaiah despite the truth of his prophecy, Micaiah's appeal to the populace as witnesses most likely saved him. In all of this, though, Micaiah was prepared to suffer for his steadfast commitment to God's Word and truth. Similarly, chaplains should realize that there may be times when their stand for God's Word will put them at odds with their secular employers' goals or policies and in the end, they could suffer as a result. There are many evangelical chaplains who have complained of persecution for their commitment to the gospel or their ethical standards. In the military, the persecution has tended to take the

22. Thus, House correctly notes that Ahab should not be seen as a victim of divine deception because Micaiah repeatedly warned him of the consequences of following the advice of his hired prophets. Micaiah even staked his own life and reputation on his words. In addition, Ahab had been given multiple opportunities to respond to true prophets (1 Kgs 18:16–19:2; 21:17–29), but he had chosen to follow his wife's lead and persecute them. Clearly, his court prophets were not a part of the separatist Yahweh movement mentioned earlier in the book as the only men who had not bowed to Baal (1 Kgs 18:1–15; 19:15–18). House, *1, 2 Kings*, 238.

form of poor officer evaluation reports and/or a pass-over for promotion. In chapters two and three, some legal cases involving alleged persecution of evangelicals will be examined. The point I wish to make here is that those called to chaplain ministry must be prepared for the possibility of persecution from the very institution within which they seek to minister, simply for doing the job they were hired to perform.

Micaiah was justified by God when his word of prophecy came true (2 Chr 18:28–34; 1 Kgs 22:29–38). It is interesting to note that Ahab took great pains to ensure that Micaiah's words would not come true, even convincing Jehoshaphat to wear his royal robes into battle while he wore the uniform of a common soldier (2 Chr 18:29; 1 Kgs 22:30). This may be due to his own fear that Micaiah could be right, so he sought to foil God's purpose, or due to some sort of intelligence he had gained about the intentions of the king of Aram to limit his attacks to the king of Israel (2 Chr 18:30; 1 Kgs 18:31). Either way, his plan failed when a supposedly random arrow landed between the joints of his armor (2 Chr 18:33; 1 Kgs 22:34). The fact that the arrow was drawn "without taking special aim" points to the providence of God in bringing about Ahab's demise. Micaiah, in spite of the unpopular nature of his word and in spite of the fact that the secular authorities sought to silence him, was shown to be right by God. Not only this, but his prophecy was not treasonous, and was instead given with the best interests of the nation in mind. Likewise, while chaplains should be prepared to suffer for their commitment to the gospel of truth, they can find solace in the fact that it is the LORD who justifies. When push comes to shove, we can trust in God's grace and we must rely upon Him for deliverance. The message of Micaiah, then, is ultimately one of hope for the chaplain who unwaveringly stands by God's word in spite of temptations or pressures to compromise.

Another compelling figure in the Hebrew Bible that a biblical account of chaplaincy must deal with is Nathan, who confronted the king with his sin. The story of King David's sin with Bathsheba is well known. David watched Bathsheba bathe from the roof of his palace and eventually had her brought to him (2 Sam 11:27). He slept with her and she became pregnant (2 Sam 11:4–5). The fact that her husband Uriah was an officer in the Israeli army and was off at war created a significant problem, as everyone would know that she had committed adultery. Under threat of death, she would most likely reveal her accomplice. So David arranged for Uriah to get some unscheduled R and R, and even urged him to sleep with his wife.

Uriah's religious sensibilities and leadership beliefs, however, would not allow him to enjoy his time at home while the Ark of the Covenant and his men remained in the field away from Jerusalem and their families (2 Sam 11:11). Even after David got him drunk, Uriah refused to go home and sleep with Bathsheba (2 Sam 11:13). So David sent Uriah back to the front lines with a sealed letter for his general, Joab. The letter instructed Joab to place Uriah at the point of the fiercest fighting and withdraw in order to ensure that he would be killed. Joab did as he was instructed, and Uriah died in battle (2 Sam 11:14–17).

When David heard the news, he prepared to marry Bathsheba after the appropriate period of mourning had passed (2 Sam 11:27). It was at this time that God sent Nathan the prophet to David. Nathan told David a parable about a poor man who had only one lamb which he loved as a child and how a rich man who had many sheep and cattle stole the lamb, butchered it, and served it to a guest (2 Sam 12:1–4). When David expressed his outrage and suggested the rich man should die for his actions, Nathan accused him of being the man in question (2 Sam 12:7)! Nathan went on to specifically catalog both the blessings God had bestowed on David and the sins of adultery and murder David had committed against God in return. He then informed David of the consequences of his sin— his household will be in turmoil, he will be plagued by conflict, and there will be treachery and adultery within his own family (2 Sam 12:10–12). David's response was immediate contrition and acknowledgement of his sin against the LORD (2 Sam 12:12), and then Nathan pronounced forgiveness (2 Sam 12:13).

Nathan's activities here are instructive for chaplains. First, Nathan confronted King David with his sin. When Nathan identified the conniving rich man with David (2 Sam 12:7), he did not shy away from an uncomfortable situation. Nathan overcame any fear of reprisal he may have had and forced the king to face his own sin and failure. He understood the grave consequences for the nation if the king were to remain in his state of unrepentant sin. Chaplains need to be ready to confront their commanders when necessary in order to aid them spiritually, but also for the good of the nation. Chaplains must be prepared to serve as the moral conscience of the command.

Second, Nathan chose a means to communicate which spoke to the king and accurately reflected the situation. In telling the story of the rich and poor men and the lamb, Nathan drew upon David's compassion.

Despite his horrid actions here, the picture of David which emerges from the narratives and his own writing (e.g., Psalms) is of a man of compassion and sensitivity. Nathan knew how to reach his commander; he spoke his language. Similarly, chaplains need to come to know the language of the commanders they serve. The better the chaplain knows his commander, the more effective he will be at gaining the commander's trust and serving as an advisor. This can take a significant amount of time and investment.

Last, Nathan did not only stand in rebuke of the king; he also proclaimed God's grace to the king (2 Sam 12:13). In fact, this seems to have been his primary purpose in the confrontation. He hoped to call the king to repentance and a proper relationship with God. When David repented, Nathan left (2 Sam 12:15). It is interesting to note, though, that Nathan later served as one of David's most trusted spiritual advisors.[23] There is no indication that he ever gave in to temptation or pressure to bless whatever the king desired. In fact, at one point, he risked his life by siding with Solomon in his dispute with Adonijah over the proper succession to the throne and confronting the king about the situation (1 Kgs 1:8, 10–12, 22–27). Chaplains must be careful to proclaim grace to commanders while advising on issues of ethics. The wise chaplain should be careful to avoid the appearance of being judgmental while retaining his integrity and commitment to God's Word. At the end of the day, though, he must reject pressure to perform divine rites when he feels it is inappropriate or may give a false sense of divine approval.

Perhaps the most common instance in which chaplains feel pressure of this kind is when a soldier requests a military wedding. Several times when I have been asked to perform wedding ceremonies, I simply did not feel comfortable doing so. My own convictions are such that I will not perform a ceremony for couples residing together, I have strong reservations about marrying couples when one or both of the individuals is divorced, and I require premarital counseling before I agree to officiate at a wedding. These requirements/restrictions are not unique; in fact, it would not be an exaggeration to say that they are standard among a large number of evangelicals, but they have engendered anger and even pressure from above on occasion. Interestingly, most couples have been understanding and gracious when I have explained my position, while

---

23. See 1 Kgs 1:26. The double emphasis on himself as the king's servant and his surprise at not being informed of Adonijah's ascent to the throne indicates a close relationship with David.

there have been some chaplains of higher rank who have suggested that I am obligated to perform the wedding and by not doing so, I am somehow shirking my duty. It is conceivable that a commander could hold the same view and attempt to require the chaplain to perform a given wedding or to give a negative evaluation of the chaplain if he does not. These problems or pressures are not restricted to chaplaincy; many pastors have experienced pressure to perform weddings for persons unaffiliated with their churches because they are relatives of prominent church leaders, but generally speaking, the problem is more acute in chaplaincy because of the command structure. That is, the church structure (no matter what denomination) typically has more protective measures in place to ensure that the pastor's job cannot be placed in jeopardy if his performance is deemed unsatisfactory or offensive to one individual. Chaplains' careers, by contrast, live or die by the yearly evaluations performed by their secular supervisor. One bad evaluation can (at least in the military) effectively end a career because of the promotion system. Any commissioned officer, including the chaplain, who is passed over for promotion (for the same rank) twice is excused from service. In the competitive world of the military officer corps, one bad evaluation almost always ensures a denial for promotion and an end to the career.

The Global War on Terror and the increased operational tempo has impacted wedding requests of chaplains. When units get the warning or alert orders for deployment, invariably there are some couples who decide to get married or to move up their wedding dates. Just after September 11th, I had to face these issues from two angles when my unit, a military police battalion, was activated in early October with three days' notice. First, I had to face them from my own perspective as an engaged person when called to service. I was engaged in August and had planned on a mid-Spring or early summer wedding. My orders were for 365 days, renewable for up to an additional 365 days, and I was unsure of what chance I would have of getting home for a wedding. Things were pretty confusing at the time as no one was sure how the National Guard would fit into the larger Army mission. In Desert Storm, most of the units deployed were combat service support, but in this case, it was conceivable that many prisoners of war could be taken and my unit could be needed on the frontlines. We were being sent to Fort Bragg for homeland security, but this did not appear to be a long-term plan. In fact, the active component seemed unsure of what to do with us when we arrived. We were eventually attached to the 16th MP Brigade and moved into the Airborne Inn, but in those three days prior to leaving home station, we were not sure if we would eventually end up overseas in a combat zone or not.

My fiancé and I spent some time discussing our options. The primary concern I had was her welfare and my ability to come home if (God forbid), something were to happen to her. Unfortunately, the Army does not recognize fiancés in its consideration of Emergency Leave policies for soldiers. So, for example, if my fiancé were in an auto accident and killed, my request for Emergency Leave to attend the funeral would most likely have been denied since she was not immediate family. This flaw in the system led me to strongly consider a legal marriage. It seemed to make sense to go ahead and get married so that she could receive benefits like health insurance and be a beneficiary if something were to happen to me, and so I could take Emergency Leave if necessary. However, we did not think it wise to rush something as important as a wedding. After all, we wanted our ceremony to be a witness of God's love and grace. We seriously considered going to a Justice of the Peace to get legally married for the paperwork purposes, while treating our relationship as if we were still engaged. We would then have our *real* wedding with our pastor officiating at a later time. We were going to take this position because we see marriage as a covenant between us as individuals with one another and us as a couple with God. If God is left out of the vow ceremony, then there is no marriage; there is only a legal contract. At the same time, I did not like the prospect of deploying when the Army considers my relationship with my fiancé as no different from that between a soldier and someone he just began dating a week earlier. But that is how the Army views all unmarried relationships, without distinction for longevity or commitment level. This approach would cover our concerns while preserving the seriousness and sanctity of biblical marriage.

We eventually came to the conclusion that the way to trust God in our situation was to wait to see what would happen. Even though we could make a case for the distinction between a legal marriage and a true, biblical marriage, we felt that moving in that direction was, at least for us, born out of a lack of faith. This is not to say that I would think ill of someone who went ahead with a legal marriage for reasons similar those I considered. On the contrary, I recommended it to at least one couple.

Second, I had to face these issues as the chaplain. One of our female soldiers who had recently had a baby with her boyfriend asked if I would perform a wedding ceremony for them before we deployed. They were engaged and were planning to get married in several months, but had decided that it would be best to get married before we left, for the same reasons I had considered it. I had a lot of sympathy for their position, especially since they had a newborn to consider, and there was pressure placed upon me to do the service. This pressure was compounded by the fact that she was a full-time worker in the unit's headquarters and was well-known to the command, but I didn't think I could do justice to premarital counseling and a ceremony in three days. In addition, I was unsure of my own feelings about conducting the ceremony, given their living arrangements. I asked them if they had spoken with their pastor (something I always ask, since I am a reservist chaplain; most reservists, if Christian, should have a local church pastor) and told them of the plan my fiancé and I had considered. But I went further: I recommended that they have a legal wedding before a Justice of the Peace and then plan their wedding at their church in Louisville. While they would have preferred for me to conduct the service there at the Armory, they understood my reluctance to do so on such short notice. They decided to go to a JP, though I do not remember if they had a religious ceremony later.

As a chaplain, I had to think through the ethical and theological issues related to marriage on short notice before a deployment. As an individual, I had to think through my own feelings about my marriage plans and the fears associated with deploying during an engagement and putting off marriage for potentially two years. In the final analysis, the chaplain must take a stand for what he believes is the proper position in accordance with his faith. In my case, my understanding of marriage as covenant and a sign of the relationship between Christ and the Church must be preserved. If we will do so with firmness of biblical conviction but also with compassion, our soldiers and commanders will respect us for it (and may even be moved by God's Spirit through the situation to look at His word). The point here, then, is that there are ways of standing firm for our convictions, but without offending. This is what we must seek to do in chaplaincy (and arguably, the pastorate as well).

MINISTRY IN A PLURALISTIC ENVIRONMENT

The issue of my reluctance to perform some weddings naturally leads into a second slogan which well describes chaplaincy work: "Perform or

Provide." It is meant to communicate the two means by which chaplains seek to serve the persons under their care. The first and most obvious is to perform religious services/rites for others; to lead persons in worship of the Lord. As a Southern Baptist, I offer religious services consistent with my own faith tradition. This is typically done in the context of the *General Protestant* worship service, though I could offer a denominationally specific service (i.e., a Southern Baptist service) if I so desired and it were deemed beneficial by the command. The second way chaplains serve those to whom they are assigned (whether soldiers/sailors, airmen in a unit, patients on a ward, inmates on a cell block, etc.) is unique to chaplaincy and is represented by the term, "provide." Since chaplains are assigned to groups which are made up of persons from diverse backgrounds and faith traditions, it is common for them to have persons under their care who have different faith commitments from their own. Put differently, chaplains minister in a pluralistic environment. It is the chaplain's role, as a sort of spiritual liaison or coordinator, to ensure that the distinctive religious needs of all the persons in the unit (or ward, or cell block, etc.) are met, at least insofar as the requests are reasonable and do not violate policies or the law.

The *provision* that a chaplain makes for those from competing faith groups can take a variety of shapes, from advocating for a soldier to get some time off on his religious holidays, to ordering books/supplies, to simply scheduling a worship time in the chapel for the group. It does mean that the chaplain must be willing to work with persons of different faiths and to avoid using his position to coerce or seek to convert the other. It is this aspect of chaplaincy that has sometimes proven to be a stumbling block to evangelicals.

When working on my Ph.D., I was commissioned as a chaplain and served as a grader for several professors at the institution. Several of the Master's students who heard that I was a military chaplain came to inquire about the nature of that ministry and the process for getting involved. I distinctly remember one conversation with a young man who was already a chaplain candidate and had attended the first phase of the U.S. Army's Chaplain Officer Basic Course. He was troubled with the idea of having to provide for the religious needs of those soldiers within his command that practice a different faith from his own. He even claimed that, in order to be a good chaplain, he must compromise his own faith. As I attempted to explain to him the rationale for taking on the role of provider, I too felt something of an inner struggle. There seems to be inherent within the concept of "provide" conflicting interests of the evangelical Christian. His zeal for the LORD seems to be at odds or tempered by his respect for others and their personal faith journeys. Whenever I consider my role in ministering to someone of another faith, I must confess that the story of Elijah on Carmel looms large; it seems to call out to us, challenging us to avoid the trappings of the typical court prophets (1 Kgs 18:21–40).

Elijah confronted the prophets of Baal (and Ashtoreth) who worked for the court of Ahab and Jezebel. His challenge to them included at least three antagonisms. First, he ridiculed and taunted them, telling them to shout louder and louder, claiming that their god could not hear them. Second, he told them to cut themselves more, intimating that, perhaps, they were not faithful enough. Third, he even made fun of their gods, suggesting that they were sitting on the toilet or that their gods were not powerful enough to do more than one thing at a time! Clearly, Elijah's approach required faith that their gods would not answer, but it also took a kind of zeal; a zeal that does not sit around and discuss the differences of the two religions in a calm fashion. It is not a zeal that is particularly concerned with political correctness or propriety in dealing with others. It is not a zeal that is careful not to offend. Instead, Elijah understood that this was a confrontation that would end badly for someone—either himself or the false prophets—and he had to have a zeal that would sustain him to the end, even if it were a bitter one. This story may be thought to suggest that this is the proper response to other faiths for the Bible-believing Christian; that we ought to have the kind of zeal Elijah has, and that we should act as he did when confronted with those of another faith. Yet, I will argue that this is not normative; that Elijah's actions were indeed appropriate for the context within which he ministered, but that they are certainly not appropriate for us, and we should not concern ourselves with questioning our own zeal for God if we fulfill our mission as chaplain by providing for the free exercise of non-Christians. The tension of holding true to evangelistic zeal, while providing for the religious requests of those to whom we are assigned, is a constant theme throughout this book. It will be addressed in some detail in chapter four, but it also impacts the discussions in chapters two, three, and six.

CHAPLAINCY—HISTORY

Identifying the beginnings of chaplaincy—and in this case, military chaplaincy—is exceedingly difficult because religious in virtually every culture have performed at least some of the functions of chaplains for the military, while no ancient cultures had official clergy positions within the military structure. So priests of Ra, for example, would offer up prayers before the Egyptian army went into battle, but to claim they were chaplains is analogous to calling a local parish pastor "chaplain" because he came to a deployment ceremony for a local reserve unit and offered a prayer.

We have already addressed the Levites who accompanied the Israelite army. They may be the closest group (to military chaplains) from the ancient world. Roman military officers provided some cultic rites/services for their troops, but this seems to have been due to the identification of the army with the state and the close ties of the state to the honoring of the gods in the state cult.[24] Mathisen notes that there is some evidence that priests of religions other than the state cult ministered to specific groups of soldiers within the Roman army. This service, however, was sporadic and localized, and few pagan priests served as soldiers; therefore, it should not be viewed as the beginnings of military chaplaincy.[25] There is also evidence that something approximating military chaplains existed in the Christian Roman army. For example, the bishop Eusebius of Caesarea (early 300s) reports that Constantine had a tent designated for worship. Likewise, Bishop Theodoret of Cyrrhus (early 400s) mentions that some priests were given duties to the military. He even names one Agapetus, who "has been appointed to guide a military regiment (*tagma*) in things divine."[26] Sozomen (5th C) describes the religious climate of Constantine's military and his attempts to inculcate a sense of worship into the soldier's weekly regimen:

> In order to accustom the soldiers to worship God as he did, he
> had their weapons marked with the symbol of the cross, and he
> erected a house of prayer in the palace. When he engaged in war,

24. For an interesting discussion of the religious role of commanding officers in the Roman military, see Mathisen, "Emperors, Priests, and Bishops," 29–43.

25. Ibid., 35.

26. Sakkelion, ed., *Forty-eight Letters of Theodoret*, no. 2.; as cited in Mathesin, 36–37. Azema translates it somewhat differently, claiming that Agapetus' "mission is to go and regulate the lives of soldiers according to godly maxims." Theodoret, *Epistula* 2 (ed. and trans. Azema, 75.

he caused a tent to be borne before him, constructed in the shape of a church, so that in case he or his army might be led into the desert, they might have a sacred edifice in which to praise and worship God, and participate in the mysteries [most likely sacraments]. Priests and deacons followed the tent, who fulfilled the orders about these matters, according to the law of the church. From that period the Roman legions, which now were called by their number, provided each its own tent, with attendant priests and deacons. He also enjoined the observance of the day termed the Lord's day, which the Jews call the first day of the week, and which the pagans dedicate to the sun, as likewise the day before the seventh, and commanded that no judicial or other business should be transacted on those days, but that God should be served with prayers and supplications. He honored the Lord's day, because on it Christ arose from the dead, and the day above mentioned, because on it he was crucified.[27]

Bachrach argues that the origins of military chaplaincy are tied to the development of the penitential system, to the move in the Church's theology from viewing penance as a one-time event to a system of penances assigned to various sins. He notes that in the middle of the fifth century, Pope Leo I expected soldiers to retire after penance (presumably due to committing the sin of killing), but by AD 742 at the *Concilium Germanicum*, bishops discussed spiritual care given to soldiers—each unit commander had a priest and army commanders had bishops serving on their staff. This was the first (at least the earliest on record) indication of priestly duties to individual soldiers. As Bachrach writes, "Indeed, it is proper to identify the *Concilium Germanicum* as the legal origin of the chaplain's office in the Latin West."[28] A Carolingian-era text (ca. 850) compiled by Benedict the Levite outlines specific duties of chaplains. Interestingly, the document was meant to protect clergy from abuse by their secular authorities. Already, then, there was an attempt at regulating the duties of chaplains in service of the state. Also, interestingly, priests were prohibited from bearing arms or shedding blood.[29] Thus, by the time of the Crusades (b. 1095), an increased emphasis on ministry to the military existed. Some of the duties of chaplains included: celebrating the Mass and preaching the Word, carrying relics into the field, hearing confession

27. Sozomen, *Ecclesiastical History* 1.8, rev. Hartranft, 245.

28. Bachrach, "The Medieval Military Chaplain," 76.

29. Ibid., 73–74.

and assigning penance, and of course, *viaticum* (final Mass, extreme unction). The duties of chaplains continued to be defined and clarified. At the Fourth Lateran Council (1215), Pope Innocent III presented a list of chaplain's duties, and in 1238, Pope Gregory IX spelled out the duties of chaplains in a papal bulletin. By the time of the Protestant Reformation, chaplains were regularly going into battle with the soldiers they served. Ulrich Zwingli, the great Swiss Reformer, worked as a military chaplain, though his zeal for that work was quelled at the Battle of the Giants, which was a disaster for the Swiss military men. In fact, this experience led him to believe that the future of the Swiss people was dependent on their ceasing mercenary activity, and it was arguably this social concern that was the origin of his life of challenging authority and championing the rights of the Swiss.

While it may not be possible to definitively identify the origins of military chaplaincy, partly due to the difficulty in determining just what activities or titles qualify as chaplaincy (over against non-chaplaincy clerical activities performed for the military), most historians of chaplaincy point to the development of the term, "chaplain," as a good starting point for historical inquiry. "Chaplain" comes from a legend associated with Saint Martin of Tours. Martin was born in Hungary, circa 315. He was a pious young man who was forced into military service for the Roman Empire to fight against the pagan Visigoths. He had reportedly refused to take up arms, which earned him a charge of cowardice by the Roman generals and governmental leaders. He responded by offering to enter the fray with no arms, but to stand beside his comrades in order to provide encouragement. He was thrown in jail until the authorities could decide what to do. It seems that they were going to take him up on the offer when the Visigoths asked for peace, so nothing came of it.

There is a rather famous story of Martin's interaction with a beggar which serves as the origin of chaplaincy. Sulpitius Severus presents it in his biography of Martin. Rather than summarizing, I will quote it at length:

> ACCORDINGLY, at a certain period, when he had nothing except his arms and his simple military dress, in the middle of winter, a winter which had shown itself more severe than ordinary, so that the extreme cold was proving fatal to many, he happened to meet at the gate of the city of Amiens a poor man destitute of clothing. He was entreating those that passed by to have compassion upon him, but all passed the wretched man without notice, when Martin, that

man full of God, recognized that a being to whom others showed no pity, was, in that respect, left to him. Yet, what should he do? He had nothing except the cloak in which he was clad, for he had already parted with the rest of his garments for similar purposes. Taking, therefore, his sword with which he was girt, he divided his cloak into two equal parts, and gave one part to the poor man, while he again clothed himself with the remainder. Upon this, some of the by-standers laughed, because he was now an unsightly object, and stood out as but partly dressed. Many, however, who were of sounder understanding, groaned deeply because they themselves had done nothing similar. They especially felt this, because, being possessed of more than Martin, they could have clothed the poor man without reducing themselves to nakedness. In the following night, when Martin had resigned himself to sleep, he had a vision of Christ arrayed in that part of his cloak with which he had clothed the poor man. He contemplated the Lord with the greatest attention, and was told to own as his the robe which he had given. Ere long, he heard Jesus saying with a clear voice to the multitude of angels standing round— "Martin, who is still but a catechumen, clothed me with this robe." The Lord, truly mindful of his own words (who had said when on earth— "Inasmuch as ye have done these things to one of the least of these, ye have done them unto me"), declared that he himself had been clothed in that poor man; and to confirm the testimony he bore to so good a deed, he condescended to show him himself in that very dress which the poor man had received. After this vision the sainted man was not puffed up with human glory, but, acknowledging the goodness of God in what had been done, and being now of the age of twenty years, he hastened to receive baptism.[30]

The cloak is rumored to have been returned whole in the morning, though this is not in the original account. It became a relic of the Catholic Church in France, especially during the reigns of the Merovingian Kings and was carried into battle, presumably to protect the French armies. The tent in which it was housed was called a *capella* (literally, "little cape"; chapel). The man charged with caring for the cloak was called the *capellanus*, which is translated as "chaplain."

Identifying the origins of other areas of chaplaincy is just as difficult but, like military chaplaincy, at least some formative events can be highlighted. For example, while prison chaplains, as official administra-

---

30. Sulpitius Severus, *Life of Saint Martin (ch. III)*, ed. Roberts, 5.

tors within the prison, are a relatively modern development, clergy have almost always had an interest in ministering to the incarcerated. While it is an unfortunate fact that in some instances, the clergy functioned more to condemn or extract confessions than to meet the spiritual needs of the condemned—during the Inquisition, this function of the clergy was notorious for its brutality and even glee at the suffering of the accused—this is not the case in most instances. The modern prison chaplaincy movement traces its roots not to the Inquisition, but rather to the prison reform movements of the late eighteenth century which grew out of the religious fervor of the revivalist movements. Perhaps the most famous individual who championed the rights of prisoners was John Howard. Howard was a wealthy English landowner in the late eighteenth century. Upon being named High Sherriff of Bedfordshire in 1773, he immediately began inspecting the prisons in his jurisdiction. His interest compelled him to travel thousands of miles, even outside of his area of responsibility, and even outside of England. He published a book describing the deplorable conditions in English prisons. The title, *The State of Prisons in England and Wales* went through three editions, and gained Howard something of a reputation for his concern for the sick and imprisoned. It was that reputation which enabled him to intervene and bring to an end a riot at a military prison in London. Howard eventually died of typhus in 1790 while visiting a Russian military hospital. He advocated for clean living conditions (including linens for the bedding), segregation of prisoners by gender, age, and offense, and for religious services. While Howard did not go into the prisons primarily as a chaplain, it was clearly his religious convictions which spurred him to spend his fortune and risk his own health to minister to prisoners. He paved the way for an organized prison chaplaincy.

The history of the chaplaincy in the United States armed forces begins even prior to the mustering of the Continental Army. Drazin and Curry point out that chaplains were a vital part of the militia forces of the British settlements in the New World. By way of example, they point to the raising of a militia for the Connecticut colony in April 1637 in order to defend against the Pequot Nation. The Connecticut legislature provided for ninety men and appointed Samuel Stone as its chaplain.[31] By the time of the American Revolution, chaplains were seen as necessary to keeping good order and for boosting the spirits of the soldiers:

---

31. Drazin and Curry, *For God and Country,* 6.

"Thus chaplains were frequently and regularly called upon, in the colonial period of this nation's history, to serve with militia forces from north to south. Examples could be endlessly multiplied, but the point has been made. The chaplaincy was everywhere recognized as a legal and necessary part of military life."[32]

In the Revolutionary Army, chaplains' roles were primarily pastoral, and there was little concern for protecting the religious rights of soldiers. Nevertheless, Washington did instruct his generals to respect the local religions of the areas in which they were stationed. For example, before an invasion of Canada, Washington told Colonel Benedict Arnold to respect Catholicism and promote free exercise. It is interesting to note that Washington's officers initially offered to pay the salaries of chaplains out of their own pockets because of the value they attached to chaplains.[33] The Continental Congress first funded chaplains at the federal level on July 29, 1775 at the rate of a captain's salary. This is normally considered the birth date of the U. S. Army chaplaincy, even though chaplains had served with various units from state militia. Within a year, a chaplain was authorized for each regiment (comparable to a modern-day battalion) with a notable pay increase of 30 percent. By 1777, Congress attempted to introduce uniformity in the chaplaincy by allocating one per brigade, but this would effectively reduce the number of chaplains by increasing the number of soldiers for which each was responsible. General Washington was concerned that this move could cause dissension, since many of the regiments had distinctive religious commitments (e.g., Anglican regiment from Massachusettes, Irish regiment from New York, etc.) while brigades were made up of regiments with a variety of religious perspectives represented. Even though Washington had some disputes with Congress over the particulars of chaplaincy, there was still general agreement that it was a vital and necessary part of the military structure both for morale and morality of the soldiers, as well as the soul of the nation.

The history of the U. S. military chaplaincy after the Revolutionary War is one of ups and downs which parallel the relative strength of the U. S. forces. During times of conflict, the army was increased in size and with that increase in ground forces came an increase in chaplains serv-

---

32. Ibid., 7.

33. Williams suggests this was due less to Washington's own personal piety and more to his view that chaplains could help institute moral order in the ranks of the colonial forces. Williams, "The Chaplaincy in the Armed Forces," 18.

ing. During times of peace, the number of troops diminished, and so did the chaplaincy. For example, soon after the end of the Revolution (ca. 1791), there were fewer than 600 soldiers serving in the Army in one regiment with no chaplains, and when a second regiment was to be stood up, Congress reluctantly agreed to one chaplain being appointed. During the War of 1812, each brigade again had at least one chaplain serving, but between 1818 and 1838, there seem to have been no chaplains serving at all! In 1838, the structure of chaplaincy saw further development as Congress authorized chaplains to serve at military posts in addition to the brigades once again. Further standardization and development took place over the years as the needs of the army (and navy) continued to develop with increases and decreases, but the basic structure of the chaplain corps was now in place.

CONCLUSION

As already noted, the chaplaincy began with a measure of concern for ecumenism, and that concern was grounded in the basic rights upon which the U. S. Constitution was founded: life, liberty and the pursuit of happiness. The First Amendment was seen as a codification of those rights with respect to religion, and it was already reflected in the attitudes of military commanders toward the diverse beliefs of soldiers and the peoples in various areas of operations for the military, even before the Revolutionary War. Despite this respect for differing religious perspectives, most regular army chaplains in the early years were from Protestant denominations. The first Roman Catholic priest served in one of the two Canadian regiments during the Revolutionary War, but most chaplains were Protestant, and all were Christian. In fact, the earliest requirements for chaplaincy included belief in the Christian faith. This seems to have been more a matter of tradition and not principle, and in July 1862, President Lincoln had the requirements for chaplains changed to make provision for those of other faiths, most notably Jewish rabbis.[34] Thus, the chaplaincy began

---

34. He did so at the request of the Board of Delegates of American Israelites. The new qualifications for chaplaincy read, "That no person shall be appointed a chaplain in the United States Army who is not a regularly ordained minister of some religious denomination, and who does not present testimonials of his good standing as such minister, with a recommendation of his appointment as an Army chaplain from some authorized ecclesiastical body, or not less than five accredited ministers belonging to said religious denomination." US Army Chaplain School, *History of Chaplaincy*, Chapter 3.

with a form of ecumenism, and took on a more diverse look by the time of the Civil War. It has increased in diversity throughout the years. It was in the twentieth century that the first Muslim and Buddhist chaplains were added to the rolls, and there is reason to believe that other religions will one day be represented in the ranks. While this may be uncomfortable for some, respect for individual religious liberty is a hallmark of the American experience. Nevertheless, liberty should not be confused with relativism or an "anything goes" mentality.

There has always been tension between allowing religious minorities to worship and legitimizing just any belief with an air of religiosity to it. This tension must be resolved ultimately in the courts, but in many cases, it is first decided by unit commanders under the advisement of the chaplain. Questions related to pluralism have plagued the chaplaincy from its inception, and have proven difficult to all who have taken them up. They are a part of virtually every chapter in this book, from issues related to the offering of sectarian prayers at secular events (chapter two), to questions related to what counts as a religion (chapter three), to the rights of evangelicals (chapter four), to how evangelicals can relate to those who practice other faiths or no faith (chapter five), to interaction with local religious leaders (chapter six), to the offering of spiritual counsel to all soldiers, no matter what their background (chapter seven). Evangelical chaplains must seriously consider the nature of their commitment to Christ, of their calling to ministry, and of their role as minister-soldier. If they do not, the results may prove disastrous for the U. S. military, for their own careers, and most importantly, for the Gospel. These tensions and the theological issues at stake are what I hope to address in this book.

2

"In Jesus' Name"

Christian Prayers at Command Events

. . . at the name of Jesus every knee should bow—of those who are in heaven and on earth and under the earth—and every tongue should confess that Jesus Christ is Lord, to the glory of God the Father.

—The Apostle Paul,
Letter to the Philippians (2:10–11)

INTRODUCTION

ONE OF THE MOST oft-asked questions I have fielded since my return from Kosovo has been whether chaplains are allowed to pray in Jesus' name. I found it strange that so many people were asking the same question, but I quickly realized the belief that military chaplains are so constrained is due to the publicity given to the lawsuit filed by Lieutenant Gordon Klingenschmitt, a Navy chaplain who was seemingly disciplined and eventually court-martialed for his evangelical commitments.

Klingenschmitt has been referred to as "the chaplain who prayed in Jesus' name," and has received much press coverage as a spokesman for chaplains who have purportedly been persecuted for their Christian beliefs. In 2006, he was prosecuted and found guilty at a special court-martial for, in his words, "praying in Jesus' name while in uniform," and in 2007 was removed from the Navy. He has since begun an advocacy campaign to fight for the free speech of institutional chaplains, to fight religious persecution (specifically of Christians in the military), and to lobby for his reinstatement as a chaplain in the United States Navy. He has joined with former Ambassador to the United Nations and Assistant Secretary of State Alan Keyes and Pastor Rick Scarborough in a "70 Weeks to Save America" campaign, whereby they speak to local church congregations about the religious heritage of the United States in an effort to encourage Christians to participate in the political process, voting their values.

The details of the Klingenschmitt case are sordid and rather difficult to piece together, but it seems that he was first reprimanded by his commander and senior chaplains for preaching a strongly evangelical sermon at the funeral of a [formerly] Catholic soldier. Klingenschmitt told the audience at the funeral that he had led the soldier to saving faith in Jesus Christ and noted that, according to John 3:36, those who do not accept Jesus are condemned for eternity. Klingenschmitt defends his actions, noting "My sermon was in the base chapel, it was optional attendance, and it was by invitation. If we can't quote certain scriptures in the base chapel when people are invited to church, where can we quote them? . . . Don't paint me as a person who's going around forcing my faith on people. I've never done that."[1] That was in July 2004, and in March the following year, his commander recommended against extending his tour in the Navy, arguing that Klingenschmitt had expressed continuing confusion over the chaplain's role in the military. It should be noted, though, that at least with respect to his claim for protection at a memorial service, Klingenschmitt was in the right. Even Chaplain (RA) Louis V. Iasiello, then Chief of Navy Chaplains and a Catholic priest, noted that chaplains are free to preach however they wish in their base chapels or at sectarian worship services. It is only at ceremonies and mandatory-attendance events that a more pluralistic prayer is advisable: "We train our people to be sensitive to the needs of all of God's people. We don't direct how a person's going to pray. Because everyone's own denomination or faith group has certain directives or certain ways of doing things, and we would never—it's that whole separation-of-church-and-state thing—we would never want to direct institutionally that a person could or couldn't do something."[2]

1. Cooperman, "Military Wrestles with Disharmony": A01.
2. Ibid.

It is true that Klingenschmitt has caused much concern over/interest in the issue of praying "in Jesus' name" at mandatory-attendance meetings. In fact, he held a hunger strike in an effort to get President Bush to sign an executive order allowing chaplains to offer sectarian prayers at public mandatory meetings, contrary to the guidance that had recently been published by the Secretary of the Navy.[3] It should be noted that this is *guidance*, and not a direct order, though a commander of any given unit certainly reserves the right to make such an order. Klingenschmitt asked for permission to wear his Navy uniform at a public protest in front of the White House following his hunger strike, and tacit permission was given by his commander, with the proviso that the uniform be worn only for an official religious service. When Klingenschmitt wore the uniform at the public gathering in order to offer a prayer, he was court-martialed and found guilty of violating a direct order to not wear the uniform. Klingenschmitt has argued that the offering of the prayer in public was a worship service, but the judge in the case disagreed, arguing that chaplains can be ordered to refrain from public worship outside of the regularly scheduled Sunday morning observance.[4]

But was he *really* court-martialed for praying in Jesus' name? Was the content of his prayer really the issue? There are currently approximately 2200 men and women serving as chaplains in the Armed Forces of the United States who identify with conservative and/or evangelical groups, yet very few have complained of such blatant persecution. In fact, many find Klingenschmitt's claims not only hard-to-believe, but offensive, presumably because they suggest that no other chaplains are daring to pray in Jesus' name.[5] A more detailed examination of the event is required in order to determine if the issue at heart really does have to do with the content of prayer.

---

3. See, for example, "Navy surrenders:" http://www.WorldNetDaily.com.

4. "Chaplain who prayed 'in Jesus' name' convicted" http://WorldNet Daily.com posted September 13, 2006.

5. See, for instance, the arguments presented in the blog: http://www.shameful-chaplain.blogspot.com/. While many of the comments and humor surrounding the Klingenschmitt case on the blog are unsubstantiated and hurtful, the point is still made that resentment among other chaplains for Klingenschmitt's claims does exist. In fact, my own attitude toward the case began with a sense of disbelief and defensiveness. After all, I am a chaplain serving in the United States military, and I have not been court-martialed. Some people in churches almost seem to ask me, "Why not!?"

KLINGENSCHMITT'S CASE

The evidence is clear that Klingenschmitt was not, in actuality, court-martialed for offering a prayer in the name of Jesus, but instead for violating a lawful order to refrain from participating in a political rally while wearing his Navy uniform. The Punitive Letter of Reprimand placed in Lieutenant Klingenschmitt's official personnel record by Admiral F. R. Ruehe, Commander of the Navy's Mid-Atlantic Region, specifically states that he was convicted of violating a lawful order when he "participated in a political press conference in Washington, DC, while in uniform."[6]

In the findings of Lieutenant Klingenschmitt's special court-martial, one can begin to see why naval prosecutors and commanders saw his actions as a violation of a lawful order in addition to a violation of Navy regulations. The order in question was issued by Captain Lloyd Pyle, Commander of Naval Station Norfolk (VA), who forbade Klingenschmitt from wearing his uniform on the Bill O'Reilly television show and directed him to seek express permission to do so for any other media appearance. Despite the fact that Klingenschmitt applied for protection under the Federal Whistleblower Statute, presiding Judge Lewis T. Booker agreed that the order was not given for vindictive reasons as Klingenschmitt maintained, but instead concluded that it was issued to protect Klingenschmitt from unwittingly violating Navy and Department of Defense Regulations and Policy: "As CAPT Pyle testified, moreover, he was interested in ensuring that LT Klingenschmitt did not run afoul of other statutes or regulations governing his conduct as an officer, for example, the Department of Defense prohibition on engaging in certain partisan political activities, DODDIR 1344.10 of 2 August 2004, or the Joint Ethics Regulation, DOD 5500.7-R of 30 August 1993. The order was therefore directed toward a military purpose, not toward a private end."[7] Klingenschmitt maintains that he was, indeed, given permission to wear his uniform at the event, though he admits that he received "conflicting orders." In a letter to Captain Pyle dated 03 April 2006, he wrote, "On Wednesday 29 Mar 06, Chaplain Holcomb verbally directed me not to wear my uniform at the 30 Mar 06 event. But on 6 Jan 06, your Executive Officer gave me express written permission to wear my uniform during

6. Ruehe, "Punitive Letter", www.persuade.tv., accessed July 25, 2007.

7. Booker, "Ruling on the Lawfulness of the Order," www.persuade.tv, accessed July 25, 2007.

all 'public worship' events (such as the 30 Mar 06 event)."[8] Klingenschmitt goes on to quote at length the letter he received from the Naval Station Executive Officer (i.e., Second in Command) demonstrating that he did, technically speaking, have permission to wear his uniform at the event. Klingenschmitt then summarizes his own line of reasoning:

> Since I received two conflicting orders from you, I obeyed your written lawful orders (signed by the higher ranking XO, who did represent your view) and disobeyed the verbal unlawful orders (of lower ranking chaplain who merely claimed to represent your view). In this way, I did not disobey you at all, I simply obeyed your more authoritative (written) orders, and disregarded Chaplain Holcomb's claim to speak as your representative, when his guidance conflicted with your previously written orders. As your XO agreed in writing, my prayers in Jesus name were 'bona fide religious observance' in full compliance with uniform regs. [regulations][9]

There are several items worthy of note in these comments. First, Klingenschmitt is right to be wary of orders given by a chaplain since chaplains do not have command authority, except in very unusual circumstances (e.g., Administrative Chaplains at the Armed Services Chaplain's Schools have limited command authority). However, since there was confusion, it would have been prudent to seek clarification from the Commander or Executive Officer; to simply assume that he knows the mind of the commander in such a situation is dangerous at best. All staff officers know that, in the absence of clear commands or orders, a commander's intent and commander's guidance give some insight into his/her thought process(es) regarding a given question, operation, or situation. In this case, the original command to seek permission gives insight into Captain Pyle's reluctance to allow Klingenschmitt to wear his uniform at any media event. The fact that the permission he received was tenuous (see below) should have alerted him to the concern of the command with his participation in the event.

Second, and this really gets to the heart of Klingenschmitt's claim and his involvement at the event, is his characterization of the event as a "bona fide religious observance." This language is not incidental—it is taken directly from the Executive Officer's letter, which came from the U.S. Navy's

---

8. Letter from G.J. Klingenschmitt to Commanding Officer, Naval Station Norfolk, 3 Apr 06, www.persuade.tv, accessed July 25, 2007.

9. Ibid.

regulations concerning the wear of the naval uniform. While it is true that the heartfelt offering of a prayer is a worshipful act (or at least ought to be), it seems disingenuous to claim that all events which begin with an invocation or include a prayer or blessing of some sort are thus transformed into bone fide worship services. If that were the case, then every change of command ceremony, every ribbon-cutting ceremony, or every baseball game (to name a few) which includes a prayer at the beginning would have to be considered a worship service for legal purposes. This does not seem to be a reasonable assertion under most conceptions of worship.

Third, as already noted, the permission given to Klingenschmitt by the Executive Officer was tentative, as the wording of his written response to Klingenschmitt's request makes clear. While Klingenschmitt did have permission from the XO to wear his uniform at the event in front of the White House on March 30, 2006, it is far from clear that such permission would have been given had the XO known the detailed plans for the event. In fact, he specifically warned Klingenschmitt of the danger of participation in an event which could be deemed "political." His words make his reservations about Klingenschmitt's participation clear:

> b. Based on the limited information about this event that you have provided, including your statement to the Executive Officer that the event was being organized by a clergy lobbyist group, I have strong reservations about whether this event will, indeed, be a bona fide religious service or observance, rather than a demonstration or assembly to promote personal or partisan views on political, social or religious issues. Accordingly, I recommend that you not wear your uniform for this event. c. Notwithstanding my recommendation, you must use your own best judgment to evaluate the facts and conform your conduct to regulations. d. If, despite my recommendation, you choose to participate in the event in uniform, you should limit your participation, while in uniform, to the 'bona fide religious service or observance.' If the event becomes a demonstration or assembly of personal or partisan views you are directed to ensure that you conform to the guidance as specified in reference (c). You should not, while in uniform, give interviews, make speeches, or otherwise engage in public advocacy of personal or partisan views on political, social or religious issues.[10]

Klingenschmitt has defended his actions by noting that he did not give interviews or make speeches until he had changed out of his uniform,

10. Ibid.

and that he merely offered the prayer at the event. However, it should be noted that item (d) in the Executive Officer's guidance only specifies a few examples of the kind of activity he was directing LT Klingenschmitt from engaging in; it was clearly not meant to be taken as an exhaustive list. In fact, item (c) in the letter makes it clear that his intent was for LT Klingenschmitt to not participate in any way in an event that could be characterized as political in nature.

The Armed Services' uniform regulations clearly state that commissioned officers (or any other members of the armed services) may not wear their uniforms at events or rallies which may be construed as political in nature. The Department of Defense has explicitly rejected such use stating,

It is DoD policy that:

> 3.1 The wearing of the uniform by members of the Armed Forces (including retired members and members of the Reserve components) is prohibited under any of the following circumstances:
>
>> 3.1.2 During or in connection with furthering political activities, private employments or commercial interests, when an inference of official sponsorship for the activity or interest may be drawn.
>>
>> 3.1.1 . . . when participating in activities such as unofficial public speeches, interviews, picket lines, marches, rallies or any public demonstration, which may imply Service sanction of the cause for which the demonstration or activity is conducted.[11]

In fact, the Navy regulations are even more restrictive. They state, "Exercising the rights of freedom of speech and assembly does not include the right to use the inherent prestige and traditions represented by the uniforms of the naval service to promote privately held convictions on public issues."[12] Interestingly, the regulation does give allowance to those who are involved in such activities that are "incident to attending or participating in a bona fide religious service or observance."[13] It should

---

11. Department of Defense Instruction 1334.01 (October 2005).

12. Navy Regulations, NAVPERS 15665I, Chapter One, "General Uniform Regulations" Section 4, "Laws, Directives, U.S. NAVY Regulations Pertaining to Uniforms" 1401.3.b (4) (a).

13. Ibid., 1401.3.b (4) (b).

be noted, though, that of the political and partisan activities listed as prohibited while in uniform, religious issues are included. Thus, if an event can be construed as a religiously motivated partisan event, it would still not meet the "bone fide religious service or observance" test. This was Klingenschmitt's argument, but it is a weak one.

Even though Klingenschmitt continues to maintain that he was court-martialed for praying in Jesus' name, he admits that his actions in response to his superiors was "activism." In his recorded personal testimony of his faith journey, he claims that when he saw that a lawsuit by evangelical chaplains against the Navy was not producing the desired results, he decided that he had to become a political activist. As he told me in personal conversation, "If you want politicians to hear you, you have to become an activist."[14] So it is clear that the findings in Klingenschmitt's court-martial were justified with respect to naval regulations and rules and that he was not court-martialed for praying in Jesus' name. He violated orders and engaged in inappropriate political activity as a commissioned officer in the United States military. Yet, in Klingenschmitt's defense, he argues that he would not have had to become an activist if he were not already being punished for praying in Jesus' name and for his evangelical beliefs and activities. In fact, he claims, the court-martial was really the culmination of a history of persecution of evangelical Christians generally and of himself specifically, which had already effectively ended his 14-year military career.

INTOLERANCE, LIBERALISM
AND FORCED UNIVERSALISM IN THE NAVY

Klingenschmitt argues that, while the Navy claims to foster a culture of religious tolerance and inclusion, in actuality it breeds intolerance for anything that smacks of exclusivism. He claims that the Navy's position on the offering of prayers at mandatory events points to its deeply held commitment to the religion of liberalism and universalism. By way of example, Klingenschmitt points to the training he received at the naval chaplain's school on how to pray at mandatory-attendance events. He notes that students are encouraged to offer non-sectarian prayers, and are evaluated by senior chaplains. Students who offer prayers with an exclusivist ending

---

14. Personal conversation at First Baptist Church in Houston, TX; Wednesday, July 11, 2007.

(e.g., "in Jesus' name," "in the name of the Father, of the Son, and of the Holy Spirit," etc.) are retrained, while those who offer prayers to a generic "God" are praised.[15] Perhaps the most damning evidence against the Navy was an assignment for students to visit the Harvard Seminary website on the "Pluralism Project" for more information on the proper way to pray. While Harvard Seminary claims to be "non-sectarian," Klingenschmitt has demonstrated that both it and the pluralism project are decidedly anti-sectarian in theology.[16] If sectarian beliefs are to be frowned upon, then it may be the case that Klingenschmitt's claims that the naval school actually establishes a religion by forcing Unitarianism upon junior chaplains may very well be sustained, even if the ties to Harvard are irrelevant.[17] However, the training at the chaplain's school is not the only evidence he points to.

In a letter disseminated in May 1998, Admiral A. Byron Holderby, Jr., Acting Chief of Chaplains for the Navy, encouraged naval chaplains to follow the guidelines of an information paper entitled "Public Prayer in Military Ceremonies and Civic Occasions" and produced by the Executive Director of the Armed Forces Chaplains Board. This paper is meant to cover the prayers of all military chaplains at events where attendance by soldiers/sailors/airmen is compulsory. It should be noted that the paper can only provide *guidance* and is not a statement of Department of Defense or any of the Armed Services' doctrine. Still, as Klingenschmitt correctly points out in personal comments attached to Admiral Holderby's letter, "Any time a two-star Admiral who sits on your promotion board says, 'I cannot tell you what to do, but . . .' you read between the lines, and you know exactly what you must do, if you want him to promote you."[18] Klingenschmitt refers to this document as a "smoking gun of religious intimidation" and claims that it "establishes government-religion" in the form of Unitarian Universalism as taught and endorsed by Harvard Divinity School.[19]

---

15. Appendix J, www.persuade.tv, accessed September 14, 2007.

16. Appendix S, www.persuade.tv, accessed September 14, 2007.

17. See footnote 19 below.

18. Appendix N, www.persuade.tv, accessed July 25, 2007.

19. Ibid., N1. Klingenschmitt's claim that Harvard University endorses Unitarian Universalism can be neither affirmed nor denied. Officially, Harvard is an independent school without ties to the Unitarian Church. However it appears that Klingenschmitt has had to defend his claim of a Harvard connection to Naval Chaplaincy Training and its ties to the Unitarian Church. He has shown that there is at least a tendency toward

Yet, as one reads the paper, it is difficult to find evidence of religious intimidation and/or an attempt to establish any religion, let alone Universalism. The paper does affirm the pluralistic context within which military chaplains must serve and it does note the unique position of chaplains (in this case, military chaplains, though it could just as easily refer to hospital, prison, or other institutional chaplains; anyone working as a minister for a secular or non-religious organization or entity) with regard to offering prayers at otherwise secular events (typically in the form of an invocation, benediction, or both). For example, the paper states,

> We are often invited to contribute with the offering of public prayer. These occasional ministries, whether they take the form of evening prayers at sea aboard ship or during a formal change of command, almost always take place in a religiously plural context. Unlike our role within the context of faith-specific worship settings, the offering of public prayer at these more secular events calls for a particular sensitivity. This is a burden unique to those who perform their ministries outside the traditional parish setting and in the institutional environment of the military.[20]

The paper goes on to make several pertinent comments concerning the context of such prayers which chaplains ought to keep in mind, along with suggestions of which commanders and organizers should also be cognizant. Among these notations are that the commander/organizer is in charge of the event; that the chaplain should be aware of the pluralistic nature of the audience; that chaplain involvement should be voluntary and that, if a chaplain should refuse to participate on religious grounds, he should not be subject to retribution or recrimination; and that chaplains should not "transform such non-faith-specific observances to reflect the chaplain's denominational commitment without providing for the distinction in a manner consistent with a religiously plural gathering."[21]

Unitarianism at Harvard and that Harvard is favorably received by the Unitarian Church, even if an official endorsement by Harvard cannot be demonstrated. At any rate, the origins of the faith allegedly being promulgated by the Armed Forces Chaplains Board and by extension here, the Naval Chief of Chaplains, is not relevant, but instead the question of the veracity of Klingenschmitt's complaint of religious intimidation and official establishment of one religion.

20. "Talking Paper: Public Prayer in Military Ceremonies and Civic Occasions" Armed Services Chaplains Board, 1.

21. Ibid., 2.

One of the suggestions/comments is particularly noteworthy for consideration: "If the chaplain cannot discover a way to be inclusive of all participants, the chaplain ought not to participate in the secular event as a prayer giver."[22] Interestingly, it is this comment that Klingenschmitt sees as a violation of his own religious rights. In personal notes amended to the paper, he writes, "SMOKING GUN. Here the two star admiral tells us we cannot have equal access or equal opportunity if we pray publicly 'in Jesus name.' He directly prohibits the free exercise of religion, and denies us equal access."[23]

This interpretation, though, is hardly convincing. It is difficult to see how excluding a sectarian prayer from a change of command ceremony is a denial of free exercise or equal access. In fact, I imagine that Klingenschmitt would not appreciate a prayer offered to Allah at a change of command ceremony. Nevertheless, the point is that the paper does not suggest restricting the religious rights of groups that have distinctive claims, but only to disallow such claims from being made in prayers in the context of a mandatory-attendance event. Instead, the paper suggests that chaplains should seek to offer prayers consistent with their faith traditions but inoffensive to all members of the audience; in sum, they should seek to avoid offending any member of the audience and try to utilize the "highest common denominator" of the persons in attendance.[24]

This search, though, may prove exceedingly difficult if the prayer offered is directed at God, since an increasing number of soldiers/sailors/airmen are claiming atheism as their religious preference. When I first attended Basic Training at Fort Knox, Kentucky, I was an avowed atheist, but I was not allowed to make that claim on my dog tags. I was told by my drill sergeant that I could put "No Religious Preference" instead. I told him that I did have a preference and that it was Atheism. I was "dropped" [push-ups]. During the train-up for my most recent deployment, the members of my unit were allowed to go home for a three-day pass on a few occasions. Before we left Fort Hood, our commander got the troops together for a safety briefing and to say a few words, and each time he did, I offered a prayer for safe travels and restful visits with family and friends. The prayers were offered to God and were ended "in Your Name." Still,

22. Ibid.

23. Appendix N, N3.

24. "Talking Paper: Public Prayer in Military Ceremonies and Civic Occasions" Armed Services Chaplains Board, 3.

some soldiers complained to the Sergeant Major because they were atheists and felt that they should not have to listen to prayers. The point is this: while Klingenschmitt's claim of persecution because of such guidance cannot be sustained, it should also be admitted that, taken to its logical conclusion, the guidance offered could lead to such censorship of prayers that nothing closely resembling a prayer may be offered at any ceremony or other secular event. Such a loss would represent one not only of divine blessing, but also of a tradition that stems from the very beginnings of the American Republic. There is, however, no reason to think that the logic will be pushed so far, but it is something to consider.

It is also noteworthy that the paper is presented as tentative in its conclusions. In point of fact, it expressly states, "Our conclusion is: there is no conclusion!" The paper raises several questions that are worthy of continued discussion, even though its content seems to have already decided on some. Three such examples should suffice: "Is the chaplain praying in behalf of the assembled audience, or is the chaplain leading the audience in prayer? Is public prayer 'our own prayer,' a private prayer, or does it somehow belong to the moment or to the occasion? Who is requesting the prayer? What are the expectations of the requester(s)?"[25] It seems that the authors of the paper have already decided that the prayer is not *private* and the chaplain is not *leading* the people in prayer, but is instead offering the prayer *on behalf of* the people. In fact, while the authors of the paper state that the commander/organizer is in control of the prayer, they suggest that the audience really has ownership of the prayer. Such inconsistencies do lead to some troubling questions regarding the nature of prayer and religious programs within the military organizations of the United States (and the church for that matter).

While the conclusions of the paper were tentative and suggestive in nature, the statements regarding proper prayer at mandatory-attendance command events found in the Secretary of the Navy's letter of instruction regarding religious ministry within the Department of the Navy (SECNAVINST 1730.7c) were not. In paragraph 6, subparagraph c, responsibility for any prayers offered at such an event is placed squarely on the shoulders of the commanding officer. Specifically, it states, "In planning command functions, commanders shall determine whether a religious element is appropriate. In considering the appropriateness for

25. Ibid., 4.

including a religious element, commanders, with appropriate advice from a chaplain, should assess the setting and context of the function; the diversity of faith that may be represented among the participants; and whether the function is mandatory for all hands."[26] Yet, the letter of instruction goes further to dictate the nature and content of most prayers in settings such as those previously mentioned. It states that, outside of religious services, religious elements for a command event should in most cases be non-sectarian in nature. It then proceeds to note that, by the mere inclusion of a prayer or the participation of a chaplain, the event cannot be construed as a public worship event: "Neither the participation of a chaplain, nor the inclusion of a religious element, in and of themselves, renders a command function a Divine Service or public worship."[27] Klingenschmitt took exception to the guidance given commanders for scrutiny of the content of prayers offered at these events because he saw it as a violation of Title 10 of the U. S. Code, which specifically states that chaplains are free to conduct public worship according to forms and manners consistent with their denominational beliefs. He also took exception to the statement which followed the quote above because it offered an official definition of public worship inconsistent with his own theological beliefs and convictions.

Two items are worth noting regarding the letter of instruction and its fallout on this issue. First, the very paragraph Klingenschmitt complained about also offered chaplains a way out of performing prayers which violate their consciences. It specifically states that the chaplain may choose to refrain from participating and do so with no adverse consequences, and that if he does accept the invitation, he must follow the commander's guidance. This was most likely meant to preclude conflict within chaplains between their consciences and duties to the command, as well as protect commanders who discipline chaplains who offer prayers (at such command events) that are not in keeping with the commander's intent and instead offer sectarian prayers. But it also means that if a commander has a Christian chaplain and expressly wants a prayer offered in Jesus' name, the chaplain can/should do so; the commander will bear responsibility for the prayer. Likewise, if the commander wants a non-sectarian prayer and the chaplain objects to offering such a prayer, then he has the right and ability to refuse without fear of reprisal. Second, the letter of instruc-

26. SECNAVINST 1730.7C, 6.c.
27. Ibid.

tion was eventually rescinded by the Secretary of the Navy, presumably due to some of the objectionable conclusions.

KLINGENSCHMITT'S PROBLEMS WITH THE COMMAND

Klingenschmitt argues that there were three events or actions on his part which led to his falling out of favor with his commander prior to the March 30th event in Washington: (1) his advocacy for specific religious requests/practices among minority religions, (2) his inability to support a command function because of his personal religious beliefs, and (3) his choice of words in a sermon delivered at a memorial service for a soldier on the ship he served.

Religious Discrimination Onboard

First, Klingenschmitt charges that his commander engaged in religious discrimination and reprimanded him for his actions in support of Jewish sailors, Muslim sailors, and sailors of other under-represented faith groups. This can be seen in an analysis of Captain Carr's reactions toward some components of the religious program Klingenschmitt implemented in an effort to foster interfaith dialogue and respect. One example has to do with evening prayers voiced over the loudspeaker of the ship. It was apparently a tradition for the chaplain to offer a prayer for the officers and sailors at the end of the duty day. In an effort to be more inclusive, Klingenschmitt planned to ask for volunteers from various faith groups to voice prayers on a rotating basis. Captain Carr rejected the plan, though, and directed Chaplain Klingenschmitt to do the evening prayer himself in a more general way to God (what Carr apparently called, "Jewish prayers").[28] Similarly, when Klingenschmitt drafted a plan for a religious education program which asked sailors of non-Protestant faith groups to volunteer to teach about their respective beliefs, Captain Carr first rejected Wicca and Paganism as viable options and instead only approved Islam, Buddhism, Mormonism, and Catholicism. This plan was meant to encourage open discussion, and it explicitly discouraged arguing. Yet Captain Carr's exclusion of pagan religions is viewed by Klingenschmitt as symbolic of his wider failure to support persons' true faith convictions.[29]

28. Appendix R, R1, www.persuade.tv, accessed July 27, 2007.
29. Ibid., R2.

The most troubling example of alleged discrimination can be seen in Klingenschmitt's advocacy for an orthodox Jewish sailor to receive kosher food and allowance for Sabbath observance while serving aboard the USS Anzio. Klingenschmitt apparently went to the supply officer and then his superiors in the chaplain corps to complain about the lack of kosher rations on board. According to Klingenschmitt, the sailor lost 14 pounds while at sea for six months because of a lack of acceptable food. This caused Klingenschmitt concern, and he even used his own funds to buy the sailor some food while he was in port in Scotland. He also went to the sailor's immediate supervisor and requested that he receive an exemption from duty on Saturdays. Yet the sailor was never removed from the Saturday duty roster and apparently had to bribe others to trade with him (at $100/day!). It was not until the Executive Officer of the ship saw that the sailor was being harassed by higher-ranking non-commissioned officers that action was taken to protect his religious observance. However, his continued movement toward the orthodox position had led the sailor to grow out his sideburns in violation of Navy uniform regulations. He has apparently requested an early release from duty because of the Navy's inability to accommodate his dietary needs. Abraham Foxman, National Director of the Anti-Defamation League, wrote a letter to Secretary of the Navy Gordon England in support of Klingenschmitt and expressed disappointment with the Navy command for its lack of support and understanding of the sailor's plight.[30]

Response

Several comments are worth noting with regard to this issue, some critical of Klingenschmitt's actions, and some laudatory. At its most basic, Chaplain Klingenschmitt's desire to ensure that a soldier under his care has his religious needs met was at the heart of what military chaplain service entails. His willingness to support the equal opportunity of Muslim, Mormon, and even Pagan sailors indicates that his insistence on praying in Jesus' name is not indicative of his own exclusivism with a vengeance; that is, he does not insist on praying in Jesus' name because of his belief that only prayers in Jesus' name should be allowed, but instead because he wants to pray in accordance with his own faith tradition and personal convictions.

30. Personal letter, found on www.persuade.tv.

It is not completely clear what took place with regard to this case. It seems that Klingenschmitt may have complained to chaplains above him without first talking to his commander about the issue. While chaplains can surely communicate with their supervisory chaplains about any issues of concern, problems within the command they serve should always first be discussed with the commander or executive officer. From the letter of instruction that Captain Carr gave Chaplain Klingenschmitt, one gets the impression that CAPT Carr was blindsided by the complaint.[31] In this case, the two senior chaplains with whom Klingenschmitt addressed the issue should have advised him to talk with his commander first before they took any action. By allowing the complaint to reach CAPT Carr by any means other than his own chaplain, they did Klingenschmitt a disservice.

Yet, according to Klingenschmitt, there is evidence that CAPT Carr would not have looked favorably upon the request and in fact initially asked him to find a way out of providing for the sailor's religious needs. Klingenschmitt cites a series of e-mail correspondence between his commander, CAPT James Carr, and senior chaplain (CAPT) Stephen Gragg as evidence that he was punished for advocating for the Jewish sailor's desires against the advice of Naval Chaplain Rabbi Kaprow, who is of the Reformed Jewish tradition. Chaplain Kaprow apparently advised the sailor to put up with concessions of his faith in order to conform to the Navy's uniform requirements and dietary constraints. Personal correspondence from the sailor to Chaplain Klingenschmitt makes it clear that he was not impressed with Chaplain Kaprow's faith or integrity.[32] Such stories

31. In his non-punitive letter of instruction to Chaplain Klingenschmitt, Captain Carr indicated that the command would have been receptive to the soldier's plight, if he had been informed: "On 09Mar04, you scheduled a conference with the CNSL and CFFC Chaplains complaining of the lack of kosher rations available onboard ANZIO. In doing so, you misrepresented the Command concern for this issue, stating that the command supported your position, when you had not in fact discussed it with either the Commanding Officer or the Executive Officer. The issue was easily resolved once the Commanding Officer became involved, but only after senior leadership in the Navy Chaplain Corps gained an (incorrect and unwarranted) impression of unrest or dissatisfaction with ANZIO concerning the issue." Appendix D, D17-D18, www.persuade.tv, accessed July 25, 2007.

32. The full text of the e-mail from the sailor to Chaplain Klingenschmitt reads as follows [spelling and capitalization errors unchanged]: "thanks a lot chaps. but the EAOS that they are qualifying this program for is before 01OCT05 and mine is not till 23JAN06. but i am still going to ask to see what i can work out. i have a question about the captain. am i caught in a power struggle with him and the xo? cause one is for it and the other is not. when the captain just last week said yes we want to help me out. so if they have their

are disappointing and if Klingenschmitt's account is accurate, a cause for concern, but as noted previously, religious accommodation must always be weighed against the needs of the service and is ultimately the call of the commanding officer.

Fleet Week Incident and Naval Support of Homosexuality

The second incident to which Klingenschmitt points as creating tension between him and naval leadership occurred as a result of a command event which he could not, in good conscience, support. Fleet Week is a public relations boon for the Navy. Each year, several ships dock in New York City's harbor and sailors enter the city in uniform for some much needed rest and relaxation, while civilians are encouraged to visit the ships and witness demonstrations of naval power and capability. Many special events are planned throughout the week with the intent of encouraging interaction between the civilian population and naval personnel. Sailors are invited and encouraged to attend local houses of worship as part of the Fleet Week activities. In this case, an arrangement was made by the fleet chaplain, Captain Jane Vieira for Protestant sailors to attend worship services at Marble Collegiate Church, a historic Dutch Reformed Church (Reformed Church in America) with roots in New York dating back to 1628. The church was reserving room at the front of the sanctuary for ISO sailors from the six ships involved, and even planned a special barbeque meal for the sailors following the services. Chaplain Klingenschmitt was tasked by his commander to recruit volunteers to represent the U.S.S. ANZIO, but when he discovered that Marble Church has a ministry program to gay, lesbian, bi-sexual, and trans-gendered person which supports

---

thing going on and i am caught up in the middle of it, that is really affecting me. now this garbage rabbi talked him out of it some how. that meeting i had with him was the worst ever. he grilled me about making a big deal. then pulled my aside and tried to be my friend. that is not a guy i can go to for anything.

I mean he just helped another guy get out a couple months ago and he wont help me. not to mention the lack of enthusiasm he had when he found out how orthodox i am. like he has some sort of grudge against orthodox in general or something. and i am feeling it. thank you for you help. i am going to be still perusing this and not stop cause the man has a problem with it." Appendix U, U7, www.persuade.tv, accessed July 25, 2007. While there are some grammatical and syntactical errors in the correspondence, it is clear that the soldier feels that Chaplain Klingenschmitt is the only person attempting to take his faith tradition seriously. It is worth noting that Chaplain Klingenschmitt received letters of thanks from Jewish leaders, including the Anti-Defamation League, for his advocacy of this sailor's religious rights, the advice of the Jewish naval chaplain notwithstanding.

their choice to follow a homosexual lifestyle, he sent an e-mail to his supervisory chaplain expressing his inability to support the event.[33] In addition, he proposed an alternate church for protestant worship and volunteered to coordinate sailor involvement. This effort was not met with the approval of Chaplain Klingenschmitt's superiors. When Chaplain Vieira saw the e-mail, she purportedly called Captain Chaplain Steve Gragg, and directed him to silence the junior chaplain [Klingenschmitt]. Chaplain Gragg called Klingenschmitt's commander, Captain Carr, to voice his and Chaplain Vieira's concerns about Klingenschmitt. When volunteers for attendance at the Marble Church event were not forthcoming, the two-star admiral (CCDG-2) purportedly directed that each ship provide bodies. In an e-mail sent out to the executive officers and chaplains of the ships, a senior chaplain in the fleet, Chaplain M.W. (LCDR) noted the number of sailors from each ship expected to attend the events at Marble Collegiate Church: "IWO will provide 50 and each of the other ships will provide 20. This is per CCDG-2 direction that this be done. Obviously, it is preferable to fill with volunteers if at all possible. Understand that for some this raises questions, but as I pulled the string on this request at the conference it was made clear that this is how the Admiral wants it done."[34]

Klingenschmitt took exception to this, lodging a formal protest with Captain Carr, and warning him of the possible fallout if word leaked that the Navy forced on-duty sailors to attend pro-gay church. According to Klingenschmitt, Captain Carr told him that the press would never find out and that he could voice his concerns at the After Action Review. He did so, and as an informal (and largely quiet) personal protest, took five soldiers to the interdenominational Times Square Church for Fleet Week Worship.

Yet this was not the end of the incident, as Klingenschmitt's refusal to participate in the official Fleet Week Worship opportunities was cited as a performance deficiency by his commanding officer in both a private

33. The ministry program to gay, lesbian, bi-sexual, and trans-gendered persons is "GIFTS," and is described on the church website as seeking "to reconcile spirituality and sexuality through God's as seeking "to reconcile spirituality and sexuality through God's love." It goes on to note that the ministry is open to all: "By celebrating the common threads between our lives and faith journeys, we embrace our spiritual inheritance." http://www.marblechurch.org/Programs/GayLesbian/tabid/95/Default.aspx., accessed July 25, 2007. Marble Collegiate Church has a heritage steeped in the Positive Thinking theology of Norman Vincent Peale. It should be no surprise that sin has been redefined as negative mental states rather than activity contrary to God's Word and/or nature.

34. Ibid.

performance counseling session and a formal performance evaluation. Klingenschmitt had, up to that point, kept the proceedings confidential, but made them public because of the disciplinary actions taken against him. He has charged Chaplain Vieira with abuse of power and a violation of sailor's constitutional rights, arguing that she has forced her own liberal version of Christianity upon the sailors (Chaplain Vieira is ordained and endorsed by the liberal United Church of Christ). He writes, "CAPT Chaplain Jane Vieira not only violated the U.S. Constitution to force her faith upon my young sailors, she hijacked the rank of the entire line community, getting them to violate the constitution."[35]

Response

The Fleet Week incident raises a number of questions relevant to evangelical service in military and institutional chaplaincy. The immediate concern has to do with the alleged violation of the sailors' religious rights by the command with the compliance of the majority of chaplains within the command. If soldiers were ordered to attend religious services of a particular sort without regard to their personal religious and/or denominational affiliation and without regard to their personal religious convictions, then it seems that a violation of the First Amendment and of naval and Department of Defense regulations was made.

Military chaplains are trained to inform commanders and senior enlisted officers that they cannot order soldiers/sailors to attend religious services. In fact, when I have suspected that a platoon or company (or any other identifiable unit/group) has been ordered into my worship service, I have always dismissed the group and invited those who wish to participate in a worship service to return in ten minutes. This is done to protect the soldiers from religious discrimination and the commander from complaints being filed with the Inspector General's office.

However, the issue is not really as clear as one may be initially inclined to think. That is, it may be that the rights of the sailors ordered to attend the service at Marble Church were not actually trampled underfoot. While a good case can be made that any direct orders to attend a religious function of any sort is, by its very nature, a violation of soldiers/sailors constitutional rights, a good case can also be made for the claim that it is not any more a violation of their rights than mandatory atten-

35. Appendix L, L2, www.persuade.tv, accessed October 15, 2007.

dance at any other command function which includes religious elements (e.g., a change of command ceremony opened with an invocation and/or closed with a benediction). In fact, many of the groups fighting against Klingenschmitt's desire to be allowed to pray in Jesus' name at command functions make this same argument. The legitimacy of many chaplaincy activities within the command came under attack on this basis. Thus, Klingenschmitt's claims that merely offering a prayer at a ceremony constitutes worship and that he ought to be allowed to pray "in Jesus' name" in such situations seem to contradict his argument against the forced attendance of sailors at the religious service while on duty.

It may be that the command made a distinction between ordering people to *attend* the event (characterized as a command event) and ordering them to *participate* in worship. This was part of the government's argument in the Federal District case of *Anderson v. Laird*, a class action lawsuit which challenged the Constitutionality of compulsory chapel attendance at the armed services' academies. Cadets at each of the Army's, Navy's, and Air Force's academies were required to attend chapel services on Sunday mornings each week unless they were given a waiver for which their parents (if under 21 years old) had to agree. They were not permitted to attend various services, but were required to attend the same service every week. If they sought to change the service they wished to attend, they had to produce evidence that they wished to affiliate with the faith of the service now attended, and needed permission from both chaplains and their parents. The Department of Defense argued that the chapel attendance policies served a secular function, namely to train future military commanders to be aware of the impact of religious devotion in the lives of many of the soldiers they would one day lead. In addition, the defense claimed that it does not require students to participate in worship, but only to attend a worship service.

District Court Judge Corcoran agreed with the armed service schools' distinction between mandatory attendance and compulsory worship, as well as the claim that the War Powers Clause in the Constitution allows the military flexibility with regard to service members' rights when combat readiness is at stake.[36] However, on Appeal, the Defense Department lost in a 2–1 decision. In his ruling, Appellate Court Chief Justice Bazelon argued that the Establishment Clause is clearly violated by "compulsory

---

36. *Anderson v. Laird*, 316 F. Supp. 1081, 1090,93 (D.D.C. 1970).

attendance at worship and prayer, profession of belief and payment of tithes," among other things.[37] Bazelon's ruling is relevant to the issues under consideration here for two reasons. First, he argues that the distinction between *attendance* and *worship* is artificial and cannot stand up to Establishment scrutiny. In this, he correctly notes that the defense gave no clear explanation of how the two would look differently, except in terminology.[38] Second, he seems to suggest that mandatory attendance at any event which includes a prayer is unconstitutional. This, of course, has grave implications, if correct, for prayers offered at military ceremonies and other unit formations. For example, he argues that Establishment prevents the government from compelling persons to "engage in religious practices or be present at religious exercises."[39] While he allows that a secular purpose for an event could conceivably make the event permissible, he also suggests that no secular purpose can negate or override an activity's religious nature.[40] These arguments, of course, could have serious and negative implications for prayers offered by chaplains at military ceremonies and other unit formations.

In his dissenting opinion, Judge MacKinnon accepted the distinction between attendance and participation, largely due to the secular purpose of the requirements as articulated by the service schools' representatives.[41] He also exhibited a strong deference to the military leadership's judgments about what is necessary to train future military commanders.

37. *Anderson v. Laird*, 466 F. 2d 283 151 U.S. App.D.C. 112 (1972), paragraph 28.

38. He writes, "The Government's contention that there is a difference between compelling attendance and church and compelling worship or belief is completely without merit. Neither appellees, nor the dissenting opinion infra, reveal how a government could possibly compel individual worship or belief other than by certain overt actions— for example, profession of belief in God; recitation of prayers; or mere presence during Bible readings. Attendance during chapel services is indistinguishable from these other overt actions, the compulsion of which has been declared unconstitutional in Torcaso v. Watkins, School District of Abington Township v. Schempp, and Engel v. Vitale." 466 F. 2d, paragraph 29.

39. 466 F. 2d, at paragraph 30.

40. 466 F. 2d, at paragraph 32. Bazelon writes, "Again, no finding of a secular purpose or effect could justify this form of governmental imposition of religion," speaking of Bible readings in public schools.

41. He suggests that the majority has assumed that the representatives of the armed services' schools have committed perjury in their claim that he compulsory attendance requirements are purely secular and do not have a goal of convincing cadets of the value of religion in their own lives.

The most relevant aspect of his dissent has to do with his *quantification* of the cadets' exposure to religion by compulsion. MacKinnon suggests that required attendance for only one hour per week is a *minimal exposure* and that, along with a secular purpose (as well as military leadership's qualified judgment regarding its value) is what enables him to see this compulsory attendance as Constitutionally allowable.[42] This, of course, may be the route naval leadership could follow in order to defend their requirement for sailors to attend the Marble Church event, that is *if* they were to admit that sailors were, indeed, ordered to attend as Klingenschmitt contends.

Nevertheless, it can reasonably be shown that, even if the requirement placed upon some of the sailors to attend the Fleet Week event could be seen as a general violation of their constitutional rights, a case can be made for a different standard for members of the military, the findings in *Anderson v. Laird* notwithstanding. After all, many of the orders given by military commanders seem antithetical to even the most basic human rights upon which the specific constitutional rights are based. For example, the constitution takes it as a given that all persons have a right to life, liberty and the pursuit of happiness, and these rights are seen as God-given, not state-granted. Yet, when a commander orders the soldiers of his command to run head-long into enemy fire, he surely violates those persons' rights to life and pursuit of happiness (or at least places them in jeopardy).

This raises a further, but related issue—that of the rights of military personnel. While a complete discussion of the philosophical and legal issues pertaining to the rights given up by individuals in a volunteer military is beyond the scope of this study (and the expertise of the author!), of particular concern to military chaplains are those issues related to questions of religious accommodation. Klingenschmitt seems to be under the impression that military personnel have the same rights regarding religious accommodation as any citizen of the United States. He also seems to think that military personnel have the same rights regarding religious freedom enjoyed by all persons residing in the United States, but as we shall see in chapter three, this is not the case. The question of when, and to what extent, a commander may deny military personnel freedom of

---

42. MacKinnon refers to the mandatory chapel attendance as a minimal exposure at least five times in his dissent. 466 F. 2d at paragraphs 95, 99, 114, 117, and 126. He also highlights that it is only a one hour requirement each week, suggesting that the quantity of exposure plays a part in Constitutional questioning. 466 F. 2d at paragraph 96.

religious expression will be examined with particular attention to the impact it can have on evangelical beliefs and/or commitments.

The Fleet Week incident also touches upon one of the recurring concerns of this chapter: the possibility of a state-sponsored liberal religion. Klingenschmitt has raised the question of why those in a position of power over him were so concerned about his objections and has suggested that there was something more insidious going on than mere advocacy for a public relations program. Instead, he believes that this was just another instance of the promotion of a government-endorsed Unitarian religious system over against evangelical Christianity: "Why should a junior chaplain be disciplined, silenced, and kicked out of the active duty Navy, for privately protesting the religious abuse of his on-duty sailors, for declining on religious grounds to attend mandatory worship at a pro-gay church, and for proposing the option to invite off-duty sailors to an optional evangelical church instead?"[43]

While it is virtually impossible to substantiate the claim that this was an official endorsement of a religion of pluralism or universalism, it does raise some concern about how evangelicals are to support such events in the future. If the chaplain encourages soldiers/sailors to attend worship services at such a church, it may be construed as an endorsement of the beliefs of the church. Such a perception could hamper the chaplain's ability to minister effectively as he very well could be thought a sell-out. Clearly many evangelicals would see a requirement to encourage persons to attend what they consider to be a false church as a violation of their own consciences and religious beliefs. Some may even feel that by supporting a command event such as this, they would be possibly leading those in their charge straight to Hell.

At the end of the day, two comments must be made with regard to Klingenschmitt's actions in response to this event. First, as a commissioned officer in the military, he should have known that an immense amount of pressure had been placed upon the shoulders of his commander, Captain Carr, for a successful event. Since the whole of Fleet Week belongs to a two-star Admiral, the success of the events planned are vitally important to him. Each member of the Admiral's staff has a piece of the pie—an area of responsibility—and the chaplain's is worship services. The pressure placed upon ships' commanders to get their sailors

43. Ibid.

to the events, including the worship service at marble Church, was really just a manifestation of the fleet commander's support of his chaplain. So Captain Carr felt compelled to have a good turnout of sailors from the USS ANZIO at the worship event, to the extent that it could have ramifications for his own career.

In fact, the success of events of this nature is almost always evaluated by means of head-count, and is almost always included on the commander's yearly evaluation. That is, it would not be surprising if Captain Carr had a good turnout of ANZIO sailors for Fleet Week events listed among his accomplishments for the year on his Fitness report. Thus, a poor turnout by ANZIO sailors could adversely affect his career, or at least call into question his leadership abilities in the eyes of his commander. The implications of this should be obvious: by protesting the event and encouraging sailors to attend an alternate church, Klingenschmitt not only put him at odds with the religious leadership of the fleet, but also jeopardized his commander's own career. One can see why Captain Carr may have been inclined to view Klingenschmitt's activities in a negative light, especially given the job of the command staff to make the commander look good. In this case, Klingenschmitt did not work with the goal of making the commander "look good," but instead worked contrary to his commander's desires and intentions.

Of course, both the belief that chaplains should strive primarily to make their commanders look good and the claim that Klingenschmitt did not work to that end can be questioned. As noted in the introductory chapter, one of the unique aspects of chaplaincy ministry is its accountability to a secular employer whose goals are not always immediately (or even clearly) connected to growth in holiness, salvation of the lost, or the magnification and proclamation of the glory of God. It is the wise chaplain who learns how to meet the needs of that secular employer (in this case, the Navy or a particular Commander) while still serving God. Ultimately, and perhaps singularly, the evangelical chaplain must not see his goal as making the commander look good or succeed, except insofar as the commander just will "look good" and have *true success* if his/her command brings glory and honor to God. This understanding, then reshapes the chaplain's advisory role to the commander into one which helps the commander to make godly decisions, not necessarily decisions which lead to the most efficient accomplishment of the mission.

In this sense, then, Klingenschmitt can rightly claim that he *was* seeking to make the commander look good by helping him see a godly response to the situation. Even if this argument is not accepted, though, it may still be claimed that Klingenschmitt was justified in at least pointing out the concern over religious persecution to his commander and offering an alternate course of action. In this, he was not only looking out for the spiritual well-being of his sailors, but also for the careers of the commanders. If a complaint of religious coercion were filed by even one of the sailors involved and an investigation found evidence of such, it seems that the ship commander(s) would take the fall. The memorandum from the Admiral's staff was not specific enough to be construed as a directive to order sailors to attend the event. Instead, such an order would most likely be deemed an erroneous interpretation of the Admiral's intent in a court-martial hearing. Klingenschmitt's actions were, in all actuality, consistent with a desire to protect his commander and consistent with chaplaincy training.

The second comment is related and has to do with whether he did the right thing. It seems that, on purely theological grounds, his actions were at least justified. A concern for theological fidelity and purity of devotion for the one true God permeates the Scriptures. The Israelites were constantly and consistently warned against the two dangers of gentile influence: false worship, which could take the form of either devotion to foreign gods or improper modes of devotion to Yahweh, and immorality. No compromises were allowed because matters of ultimate truth and holiness were at stake, and it seems that this same attitude drove Klingenschmitt's decision here. Still, in order to accurately evaluate his actions, alternate courses of action need to be considered. While it is clear that due to his own personal convictions and on biblical grounds, he should not have participated in the Marble Church event, it is not as clear that the best approach was to actually take a contingent of sailors to the Times Square Church.

One option available to Klingenschmitt was to take sailors to the Catholic worship opportunity for Fleet Week. Klingenschmitt was himself recognized by a bishop in the Roman Church as able to provide the sacraments to Catholic soldiers, presumably because of his position as an Episcopal priest. Since Episcopalianism practices open communion with Roman Catholicism, the Catholic worship opportunity was certainly a viable option for Klingenschmitt. He could have lodged his protest with his commander and the chaplains senior to him in the fleet, and then attended the Mass. In this way, he would have preserved his own integrity while still supporting the Fleet Week religious activities. Yet, this solution seems to really skirt the issue for at least three reasons. First, it only serves as an answer to Klingenschmitt's case, but does not offer anything by way of instruction for other Protestant Chaplains who come from traditions less open to Catholicism. This, of course, includes most evangelical chaplains. Second, it neglects Klingenschmitt's own denominational affiliation. Under the Department of Defense divisions for chaplaincy, Klingenschmitt was a Protestant Chaplain and it seems that an effort to promote a Catholic worship service could undermine his position in the eyes of at least some of his congregants. Third, for Klingenschmitt to not offer an alternative for Protestant sailors could have been seen as a tacit endorsement of the Marble Church event. So it seems that Klingenschmitt needed to offer an alternative Protestant worship opportunity. The only viable course of action was to do what he did, or alternately, offer a Protestant worship service on board the USS ANZIO for all the soldiers remaining on the ships. This, though, may not have been allowed by his commander or senior chaplains. Thus, it seems that in this case, devoid of command support, Klingenschmitt was left with little choice—either violate his conscience or detract from the command program. Neither option is good, and (at least it seems to me) he did the right thing. By contrast, the commander should have allowed Klingenschmitt to stay on board for the duty sailors and conscripted his personnel officer to take sailors to the event (assuming they would have been willing participants).

Unacceptable Memorial Service Sermon

The final and perhaps most disturbing issue which led to friction between Klingenschmitt and the command of the USS ANZIO involves the content of a sermon he preached at a memorial service for one of the sailors of the ship killed in a motorcycle accident. The sailor was Catholic, but had recently confessed Jesus as his personal Lord and Savior during an onboard worship service over which Klingenschmitt presided. The sailor became a regular worshipper in Klingenschmitt's services and thought of him as his pastor. As he considered what to preach for the memorial service and the number of non-Christian sailors who were likely to attend, Klingenschmitt felt led of the Lord to preach the very same sermon that he preached the Sunday morning that sailor confessed Christ. As Klingenschmitt recounts, "When ship's Commanding Officer (CO) and the Executive Officer asked Chaps to preach at D.R.'s memorial service, Chaps was honored to be invited. He immediately knew what sermon to give, thinking, 'What better way to honor D.R.'s personal religion, than to preach the same sermon D.R. personally loved and embraced before he died?'"[44]

The sermon, though, was not well received by all who attended the memorial service. In fact, according to Klingenschmitt, the commander was personally offended and cited the sermon as the precipitating event leading to the negative evaluations of his chaplaincy work which resulted in his removal from active duty. Klingenschmitt also claims that several senior chaplains reviewed the sermon and concluded that he should be punished for the content. Klingenschmitt argues that the content which was so offensive to so many is the simple gospel of Jesus Christ.[45] In an effort to evaluate this claim, I have conducted my own analysis of the content of the sermon. I found three possible areas of contention, but noted that none should have resulted in punitive action against Klingenschmitt.

The first possible source of contention has to do with what may have been construed as accusations by Klingenschmitt leveled at the deceased sailor and perhaps the audience. Several times in the sermon, in an apparent effort to explain the grace of God, Klingenschmitt mentions both his own and the deceased sailor's sins and sinfulness. The multiple allusions to the deceased's sins and his concomitant deserving of Hell could have led many in attendance to fail to listen to what followed—the gospel. For example, consider the following excerpt:

> Because we choose sin, because we choose selfishness, because we choose lust or drunkenness or immorality, or any of the number of things that I myself am guilty of in this life, that we in this church are guilty of, that D.R. [the deceased sailor] was guilty of, these things are not the end of the story![46]

Here, then, Klingenschmitt suggests that the sailor whose loss is being grieved was selfish, lustful, immoral, or the like, and it is quite possible that some in the audience found this offensive and inappro-

---

44. Appendix H, H1, www.persuade.tv, accessed January 5, 2008.

45. Ibid.

46. Ibid., H2.

priate. Yet such reactions are unreasonable, since Klingenschmitt also identifies these weaknesses with himself and even universalizes them; he notes that all persons are guilty of them. Such rhetorical approaches are explicitly taught in preaching classes in seminary and (more importantly) in the armed services chaplain's schools. As indicated in the quote, Klingenschmitt did not leave the audience to think that he and D.R. (and themselves) are simply sinful, but went on to point out that Jesus came to provide redemption for them all. He was not condemning or judging D.R., but was instead pointing out that all persons are in the same situation with regard to sin, and that D.R. had done something about it by placing his faith in Jesus Christ.

Another possible place where there could have been offense involves a misunderstanding of Klingenschmitt's point regarding the meaning of our confidence in Christ (Rom 8:31). Klingenschmitt suggests that some in attendance at the funeral may think that D.R. went to Hell. His point, of course, is that it does not matter what humans think because the only opinion that matters with regard to salvation is God's, and he goes on to indicate that there is good reason to think that God forgave D.R. of his sins.[47] Some in attendance, though, may have only heard the suggestion of D.R.'s condemnation without the further explanation of his salvation.

A third point of possible contention in the memorial service sermon was Klingenschmitt's suggestion that it may be inappropriate to mourn the loss of D.R. While it should be noted that he did not explicitly say that his death should not be mourned, Klingenschmitt did indicate that celebration (of D.R.'s new life in eternity) could be at least an equally valid response. It seems that any tension over this point could have much to do with denominational affiliation and differences in worship style. Even though Klingenschmitt was, at the time, endorsed as an Episcopal priest, he himself has strong charismatic tendencies and so it is not surprising that he would bring the celebrative component into even a memorial service. Yet, some may have felt like he was judging them for grieving and for failing to view D.R.'s motorcycle accident as an occasion for joy.

Thus, it seems that none of the proposed points of contention may serve as valid reasons for complaint with regard to the content of Klingenschmitt's memorial service sermon. They have to do mostly with either a partial understanding of his point or a disagreement over style/

47. Ibid., H5.

worship for a memorial service. The only other alternative is that which Klingenschmitt himself suggests—that it was the Gospel itself which offended. This very well may be the case, as he gave a very clear invitation at the end of the service. The Apostle Paul makes it clear that the Gospel is inherently offensive and inexplicable to carnal people (1 Cor 1:18-29). This, though, is a religious issue. The command has no right to punish a chaplain for the content of a sermon preached in a worship service, even if the commander disagrees with the theology or feels like he is somehow being told that he needs to repent.[48] The bottom line is that his attendance, just as for everyone else, is *voluntary*. If he does not like what is shared, then he is under no obligation to remain. It should also be noted, though, that a chaplain could conceivably be disciplined for the content of his sermon by his endorsing agency. That is, if a sermon is deemed to promote doctrine (or ethics) which is out of step with that chaplain's denomination, he could lose his endorsement and thereby, his position and career. But this is not what happened in this case—Klingenschmitt's sermon was in keeping with Christian doctrine generally and Episcopal theology specifically. The sermon should not ever have been an issue for his continuance in Naval chaplaincy, and the chaplains who advised the command to punish him for it should themselves be investigated for religious discrimination, something chaplains are supposed to ensure does not occur and in fact exist to prevent.

CONCLUSION

There are several issues that I believe are worth noting with regard to this case, and I would like to address each, along with my own thoughts on the implications of the case and with consideration to my own experiences as an evangelical military chaplain. First, my own experience as an evangelical serving as a chaplain in the United States military has been largely posi-

48. The military makes a clear distinction between a memorial service, which is a religious worship service, and a memorial ceremony, which, while often times led by a chaplain (but not necessarily), is not religious but instead patriotic in nature. Soldiers/sailors may be required to attend a memorial ceremony, but cannot be compelled to attend a memorial service. D.R.'s service was a memorial service (and thus, religious). Even though persons cannot be ordered to attend such a service, they often times choose to do so out of love/ respect for the deceased. On a personal note, I always recommend a service (as opposed to a ceremony) to commanders so that Scripture can be read and the gospel may be presented. Most soldiers/sailors want to hear a word from God when mourning the loss of a brother-in-arms. A memorial ceremony does not adequately provide that opportunity.

tive; I have rarely experienced pressure to compromise my own evangelical commitments; the few times I did were not due to secularly-minded commanders, but rather to pluralistic-conscious senior chaplains who were, for the most part, understanding when I voiced my concerns over what they were asking me to do or not do. Some may think that my experience is unique or radically different from Lt. Klingenschmitt's because I am a member of the Army National Guard and not the Active Component, the thought being that the reserves are more evangelical-friendly than the active component(s). Interestingly, this was my own thinking early in my career as a chaplain. My perception of most active duty chaplains was that they were neo-orthodox at best, outright universalists at worst, and classical liberals for the most part. When I was deployed to Fort Bragg in October 2001 as part of Operation Noble Eagle 1, I imagined being persecuted by the active duty chaplains for being a reservist and an evangelical. Nothing could have been further from the truth. While I would estimate about thirty percent of the chaplains at Fort Bragg had some evangelical leanings, there was never pressure from above to compromise evangelical commitments, except insofar as monetary giving to the consolidated chaplain's fund was strongly encouraged, and participation in a joint Christian (Protestant) Sunrise Easter Service was mandatory unless compelling reasons could be given for abstaining [I had no problem with participating]. So my own experience was positive.

It should be noted, though, that I can only speak of the Army. It does seem that there are differences in the religious climates of the services. The fact that the case against the Air Force [Academy] is based on a complaint that it fosters a climate only hospitable to evangelicals and the cases against the Navy are based on complaints that it has a religious climate which is hostile to evangelicals should suffice to establish this point.[49] It should come as no surprise to find that Lt. Klingenschmitt served as a missile officer in the Air Force for 11 years before accepting a commission

---

49. There are several cases currently in litigation against the Navy. For example, there is a class-action suit filed by a group of 17 evangelical chaplains, representing potentially over 1,000 chaplains. The case suggests that the Navy's promotion system for chaplains has favored chaplains from liturgical Protestant groups and Catholics over evangelicals. See Hamilton, "A Religious Bias Suit" at http://writ.news.findlaw.com/hamilton/20020829. html. See also AP, "Federal lawsuits accuse Navy" http://www.freedomforum.org; AP, "Navy religious-discrimination lawsuits given class-action status," http://www.freedomforum.org; Leaming, "Chaplains sue Navy" (04.20.2000), http://www.freedomforum.org. Some of these suits will be examined in the following chapter.

as a Navy chaplain (which included a reduction in rank/pay grade). So it could be the case that Lt. Klingenschmitt was still operating on the model presented to him as an Air Force officer, regardless of the Navy training he received.

I wish to make two additional comments with regard to Klingen-schmitt's case, one questioning, at a minimum, his wisdom if not his motivation, and one in his defense. First, I cannot help but wonder at Lt. Klingenschmitt's actions in response to those in authority over him. While he has presented himself to the media as accepting those who God has placed over him, he has pushed to the limit the legal statutes by which he agreed to abide on more than one occasion. For example, Klingenschmitt was found guilty in a summary court-martial for refusing to obey a lawful order. His decision to wear his uniform at the White House demonstration and call it a worship service is hardly commendable. While it seems that the events that day merely included a prayer, some Scripture, and then media statements/interviews by Judge Roy Moore, among others, the fact that involvement in the event could be *perceived* to be a demonstration should have alerted him to the potential for (at best) misunderstanding between himself and his commander. His claim that the offering of a prayer at a public gathering qualifies as a worship service is not compel-ling. Even so-called "worship services" held in front of abortion clinics, for example, cannot be so innocently construed; though the participants are communing with God, there is still an element of civil discord involved; the choice of the site for the religious observance included consideration of political impact, and it is here that Klingenschmitt was wrong-headed. He was not convicted of "praying in Jesus' name," but rather of wearing his uniform at a political event, which is a violation of the Uniform Code of Military Justice and military regulations. So Klingenschmitt was not justified in his actions of protest. Even civilian courts have noted that the same rights to protest are not accorded to members of the military as to members of the civilian populace.

I should be honest and note that, on first reading of Klingenschmitt's arguments and complaints, as well as his actions, I immediately thought of him as a trouble-maker. It has been my experience, over the years, that there are some evangelicals who, due to their personalities and zeal for evange-lism, are unable to work within a pluralistic environment. Those persons probably should not seek to enter military chaplaincy from the start. There are some evangelicals who seek to make every issue a hill worth dying on, but we must remember that when we do this, we very well may die! Lt. Klingenschmitt saw praying "in Jesus' name" at mandatory-attendance events one such item, and he should be commended for his convictions. However, I should note, in Klingenschmitt's defense, that he does not seem to be the sort of chaplain that cannot function within a pluralistic environment. In fact, as already noted, he took a stand for both Jewish and Muslim soldiers within his command: "Aboard the USS Anzio, his first post, he backed a Jewish sailor's request to receive kosher meals and tried to get permission for a Muslim crewman to take a turn offering the nightly benediction over the ship's public address system."[50] So, it seems that there are some rather strange things taking place with respect to Klingenschmitt's career; it may be that he got on the bad side of a commander or supervisory chaplain, and has felt constrained to make the issue a legal one due to a lack of recourse within the Naval command structure.

The big issue of concern—the offering of prayers in Jesus' name, and the attendant concern over sanctions against evangelistic preaching—has been an issue discussed and debated at the armed services' chaplain's schools for years. The demand for non-sectarian prayers at mandatory-attendance meetings has been dubbed "ceremonial deism" since Eugene Rostow, Dean of the Yale Law School, used the term in a public address at Brown University in 1962. It is a legal term for nominally religious statements and practices deemed to be within the confines of the establishment clause. It would be valid for evangelicals to question the constitutionality of such a position, though it may not be advisable. These issues will be examined in more detail in chapter four.

Should evangelicals offer prayers that are not "in Jesus' name?" That is, should evangelicals refrain from appending the phrase, "in Jesus' name" at the end of the prayers they offer for mandatory-attendance meetings and ceremonies? Or, more to the point, should evangelicals fight, along with Lt. Klingenschmitt, for the right to offer such prayers at mandatory-attendance meetings? It seems to me that the answer to some of these questions depends upon the leading of the Holy Spirit in one's life, and the common practice of the individual chaplain's faith. For my own practice, I often, even in the confines of my own home, offer prayers "in Your Name," and so, the encouragement of the Army leadership for chaplains to offer similar prayers has little effect on the way I pray. However, those

50. Cooperman, A01.

chaplains whose faith commitments require prayers to end with the phrase, "in Jesus' name," should not compromise their faith commitments. Instead, they should inform their commanders (or whoever is asking them to pray at a mandatory-attendance event) that, in order to faithfully execute their responsibilities, they must pray in that way. Additionally, though, those chaplains have a responsibility to their commanders to advise them about the potential conflict with the establishment clause and the possibility of offending soldiers within the command. It is then the responsibility of the commander to decide what he wants to do—have a sectarian prayer by the chaplain, no prayer at all, or a non-sectarian prayer by someone else. This, of course, is an ideal situation, but it seems to me that most commanders, once informed that chaplains must be good examples of the clergy from the denominations and ecclesiastical groups which endorse them [e.g., I must be a good example of a Southern Baptist preacher], do not resist the requests of chaplains for respect for their personal religious commitments.

The chaplain who chooses to take a stand on this issue should realize that he may be missing opportunities to offer public prayers that could have an impact on soldiers within the unit he serves. He should realize that, by insisting on a sectarian prayer, he may be cutting his feet out from under himself, as far as ministry opportunities go. Thus, it seems to me that it is better to offer a prayer to the Lord in front of the soldiers of the unit, than to not offer a prayer at all. Again, this is subject to one's own conscience.

It should be noted, though, that the Department of Defense has compelling reasons for its guidance that public prayers at ceremonies and other mandatory-attendance events should be non-sectarian: "This provision [a bill under consideration by Congress which allows chaplains to offer sectarian prayers; e.g., 'in Jesus' name'] could marginalize chaplains who, in exercising their conscience, generate discomfort at mandatory formations. . . . Such erosion of unit cohesion is avoided by the military's present insistence on inclusive prayer at interfaith gatherings—something that the House legislation would operate against."[51] While we may not be terribly concerned that offering a prayer "in Jesus' name" would destroy unit cohesion (and it is doubtful that it would), we should have concern for unit cohesion when a Muslim chaplain offers a prayer to Allah at a mandatory-attendance ceremony. That is, most of us would balk at the

51. Written statement from the Pentagon, quoted in Banerjee, "Proposal on Military Chaplains" *New York Times* (September 19, 2006).

suggestion that we could be forced to pray to the god of Islam, and rightly so.[52] Thus, we may want to think through the desire to force commanders to allow chaplains to pray sectarian prayers at such gatherings.

Prohibitions against evangelistic sermons during religious services are unconstitutional. Any suggestion that evangelicals not have an altar-call or claim that faith in Jesus is required for salvation should be rejected. Any reprimands or legal injunctions against such preaching within or without the military should be fought. Under Title X of the U.S. Code, chaplains are required to be representative of their respective religious denominations. The requirement of outside endorsement and ordination make clear that necessary allowance for sectarian statements within the confines of the chapel service. Evangelicals should not shrink from preaching the penal substitutionary death of Christ for the sins of humanity, and the fires of Hell as the destiny of those who die apart from a personal relationship with Jesus Christ by faith. To do anything less is to shirk the responsibility placed upon them by their respective denominations and to violate their own consciences (not to mention the demands of the Word of God!).

In the subsequent chapters many of these issues will be explored in more detail. Questions of the legal rights of soldiers/sailors, as well as the Constitutional basis for a tax-funded chaplaincy program will be addressed in chapter three. Questions raised in the Klingenschmitt case regarding theological liberalism and an ad hoc establishment of universalism or ceremonial deism will be addressed in chapter four. These issues also impact views of proper worship and counseling and will be discussed in chapters five and seven respectively.

---

52. In fact, Klingenschmitt himself opposed the much publicized offering of a Hindu prayer in the United States Senate, lauding the individuals who illegally interrupted the prayer. Klingenschmitt, "Hindu chaplain prays," www.worldnetdaily.com/news/article.asp?ARTICLE_ID=56688, accessed January 25,2008.

3

"Separation of Church & State"

Legal Issues in Military Chaplaincy

*It is in the space between the Constitutional command against practices
respecting an establishment of religion and the command against practices
which prohibit the free exercise thereof that the military chaplaincy rests.*

—U. S. District Judge Richard M. Urbina,
Larsen v. U. S. Navy (2007)

INTRODUCTION

MINISTRY IN A PLURALISTIC environment has many unique challenges. It can be difficult for the evangelical chaplain to follow
the dictates of perform/provide while retaining his commitment to
evangelism and the exclusivity of the gospel proclamation. Related to
these competing concerns are legal issues which stem from the First
Amendment, which states, "Congress shall make no law respecting an
establishment of religion, or prohibiting the free exercise thereof."[1] The
amendment is generally viewed as being composed of two separate clauses: the Establishment Clause and the Free Exercise Clause. Each of these
clauses is designed to protect those fundamental human rights which are
so foundational to the ideals of our nation: life, liberty and the pursuit of
happiness. Questions regarding violations of either of these clauses occa-

1. U. S. Constitution, Amendment I.

69

sionally come up in chaplaincy. For example, there have been challenges, based on the Establishment Clause, to the constitutionality of government-funded chaplaincy programs and/or religious activities. Questions related to the Free Exercise Clause generally take one of two forms: either there is a question about the religious rights of individuals within the organization or there is a question about the free exercise of the chaplain. While both clauses relate specifically to governmental actions (and so are of particular concern to chaplains working for governmental agencies/ organizations), they are still relevant to all forms of chaplaincy, as most private institutions follow the government's lead with respect to pluralism and given the litigious nature of the current work environment.

FREE EXERCISE

As noted, legal cases related to military chaplaincy which charge a violation of the Free Exercise Clause generally take one of two forms. First, they may involve a claim by a service member that his/her free exercise rights were violated due to a specific order given by the command or to a regulation or policy set by the service member's branch. Second, they may take the form of a complaint by a chaplain who has been asked to do something which violates his/her religious commitments, or who has felt it necessary to refrain from activity that he/she believes is entailed by his/ her faith. In either case, the complaint suggests that there may, indeed, be limits upon the government's ability to regulate the activities and/or speech of service members.

Goldman v. Weinberger

Goldman v. Weinberger is perhaps the most important case for resolving questions of religious accommodation and serves as the quintessential case for free exercise challenges by service members. The facts of the case are clear and undisputed. Captain S. Simcha Goldman, an orthodox Jew and ordained rabbi, was ordered to refrain from wearing a yarmulke indoors while in uniform because doing so violated the Air Force regulation governing the wear of uniforms (AFR 35-10). Specifically, the regulation states, "headgear will not be worn . . . while indoors except by armed security police in the performance of their duties."[2] Goldman's superiors at the military hospital in which he worked as a clinical psychologist had overlooked

2. AFR 35-10 (1980), para. 1–6.h (2)(f)

his wear of the yarmulke indoors for almost five years, but after a complaint was lodged when he wore it with his uniform in a court-martial proceeding, he was told to only wear it in the hospital or under his service cap when outdoors. Goldman refused and filed suit in Federal Court.

He argued that the regulation violates his free exercise rights because the wearing of the yarmulke is required by his religious beliefs. The Air Force's defense rested on the argument that military uniform requirements (including uniformity in outward appearance) are designed to both encourage group mentality and foster obedience among service members. To allow individuation in the wear of visible religious clothing or symbols could lead to a breakdown in military order in at least three ways. First, it could detract from the individual service members' identification with the community of soldiers. Second, it could cause friction between adherents of competing religions. Third, it could create resentment due to perceived preferential treatment. The concern over the perception of preferential treatment of some religions raised an additional concern: if allowances were made with respect to the yarmulke, then other similar allowances may be requested by adherents of other faiths, some which may not be possible to accommodate.[3] This could lead to cries of discrimination or worse, charges that by accommodating some religions and not others, the government (in this case the Air Force) is in effect *establishing* a religion.[4]

The Supreme Court found in favor of the Air Force. While the specific finding in the case is virtually inconsequential in the current military context (given that the Department of Defense has since published guidance for the Accommodation of Religious Practices; DoD Directive 1300.17 (1988); DA PAM 600-75 (1993); SECNAVINST 1730.9 (1997); AFPD 52-1 (2006)), the ruling in the case still serves as a benchmark for judicial review of military policy and regulations, even with respect to the Free Exercise Clause. It demonstrates the Court's reluctance to question the wisdom and/or judgment of military leaders and policy makers even when regulations and policies infringe on service members' first amendment rights. The unique role and mission of the military serves as much

3. Air Force counsel argued that "while a yarmulke might not seem obtrusive to a Jew, neither does a turban to a Sikh, a saffron robe to a Satchidananda Ashram-Integral Yogi, nor do dreadlocks to a Rastafarian." Post at 519.

4. This line of reasoning may seem far-fetched to some, but it follows similar logic to that used in one of the Navy chaplaincy cases discussed in the next chapter.

of the basis for this deference. Writing for the majority opinion, Justice Rehnquist makes it clear that the military is given exceptional leeway in constitutional issues:

> Our review of military regulations challenged on First Amendment grounds is far more deferential than constitutional review of similar laws or regulations designed for civilian society. The military need not encourage debate or tolerate protest to the extent that such tolerance is required of the civilian state by the First Amendment; to accomplish its mission the military must foster instinctive obedience, unity, commitment, and esprit de corps.[5]

Not all justices were convinced by the Air Force's claim or by the general reluctance among the judiciary to question military procedure or policy. Writing for the dissenting opinion, Justice Brennan (joined by Justice Marshall) wrote, "When a military service burdens the free exercise rights of its members in the name of necessity, it must provide, as an initial matter and at a minimum, a credible explanation of how the contested practice is likely to interfere with the proffered military interest."[6] In other words, Justices Brennan and Marshall believe that the courts have a right to evaluate military policies which infringe on individual service members' constitutional rights, and the Air Force failed to demonstrate that Goldman's wear of the yarmulke would diminish Air Force readiness. In this case, then, the burden of proof falls upon the respective service. Also dissenting was Justice Blackmun, who argued that the Air Force's claim could not be substantiated in light of the fact that Goldman had worn his yarmulke for so many years without incident:

> In my view, this case does not require us to determine the extent to which the ordinary test for inroads on religious freedom must be modified in the military context, because the Air Force has failed to produce even a minimally credible explanation for its refusal to allow Goldman to keep his head covered indoors. . . . Goldman's modest supplement to the Air Force uniform clearly poses by itself no threat to the Nation's military readiness. Indeed, the District Court specifically found that Goldman has worn a yarmulke on base for years without any adverse effect on his performance, any

---

5. *Goldman v. Weinberger*, 475 U.S. 503, 507 (1986).

6. Ibid., at 516.

disruption of operations at the base, or any complaints from other personnel."[7]

Justice O'Connor also penned a dissenting opinion, arguing that the court should "attempt to articulate and apply an appropriate standard for a free exercise claim in the military context, and should examine Captain Goldman's claim in light of that standard."[8] Ultimately, Justice O'Connor argued that precedent requires that restrictions by the state on individual constitutional rights, even those of military service members, can only be justified by particularly compelling reasons and that no such reasons exist (or at least were presented) in this case:

> One can, however, glean at least two consistent themes from this Court's precedents. First, when the government attempts to deny a free exercise claim, it must show that an unusually important interest is at stake, whether that interest is denominated 'compelling,' 'of the highest order,' or 'overriding.' Second, the government must show that granting the requested exemption will do substantial harm to that interest, whether by showing that the means adopted is the 'least restrictive' or 'essential,' or that the interest will not 'otherwise be served.'[9]

The latitude given to the military regarding restrictions of individual soldier's free exercise rights does have its limits. As noted in the dissenting opinions in *Goldman*, governmental restrictions of fundamental rights must be based on an overriding government interest. Questions of what sorts of government interests qualify to override *God-given* rights sit as the basis of all cases related to free exercise and have been a source of increased tension in recent years.

Of particular concern to evangelical chaplains is the issue of command regulation of speech within the context of chapel worship services. Evangelical concerns over restrictions on free speech from the pulpit are not confined to the military. Reports of pastors in Canada and Sweden

---

7. Ibid., at 526. Of course, the Air Force leadership was not so much concerned with the wearing of the yarmulke, though it did believe there are reasons for not allowing it. What is of primary concern is the individual's (Goldman's) refusal to follow a lawful order. Such behavior, especially by a commissioned officer, sets an example of individualism and free thinking and a willingness to disobey orders that cannot be tolerated. Goldman should have sought redress, the argument goes, through proper military channels.

8. Ibid., at 529.

9. Ibid., at 530.

languishing in prison for violating so-called "hate-speech" legislation because they spoke out against the morality of homosexuality, have set evangelicals in the United States on edge, especially when reports circulate about similar legislative attempts and lobbying in the U.S.[10] Many evangelicals fear that their right to free speech is in danger from overzealous governmental regulators. In the next chapter, concerns about persecution of evangelicals will be addressed, if only briefly, but here it is important to examine the case law with respect to such regulation, especially in the context of the military chaplaincy.

Rigdon v. Perry

The Supreme Court has not reviewed any cases regarding restrictions on free speech within the chapel setting, but one noteworthy case was decided by the U.S. District Court for the District of Columbia. The case, known as *Rigdon v. Perry*, arose out of an attempt by the Armed Services to prevent Catholic chaplains from participating in the "Project Life Postcard Campaign."[11] The campaign was organized by the Catholic

10. Swedish pastor Ake Green, a Pentecostal, was sentenced to a month in jail for reportedly preaching against the morality of homosexuality. See, for example, "Swedish Pastor Sentenced," accessed 10 March 2008. Interestingly, his sentence was eventually thrown out and he served none of the time. A Canadian pastor was sentenced to probation and community service following his involvement in organizing a protest against Islam; specifically against what he perceived as preferential treatment Islam was receiving in the local high school. He was never jailed for his actions and they did not have anything to do with the content of his sermons. See, for example, the article by Janet Folger expressing concern over limitations on Christian activity in the public arena by Canadian pastor Mark Harding. Folger, "When grandmas go to jail," accessed 10 March 2008. Yet evangelicals continue to believe that pastors are, in actuality, being jailed for the content of their sermons in countries which supposedly value free speech.

11. Another case which impacts questions of chaplains' rights to preach according to the dictates of their faith traditions and/or consciences is that of *Veitch v. England* (formerly *Veitch v. Danzig*). Following a series of alleged harassments by a senior naval chaplain, a subsequent confrontation, and an Equal Opportunity (EO) investigation, and facing an upcoming court-martial for insubordination, Chaplain D. Philip Veitch resigned his commission from the Navy. He then brought suit against the Navy, claiming he was effectively forced out because of his evangelical beliefs.

According to Veitch, his supervisory chaplain at the Naval Station in Naples, Italy, Captain Buchmiller (a Catholic priest) repeatedly criticized him for his beliefs and preaching, and gave him reduced responsibilities and a poor working environment as punitive measures. Veitch filed an EO complaint, but the officer in charge of the investigation, Commander Lawrence Zoeller, a medical service officer, found in favor of Buchmiller because he believed Veitch had violated what he perceived to be the Navy's

Church leadership to get parishioners to send postcards to Congressional Representatives and Senators in an effort to lobby them to override President Clinton's veto of HR 1833, commonly referred to as the Partial

policy of requiring pluralism among religions. Zoeller believed Buchmiller had been correct to counsel Veitch because Zoeller viewed Veitch's preaching as derogatory to other religions. In response and after another confrontation in which Buchmiller allegedly tore a Reformation poster from Veitch's office wall, Veitch wrote a harsh e-mail to Buchmiller. In the Appellate Court's findings, it is described as a "rebarbative missive" and a "four-page broadside attach on Buchmiller's command and character." (*Veitch v. England,* p. 3). As a result, Veitch faced a court-martial for, among other things (missing four staff meetings), disrespect towards a superior commissioned officer. Rather than face a court-martial, he resigned and then sought injunctive relief in Federal Court.

Both the District and the Appeals Courts denied his request for summary judgment and found in favor for the Navy. The reasons are many, but they basically boil down to three: (1) Veitch lacks standing to sue the Navy for continuing Constitutional violations because he is no longer a member; (2) Veitch was rightfully disciplined for his insubordination, which could have (I would say, most likely would have) led to his involuntary removal from the Navy; and (3) the alleged instances of harassment did not rise to the level of *constructive discharge*; that is, his resignation because of said harassment was not the only reasonable alternative—in fact, he did not even exhaust his options in the Naval legal system before turning to the civilian. These factors led the Courts to determine that the Navy was well within its rights in accepting his resignation.

The case raises many issues of concern. For example, the alleged actions of Chaplain Buchmiller and the Navy's failure to intervene are particularly troubling. A chaplain of his rank and position should surely not act in such childish ways and ought to have a spiritual maturity and skill with people so that such caustic relationships as the one he had with Veitch would not be possible. It is worth noting that Veitch's complaints about Buchmiller's leadership and personal skills are not the only ones on official record. Several affidavits from junior naval chaplains, naval personnel, and even family members of service members and other civilians involved in the Protestant chapel programs at Naval Station, Naples, have been entered into the public record. Some of the most disturbing note persons traumatized by his invective towards their beliefs. This evidence at least suggests coercion in matters of faith at the Naval Station.

As disconcerting as this is, the content of the Zoeller Report is moreso, as it seems to justify Veitch's complaint that he was punished for the content of his sermons. Generally speaking, chaplains cannot be forced to preach pluralism as Zoeller concludes Veitch should have done. Quite the contrary—chaplains must preach according to the dictates of their respective faiths. As noted in chapter one, for some, that means preaching salvation exclusively through personal faith in Christ. However, as also noted in chapter one, free speech has its limits, even in chapel sermons. In the military context, those limits may be viewed as entailing a prohibition on explicitly criticizing specific faith groups (e.g., calling Islam "of the Devil"). Thus, it is difficult to offer a complete evaluation without the specific objectionable content of Veitch's sermons. Nevertheless, it seems to me that the civilian courts failed here, for a correct understanding of the military culture would lead most reasonable persons to view Veitch's complaints as meritorious or at least worthy of unbiased (non-Naval) review. The problem here is that Veitch let his emotions get the best of him and, by sending the e-mail, effectively disallowed any further review.

Birth Abortion ban. About a month before the postcard campaign was set to begin, the Archdiocese for the Military Services sent a letter to Catholic chaplains suggesting they encourage parishioners to participate in this national Catholic effort. Approximately a week later, on June 5, 1996, an Air Force Judge Advocate General issued an opinion letter advising against chaplain participation. Three reasons were given: first, it appeared to violate Air Force regulations and Department of Defense directives which prohibit Active Duty service members from using their official authority to solicit votes for a particular political issue; second, it also seemed to violate Air Force regulations against service members engaging in partisan political activity; and third, it was in conflict with Department of Defense Instruction 5500.7-A 6-100, which states that service members "may not participate in political activities while on duty; while wearing a uniform, badge insignia or other similar item that identifies his position; or while in any building occupied in the discharge of official duties by an individual employed by the United States Government."[12]

Father Vincent Rigdon, an Air Force Reserve chaplain, sued, claiming that he felt that the prohibition from the Air Force inhibited his ability to preach according to the dictates of his religion (even to violate a direct order by his church's leadership). Others joined the suit, including Rabbi Kaye, an active duty Air Force chaplain, who argued that "it is impossible, indeed incoherent, to separate moral teachings from Judaism. And when a law is immoral, I believe that as a Rabbi, I must not remain silent."[13]

The Air Force initially tried to have the case thrown out, arguing that Chaplain Rigdon does not have standing since he is only a reservist, and that the case is moot because by the time the court reviewed the case, the postcard campaign was long over and the bill no longer in Congress. The court disagreed because Chaplain Kaye is active duty and because a similar bill was being considered in Congress at the time.[14] The case went forward, and Judge Stanley Sporkin presided.

---

12. *Rigdon v. Perry,* 962 F. Supp. 150 (D.D.C. 1997).

13. Ibid.

14. It would be interesting to know if the case would still have been considered had Chaplain Kaye not joined in the suit or if the similar bill were not already being discussed in Congress. There is evidence that Judge Sporkin would have allowed it to proceed since the regulation was being imposed on Chaplain Rigdon, who, although a reservist, still fulfilled duties in an Active Duty base chapel about 40 percent of Sundays in a year.

In arguing the case, the Air Force relied most heavily upon DOD Directive 1344.10, *Political Activities of Members of the Armed Forces on Active Duty* (June 1990), arguing that it clearly states that members of the armed forces may not use their official military authority for soliciting votes, understood more broadly as lobbying. The court found that the specific activity under consideration, encouraging parishioners to send postcards, is not direct lobbying because it is not urging congregants to vote for a particular candidate or a particular ballot initiative. Instead, it was directed at their influencing members of congress to vote a particular way. The court also dismissed the Air Force's claim that chaplains have official authority because they are commissioned officers. All the Air Force counsel could demonstrate is that chaplains hold rank, not that they wield authority that may be viewed as commanding. The Air Force attempted to argue that, because chaplains' primary duties are religious, all religious speech is "official," and therefore, may not touch on political issues. The court, however, did not accept this logic, and drawing upon AR 165-1, *Chaplain Activities in the United States Army* (para. 4-4a), concluded that the chaplain's dual roles as spiritual leader and commissioned officer point to two types of acts: "While military chaplains may be employed by the military to perform religious duties, it does not follow that every word they utter bears the imprimatur of official military authority; if anything, the content of their services and counseling bears the imprimatur of the religious ministries to which they belong."[15]

The Air Force argued that some service members could perceive a chaplain's encouragement to lobby Congress as an order, since the chaplain holds rank greater than many who attend services. In this way, then, the admonitions in a sermon would become direct orders and would be an unauthorized use of official authority. The Court found this suggestion to be ridiculous, and cited the plaintiffs' response as sufficient to dispense with the argument.[16]

15. Ibid. This statement is meant to refer to denominations, as referenced in AR 165-1, para. 4-5e (1).

16. In his reply to this argument, Chaplain Rigdon explained, "If a chaplain were to say to a congregant who had confessed to having a bitter argument with his wife, 'Go and forgive her, and say ten Hail Mary's,' surely this could not by any stretch of the imagination be considered the issuance of a military order, the disobedience of which opens the service member to prosecution under the Uniform Code of Military Justice. . . . If what a chaplain tells his congregants to do or believe while preaching is an order, then for years orders have being [sic] issued from all the branches of the military for service members

The Court found that the plaintiffs are entitled to redress under the Religious Freedom Restoration Act, which prohibits the government from substantially burdening a person's exercise in religion unless it has a compelling interest in restricting the exercise and it has no other recourse to meet its interest that is less restrictive. In essence, the Court agreed with the plaintiffs that they have the right to determine if opposition to partial birth abortion is an important part of their faith. While the government does have an interest in having a politically-disinterested, well-ordered and disciplined military, it has provided no evidence that the preaching activities (or exhortation to participate in the postcard campaign) will lead to political conflicts within its ranks. This led Judge Sporkin to conclude that the rights of the plaintiffs cannot be diminished: "Here, the compelling interests advanced by the military are outweighed by the military chaplains' right to autonomy in determining the religious content of their sermons, especially because the defendants have failed to show how the speech restriction as applied to chaplains advances these interests."[17]

The defendants disputed Chaplain Rigdon's claim that urging parishioners to participate in the campaign is an essential part of his faith by pointing to another Catholic chaplain (of a higher rank, Navy Captain John F. Friel) who did not think it necessary, and instead simply informed his parishioners of the dispute and said they can decide for themselves what they would like to do about the bill in Congress. Judge Sporkin found this argument to smack of government authorization of certain forms of religion and to border on a violation of the Establishment Clause. At the very least, it is a violation of Free Exercise. In commenting on this argument in his finding, he wrote,

> While Captain Friel's speech is permissible, Father Rigdon's speech is not. Therefore, although the defendants claim otherwise, they have sanctioned one view of Catholicism (it is not necessary to write to Congress) over another (it is necessary). Such favoritism not only impinges on Father Rigdon (and on Rabbi Kaye because of his view of Judaism), but on their congregants, because these chaplains are not free to advocate what they believe to be appropriate religious conduct. If, after an emotional sermon about the

---

to believe in the resurrection of Jesus, to believe that the Torah was written by Moses who was inspired by God, that Moslem soldiers must pray daily, and that Catholic service members must go to Mass every week." Ibid., *Plaintiff's Reply* at 4.

17. Ibid.

'abomination' of partial birth abortion, congregants were to rise from the pews and ask Father Rigdon or Rabbi Kaye what they can do to stop this practice, these chaplains would have to respond, 'I cannot say.' This muzzling of religious guidance is the direct result of the defendants' viewpoint discrimination.[18]

Ultimately, Judge Sporkin contends, the line between political or religious speech, when issues of a moral nature are under consideration, is too fine for the Court to delimit. It is a question of theology, not law, and therefore, one to be answered by theologians, not lawyers and judges.[19] In the conclusion to his ruling, he chastised the government's attempts to regulate religious speech given in the context of worship by the clergy:

What we have here is the government's attempt to override the Constitution and the laws of the land by a directive that clearly interferes with military chaplains' free exercise and free speech rights, as well as those of their congregants. On its face, this is a drastic act and can be sanctioned only by compelling circumstances. The government clearly has not met its burden. The "speech" that the plaintiffs intend to employ to inform their congregants of their religious obligations has nothing to do with their role in the military. They are neither being disrespectful to the Armed Forces nor in any way urging their congregants to defy military orders. The chaplains in this case seek to preach only what they would tell their non-military congregants. There is no need for heavy-handed censorship, and any attempt to impinge on the plaintiffs' constitutional and legal rights is not acceptable.[20]

18. In a footnote appended to the ruling at this point, Judge Sporkin pointed out that the anti-lobbying legislation is not content-neutral, for under the Air Force's interpretation, chaplains cannot encourage parishioners to lobby their Representatives, but can discourage parishioners from lobbying their Representatives. Thus, it does not prohibit all religiously-motivated political speech in the chapel, but just certain forms of that speech.

19. He writes, "Even assuming *arguendo* that Father Rigdon's intended speech is in some sense political, it is not the role of this Court to draw fine distinctions between degrees of religious speech and to hold that religious speech is protected, but religious speech with so-called political overtones is not. See *Widmar v. Vincent*, 454 U.S. 263, 270 n. 7, 102 S. Ct. 269, 274 n. 7, 70 L. Ed. 2d 440 (1981) (refusing to hold that 'religious worship' is unprotected speech while speech about religion is protected; 'even if the distinction drew an arguably principled line, it is highly doubtful that it would lie within the judicial competence to administer'). Accordingly, Father Rigdon's and Rabbi Kaye's intended speech lies within the limitations on the religious forum in which they speak." 962 F. Supp. 150 (D.D.C. 1997).

20. Ibid.

The finding states that the military has to prove compelling interest for restricting speech in worship if that speech is religiously motivated, even if it has implications for politics. The court found that "the compelling interests advanced by the military are outweighed by the military chaplains' right to autonomy in determining the religious content of their sermons . . ."[21] According to Wildhack, this means that the current litigation in the Navy over concerns regarding free speech should find in favor of the chaplains.[22]

ESTABLISHMENT

Lemon v. Kurtzman

The Supreme Court case of *Lemon v. Kurtzman* is arguably the most important litigation for judicial review of the Establishment Clause. Argued in early March and decided in late June of 1971, the case actually involved questions of the constitutionality of two separate state laws which provided state funds to support sectarian educational programs in various ways.

Rhode Island's 1969 Salary Supplement Act made a 15 percent salary supplement available to teachers at nonpublic schools. Approximately 25 percent of the state's elementary school students attended nonpublic schools. In order to receive the pay, teachers had to limit their teaching to courses offered in the public schools (using only materials used in public schools), and had to agree to refrain from teaching courses in religion. All payments made under the Act were to teachers at Catholic schools, many of whom were nuns.

Pennsylvania's Nonpublic Elementary and Secondary Education Act of 1968 allowed the State Superintendent to pay nonpublic schools for secular educational services by reimbursing them for teacher's salaries, textbooks, and other materials directly related to instruction of certain courses. Those courses approved for the program had to be secular in nature, and the textbooks (and other materials) were subject to approval by the superintendent. Over 20 percent of the state's student population attended nonpublic schools. Alton J. Lemon, a resident and taxpayer of Pennsylvania, brought suit in Federal Court. After the case was dismissed,

21. Ibid., at 162.
22. Wildhack, "Navy Chaplains at the Crossroads," 7.

he appealed to the Supreme Court. When the Court agreed to review the case, it was combined with two other suits related to the Rhode Island Statute.[23] The Court held that both statutes violate the First Amendment because "the cumulative impact of the entire relationship arising under the statutes involves excessive entanglement between government and religion."[24]

Lemon v. Kurtzman is most important for its findings with regard to evaluating legislational challenges based on the Establishment Clause. The Court's decision presented a three-pronged test for evaluating government actions, now known as the "Lemon test":

1. Must have a legitimate secular purpose;

2. Must not have the primary effect of either advancing or inhibiting religion; and

3. Must not result in excessive government entanglement with religion.

Two of the three prongs came from earlier decisions. First, the requirement that the law's "principal or primary effect must be one that neither advances nor inhibits religion" came from *Board of Education v. Allen,* 392 U.S. 236, 243 (1968), in which the Court ruled that state funds could be used to purchase textbooks for loan to students (grades seven to twelve) attending private schools, including religious schools. These findings were based largely on the Court's decision in a similar case, *Everson v. Board of Education* 330 U.S. 1 (1940), which allowed state funds to pay for bus fare of students attending parochial schools. Second, that the statute must not foster "an excessive government entanglement with religion" came from the findings in *Walz v. Tax Commission* 397 U.S. 664, 668 (1970), which allowed property tax exemptions to religious organizations.

Chief Justice Warren Burger, et al., acknowledged that in both Rhode Island and Pennsylvania, the intent of the statute was secular; it was not meant to promote religion. However, both statutes faltered on the second and third criteria. As Chief Justice Burger noted, the two state legislatures acknowledged the religious mission of parochial schools and took measures to limit that mission as it pertained to the use of state funds. In their effort to ensure that state monies were not used to promote religion,

23. *Earley v. DiCenso;* and *Commissioner of Education of Rhode Island v. DiCenso.*

24. *Lemon v. Kurtzman,* 403 U.S. 602, 603 (1971).

both statutes included oversight of the programs which led to excessive entanglement. In his majority opinion, Chief Justice Burger wrote,

> The two legislatures, however, have also recognized that church-related elementary and secondary schools have a significant religious mission and that a substantial portion of their activities is religiously oriented. They have therefore sought to create statutory restrictions designed to guarantee the separation between secular and religious educational functions and to ensure that State financial aid supports only the former. All these provisions are precautions taken in candid recognition that these programs approached, even if they did not intrude upon, the forbidden areas under the Religion Clauses.[25]

Justice Douglas penned a concurring opinion, in which he argued that taxpayer funding of *any* aspect of parochial education necessarily involves excessive entanglement because of the original purpose of parochial schools: to win converts. In order to ensure that the secular purpose of the money is met, the government must prevent the school from performing its originally intended mission:

> The surveillance or supervision of the States needed to police grants involved in these three cases, if performed, puts a public investigator into every classroom and entails a pervasive monitoring of these church agencies by secular authorities. Yet if that surveillance or supervision does not occur the zeal of religious proselytizers promises to carry the day and make a shambles of the Establishment Clause.[26]

Douglas is not only concerned for the integrity of the school, but also seems suspicious of the suggestion that secular subjects will be taught secularly in parochial schools. That is, he believes the teachers (many of whom were nuns) would use the opportunity to teach doctrine even in the non-religious courses. This is not to say that they are intentionally deceiving the State, but it is to say that they can divorce neither their personal religious beliefs and commitments, nor their pedagogical philosophy (which seems to necessarily include the teaching of religion within the so-called secular subjects), from their work for the schools:

25. Ibid., at 613.
26. Ibid., at 627.

Sectarian instruction, in which, of course, a State may not indulge, can take place in a course on Shakespeare or in one on mathematics. No matter what the curriculum offers, the question is, what is taught? We deal not with evil teachers but with zealous ones who may use any opportunity to indoctrinate a class. It is well known that everything taught in most parochial schools is taught with the ultimate goal of religious education in mind.[27]

Or again, Justice Douglas notes, "In the present cases we deal with the totality of instruction destined to be sectarian, at least in part, if the religious character of the school is to be maintained. A school which operates to commingle religion with other instruction plainly cannot secularize its instruction."[28] Justice Douglas, however, also expresses concern over the sort of oversight required by the government in this case, for it seems that it could evolve (devolve?) into a problem for free exercise. If the state is allowed to restrict religious instruction in religious schools, then problems seem inevitable: "The subtleties involved in applying this standard [no religious teaching in secular courses] are obvious. It places the State astride a sectarian school and gives it power to dictate what is or is not secular, what is or is not religious. I can think of no more disrupting influence apt to promote rancor and ill-will between church and state than this kind of surveillance and control."[29]

Ultimately, he argues, to subsidize parochial school teachers' salaries with tax dollars is to fund sectarian education, even if it is meant to only help fund secular subjects. The religious character of the school, or at least the religious commitments of its faculty, makes separating out some subjects as secular virtually impossible:

> . . . there are those who have the courage to announce that a State may nonetheless finance the secular part of a sectarian school's education program. That, however, makes a grave constitutional decision turn merely on cost accounting and bookkeeping entries. A history class, a literature class, or a science class in a parochial school is not a separate institute; it is part of the organic whole which the State subsidizes.[30]

27. Ibid., at 635.
28. Ibid., at 636.
29. Ibid., at 637.
30. Ibid., at 637.

The findings in *Lemon v. Kurtzman* may be viewed by some as a set-back for religion in the culture, or more to the point, as setting precedent whereby Christianity may be excluded from society. However, it seems that Douglas' words should give evangelicals considering a request for government funds reason for pause. The price for those funds may be too high.

Katcoff v. Marsh

The most important litigation questioning the use of government funds for religious programs is arguably the case of Katcoff versus Marsh. Two Harvard law students, Joel Katcoff and Allen Weider, sued the Secretary of the Army, stating that the Army chaplaincy programs were/are a violation of the Establishment Clause of the Constitution.[31] The case was first filed in November 1979, and was not settled until 1986. It was first considered in Federal District Court and, after that, the Second Circuit Court of Appeals, which concurred with most of the District Court's findings, but also remanded part (e.g., chaplaincy ministry to veterans) back to the District Court, finding that Congress and the Army do not, for the most part, violate the Constitution by providing chaplains with taxpayer funds. The case was not appealed again, seemingly due to Katcoff's and Wieder's weariness and need to focus on their newfound careers, and therefore, the issues in question could still conceivably be argued before the Supreme Court. Nevertheless, the findings of the District and Appeals Courts still serve as the legal basis for government-sponsored chaplaincy within the United States Armed Forces.

In responding to the initial complaint, the government moved for a dismissal on several grounds. First, it was argued that Katcoff and Wieder did not have standing because they did not pay taxes (at least at the time of the initial complaint, since they were full-time students) and therefore, did not have a right to raise a complaint about how tax dollars are used; second, the government claimed that the lawsuit was frivolous because any possible injury would be insignificant since the chaplaincy budget is so small compared to the overall Army budget (0.189 percent); third, even

31. As an interesting side note, when Katcoff and Wieder asked the Navy for statistical information on its chaplaincy program under the Freedom of Information Act, naval leadership informed them that they would have to pay for the man-hours and other expenses associated with obtaining the requested information. They withdrew their request and did not pursue a case against the Navy. The Army provided the information free of charge.

if the Army chaplaincy is a violation of the First Amendment, according to their own argument that the government and not the denomination or ecclesiastical agencies promotes chaplains, Katcoff and Wieder were not personally injured; fourth, the War Powers Clause of the Constitution precludes courts from ruling on military affairs; and fifth, the unique nature and history of the chaplaincy, going back to the nation's Founders prior to the Constitution, demonstrates that it is not a violation of the Establishment Clause. Federal District Court Judge Jacob Mishler denied the Army's motion to dismiss, but ultimately ruled in favor of the Army. In so doing, he also indicated the basis upon which the Army Chaplaincy may pass Constitutional muster: it may be Constitutional if it is reasonably necessary in order to ensure the protection of the free exercise rights of military personnel.

This proved prophetic, as concerns over free exercise for service members ultimately came to be seen as the legal basis for allowing a military chaplaincy. Katcoff and Wieder granted that free exercise of service members is a legitimate concern, but also argued that those religious needs of military personnel could be met by a civilian-funded, manned, and managed chaplaincy program to the military. They cited a study conducted by the United Church of Christ, which seemed to suggest that military chaplaincy is unnecessary, and produced an affidavit from Wisconsin Synod Lutheran Church President Reverend Carl Mischke, who argued that his denomination funded its own civilian chaplaincy program for the military, since its bylaws precluded ministers from serving in the military.

The United Church of Christ study did not have credibility, since even the leadership of that denomination did not take it seriously, but the example of the Wisconsin Synod's civilian chaplaincy program to the military looked to be a promising alternative to the government-sponsored program, and so Katcoff and Wieder made it the linchpin of their argument. They reasoned that, since the Wisconsin Synod provided ministry to its members in the military at its own cost, other faith groups could do the same for their members. Reflecting on this move, Drazin and Currey note,

> . . . Katcoff and Wieder had made a critical and decisive strategic error. Until the appearance of Mischke's statement, both the government and the plaintiffs could only argue abstractly that a civilian chaplaincy was or was not feasible. Now the plaintiffs had

presented a concrete example of a civilian chaplaincy and naively based their entire case on this model. . . . [Advisors to the Army Chief of Chaplains] were certain that if they could disclose the truth about the Wisconsin Synod's program to the court, any reasonable person would see and understand that it was limited in scope, inept in performance, and unable to meet soldiers' needs.[32]

The Appeals Court seemed to agree with this assessment, and concluded that a civilian chaplaincy program on a scale large enough to meet the diverse religious needs of the military is infeasible for a number of reasons. In the majority opinion, Circuit Judge Mansfield considered the Wisconsin Synod's program and found it wanting. First, it was misleading for Mischke to claim that the program was fully funded with denominational dollars. The Army provided a significant amount of logistical and physical support for the Wisconsin Synod chaplains, including transportation, housing, and food, among other things. It is impractical to suppose that each of these items could be charged back to the Church and therefore, they represent an incursion of expense on the part of the government. Second, according to affidavits submitted by two senior Army chaplains from the Missouri Synod Lutheran Church, the Wisconsin Synod's program was ineffective because it could not provide enough personnel to cover the area in which the Army served, and those chaplains that did have opportunity to visit soldiers were unable to do so with enough regularity to provide on-going pastoral care. Third, the Wisconsin Synod's program was unreliable due to the civilian status of its chaplains. Since the chaplains were civilians, they would have to be evacuated along with other civilians in an area of operations if combat ensued. The net effect is that there would be no chaplain for the soldiers in the time of greatest need.

The Appeals Court went further, though. Even if a good example of a civilian program could be given, there are still doubts about the feasibility of a total program. That is, just because one denomination can meet the needs of its soldiers, there is no reason to expect that all religious groups could do so. The complexities associated with military service and the function of the military make such programs virtually prohibitive. For example, military chaplains receive specialized training for military service, something that seems necessary given the operational environ-

32. Drazin and Currey, For God and Country, 165.

ment of military actions, but that civilian groups are ill equipped to provide. A civilian program like that proposed by Katcoff and Wieder could not ensure standardization of training, since each denomination or ecclesiastical agency would be responsible for training its own chaplains, and many would not have the necessary equipment to adequately train their chaplains. If the program set up a standard training program, the potential for conflict over funding seems never ending (see below). In addition to these considerations, the Appeals Court noted that there are also unanswered questions about command and control—it is unclear if military commanders could demand that civilian chaplains minister to their soldiers on the battlefield. If a chaplain refused, there seems to be no recourse for the military, and it is the soldier who is left without help.

The feasibility of a civilian chaplaincy was also called into question based on questions of funding. For example, it seems likely that many smaller denominations could not fund chaplains for their members serving in the military and would thereby be excluded from providing any support to their personnel. Additionally, funding for a civilian program would be problematic because the government could not require religious organizations to support the program without violating Free Exercise, not to mention the difficulty in assigning proportions to each denomination or faith group.

In addition to these considerations, the Appeals Court also noted that the underlying problem with Katcoff's and Wieder's complaint is that it fails to consider the complexity of Establishment Clause considerations. In considering the Establishment question, Mansfield noted that one could actually argue that military service without something like a chaplaincy program would itself be a violation of the Establishment Clause because it would, in effect, prevent Free Exercise on the part of service members when they are serving overseas in areas where the local community cannot meet their religious needs. This problem could be seen as suggesting a government preference for non-religion over religion: "Indeed, if the Army prevented soldiers from worshipping in their own communities by removing them to areas where religious leaders of their persuasion and facilities were not available it could be accused of violating the Establishment Clause unless it provided them with a chaplaincy since its conduct would amount to inhibiting religion."[33]

33. *Katcoff v. Marsh*, 755 F.2d, at 230.

At the end of the day, Mansfield, concluded that Katcoff and Wieder failed to offer a legitimate alternative to military chaplaincy while they acknowledged its value and need:

> In short, plaintiff's proposal is so inherently impractical as to border on the frivolous. Absent some substantial evidence that it might be within the realm of the feasible, we do not believe that taxpayers, merely by instituting a lawsuit, are entitled to engage in a costly and time-consuming broad-scale investigation into an entirely speculative suggestion, made without an evidentiary basis for believing that the claim is well-grounded in fact. See Fed.R.Civ.P. 11. The sole evidence in support of plaintiffs' claim, the affidavits of the Rev. Carl H. Mischke of the Wisconsin Evangelical Lutheran Synod, even if accepted at face value, can hardly serve as an indication that the Catholic Church, the Jewish Religion, and the numerous other Protestant denominations would favor, much less financially support, a civilian chaplaincy.[34]

Since there are doubts about civilian chaplaincy and virtually no evidence that it could work, deference to Congress' use of its War Powers function must come into play: "Any doubt as to the feasibility of a civilian chaplaincy must in our view be resolved in favor of judicial deference to Congress' decision in this area, which is closely tied to the efficient functioning of our armed forces."[35] The military chaplaincy survived the Constitutional challenge.

This victory for military chaplaincy has not quelled all criticism, as some legal scholars have continued to question its legitimacy. For example, Kaplan argues that the Constitutionality of military chaplaincy has never seriously been considered (even in the Katcoff case) and she maintains that it violates Establishment on several counts. The clearest violations are related to the excessive entanglement with religion involved in its promotion system and in its supposed Constitutional basis: it serves a secular purpose.

First, she argues that the chaplaincy promotion system is problematic because chaplains are evaluated on their military performance as officers rather than on their performance as clergy, but armed services regulations state that their primary function is clerical. According to Kaplan, this system encourages chaplains to focus on professional development

34. Ibid., at 236.
35. Ibid., at 236.

as officers to the detriment of their ministerial skills, and thereby detracts from the value of the chaplaincy programs (which is grounded in their provision of highly trained and skilled clergy to meet the religious needs of military personnel). If chaplains were evaluated on their performance as clergy, then commanders with (at least in most cases) no formal theological training would be evaluating personnel on their performance in an area in which they are not the subject-matter experts. In that case, Kaplan argues, governmental representatives (i.e., commanders) would then be sitting in judgment of religion.[36]

Its secular purpose is problematic because it encourages commanders to view the chaplaincy as a tool for what is typically referred to as "combat multiplication." She writes, "In the military chaplaincy, government influence threatens the religious independence of chaplains, impermissibly subsuming religions' goals within the military's agenda."[37] Thus, she argues that this causes the state to place undue pressure upon the chaplain to serve the desires of the command rather than the dictates of his faith. As evidence for her claim, she points to the military's rejection of a civilian chaplaincy program in *Katcoff* and argues that it was due not to the infeasibility of such a program, but rather to its desire to have a chaplaincy it can control.

Kaplan's evaluation of the promotion system is erroneous for several reasons. First, while it must be admitted that some chaplains are rightly perceived as being overly concerned with their status and/or professional development as officers, this is neither endemic to the system nor true of all (or even the majority) of chaplains.[38] In this criticism, she fails to give

36. Kaplan, "Military Mirrors," 1228.

37. Ibid., 1227. Kaplan here, as throughout the paper, relies much too heavily upon the United Church of Christ report, accepting its findings uncritically.

38. A more accurate assessment would note that all chaplains have some measure of concern for their career progressions and professional development, in addition to concern for ministry enhancement. Some are more inclined to emphasize their roles as commissioned officers ("wear the rank" as some enlisted soldiers say), while others are more inclined to emphasize their roles as ministers. I have long suspected that some of these differences in emphasis have their roots in the ecclesiology of the individuals—those from a more high church tradition where seminary and formal training are necessary for ordination, and both are required for the pastoral office, along with a hierarchical church structure being more inclined toward emphasizing rank; and those from a more free church tradition, where seminary and formal training are not required for the pastoral office, and where ordination is optional being more inclined toward emphasizing their position as minister to the unit—but I have no evidence that this is the case, and I am

due weight to the sense of calling or divine commission which motivates most chaplains to serve in the armed forces. In addition, even if the current promotion system did result in a chaplaincy overly concerned with professional development, it would have no impact on the legal status of the chaplain corps. It may be the cause of consternation of many godly persons in the services, but it does not violate the Constitution. Second, Kaplan fails to note that supervisory chaplains are usually involved in some way, even if only in an advisory role, in the evaluation process of chaplains to subordinate units.[39] Third, she does not give senior military officers enough credit by suggesting that they are ill-equipped to evaluate chaplains in their clerical duties. Such evaluations would be less theological and instead more focused on results. That is, there is no good reason to think that a commanding officer does not have the ability to evaluate the effectiveness of a chaplain in his ministerial role because such an evaluation would include examination of the programs the chaplain leads, the tasks he performs, his ability to communicate effectively, the willingness of soldiers within the command to go to the chaplain when in need, etc. While it may be hard to identify a good versus adequate chaplain, it is not difficult, upon these criteria, to identify an outstanding or deficient chaplain. In addition, other professions in the military are similarly evaluated without problems (e.g., medical and legal personnel). Thus, Kaplan's complaints about the promotion system are without warrant.

Kaplan's concerns with the secular use of the chaplaincy are not completely unfounded, as shown in the first chapter, but this should not lead to a questioning of the chaplaincy. The military has taken some measures to protect against abuse, but some issues could potentially fall through the cracks. However, her suggestion of a civilian chaplaincy program is really no improvement over the failed suggestion of Katcoff and Weider.

---

not sure how any such evidence would be gathered or obtained. Of course, there would always be exceptions, even if it could be proven.

39. In the Army, the chaplain is typically *rated* by the commanding officer or the executive officer for the unit he serves. He is *senior rated* by his rater's rater (i.e., either the unit commander, or the commander of the next higher unit), but his supervisory chaplain serves as his intermediate rater. The supervisory chaplain can thereby write comments on the evaluation report which will become part of that chaplain's permanent file. It is interesting to note that some naval chaplains have complained about chaplain involvement in the evaluations process, arguing that they are more susceptible than secular commanding officers are, to temptations to discriminate on religious grounds. See the legal cases against the Navy in the next chapter.

For instance, she fails to account for the need to have chaplains in hostile operational environments and the requirement for unit commanders to have positive control over personnel in those environments.[40] She also offered no answers to the inability of civilian organizations (denominations) to provide for a consistent, well-trained, and adequately diverse chaplaincy that offers support to the entire military community, or to the problem of excessive entanglements that would result from a civilian chaplaincy when the government attempts to require denominations to provide clergy or funds for the chaplaincy program.[41]

THE QUESTION OF SECTARIAN PRAYERS

As noted in the previous chapter, the question of offering sectarian prayers or performing religious rites at command ceremonies and other mandatory-attendance events is a particularly controversial and current topic among military chaplains (as well as chaplains serving other secular institutions such as legislatures, hospitals, or corporations). This question can best be viewed as a special case of the Constitutionality question, since it impacts both Establishment jurisprudence, when such prayers are viewed as communicating a government (or institutional) preference for one religion over others or non-religion, and Free Exercise jurisprudence, when the prayers of chaplains are censured in an effort to project a more pluralistic work environment.

Marsh v. Chambers

Perhaps the most important case for considering the constitutionality of chaplain activities at official ceremonies and events is *Marsh v. Chambers*, which considered the legality of chaplain-led prayers to open the Nebraska State Legislature. Ernest Chambers, a member of the Nebraska Legislature (and taxpayer) sued in Federal District Court, arguing that both the prac-

40. The current military context provides a better example of how this may work than it did when Kaplan wrote her article (or when Katcoff and Weider brought suit). The use of civilian contractors in Iraq and Afghanistan has at least provided a model for such an endeavor, but it also brings to the fore some of the very problems that were a cause of concern for the judges in *Katcoff*.

41. Interestingly, this very issue comes up with regard to Catholic chaplains. Even when an individual has volunteered to serve in the reserve forces, the military must still obtain permission from the Catholic chaplain's superiors in order to deploy him. I have thought this odd, but the policy is probably grounded in fear of excessive entanglement.

tice of prayers at the assembly and the payment of a chaplain with public funds violate the Establishment Clause. The District Court ruled that the practice itself is not a violation, but that paying the chaplain from taxpayer funds is, and enjoined the legislature from using public funds for such purposes. Both parties appealed to the Eighth Circuit Court of Appeals, which considered both the practice and the payment as one issue (contrary to the District Court's approach). It applied the Lemon Test and held that the chaplaincy practice violated all three prongs: the primary purpose and effect were religious (and because the same minister had served in that role for sixteen years, despite the legislature's policy of selecting the chaplain biennially, it seemed to be purposed to promote a particular religious expression), and the use of public funds to pay the chaplain and to publish the prayers led to excessive entanglement. The Supreme Court heard the case on April 20, 1983, and rendered its decision on July 5 that same year. In a 6-3 vote, the Court held that the practice is not a violation of Establishment and thereby overturned/reversed the findings of the District Court and the Appeals Court. Chief Justice Warren Burger delivered the opinion of the Court.

One of the factors impacting the Court's opinion here was the demonstrable history of legislative prayers in this country as well as the intent of the Framers with regard to the Establishment Clause. The practice of opening legislative sessions with prayer is not confined to the Nebraska State Legislature or to the state level for that matter, but was also observed at the Federal level. The very men who drafted the Constitution and authored the First Amendment did not see such activity as a violation of its principles since they countenanced prayers before their own sessions and voted to fund legislative and military chaplains. Writing for the majority, Chief Justice Burger noted, "It can hardly be thought that in the same week Members of the First Congress voted to appoint and to pay a chaplain for each House and also voted to approve the draft of the First Amendment for submission to the states, they intended the Establishment Clause of the Amendment to forbid what they had just declared acceptable."[42]

In an effort to interpret the reasoning of the Framers, Burger cites an exchange between John Jay and John Rutledge on the one hand, both of whom were concerned that legislative prayers could cause division since representatives were of many different faiths, with Samuel Adams

---

42. *Marsh v Chambers*, 463 U.S. 783, 790 (1983).

on the other hand, who suggested that any prayer offered by a person who loves the country ought to be welcomed by the Congress. Burger takes this exchange as important for consideration because it suggests that the Founders had carefully considered the very question at issue here, that Adams' answer was deemed sufficient by Jay and Rutledge, and that such prayers were seen as neither endorsing nor advancing the faith of the one who prayed.[43] The long history of legislative prayers in this country (and thus, in the Nebraska legislature; almost 200 and over 125 years respectively) represents "a tolerable acknowledgment of beliefs widely held among the people of this country."[44]

Complicating consideration of the practice in the Nebraska legislature were the long tenure of the chaplain voicing the prayers (e.g., sixteen years), and the sectarian nature of some of the prayers he offered. On the first issue, the majority found that length of tenure, in itself, says nothing about a preference for the particular religious beliefs of the chaplain. In fact, the legislature could have replaced the chaplain with someone else on many occasions when his contract was renewed, if the members had so chosen. The fact that they did not suggests that he did a good job. In order to make the case, the plaintiff would need to demonstrate that the continued reappointment was due to an attempt to give preference to one particular faith tradition. No such proof was offered and so the charge was viewed as speculative. In addition, chaplains of other faith groups were heard by the legislature on special occasions or when the normal chaplain was absent.

On the second issue, the content of the prayers, Burger's comments were surprisingly brief and disappointingly vague. He allowed for prayers in the Judeo-Christian tradition as long as they are not used for an agenda (e.g., criticizing other faith groups, or evangelizing the audience). Burger writes, "The content of the prayer is not of concern to judges where, as here, there is no indication that the prayer opportunity has been exploited to proselytize or advance any one, or to disparage any other, faith or be-

43. Burger writes, "This interchange emphasizes that the delegates did not consider opening prayers as a proselytizing activity or as symbolically placing the government's 'official seal of approval on one religious view,' cf. 675 F.2d, at 234. Rather, the Founding Fathers looked at invocations as 'conduct whose . . . effect . . . harmonize[d] with the tenets of some or all religions.' McGowan v. Maryland, 366 U.S. 420, 442 (1961)." Ibid., at 792.

44. Ibid.

lief. That being so, it is not for us to embark on a sensitive evaluation or to parse the content of a particular prayer."[45]

While evangelicals certainly appreciate the reluctance of the Court to engage in theological analyses of the content of prayers, there is still reason to find Burger's words to be at least potentially disconcerting. The lack of clarity in Burger's qualifications for when the Court may take issue with the message of one's prayer is unsettling, for it seems that some may view, for example, any form of sectarian prayer as an attempt at proselytization. Similarly, one could argue that certain forms of sectarian prayer are disparaging of other faiths. Clearly, what makes any given prayer sectarian is, at a minimum, an implied claim to exclusive truth. For example, a Hindu prayer to Brahman includes in its structure a claim that Brahman exists (or at least that Brahman is an appropriate name for God), and that the Christian belief that he is a false god is itself false. Some Christians, then, could consider such a prayer as an affront to their own beliefs. While I doubt that such an argument would gain a serious hearing by the Court, there is nothing in Burger's words to disallow it.

These considerations aside, it should be noted that Burger's words suggest that more general prayers are preferred because they could not be construed as attempts to proselytize or to criticize other faiths.[46] This, then, is the concern: Burger's words could be interpreted as suggesting generic prayers be offered at government-sponsored events. They certainly stop short of affirming the right of the one leading the prayer to pray according to the dictates of his own conscience or faith tradition. Nevertheless, they also do not dictate proper forms for prayers or restrict sectarian prayers. In the findings of *Marsh v. Chambers*, the content of prayers were not considered by the majority, yet this same issue came up in the dissent.

In his dissenting opinion, Justice Brennan noted that his view had changed from an earlier case in which he reasoned in much the same way to the majority here. He has since changed his thinking about these cases. He points to the somewhat obvious fact that the Court, in this decision, did not follow its own Establishment Clause jurisprudence, ignoring the Lemon Test, and in essence, was "carving out an exception to the Establishment Clause rather than reshaping Establishment Clause doc-

45. Ibid., at 794–95.
46. See footnote 43 above.

trine to accommodate legislative prayer."[47] Interestingly, Brennan argues that the practice of employing legislative chaplains and allowing prayer in the legislature leads to excessive entanglement because the state must ensure that the chaplains and their prayers do not violate the principles the majority set forth: "In the case of legislative prayer, the process of choosing a 'suitable' chaplain, whether on a permanent or rotating basis, and insuring that the chaplain limits himself or herself to 'suitable' prayers, involves precisely the sort of supervision that agencies of government should if at all possible avoid."[48]

In his separate dissenting opinion, Justice Stevens takes it a step further, suggesting that the reason Nebraska's chaplain had such a long tenure was that his sectarian prayers were accepted by the "silent majority" in the legislature and that the majority refrained from examining the content of prayers because it could not do so and continue to hold its position.[49] Stevens also points to the democratic nature of the legislative actions to argue that the tenure of the chaplain does denote a preference for the religion of the chaplain. His point is that the faith of the majority (or their constituents) will most likely be reflected in the faith tradition of the chaplain.[50]

CEREMONIAL DEISM

The issues raised in the findings of *Marsh v. Chambers* naturally lead to consideration of *ceremonial deism*, since it actually serves as the legal basis for the constitutionality of instances where religion and government mix. That is, religious speech at government-sponsored events, religious symbols on government-owned property, or religious practices led by

47. 463 U.S. at 796.

48. Ibid., at 799.

49. Ibid., at 823.

50. He writes, "In a democratically elected legislature, the religious beliefs of the chaplains tend to reflect the faith of the majority of the lawmakers' constituents. Prayers may be said by a Catholic priest in the Massachusetts Legislature and by a Presbyterian minister in the Nebraska Legislature, but I would not expect to find a Jehovah's Witness or a disciple of Mary Baker Eddy or the Reverend Moon serving as the official chaplain in any state legislature. Regardless of the motivation of the majority that exercises the power to appoint the chaplain, it seems plain to me that the designation of a member of one religious faith to serve as the sole official chaplain of a state legislature for a period of 16 years constitutes the preference of one faith over another in violation of the Establishment Clause of the First Amendment." Ibid., at 822–23.

government employees functioning in their official capacity, are deemed Constitutional because they are thought to be cases of ceremonial deism. Of course, the applicability to the question of allowing sectarian prayers (e.g., "In Jesus' Name") by military chaplains at official events and ceremonies should be obvious. Such prayers are typically justified by an appeal to *ceremonial deism.*

"Ceremonial Deism" is the legal term used to describe activity (primarily speech) that, "though religious in nature has a secular purpose and hence is constitutional."[51] The term originates with Eugene Rostow, then Dean of the Yale Law School, who explained in his 1962 Meiklejohn Lecture at Brown University that certain types of speech were "so conventional and uncontroversial as to be constitutional."[52] Since Rostow introduced the term, it has been used by several Supreme Court Justices in Establishment cases, sometimes by explicit reference, and sometimes by allusion. It was specifically mentioned by Justice William Brennan in his dissenting opinion in *Lynch v. Donnelly* to argue that some phrases, through rote repetition, have lost their significant religious content, and by Justice Sandra Day O'Connor in her opinion in *County of Allegheny v. ACLU* (1989), a case involving religious symbols in holiday displays, and in *Elk Grove Unified School District v. Newdow* (2004), a case which questioned the constitutionality of the phrase, "under God" in the Pledge of Allegiance.[53] In both cases, O'Connor claimed that a secular purpose, along with a history of institutional use, can allow religious speech or symbols to pass constitutional muster.

The basic reason for accepting ceremonial deism has to do with the function some religious references and symbols have played in the history and cultural development of the United States; they have, through continued use, become part of the American identity and consciousness. Yet, even among its adherents/proponents, there is little agreement over what constitutes legitimate cases. For example, Frank Ravitch argues that ceremonial deism should be limited to items of a generic religious nature associated with public property or government-sponsored events, such as patriotic songs with references to the divine, "In God We Trust" on U.S. currency, and even

51. Douglas, "Ceremonial Deism," 1:258.

52. Rostow, Meiklejohn Lectures.

53. Justice Harry Blakckmun, in *County of Allegheny v Greater Pittsburgh ACLU*, argued that all people realize that the government is not promulgating particular religious beliefs by simply allowing religious symbols in a holiday display.

Christmas trees on public property, but it should not include items with theological content such as nativity scenes, Ten Commandments displays, or legislative prayers because they are too specific, and to so identify them is to detract from their religious meaning.[54] Others, though, have even viewed at least some prayers (e.g., invocations at the opening of legislature, invocations and benedictions at military and other governmental ceremonies, etc.) as instances of ceremonial deism. In order to gain an appreciation for the complexities associated with the concept of ceremonial deism and to see how it has been used in Establishment Clause jurisprudence, it may be helpful to examine, in some detail, the rulings in the three cases in which it was specifically mentioned.

Lynch v. Donnelly

Two separate cases involving religious displays set up and maintained by local governments have included references and/or allusions to ceremonial deism. The first case, *Lynch v. Donnelly*, arose when the city of Pawtucket, Rhode Island, erected a nativity scene as part of a larger Christmas holiday display. The display included many secular items such as a banner which read, "Season's Greetings," a Santa Claus house, and a Christmas tree, and was erected on the grounds of a park owned by a nonprofit organization in the heart of the city's downtown shopping district. It had been an annual display for forty years before the local chapter of the American Civil Liberties Union brought suit, claiming the crèche violated the First Amendment.

The city claimed that the crèche served a purely secular purpose as part of the larger holiday display designed to attract people to the downtown shopping district in order to boost retail sales. It also stated that it hoped to engender the spirit of goodwill and neighborliness which is a common result of the Christmas season. The Court ruled in favor of the city, arguing that the display of the crèche is not a violation of Establishment because it serves a secular purpose and does not advance religion.

In the majority opinion, Chief Justice Warren Burger noted that it is the *purpose* of any given governmental activity which determines its constitutionality: if it has a religious purpose, then it is unconstitutional: "Focus exclusively on the religious component of any activity would in-

54. Ravitch, *Masters of Illusion*, 101.

evitably lead to its invalidation under the Establishment Clause."[55] Justice Burger points out that, just because a given action or item is religious in nature, it does not necessarily mean that it is a violation of Establishment. In fact, he argues that Ten Commandments displays or required Bible reading in public schools could be constitutional if they served a secular purpose.[56] The religious content is not the primary concern; rather, the *purpose* and as will be noted later, the *effect* are most important in Establishment Clause questions.

It is interesting to note that Burger admits that, even though the crèche serves a secular purpose for the city (namely, to celebrate a national holiday and point to its historic origins), it may still indirectly advance a particular religion (i.e., Christianity). This indirect aid, though, does not in itself make the display a violation of the Constitution: "Here, whatever benefit there is to one faith or religion or to all religions, is indirect, remote, and incidental; display of the crèche is no more an advancement or endorsement of religion than the Congressional and Executive recognition of the origins of the Holiday itself as 'Christ's Mass' . . ."[57] So advancement of religion, at least under Burger's analysis, may be Constitutional, so long as it is incidental to a larger secular purpose and can be fairly judged minor in scope or effect.

Justice Sandra Day O'Connor, in her concurring opinion, notes that Establishment questions cannot be decided by a single test, but that the endorsement test is particularly helpful nonetheless. The endorsement test disallows situations in which an individual's inclusion in the political community or process is contingent upon some form of religious belief, confession, or practice. However, the evaluation of contingency must be based upon what a reasonable observer would be expected to think about the relationship between inclusion and the activity, and the religious nature of the activity.[58] The upshot of this requirement is a denial

55. *Lynch v. Donnelly,* 465 US 668, 680 (1984).

56. Ibid., at 679.

57. Ibid., at 683.

58. O'Connor notes that the endorsement test must assume the viewpoint of a reasonable observer because there could always be unreasonable objections to any supposedly religious event or requirement. She writes, "Given the dizzying religious heterogeneity of our Nation, adopting a subjective approach would reduce the test to an absurdity. Nearly any government action could be overturned as a violation of the Establishment Clause if a 'heckler's veto' sufficed to show that its message was one of endorsement. . . . Second, because the 'reasonable observer' must embody a community ideal of social judgment,

of an absolute separation of all references to religion and public life. In this case, O'Connor makes a distinction between the intent of city leaders in displaying the crèche, and what they actually communicated in the display. Thus, for the Court, the hermeneutical issue includes both authorial intent and the meaning of the words/actions themselves. Even if the intent is secular, there could still be a violation of Establishment (if the outcome is that a particular religion is promoted, or religion is promoted over non-religion, or vice versa).[59]

In the case of Pawtucket's Christmas display, the fact that it was included alongside non-religious holiday images supported the city's claim that the nativity display was not meant to promote religion, but instead to celebrate the holiday. O'Connor concluded that this case was no more a violation of Establishment than other government acknowledgements of religion such as the recognition of Thanksgiving, "In God We Trust" on coinage, or opening courts with the declaration, "God save the United States and this honorable court." According to O'Connor, these sorts of government acknowledgement of religion solemnize public occasions, express confidence in the future, and encourage the recognition of what is worthy of appreciation in society. She concludes, "For that reason, and because of their history and ubiquity, those practices are not understood as conveying governmental approval of particular religious beliefs. The display of the crèche likewise serves a secular purpose—celebration of a public holiday with traditional symbols."[60]

The dissenting opinion was written by Justice William Brennan, who was joined by Justices Marshall, Blackmun, and Stevens. Their principle objection was due to the sectarian nature of the crèche. It is simply hard to

---

as well as rational judgment, the test does not evaluate a practice in isolation from its origins and context. Instead, the reasonable observer must be deemed aware of the history of the conduct in question, and must understand its place in our Nation's cultural landscape." *Elk Grove Unified School District et al v. Newdow et al,* 542 U.S. 1, 85 (2003).

59. O'Connor writes, "If the audience is large, as it always is when government 'speaks' by word or deed, some portion of the audience will inevitably receive a message determined by the 'objective' content of the statement, and some portion will inevitably receive the intended message. [Note: She neglect to mention that some, no doubt, will fail to properly discern either, but perhaps this is irrelevant to her point.]. Examination of both the subjective and objective components of the message communicated by a government action is therefore necessary to determine whether the action carries a forbidden meaning." *Lynch v. Donnelly,* 465 U.S. at 690.

60. Ibid., at 693.

believe, they noted, that the city leaders' motives for including a nativity scene in the holiday display was purely secular, but that notwithstanding, it is even more difficult to claim that it does not have the primary *effect* of advancing religion. This fact leads to excessive entanglement, and there does not seem to be a compelling state interest in retaining the crèche. As Justice Brennan notes, the secular goals can be met without the nativity scene: "Plainly, the city's interest in celebrating the holiday and in promoting both retail sales and goodwill are fully served by the elaborate display of Santa Claus, reindeer, and wishing wells that are already a part of Pawtucket's annual Christmas display. More importantly, the nativity scene, unlike every other element of the Hodgson Park display, reflects a sectarian exclusivity that the avowed purposes of celebrating the holiday season and promoting retail commerce simply do not encompass."[61]

Justice Blackmun wrote an additional dissenting opinion in which he was joined by Justice Stevens. In it, he suggests that, in addition to an improper application of the Lemon Test, the Court's ruling does an injustice to the religious value and meaning of the nativity scene. That is, to see the nativity scene as just one more item in a secular display designed to make money for community merchants is to detract from its true significance:

> While certain persons, including the Mayor of Pawtucket, under-took a crusade to 'keep 'Christ' in Christmas,' App. 161, the Court today has declared that presence virtually irrelevant. The majority urges that the display, 'with or without a crèche,' 'recall[s] the religious nature of the Holiday,' and 'engenders a friendly community spirit of goodwill in keeping with the season.' Ante, at 685. Before the District Court, an expert witness for the city made a similar, though perhaps more candid, point, stating that Pawtucket's display invites people 'to participate in the Christmas spirit, brotherhood, peace, and let loose with their money.' See 525 F. Supp. 1150, 1161 (RI 1981). The crèche has been relegated to the role of a neutral harbinger of the holiday season, useful for commercial purposes, but devoid of any inherent meaning and incapable of enhancing the religious tenor of a display of which it is an integral part. The city has its victory—but it is a Pyrrhic one indeed.[62]

61. Ibid., at 699–700.

62. Ibid., at 726–27. My concern is that a victory in the opposite view—to declare that an activity is religious may win the battle—it is Unconstitutional to require generic prayers since to do so would violate the person's (giving the prayer) free exercise rights—

This complaint of Blackmun and Stevens, I suspect, will resonate with many evangelicals regarding a capitulation to ceremonial deist requirements for pluralistic, or at least nonsectarian, prayers.

Allegheny County v. Greater Pittsburgh ACLU

The second case, *Allegheny County v. Greater Pittsburgh ACLU* (1989) arose when the American Civil Liberties Union sued the county of Allegheny, claiming that two holiday displays on county-owned land violated the Establishment Clause. The first display, a nativity scene, was placed on the Grand Staircase of the Allegheny County Courthouse, a place described as the "main," "most beautiful," and "most public" section of the courthouse. The second, an 18-foot menorah, was erected outside the City-County Building next to the city's 45-foot decorated Christmas tree and a sign with comments by the city mayor which connected the display to the city's "Salute to Liberty." The crèche was donated by the Holy Name Society, a Roman Catholic group, and the menorah is owned by Chabad, a Jewish group, though it is maintained, stored, and erected by the city.

The Court found (5-4) that the nativity scene violates the Establishment Clause, but that the menorah (6-3) does not. While it may be tempting to interpret these findings as just another example of anti-Christian attitudes in the culture, such an interpretation is unwarranted. The reason for rejecting the crèche while accepting the menorah has to do with the setting of each display and what it communicates about the government's endorsement of a particular religion (or religion in general). The crèche was seen as endorsing Christianity because it was alone with no secular message and included a "patently Christian message: Glory to God for the birth of Jesus Christ."[63] As Justice Blackmun notes in his summary of the judgment, "Although the government may acknowledge Christmas as a cultural phenomenon, it may not observe it as a Christian holy day by suggesting that people praise God for the birth of Jesus."[64] The menorah's position next to the secular symbol of the Christmas tree, along with the

---

but lose the war. The result may be that, since all prayers are religious expressions of the individual leading the prayer, prayers at all government events will be prohibited. This would be a Pyrrhic victory, but even more so.

63. *Allegheny County v. Greater Pittsburgh ACLU*, 492 US 573, 574 (1989).

64. Ibid., at 574.

largely secular interpretation of the symbols on the city's accompanying sign, detracted from its purely religious significance and communicated a sense of pluralism that makes its display pass constitutional muster.

In her concurring opinion, Justice O'Connor responded to some criticisms of her position in *Lynch v. Donnelley*. She points out that an appeal to historical use of religious language, practices, or symbols does not, in itself, allow the continued use to survive Establishment questioning, but it does contribute to an overall evaluation of the meaning of that language or those practices/symbols. Commenting on such examples as legislative prayers and opening court sessions with "God save the United States and this honorable Court," she reaffirmed her earlier contention that they solemnize the occasion and express confidence in the future, but then added, "These examples of ceremonial deism do not survive Establishment Clause scrutiny simply by virtue of their historical longevity alone."[65]

For O'Connor, longevity of use combined with a nonsectarian nature allow for the use of religious language, practices, and symbols by government because they are then viewed as a recognition of the nation's history and therefore serve a secular function: "It is the combination of the longstanding existence of practices such as opening legislative sessions with legislative prayers or opening Court sessions with 'God save the United States and this honorable Court,' as well as their nonsectarian nature, that leads me to the conclusion that those particular practices, despite their religious roots, do not convey a message of endorsement of particular religious beliefs."[66]

For O'Connor, then, the importance of the menorah's being stationed next to the (in her words) "secular" symbol of the Christmas tree, is found in the message of pluralism that the arrangement sends to the reasonable observer. The menorah does not need to be viewed as a secular symbol and Chanukah need not be seen as a secular holiday for the display to serve a secular purpose and/or to convey a secular message, and thereby

---

65. This should be obvious. In fact, Justice O'Connor goes on to point out the clear counter-example to such a claim in discrimination: "Historical acceptance does not in itself validate that practice under the Establishment Clause if the practice violates the values protected by that Clause, just as historical acceptance of racial or gender based discrimination does not immunize such practices from scrutiny under the Fourteenth Amendment." Ibid., at 630.

66. Ibid., at 630–31.

avoid the appearance of a government endorsement of religion (in this case, Judaism), contrary to Justice Blackmun's contention, in *Lynch v. Donnelly* that the majority had relegated the menorah to the status of a secular holiday symbol. However, she contends that the menorah does need to be in a setting which clearly conveys a message of pluralism and freedom of choice with respect to religion.[67] Thus, she notes that, for example, a menorah standing alone at city hall would violate the First Amendment, just as the crèche at the Allegheny Courthouse did. In this case, it is the combination of the secular symbol of the Christmas tree and the sign saluting liberty alongside the menorah which communicates the government's intent to commemorate the religious liberty and diversity enjoyed in this country. She writes, "By accompanying its display of a Christmas tree—a secular symbol of the Christmas holiday season—with a salute to liberty, and by adding a religious symbol from a Jewish holiday also celebrated at roughly the same time of year, I conclude that the city did not endorse Judaism or religion in general, but rather conveyed a message of pluralism and freedom of belief during the holiday season."[68] Justice O'Connor also argues that the display does not endorse religion over nonreligion by virtue of the inclusion of secular symbols alongside the distinctively religious. She continues:

> Here, by displaying a secular symbol of the Christmas holiday season rather than a religious one, the city acknowledged a public holiday celebrated by both religious and nonreligous citizens alike, and it did so without endorsing Christian beliefs. A reasonable observer would, in my view, appreciate that the combined display is an effort to acknowledge the cultural diversity of our country and to convey tolerance of different choices in matters of religious belief or nonbelief by recognizing that the winter holiday season is celebrated in diverse ways by our citizens.[69]

In his dissenting opinion, Justice Brennan (joined by Justices Marshall and Stevens) argued that the Christmas tree is, indeed, a religious symbol and therefore, violates Establishment because the combined display seemingly endorses Christianity and Judaism. He bases his argument on three points: first, it is unquestionably symbolic of, and has historically

67. Ibid., at 633–34.
68. Ibid., at 635.
69. Ibid., at 635–36.

been associated with, the celebration of Christmas, a Christian holiday; second, Justice O'Connor's argument that the menorah combined with the Christmas tree communicates pluralism requires the tree be a religious symbol; and third, the context within which the tree sits (i.e., next to the menorah) makes it a religious symbol; that is, the religious nature of the menorah at least suggests a religious dimension to the tree (the only other holiday symbol present, unlike in *Lynch v. Donnelly*).[70] On the third point, Brennan notes, one cannot claim to know with certainty what a "reasonable observer" would conclude about the symbolic significance of the tree (or the display):

> I would not, however, presume to say that my interpretation of the tree's significance is the 'correct' one, or the one shared by most visitors to the City County Building. I do not know how we can decide whether it was the tree that stripped the religious connotations from the menorah, or the menorah that laid bare the religious origins of the tree. Both are reasonable interpretations of the scene the city presented.[71]

He continues, noting the subjective aspect of the majority opinion: "I shudder to think that the only 'reasonable observer' is one who shares the particular view on perspective, spacing, and accent expressed in Justice Blackmun's opinion, thus making analysis under the Establishment Clause look more like an exam in Art 101 than an inquiry into constitutional law."[72]

Brennan also concludes that a message of pluralism can still favor religion over nonreligion and thus, violate the Constitution. In fact, he suggests that the only pluralism O'Connor has in mind is religious pluralism. This is problematic, he argues, because the display suggests a government preference for religious homogeneity or cooperation which seems to go afoul of Free Exercise:

---

70. Brennan writes, "Positioned as it was, the Christmas tree's religious significance was bound to come to the fore. Situated next to the menorah . . . the Christmas tree's religious dimension could not be overlooked by observers of the display. . . . Consider a poster featuring a star of David, a statue of Buddha, a Christmas tree, a mosque, and a drawing of Krishna. There can be no doubt that, when found in such company, the tree serves as an unabashedly religious symbol." Ibid., at 641.

71. Ibid., at 642.

72. Ibid., at 643.

The uncritical acceptance of a message of religious pluralism also ignores the extent to which even that message may offend. Many religious faiths are hostile to each other, and indeed, refuse even to participate in ecumenical services designed to demonstrate the very pluralism Justices Blackmun and O'Connor extol. To lump the ritual objects and holidays of religions together without regard to their attitudes toward such inclusiveness, or to decide which religions should be excluded because of the possibility of offense, is not a benign or beneficent celebration of pluralism: it is instead an interference in religious matters precluded by the Establishment Clause.[73]

Elk Grove Unified School District v. Newdow

Another case involving the issue of ceremonial deism has to do with the Constitutionality of the inclusion of the phrase, "under God" in the Pledge of Allegiance. In *Elk Grove Unified School District v. Newdow*, Michael Newdow, an atheist living in California, sued the school district in which his daughter attended school because children in the schools were forced to recite the Pledge of Allegiance daily, and he believed the phrase, "under God" violated both her First Amendment rights and his rights as a parent to direct the religious education of his daughter. At the time, California law required public schools to begin the day with some form of patriotic act, and the recitation of the Pledge was seen to fulfill that requirement. It should be noted that students were permitted to opt out for religious reasons without fear of reprisal. Ultimately, Newdow's complaint was not allowed to go forward in argument because the Supreme Court found that he did not have standing since he did not have any form of custody of his daughter; and therefore, he could not sue as a *next friend* for her, and it is not the place of the federal court to decide matters of paternity, custody, or parental rights.[74]

In her concurring opinion, Justice O'Connor, nevertheless, sought to address the issues at stake in the suit and appealed to ceremonial deism as her basis for upholding the Constitutionality of the phrase, "under God" in

73. Ibid., at 645.

74. The child's mother, to whom Newdow was never married and who had sole legal custody of the child, enjoined the court to remove the child from the complaint. She did so for three reasons: first, their daughter was a Christian; second, she did not object to the practice; and third, there was concern that her remaining on the complaint could cause problems for her at school with teachers as well as other students.

the Pledge. She begins by reasserting her claim that the reasonable observer is the standard for evaluating the perception of coercion by the government or of one's inclusion in or exclusion from the political community because of religion. She also reiterates the fact that the Court has allowed religious references in the public square because they serve the secular purpose of commemorating the role of religion in our nation's history. Taking this a step further, though, O'Connor argues that even invocations of divine assistance can serve such a secular function and are therefore, not viewed as a government preference for religion. She writes,

> For centuries, we have marked important occasions or pronouncements with references to God and invocations of divine assistance. Such references can serve to solemnize an occasion instead of to invoke divine provenance. The reasonable observer discussed above, fully aware of our national history and the origins of such practices, would not perceive these acknowledgments as signifying a government endorsement of any specific religion, or even of religion over nonreligion.[75]

O'Connor's claim here seems to represent something of a departure from earlier arguments that the religious aspect of instances of ceremonial deism may still be Constitutional so long as they are incidental to the secular purpose. Here, though, O'Connor seems to suggest that the prayer itself not only serves a secular purpose, but is itself a secular act! Such an interpretation of prayer may be disturbing to some, and certainly, if a correct understanding of her words, is theologically suspect.

In perhaps the most developed discussion of ceremonial deism by a Supreme Court Justice, O'Connor outlined four factors for consideration: 1) History and ubiquity, 2) Absence of worship or prayer, 3) Absence of reference to particular religion, and 4) Minimal religious content. Other justices did not join her in this assessment, even though she found that the phrase meets the criteria and hence, passes constitutional muster.

First, O'Connor maintains that one way to evaluate the viewpoint of the reasonable observer is to examine the historical response of Americans to religious speech, acts, or symbols that have broad appeal and have been in use for some time. She writes, "The constitutional value of ceremonial deism turns on a shared understanding of its legitimate nonreligious purposes. That sort of understanding can exist only when a

---

75. 542 U.S. at 36.

given practice has been in place for a significant portion of the Nation's history, and when it is observed by enough persons that it can fairly be called ubiquitous."[76] In the case of the Pledge, there have been virtually no challenges to its Constitutionality since the words, "under God" were added approximately 50 years ago.

Second, O'Connor cites the findings in another case to make the point that ceremonial deism almost never includes prayer or worship because such activities seem to detract from the secular purpose.[77] The one exception was prayer by a chaplain to open the legislature, and this due largely to its historical longevity.[78] But generally speaking, prayers and other forms of religious speech associated with worship cannot count as ceremonial deism: "Any statement that has as its purpose placing the speaker or listener in a penitent state of mind, or that is intended to create a spiritual communion or invoke divine aid, strays from the legitimate secular purposes of solemnizing an event and recognizing a shared religious history."[79] Thus, while prayers do not usually count as ceremonial deism, the fact that prayers considered in *Marsh v. Chambers* do, and that chaplain-led prayers at mandatory events are justified on the basis of that case, it is reasonable to assume that they would also be so construed.

Third, O'Connor notes that the Establishment Clause does not allow for one denomination to be officially preferred over another.[80] Thus, practices cannot be deemed ceremonial deism if they explicitly favor "one particular religious belief system over another."[81] In most cases, ceremonial deism must keep its theological claims general. The reference to God

76. Ibid., at 37.

77. She cites *Engel v Vitale*, 370 U.S. 421, 429 (1962): "[O]ne of the greatest dangers to the freedom of the individual to worship in his own way [lies] in the Government's placing its official stamp of approval upon one particular kind of prayer or one particular form of religious service."

78. 463 U.S. at 783.

79. 542 U.S. at 40. O'Connor bolsters her opinion here by quoting from *Santa Fe Independent School District v Doe*, 530 U.S. 290 (2000), a school-prayer case, which concluded that invocations cannot be used to solemnize occasions if they were, in actuality, prayers. This, of course, is confusing, to say the least, as it is hard to see how a reasonable observer would not view an invocation to open a legislative session as an actual prayer. What O'Connor almost seems to suggest is that the reasonable observer knows enough to not take prayer seriously if offered at a government event by a chaplain.

80. *Larson v Valente*, 456 U.S. 228 (1982).

81. 542 U.S. at 42.

in the Pledge meets this criterion. However, this has serious implications for the desire to offer sectarian prayers at public events. It does not seem that prayers "in Jesus' Name" would meet the criterion.

Fourth, O'Connor suggests that ceremonial deism includes minimal reference to God. This seems to be largely a test for exclusion rather than inclusion: a case which has too many references to God or religion will not be deemed ceremonial deism. As O'Connor puts it,

> ... the brevity of a reference to religion or to God in a ceremonial exercise can be important for several reasons. First, it tends to confirm that the reference is being used to acknowledge religion or to solemnize an event rather than endorse religion in any way. Second, it makes it easier for those participants who wish to 'opt out' of language they find offensive to do so without having to reject the ceremony entirely. And third, it tends to limit the ability of government to express a preference for one religious sect over another.[82]

In her summary statement, she concludes,

> Certain ceremonial references to God and religion in our Nation are the inevitable consequence of the religious history that gave birth to our founding principles of liberty. It would be ironic indeed if this Court were to wield our Constitutional commitment to religious freedom so as to sever our ties to the traditions developed to honor it.[83]

Assessment

Since these cases were decided, the concept of ceremonial deism has been the topic of much debate. Under a legal analysis, many Constitutional scholars have argued that it fails to pass muster, but they nevertheless admit that there are some instances, rare though they are, where allowance of violations of Establishment exists in order to protect Freedom of Religion (e.g., military chaplaincy). For example, Ravitch correctly notes that the principle of accommodation is what has guided the Court's judgment in Establishment cases; those items that have passed the bar as ceremonial deism (and therefore constitutional) have really been concessions by the Supreme Court to the broader public which is religious in

82. Ibid., at 43.
83. Ibid., at 44–45.

leanings: "What is really going on is a form of pragmatic accommodation that recognizes the religious heritage and nature of our society, or at least many people in it. If one wants to be consistent with established doctrine, either most ceremonial deism would be unconstitutional or much of what the Court has found unconstitutional would be constitutional."[84] While Ravitch's analysis may be a bit overly simplistic, his underlying point is correct: accommodation is at least one of the bases for judging ceremonial deism as constitutional, though it is not mere condescension to an ignorant public.

Others have echoed Ravitch's point about the unconstitutional nature of ceremonial deism. Epstein argues that none of the arguments posited in favor of the constitutionality of ceremonial deism hold water. For example, he points out that the accommodation argument does not work because violations of the Establishment clause are only permissible when they lift a burden or barrier to someone's free exercise rights, but this is never the case in those areas already accepted as ceremonial deism. Commenting on Christmas as a national holiday, he notes, "Even if the government did not declare Christmas a holiday, Christians would still be able to exercise their religion on that day just as freely as they do on Christian holidays not recognized by the federal and state governments, such as Good Friday, and just as Muslims, Hindus, and other religious minorities do on their nongovernmentally endorsed religious holidays."[85]

There are good reasons for doubting this claim, at least as it pertains to a major holy day of the majority religion in any society, for consider the implications if, on a normal workday, fifty-percent (which is probably low regarding Christmas in America) of the workforce wished to take off. It seems that some of the requests would, out of necessity, be denied. With regard to members of minority groups who wish to take a particular religious holiday off from work, co-workers can fill in the gap, but this is simply not possible when it is a large percentage of the workforce who would like off, and let's be honest: any who do not claim Christianity as their personal religion in American culture nevertheless wish to have Christmas off from work because it has become part of the culture. It is this aspect of the accommodation argument that Epstein fails to take seriously, for if the government were to mandate that adherents

84. Ravitch, 102.
85. Epstein, "Rethinking the Constitutionality of Ceremonial Deism," 2173.

of a particular religion work on their most holy day, this would appear to be a violation of the Free Exercise Clause, and it is this, I take it, to be the argument of the accommodationists. Justice Brennan, in his dissenting opinion in *Lynch v. Donnelly*, makes this very point. Some governmental recognition of religious holidays is a pragmatic necessity, even if not required by Free Exercise. Yet, it is also a mistake to view it as a violation of Establishment:

> When government decides to recognize Christmas Day as a public holiday, it does no more than accommodate the calendar of public activities to the plain fact that many Americans will expect on that day to spend time visiting with their families, attending religious services, and perhaps enjoying some respite from preholiday activities. The Free Exercise Clause, of course, does not necessarily compel the government to provide this accommodation, but neither is the Establishment Clause offended by such a step.[86]

So, even though ceremonial deism represents a technical violation of Establishment legislation, Ravitch maintains, there are good reasons, mostly of a pragmatic nature, for the Court to remain somewhat inconsistent in its future rulings on this subject, for the peace of American society may very well be at stake. Ravitch seems to be concerned that, if the Supreme Court were to consistently enforce the Establishment Clause (as Epstein and others suggest), there could be an amendment to the Constitution to allow for public religion, or worse, revolution. That is, to enforce the Establishment Clause to the extent that it would need to be enforced under a strict reading of the Constitution could very well lead to an undermining of the Establishment Clause or the entire Constitution! So the Court allows some violations of Establishment as a legislative attempt to preserve the ideal of religious freedom: "A broad notion of ceremonial deism could swallow much of the Establishment Clause as it is currently understood. On the other hand, too narrow a definition may increase angst among the competing sides in the culture wars. Here the principle of accommodation is useful."[87] Ravitch maintains that ceremonial deism, as a category or a heuristic for a non-religious reference to the transcendent is invalid:

86. 465 U.S. at 710.
87. Ravitch, 102.

In the end, however, it all ends up being a form of mental gymnastics unless one is willing to argue that organized school prayer and the like are constitutional or that the singing of patriotic songs with religious references is unconstitutional. The reality is that maintaining intellectual consistency in this area requires an honest acceptance of doctrinal inconsistency and the fact that this inconsistency is driven by pragmatic concerns. What we basically have is a form of religious accommodation that is almost entirely driven by pragmatism even if it is sometimes justified on other grounds such as selective use of the 'traditions' of our nation.[88]

Nevertheless, he still argues that it is a beneficial accommodation; that some violations of the Constitution can be more helpful than harmful. We should just be honest about it as a violation.

Some legal scholars have been less charitable, objecting to the use of ceremonial deism because other means are available to meet those secular goals. For example, Patrick has suggested that "nonreligious invocations" can serve any of the functions (e.g., solemnity) ceremonial deism serves.[89] Unfortunately, he neither defines these terms, nor explains what form they may take. That is, the concept of a *nonreligious invocation* seems virtually devoid of meaning, apart from an interpretation similar to that given in the concept of ceremonial deism. After all, even if a prayer were offered to Liberty, some would object to it on First Amendment grounds. In fact, such an invocation would probably arouse both religious and nonreligious objectors. In the next chapter, theological concerns with ceremonial deism, as well as practical considerations associated with its adoption, will be examined.

CONCLUSION

Despite the legal objections to ceremonial deism, the clear fact of the matter is that the Supreme Court has consistently rejected a strict reading of Establishment, preferring instead to examine each case independently, and allowing religion at least some role in the public square. In fact, the Court has, on more than one occasion, noted the *impossibility* of viewing the Establishment Clause as demanding a *wall of separation of Church and State*. For example, in the majority opinion from *Lemon v. Kurtzman*, Chief Justice Burger argues that the principles enshrined in the First

88. Ibid., 103.
89. Patrick, "Ceremonial Deisms," 42.

Amendment are ill-served by the moniker, "Separation of Church and State" because it is so misleading. True separation is not possible because both religion and politics are tied to the societal structures of American life: "Our prior holdings do not call for total separation between church and state; total separation is not possible in an absolute sense. Some relationship between government and religious organizations is inevitable. . . . Judicial caveats against entanglement must recognize that the line of separation, far from being a 'wall,' is a blurred, indistinct, and variable barrier depending on all the circumstances of a particular relationship."[90] Nevertheless, the Court has also demonstrated concern over protecting the religious rights of all persons, even those who claim to prefer nonreligion. Its reluctance to rule in cases regarding religion stem from a concern to avoid theological analysis in the Court, preferring such analysis to take place within the Church, Academy, and among the ordained clergy.

90. 403 U.S. at 614.

4

"Nurture the Living, Care for the Wounded, and Honor the Dead"

Liberalism, Ceremonial Deism, and the Ideal Chaplain

INTRODUCTION

WHILE IT WAS DEMONSTRATED that Chaplain Klingenschmitt was not court-martialed because he prayed in Jesus' name, the case still raises issues of concern to evangelicals engaged in, or considering engaging in, military chaplaincy. That is, the case raises an important issue for investigation in answering the central question of this study—the question of whether or not evangelicals can continue to serve in chaplaincy positions. Specifically, Klingenschmitt charged that Unitarian Universalism is the *de facto* established religion of the United States Navy, and that theological dissent is not only frowned upon, but actually punished.

It is unlikely that, properly speaking, this charge can be sustained. Chaplaincy at its heart requires the ability to conduct ministry in a pluralistic environment, so some sensitivity to faiths other than that of the chaplain (or commander/boss for that matter) is necessary. How that sensitivity manifests itself has been the cause of much debate over the years at the Armed Services Chaplains Schools, but the fact that it must be present is not debated. It seems to me that the bulk of Klingenschmitt's complaints had to do with the training he received in pluralism, rather than forced universalist theological commitments. So in reality, the Klingenschmitt case brings to light two issues related to the pluralistic context of chaplaincy ministry: a theological question and a practical question. We shall examine the theological question first, since it impacts the answer to the practical question.

The theological question is one that has been raised in several quarters over the last ten years or so, though it has reared its head off and on throughout the history of the chaplaincy. The question of theological favoritism within chaplaincy for a wide-reaching liberal theology has been the topic of heated debate within military chaplaincy, even among some of the higher ranking officials. There is no doubt that this claim has been made by evangelical chaplains over the years. One of my best friends in the Army chaplaincy, an evangelical Methodist and a graduate of Asbury Seminary, felt that he had been denied promotion to the rank of Major the first time he came before a review board because of his theological stance. Similar claims have been made by evangelicals over the years, but such anecdotal evidence and hunches are terribly difficult to prove.

NAVY CHAPLAINS CASES

In recent years, though, some more concrete cases have developed against the Navy and they were alluded to in the second chapter. These cases, and others like them, have charged discrimination in the naval chaplaincy personnel policies, specifically arguing that there is a systematic bias against evangelical chaplains in promotion and retention, among other things. Two cases will be examined, if only briefly.

Larsen v. United States Navy

The first case has to do with acceptance into the Navy chaplaincy program. Three non-liturgical Protestant ministers, Charles Larsen, Gregory McNear and James Linzey applied for commissions in the Navy Chaplain Corps but were denied. They filed suit in the U.S. District Court in Washington, D.C., alleging discrimination in the Navy Chaplaincy hiring policies.[1] The plaintiffs claimed that the Navy used to base its allotments of chaplains from various religious groupings on the percentages of service members from those groups, but in the late-1980's (circa 1988), moved to a quota system unrelated to the representation of those faith groups among service members in the Navy. The new quota system purportedly allotted a third of chaplain slots to the Roman Catholic faith, a third to Protestant liturgical, and the final third to both non-liturgical

---

1. A fourth plaintiff, David Myers, dropped his part in the suit.

Christian and Special Worship. Since these divisions do not represent the faith make-up of the Navy as a whole, and in fact give a disproportionate number of slots to those from liturgical Protestant traditions, the plaintiffs believed it to be a deliberate attempt to minimize the career opportunities of non-liturgical clergy and to limit their influence in the Navy's Chaplain Corps. Both Larsen and Linzy claimed to have been told that they were denied because of their non-liturgical status, while McNear was told that he did not satisfy the "needs of the Navy," which he took as code for a reference to his evangelical commitments.

After some legal maneuvering in which the Navy attempted to argue that the case is moot because the plaintiffs do not have standing, cannot articulate a measurable injury, and the Navy is allowed to have Unconstitutional policies in hiring and promotion (because of the War Powers Clause), the Federal District Court for the District of Columbia heard the case. Even though the Court decided to hear the case, it did not allow the challenge to the so-called "Thirds Rule" to go forward because it was no longer in effect and the plaintiffs did not incur quantifiable damages as a result: ". . . because the Navy voluntarily abandoned its Thirds Policy and because the plaintiffs present no evidence showing that the Navy took this action merely to avoid judicial review, the plaintiff's challenge to this policy is moot."[2] Thus, the Court considered current Naval accessioning policies for chaplains which, at least according to the Navy, stipulate that the best qualified candidates are accepted.

At the heart of this case, the plaintiffs argued that the Navy's chaplaincy should reflect the religious composition of the Navy itself; that percentages of chaplains should correspond to percentages of various religions represented in naval personnel. So, for example, if 25 percent of naval personnel are Baptist, then roughly 25 percent of the chaplains should be Baptist, if 35 percent of naval personnel are Roman Catholic, then roughly 35 percent of naval chaplains should be Roman Catholic, etc. Such a one-to-one correspondence between relative percentages of personnel and chaplains is necessary, they argue, for the chaplaincy to meet the religious needs of the sailors, seamen, and officers of the United States Navy. Judge Ricardo M. Urbina saw this requirement as entailing the claim that the Navy can only legally operate a chaplaincy program if it can meet the religious needs of each and every individual member of the Navy. This, he thought, was wrongheaded; the chaplaincy program

2. *Larsen v. United States Navy*, p. 16–17.

does not need to meet every individual's religious needs, but rather it only need promote free exercise. The problem with the former suggestion is multiple: first, one sailor whose needs were not met by the chaplaincy would invalidate the whole system; in addition (though not stated in the Court's opinion), it would require the chaplaincy to be in constant flux as the religious beliefs of service members constantly change as new recruits are brought in and others fulfill their obligations and retire or attrition out. Last, it is infeasible to expect a chaplain to be available for each faith group at each Naval station. Thus, Judge Urbina concluded that the Court only need evaluate the chaplaincy's sufficiency for accommodating religious needs of the Navy as a whole.

Should the religious composition of the Navy Chaplaincy mirror the religious composition of the Navy? While the plaintiffs argued that it should, the Navy argued that it should not be required to do so, and that it in fact cannot do so. While at first glance, it may seem that the plaintiff's argument is clearly in the right, and while we may truly sympathize with their predicaments, upon further scrutiny, it should become clear that the Navy's position, at least with respect to the composition of the Chaplain Corps, is correct. Judge Urbina correctly noted that this is not practical for at least three reasons. First, individuals from religious groups with little representation may not have enough persons to warrant even one chaplain, yet with the Navy dispersed, there may be a legitimate need for overrepresentation of chaplains in order to allow access. Second, differences among religions account for differing levels of need for specific chaplain support. Some groups require an *ordained* clergy, while others may prefer, but not need, such personnel. For example, in order to offer sacraments, a Catholic priest is required, at least to consecrate the wine that a Catholic Representative may then serve, but a Pentecostal or Baptist worship service may be held without a chaplain present. Third, some groups have such distinctive worship as to need their own chaplains, while others may be similar enough to one another as to share chaplains. For example, Nazarene service members could attend a Methodist chaplain's worship service, while Latter Day Saints' service members typically want their own service. Each of these points seems reasonable and they are typical considerations in the accessioning of chaplains in all of the branches of the armed forces.

To say that the Navy's position regarding the religious make-up of its Chaplaincy Corps is correct, though, is not to defend the Constitutionality of its Thirds Policy, or to affirm its decision with regard to the plaintiff's applications, or to dispute the plaintiff's charges that they were unfairly discriminated against by being rejected. Quite the contrary, there is good reason to view the Thirds Policy as favoring more liberal denominations and as having a theological basis in addition to a pragmatic concern. This, though, would be very difficult to prove, short of producing some form of written correspondence outlining a theological agenda from the Naval Chief of Chaplains Office. No such documentation has been presented as evidence, though the ruling in the case has been appealed.

Adair v. England/Johnson

The Federal case of *Adair v. Johnson* began as Adair v. England, but was granted class action status in 2002, and the current Secretary of the Navy, Hansford T. Johnson, was named in the case. This case has to do with alleged discrimination against evangelical and non-liturgical chaplains within the naval chaplaincy.

The case presents as evidence many of the policies and procedures for promotion and selection already noted (e.g., Thirds Policy, two Catholics on each promotion board, etc.), and charges that the Navy has refused to follow its stated policy of promoting the most qualified candidates to the next rank in favor of promotions based on denominational quotas or preference for liturgical over non-liturgical chaplains. The plaintiffs also argue that the way naval chaplaincy leaders use the General Protestant worship service violates Free Exercise. They claim that non-liturgical senior chaplains often preclude Protestant worship outside of the General Protestant service, and force the General Protestant service to conform to liturgical worship and theology. The combined effect of limiting non-liturgical chaplains and disallowing non-liturgical worship services violates the religious rights of the Navy service members and their families stationed abroad. The case even suggests that this has the effect of establishing Liturgical Protestantism as an official religion. While the final charge may be difficult to sustain, these concerns are troubling.

Perhaps the issue of greatest concern is the charge that some naval personnel were denied the ability to worship by senior chaplains. Some non-liturgical chaplains and like-minded naval personnel have reportedly been denied access to Navy facilities for the purpose of conducting worship. While all admit that some standard criteria need to be met before resources are allocated for a worship service (e.g., a minimum number of committed participants before a chapel and chaplain assistant are assigned), this does not seem to be the issue here. Rather, there seems to have been a motivation to explicitly hamper the efforts of some non-liturgical Protestant chaplains in their faith-specific ministries.[3] Whether this was due to theological disagreement or professional jealousy is difficult to determine. Either way, though, the issue is one that should be of concern to all, if substantiated. In addition, some non-liturgical chaplains have allegedly been forced to conduct liturgical worship services in violation of their own belief systems and their endorsing agencies' policies. The complaint also charges that the Navy has two systems of discipline and administration within its chaplaincy corps; one set of rules for liturgical chaplains, who are not removed from service when they fail to meet minimum standards, and one set for non-liturgical chaplains. Some have pointed to this lack of equity within the chaplaincy as the source of morale and recruiting problems within the Corps.[4]

3. Two examples from the plaintiffs themselves should suffice to make the point. First, Michael Belt was a chaplain from the Church of the Nazarene denomination. He claims to have been berated by senior naval chaplains for his worship style, having one call it "hogwash." According to Belt, he and another non-liturgical chaplain got together to reformat a General Protestant service and grew the congregation from 40 to 130. At that point, the liturgical chaplain who disagreed with the worship style took over the service and drove the congregation away. *Adair v. Johnson*, III.A.3.b. Chaplain David Wilder, a Southern Baptist, had a similar experience while stationed at the Marine Corps Base at Camp Butler on Okinawa. He was pastoring the General Protestant service, which averaged about 100–125 participants each week. When a new senior chaplain, Episcopal Chaplain Williams came to the base and visited Chaplain Wilder's service, he made suggestions on how the service could be improved. Chaplain Wilder saw these suggestions as an attempt to make the service Episcopal in character, and refused. He was removed from his position as pastor of the congregation and Chaplain Williams took over. As a result, the congregation dwindled to about 12 per week. At that point, Chaplain Wilder began a Baptist service in the base chapel, which grew to about 120 attendees each week. Chaplain Williams accused him of sabotage and attempted to shut his service down.

4. At a March, 2001 Navy Chaplains' Leadership Conference in Dallas, TX, senior Catholic Chaplain Gomulka stated: "The Chaplain Corps has lied to clergy about opportunities for ministry in the sea services. When new chaplains discover how they are restricted in their ministry by senior chaplains who are jealous of their talents, they become angry and return to civilian life informing their clergy friends about the 'truth' of what they can expect if they become Navy chaplains. The recent recruiting video is a perfect example of this problem. While the video portrayed chaplains happily engaged in ministry at a particular duty station, the truth of the matter was that a number of chaplains had left the Navy after having served at that particular duty station, frus-

How can evangelical claims of discrimination by liberal leaders in military chaplaincy be evaluated if anecdotal evidence is inadmissible? Perhaps the most obvious approach to evaluating these claims is to conduct a statistical analysis of the theological commitments of those who have been promoted to the highest positions within the chaplaincy of the various branches of the military. The litigants in the Adair case have done just that for the Navy. So, for example, the position of Chief of Naval Chaplains included three Roman Catholics and four Lutherans during the period 1980–2006. One Presbyterian, one Reformed, and one Seventh Day Adventist each held the position during that time. The plaintiffs note, "You will notice that there has not been one Chief of Chaplains from a major evangelical denomination during this period. Southern Baptists, who have more chaplains on active duty than any other group, are completely absent from this list."[5] Another statistical study of key naval chaplaincy billets by Chaplain Larry Ellis found that fifty-four percent were filled by liturgical Protestants, thirty-four percent by Roman Catholic, and twelve percent by non-liturgical Protestants.[6]

A similar study of historical data related to chaplaincy promotion in the Navy seemed to reveal a bias against evangelicals and other non-liturgical chaplains. For example, Baptist chaplains appeared to be only half as likely to complete a thirty year career and rise to the rank of Captain as their Roman Catholic counterparts. Dr. Harold Leuba, who conducted the research, concluded, "The statistical evidence suggests that the Chaplain Corps personnel management system exerts a systematic pressure on non-liturgical Chaplains. This is a pressure which is strong enough to overwhelm those Chaplain's [sic] natural tendency to stay in Service, and they are both systemically and systematically denied promotion opportunity. . . . Non-liturgicals in general, and non-Baptist non-liturgicals are under promoted, for even those who survive into later periods have an average lower rank than their brethren."[7]

trated at the way they were limited by command chaplains to exercise a fulfilling and life-transforming ministry. CNRC [Chief of Navy Recruiting Command] brought in chaplains from other commands to depict them happily engaged in ministry while the 'real chaplains' at the duty station whose morale was quite low were nowhere to be seen." Cited in the complaint, *Adair v. Thompson*, V.N.114.

5. http://chaplainreform.com/ChiefsofChaplains.htm, accessed February 18, 2008. It is interesting to note that the current Army Chief of Chaplains, Douglas Carver, is Southern Baptist.

6. Ibid.

7. http://chaplainreform.com/WhatHappened.htm, accessed February 18, 2008.

Of course, there are problems with this approach, even if the results suggest favoritism for some denominations over others. First, denominational endorsement does not necessarily reveal theological slant; it does not necessarily show whether any particular chaplain is liberal or conservative/evangelical. The Methodist Church, for example, is perhaps the most diverse among Protestant groups with some very liberal strains as well as some very conservative (even fundamentalist) groups as well. Similarly, the Catholic Church has chaplains with such a wide range of theological leanings that statistics regarding Catholic chaplains are virtually inconsequential for this kind of study. Some may object and claim that all Catholic chaplains they have met over the rank/position of O-4 (Major; Lieutenant Commander) are liberal, but we would then be relying on anecdotal evidence again. Second, it has a false premise—namely that the percentages of chaplains from each denomination should remain the same through career progression. This is a failed proposition when higher-rank positions are considered, for there are not enough such positions to ensure that each denomination will have its same representation as it does at the lower echelons. Under the proposed requirements (or expectations) of the cases considered above, some denominations would never have representation at the higher ranks because they do not have a large enough representation in the Service. Nevertheless, as noted, it is at least suggestive of problematic and discriminatory policies. In addition, though, other evidence exists.

The Stafford Report

Perhaps the most damning item entered into evidence in any of the naval chaplains discrimination cases is the so-called "Stafford Report," an official memorandum for the Chief of Naval Personnel by Captain J. N. Stafford, Special Assistant for Minority Affairs, who was asked to investigate allegations that promotion boards for the rank of Commander used denominational quotas to select less qualified chaplains for promotion. In the memorandum, Stafford concludes that Lieutenant Commander S. M. Aufderheide's (the injured party) allegation of denominational discrimination "has merit" and recommends he be granted a special promotion board.

Stafford's investigation included a comparison of Chaplain Aufderheide's record with those who were selected at the two promotion boards which denied him advancement. This comparison revealed that Aufderheide's was stronger and that some of those individuals promoted had deficiencies that should have prevented their selection. The third paragraph of Stafford's memo is telling:

> Although the Secretary of the Navy's Selection Board Precepts support the practice of '. . . giving due consideration to the needs of the Navy for officers with particular skills' neither the precepts nor Navy Regulations mandate the selection of officers based on affiliation with a given faith or denomination. However, it appears that the board may have systematically applied a denominational quota system, perhaps to ensure balanced denominational representation across the Chaplain Corps. It is important to note that the precepts do mandate the application of a 'best and fully qualified' standard, and require that the board consider substandard performance that is documented in official records in determining who is best qualified for promotion.[8]

The report goes on to offer up several specific examples of Lutheran chaplains with performance or weight deficiencies who were nevertheless promoted ahead of Aufderheide. In the end, two recommendations of Stafford's are particularly noteworthy. First, he recommended that chaplains no longer be allowed to serve on promotion boards for other chaplains (a sad commentary; that chaplains would discriminate more than their secular counterparts). Second, and most significantly, he recommended that the Chief of Naval Personnel initiate an Inspector General investigation into Chaplain Corps selection board processes. In so doing, he suggests that there may have been systematic discrimination on the basis of denominational affiliation. This, he believes, is improper and out of step with naval regulations. It could also be argued that such unfair practices are certainly out of step with the teachings of all major religions as well.

Conclusion

Questions related to the composition of the Naval Chaplaincy are at the basis of several of the cases in question. Such questions are worth asking, but are more complex than initially thought. In the case of *Katcoff v. Marsh*, the Army Chaplaincy had to articulate its own rationale for its

8. J. M. Stafford, "Memorandum for Chief of Naval Personnel, RE: Request for Special Selection Board ICO LCDR S.M. Aufderheide, CHC, USN," dated 23 December 1997, accessed via link at http://chaplainreform.com/Promotions.htm, on May 2, 2009.

religious composition in light of its arguments for its Constitutionality as a program. While the Office of the Army Chief of Chaplains manages personnel and does so on the basis of a form of quota system, those numbers/quotas are set not at the complete discretion of the Chief of Chaplains (though a measure of flexibility and discretion must be allowed), and not even by the religious make-up of the Army, but rather by the religious composition of the entire civilian population. This allows for the ongoing fluctuation in the Army's religious composition due to accession and attrition, but also for a change in religious composition in the event of a full-scale draft and total mobilization of the Army. Still, the Army also considers underrepresented groups which may not have enough members to warrant a chaplain, and may grant them a chaplain slot.

It is curious that the Army has not seen the kind of litigation that the Navy in particular, and to a lesser extent, the Air Force, have encountered recently. I wonder if this is due to the fact that the Army Chaplaincy faced a serious challenge to its continuance, while the Navy did not. Perhaps the challenge of Katcoff and Wieder forced Army Chaplaincy leadership to think though its program's implementation and management more carefully, and the result has been a program that does as good a job as humanly feasible to balance the Free Exercise rights of all Army personnel, including service members and chaplains. It may also have caused those in higher positions within the chaplaincy to be more self-conscious of their own prejudices and/or the impact of their own theological commitments upon their evaluations of other chaplains. Drazin and Currey seem to indicate this as they reflect on the net effect of the Katcoff and Wieder case:

> What were the results of the years of effort on the part of so many people to defend the constitutionality of the Army chaplaincy? The lengthy litigation provided an opportunity to improve the chaplaincy, an impetus to rethink and redirect goals, allowing a more careful understanding and awareness of the possibilities for service inherent in the position. It also caused the chaplaincy to focus as never before on its responsibilities to provide for and to defend the rights of soldiers to free exercise of their faith (or lack thereof).[9]

While it cannot be demonstrated that there is systemic persecution of evangelicals in the Navy or the Navy's chaplaincy program, the sheer

9. Drazin and Currey, 205.

number of complaints and cases filed serve as convincing circumstantial evidence.[10] There are currently at least five cases filed in Federal Court by evangelicals or conservative Christian groups representing over fifty former, retired, and current naval Chaplains. These cases, do not tell the whole story, as there has been a history of litigation by evangelicals against the Navy, though many of the cases were dismissed when the Navy reconsidered its actions and the lawsuits were dismissed. For example, the 1998 case of *Yourek v. USA* was settled out of court because the individual was given a promotion with back-dating. Similarly, the 1999 case of *Sturm v. Danzig* was dismissed by the San Diego District Court as moot because Chaplain Sturm was promoted and back-dated, and therefore, there was no injury. In addition, the findings of the Stafford Report are particularly troubling. All of this suggests that the Navy has, at the very least, allowed some senior chaplains to treat evangelicals as lesser members of the chaplaincy team. Hopefully, Naval Chaplaincy leadership will reconsider the Constitutional basis for Naval Chaplaincy and will acknowledge some of the inconsistencies in policy and will rectify the problem, refusing to tolerate any form of discrimination. I fear that if it does not, more denominations will join the Full Gospel Chaplaincy in steering their prospective clergy from considering Naval Chaplaincy as a career.

CLASSICAL LIBERALISM

In order to properly evaluate claims of preference for liberal theology, a brief examination of classical theological liberalism is in order. Friedrich Daniel Ernst Schleiermacher (1768–1834) has been commonly referred to as the "Father of Modern Theological Liberalism." He was a hospital chaplain in Berlin when he published his most famous work, *Addresses on Religion to its Cultured Despisers,* in which he defended religion as a valuable aspect of human life. At the risk of oversimplification, I would argue that it is best to view Schleiermacher's theology as largely reactionary; a reaction against the rationalism of the so-called natural theologians and the creedal orthodoxy of the Pietists (out of which Schleiermacher himself had come!). It was the work of Immanuel Kant that was most influential on the rationalism of the day. The relevant contribution of Kant for an understanding of Schleiermacher comes in the form of his division

---

10. A website dedicated to the case of *Adair v. England* documents several of the problems mentioned here: http://chaplainreform.com/Prayer.htm.

of reality into two worlds: the Noumenal (real of the spiritual) and the Phenomenal (realm of the physical). For Kant, this division meant that nothing can be *known* about the spiritual realm because humans occupy the physical. The upshot of this division led Kant to deny revealed religion in favor of religion based on reason. Such a religion, at its heart, has to do with duty and moral obligation; things that can be known through rational reflection. The Pietists of Schleiermacher's day had become consumed with debates over doctrine. Thus, while rationalists argued that religion was the acceptance of natural theology and a universal morality ascertained by reason, the orthodox theologians saw religion as acceptance of revealed truths and obedience to God's will. Both seemed to be cerebral and devoid of emotion, a problem similar to that which originally gave rise to Pietism in the first place. The people of Germany in this time, following Goethe, saw religion as fundamentally separated from life, which was characterized by potentiality revealed in passion and art. Christian argues, therefore, that Schleiermacher was trying to respond to the fragmentation of religion from the whole of life that seemed to be a part of modern philosophy—religion does not merely have to do with what one knows or with what one does: "To assign religion to either of these spheres—knowing or doing—in exclusion of the other, would compromise its relation to the whole of existence, and would perpetuate the tragic separation of the world of fact from the world of value begun by Descartes and continued by Kant."[11]

Schleiermacher saw religion as a feeling; as something like an immediate awareness of God's presence through His providential sustainment and guidance of the created order. The deep reflection upon and recognition of God's immanence in that providential activity is the heart of the religious life. He writes, "The contemplation of pious men is only the immediate consciousness of the universal being of all finite things in and through the infinite, of all temporal things in and through the eternal. To seek and to find this infinite and eternal factor in all that lives and moves, in all growth and change, in all action and passion, and to have and to know life itself only in immediate feeling—that is religion."[12] He continues, "The sum total of religion, then, is to feel all that moves us in our feeling, in the supreme

11. C. W. Christian, *Schleiermacher, Makers of the Modern Theological Mind* (Peabody, MA: Hendrickson, 1979), 53–54.

12. Friedrich Schleiermacher, *On Religion: Addresses in Response to Its Cultured Critics*, trans. by Terrence N. Tice (Richmond, VA: John Knox Press, 1969), 79.

unity of it all, as one and the same, and to feel all that is individual and particular as mediated only through that unity—that is, to feel our being and life as a being and life in and through God."[13]

He further described religion as a feeling of ultimate dependence. This is not mere emotionalism, though; it is more like a sense. As Hopper explains Schleiermacher's theology, "Human religious experience is not a matter of dogmas that one believes or of moral precepts that one obeys. It is, rather, immediate experience of God's presence. . . . Religion or piety is thus not primarily a matter of knowing or doing, but of 'feeling.' This most basic and pervasive aspect of all human experience Schleiermacher called 'the feeling of absolute dependence.'"[14]

This sense of ultimate dependence comes as one realizes his own finitude—in our experience, we see that there is change everywhere, yet we also have an ideal of permanence and the unchanging . . . the world is changing and it seems therefore to be dependent on that which is unchanging. Likewise, we are changing, and as we reflect on these things, we come to sense our dependence on the Unchanging; on God. Thus, the essence of all religion is a feeling of dependence, which comes as a result of self-reflection. All religions seek to bring man into harmony with God. It is interesting to note that according to Schleiermacher, some religions do a better job of this than others do, so his system does not just lead to relativism, but it does lead to the conclusion that all religions are true *to a certain degree.* Of course, Schleiermacher argued that Christianity is the best because it fully unites man and God in the person of Jesus Christ, but this was less of a Christological statement, and more a statement about Jesus' dependence upon God. Thus, Schleiermacher made Christ's example in living primary in his Christology, to the detriment of his Being and sacrificial death as substitute.

So theological liberalism is important for this study for several reasons, if it is indeed given a place of preference among chaplaincy or military leaders. It opens the door to religious pluralism by acknowledging the common experience at the foundation of all religions, even all of life. Although it does not assess all religions the same, it is suggestive of value in all religions at their core, a claim with which most evangelicals would not wholeheartedly agree. Similarly, its emphasis on feeling as the basis

13. Ibid., 94.

14. Jeffery Hopper, *Understanding Modern Theology II* (Philadelphia: Fortress, 1987), 37–39.

for theological truth lends itself well to a pluralistic context, for it includes a de-emphasis upon dogmatic theology. Instead, commonality is highlighted and religious distinctives are dismissed or ignored. Those who refuse to compromise or who acknowledge the commonality of religions may be viewed as theologically naïve, ignorant, or worse, troublemakers.

WHY EVANGELICALS FEEL PERSECUTED

While the statistics do not demonstrate that widespread systematic discrimination is taking place, they are at least suggestive of it. Similarly, it still seems that the military chaplaincy has created an ethos which is generally hostile to evangelicals, at least by the perception of many evangelicals who serve.[15] That is, many of us *feel* as though our commitment to biblical inerrancy and the necessity of personal faith in Christ for salvation precludes us from being *ideal* chaplains in the eyes of military leadership as a whole, and chaplaincy leadership specifically. What needs to be answered are the questions, "Why is this the case? Why do evangelicals feel this way if the statistics do not bear it out?" Closely related to these questions is the question of why so many evangelicals have been quick to uncritically accept Klingenschmitt's claims of religious persecution by liberal leadership and of the establishment of an unofficial religion of the United States government. Three answers are in order. First, the history of evangelicalism has led to a self-identity of a persecuted people; second, the model held up to which chaplains should aspire is more liberal in leanings; and third, the use of ceremonial deism in some establishment questions may indicate as much, at least if ceremonial deism has religious overtones.

Self-Perception as Persecuted

First, evangelicals have always had something of a self-identity as a persecuted people. In fact, it may be argued that persecution of Christians has served as a stimulus for evangelical involvement in politics in recent years, despite a strong heritage of support for separation of church and state under the guise of religious liberty. Lindsay argues that evangelical

---

15. I suspect that Jewish and Muslim chaplains could make the same claim—that while the military speaks of pluralism and acceptance, and even bends over backwards to accommodate specific religious needs (e.g., building a Kosher kitchen in the chapel at a cost of approximately $40,000), there is still an air of exclusion regarding non-Christian religions. For the Muslim chaplain, there may even be hostility at times since 9/11.

involvement and interest in foreign policy issues stems from their commitment to missions and their identification with those Christians persecuted abroad: "Tales about the persecution of missionaries became part of evangelical lore, but as technology made communication faster and more reliable, evangelicals began to learn of episodes like these within hours or days instead of weeks or months. Under the influence of a few key individuals, the evangelical community mobilized around concerns over religious persecution." [16]

One example of this self-identity can be found in certain quarters within the Baptist church. *The Trail of Blood*, a small pamphlet written by prominent Baptist pastor J. M. Carroll in the latter part of the nineteenth century, is now in its 80th printing, and continues to influence pastors and laity alike. The basic premise of the book is that Baptists can trace an unbroken line of succession of faithful churches back to Jesus and the Apostles, and that these churches were characterized by faithful adherence to the teachings of Christ (e.g., regenerate church membership, believer's baptism, congregational, anti-sacramental, etc). As Walker, who has authored an introduction to the pamphlet comments regarding Carroll's work, "The history of Baptists, he discovered, was written in blood. They were the hated people of the Dark Ages. Their preachers and people were put into prison and untold numbers were put to death." [17] Appended to the pamphlet is a chart which is supposed to represent the history of the church from the time of Christ, with red dots signifying the persecuted, true Church. In explanation of the chart, Carroll writes,

> THE RED CIRCLES REPRESENT BAPTIST CHURCHES beginning with the first Church at Jerusalem, founded by Christ during his earthly ministry, and out of which came the churches of Judea, Antioch and others. The red indicates they were persecuted. In spite of the bitterest opposition and persecution Baptist Churches are found in every age. The first nickname given them was Christians, the next, Ana-Baptists, and so on. You will notice that the dark ages are represented by a dark space. Even during this time you will notice a continual line of churches called Ana-

16. D. Michael Lindsay, *Faith in the Halls of Power: How Evangelicals Joined the American Elite* (New York: Oxford, 2007), 42–43.

17. Clarence Walker, "Introduction" in J. M. Carroll, *"The Trail of Blood" . . . Following the Christians Down Through the Centuries . . . or The History of Baptist Churches from the Time of Christ, Their Founder, to the Present Day* (Lexington, KY: Ashland Avenue Baptist Church, 1931; 66th ed., 1992), 2.

Baptists. They were continually and bitterly persecuted even unto
death by the Catholics. Near the first of the 16th Century the Ana
was dropped and they were simply called Baptists.[18]

Of course, this is just one example of such a self identity. One could
easily substitute writings from the Church of Christ or any number of
others for the Landmark Baptist perspective here. What is of interest at
this point, is that there is a certain allure of this perspective; there is something that is a bit enticing in the idea that we are a persecuted people.
Why is that the case? It seems that there are at least three good reasons,
two theological, and one sociological. First, evangelicals have come to
believe that persecution may serve as evidence of one's faithfulness to the
teachings of Christ. Jesus' own words in the Sermon on the Mount are
suggestive of this: "Blessed are you when they insult you and persecute
you and falsely say every kind of evil against you because of Me. Be glad
and rejoice, because your reward is great in heaven. For that is how they
persecuted the prophets who were before you." (Matt 5:11–12, HCSB).
Similarly, in the farewell address recorded in John's Gospel, Jesus notes
the opposition between the world and his true followers: "If the world
hates you, understand that it hated Me before it hated you. If you were of
the world, the world would love [you as] its own. However, because you
are not of the world, but I have chosen you out of it, the world hates you.
Remember the word I spoke to you: 'A slave is not greater than his master.'
If they persecuted Me, they will also persecute you. If they kept My word,
they will also keep yours." (John 15:18–20, HCSB). Jesus then moves to
an explicit warning of persecution because of the disciples' identification
with him: "I have told you these things to keep you from stumbling. They
will ban you from the synagogues. In fact, a time is coming when anyone
who kills you will think he is offering service to God. They will do these
things because they haven't known the Father or Me. But I have told you
these things so that when their time comes you may remember I told
them to you." (John 16:1–4a). Many evangelicals have appropriated these
warnings to their own situations and have thus, expected conflict with
the world as a result of their faithfulness to Christ. Second, the perva-
siveness of pre-millennialism among many evangelicals has led some to
expect persecution and to see it as evidence of Christ's imminent return.[19]

18. Carroll, *The Trail of Blood*, chart appended to the end of the book, point #4.

19. Hankins offers a good summary of the development within evangelicals of an

Third, evangelicalism, while now a part of the mainstream, originated on the periphery of American Christianity, and as sociologists of religion have pointed out, minority groups characteristically develop their self-identities in opposition to others. Sociologist of religion Sam Reimer maintains that evangelicals, while wishing to engage the culture, have a sense of exclusion from the culture, often times the result of either subtle criticism or overt ridicule. He notes,

> Many respondents indicated that encounters such as these [where ridiculed for their morals or religious beliefs by non-evangelicals] were not isolated events. Since the majority of core evangelicals had negative encounters with nonevangelicals, the boundaries that separate them are more salient. In addition, more than ninety percent of respondents believed that the 'values in this country' are 'becoming worse.' It is likely that the distinctiveness of being an evangelical is enhanced by a sense that much of the rest of society is deteriorating.[20]

Liberal Ideal and the Four Chaplains

In addition to evangelical identification with persecution, the ideal held up in military chaplaincy is often done so in such a way as to imply that liberal approaches to theology and pluralism are to be preferred. Perhaps the most famous story of any military chaplain is that of the immortal "Four Chaplains" in the Army. One February during a deployment, Chaplain Postma, my supervisory chaplain, reminded me and the other chaplains of the anniversary of the sinking of the U.S.S. Dorchester, a

interest in eschatology generally, and of premillennialism specifically. See "Chapter four: Millennialism: Folk Religion and the Career of End-Times Prophecy" in Barry Hankins, *American Evangelicals: A Contemporary History of a Mainstream Religious Movement* (Lanham, MD :Rowman & Littlefield, 2008).

20. Sam Reimer and Samuel Harold Reimer, *Evangelicals and the Continental Divide: The Conservative Protestant Subculture in Canada and the United States* (Montreal: McGill-Queen's Press - MQUP, 2003), 53. According to the study conducted by Reimer and Reimer, the self-identity of evangelicals is tied to both belief and action, as epitomized in four areas: Biblicism (or a Bible-based faith), conversionism (or a belief grounded in a conversion experience), activism (especially with respect to church involvement and evangelism), and crucicentrism (or centrality of Christ's death on the cross). These components create a unique group identity for evangelicals, who more often than not seem to fail to distinguish between their own commitments and Christianity. Consequently, they are likely to view other Christian traditions with suspicion, while still allowing for some true believers within those traditions. Ibid., 43.

cruise ship turned military transport during WWII. It was the worst sea disaster for the military in U.S. history. Over 600 Army soldiers and Navy sailors died by drowning or hypothermia in the icy waters off the coast of Greenland when a German U-boat torpedoed the ship as it was headed for the European theater.

Disasters of this magnitude, especially when the victims are members of the military during a time of war, are prone to mythological development. Mistakes and errors in judgment are minimized, while acts of honor and valor are emphasized and even sometimes embellished. This is probably due to the fact that we need heroes to encourage us to continue putting lives on the line for the cause. The same psychological need for heroes drives a need to demonize and dehumanize our enemies. The same psychological need for heroes drives a need to reject any discussion of American military or political failures during a time of war. We cannot tolerate suggestions that our forces have committed illegal acts or have violated human rights, or have violated the laws of war. This is why so many conservatives have reacted harshly to the reporting of the Abu Ghraib Prison scandal. Some argued that the photos may have been doctored, and others suggested the media was irresponsible for reporting the events, arguing that it put American soldiers' lives in danger.

The story of the *Dorchester* includes both failure and success, but most of all, it includes a lot of simple humanity. Failures in judgment regarding rescue efforts and in procedure surely abounded. Overcrowding of the hold in the *Dorchester*, blocked exits, and insufficient U-boat response training have all been cited as contributing factors to the high death toll. However, the greatest blunder came as a result of an overdeveloped sense of duty to standard operating procedures by the convoy commander. Captain Joseph Greenspun refused permission to pull survivors from the water because of his fear that the cutters involved in rescue operations may be torpedoed. Instead, they were to protect the remaining ships in the convoy and to search out and destroy the offending submarine. The resulting 48-minute delay cost hundreds of lives. There were also failures aboard the Dorchester itself. Many soldiers failed to heed warnings and commands to sleep wearing protective gear (i.e., life vests). But the story also includes acts of courage and heroism. The crew of the coast guard cutter, *Comanche* helped the *Escanaba* retrieve survivors despite orders to the contrary. Skipper (Lieutenant Commander) Ralph Curry ignored orders to provide overwatch for the *Escanaba* and risked court-martial in order to save an additional 94 soldiers/seamen.[21] But by all accounts, the most heroic aspect of the *Dorchester* story is the story of the four chaplains who were aboard at the time of its sinking, Reverend George Fox, Reverend Clark Poling, Rabbi Alex Goode, and Father John Washington.

The senior chaplain on board was Chaplain George Lansing Fox. He had a troubled childhood, and ran to enlist in the Army when hostilities with Germany reached a boiling point in 1917. He was assigned as a combat medic, and his experience of war rekindled the faith that his mother had instilled in him as a boy. He was injured when artillery hit the hospital he served, and he had much time to think. After the war, he attended Moody Bible College, served for a short while as a circuit rider in the Methodist Church, and then attended seminary. When he heard the news that the Japanese had attacked Pearl Harbor and that Germany had declared war on the United States, he decided to volunteer for another tour of duty, a decision which immediately halted his disability benefits (a source of much-needed income in the Fox household). His sense of duty and love of country compelled him to serve, despite the difficulties associated with that decision. After receiving a medical waiver from the Department of the Army, he was commissioned as a chaplain.

Clark Poling was born into a family with a heritage of ministry. His father was a well-known evangelist, as was his grandfather. He was described as courageous and inquisitive. In fact, he struggled with his faith for a time, but eventually came to believe God had called him to preach. He had a penchant for debate, which sometimes came out in his relations with family members, but also landed him a position on the debate team of Hope College. Even though he liked a good argument, he was not a disagreeable person, having a charm and wit that endeared him to everyone he met. Interestingly, this characteristic did not lead him into conflict with others over religious issues. Even though Poling was the most evangelical of the four, there was a sense of ecumenism in his theology and practice. He even invited Rabbi Aaron Wise to speak to his growing congregation on several occasions, presumably to aid interfaith relations. His early years in the pastorate were difficult financially, but that did not dissuade Clark from being generous. Giving away his own personal necessities seemed almost natural to Poling. Some biographers have

---

21. The crew of the *Escanaba* was able to pull 132 men out of the water with all but one surviving the ordeal.

reported that, on more than one occasion, he gave away one of his two pair of trousers or shoes despite his wife's protests! These characteristics and the way they played out in his actions serve as a sort of foreshadowing of his future actions on that fateful day.

Chaplain Goode was the son of a rabbi and was brought up in Brooklyn, New York and Washington, D.C. He was always a good athlete, flourishing especially in track. He was always popular with the members of the synagogues he served, even though he was quite young. He and his wife, Theresa had an energy about them which was both infectious and endearing. By most counts, he was a progressive thinker and worked hard for interfaith relations, claiming that the best cure for religious hatred is information: "Let us know one another better and thus learn to appreciate the good inherent in every man."[22] One concrete example of his efforts at promoting good relations between persons of differing faiths occurred during his first year serving the synagogue in York, Pennsylvania. The local Lutheran church burned to the ground. He immediately offered the use of the Temple facilities, though it turned out to be too small for the congregation. He participated in and helped organize joint worship services with another local church, and worked with the superintendent of primary schools on projects to help reduce bigotry among the children. Superintendent Lyles would later write of him, "Rabbi Goode educated the whole town of York in social relations . . . it is only a question of time until his name will be remembered everywhere."[23] He was also a scholar—earning a doctorate from John's Hopkins University, and writing monthly articles for the National Jewish Monthly. But more than scholarship and athletics, Alex was a patriot, as one incident from his childhood portrays. After the Tomb of the Unknowns was dedicated, Alex decided some form of commemoration was in order. As Wales and Poling describe it, "To show his respect for America's brave soldiers and the country they defended, Alex resolved to walk from his home in Georgetown all the way to Arlington. Leaving the bicycle he had earned with his paper route leaning on the porch, he made the trip on foot, alone—a solitary pilgrim on his own personal mission of honor."[24] As the war in Europe continued to develop, he felt compelled to volunteer, and was accepted into the chaplain corps.

22. Dan Kurzman, *No Greater Glory: The Four Immortal Chaplains and the Sinking of the Dorchester in World War II* (New York: Random House, 2004), 70.

23. Ibid., 72.

24. Ken Wales and David Poling, *Sea of Glory* (Nashville: Broadman & Holman,

John Washington is described as an adventurous young boy. Of Irish descent, he was brought up in an enclave of Irish immigrants in Newark, New Jersey. He felt called to the ministry before he even got out of high school and attended Seton Hall before Darlington Seminary. Perhaps the three most formative events in his life were an incident with a bee-bee gun when playing with friends in which he almost lost an eye, the death of his sister, Mary when she was fifteen and he was in high school, and his own bout with an infection of his tonsils just prior to starting college. The infection caused him to develop an extremely high fever which eventuated in a coma. The prognosis was not good, and his mother arranged for him to receive the *last rites*. After he healed, Washington came to believe that God had a special purpose for his life (beyond the general call to the priesthood). When he heard of the Japanese attack on Pearl Harbor, he came to see that purpose—to serve God in the military. While the Navy turned down his application to enlist, the Army did not.

It is the heroism of these four seemingly ordinary men that has made the story of the *Dorchester* so compelling. After the ship was hit, the chaplains, who had organized a talent show earlier that evening in an effort to boost morale, all made their way to the top deck, helping soldiers and seamen along the way. Rabbi Alex Goode gave his gloves to Navy Lieutenant John Mahoney, who forgot his as a result of the confusion. In Mahoney's estimation, those gloves meant the difference between life and death for him: "I landed in a lifeboat that was awash and for eight hours had to hold on in [freezing] waters. I would never have made it without them. As it was, only two of us survived out of the forty who were in the boat."[25] As the boat went down, many of the young men were terrified, even unable to move. Clark Poling apparently approached one such Army Private, took off his own lifejacket, gave it to the hysterical young man, and ordered him down into the icy waters.[26] Some reports have suggested that, by the end of the ordeal, all four chaplains gave up their jackets to others who had refused to follow ship's orders to wear them to bed, and subsequently forgot them when the alarm sounded.[27]

2001), 27–28.

25. Kurzman, 141.

26. Ibid., 142.

27. Wales and Poling, 298–99.

After giving up their only earthly chance of survival, the chaplains stood on the deck in a circle, and each began to pray aloud to his God: "As the chaplains looked around the circle at one another, the same thought passed from one to the next: *We didn't plan this, didn't talk about it in advance. Yet here we are, all giving up our life jackets to others. Giving them up not grudgingly but willingly, thankful for the chance to sacrifice in the service of an all-knowing, all-loving God. Jewish, Catholic, and Protestant— different and yet the same. Separate and yet forever indivisible.*"[28] Just before the *Dorchester* went down, all four chaplains locked arms and sang hymns together.

It is truly an inspiring story. The heroism and self-sacrifice of these four men is surely worthy of admiration and their story is rightly memorialized. Stamps issued during the War depict the faces of the four men. It was unusual for the United States Postal Office to put the face of someone who had not been dead at least ten years on a stamp, but their story was such a powerful motivator to the soldiers on the front lines and an inspiration to those on the home front, that it just made sense. Other memorials include a chapel at the Veteran's Administration Hospital in Minneapolis, and stained glass windows in the chapel at the United States Military Academy in West Point and in the Heroes Chapel at the National Cathedral in Washington, D.C. In each case, the memorial is proper and befitting.

Yet, even while I acknowledge the need for such memorialization, I am somewhat disturbed by the way this wonderful story of heroism, selfless love of others, and faithfulness is often peddled. That is, there is something unsettling about the emphasis in the way the story is often told. I must admit that I am somewhat reluctant to offer any words of critique about this particular story, as it is sacrosanct among Army chaplains, but the theologian and historian in me is driven to ask the sometimes unpopular and even uncomfortable questions. Ultimately, of course, truth is what is sought, and it seems to me that, unfortunately, stories are often recounted for other purposes, especially stories which can be used to spur combat soldiers forward to victory.[29] The most troubling aspect has

28. Ibid., 300.

29. The relatively recent movie, *Flags of Our Fathers* recounts the true story (with a measure of artistic license, of course) of the famous photograph of the raising of the American flag at Iwo Jima during World War II. At the time, publicists and the Department of Defense wanted the nation to think it was raised after a decisive victory, even though this was not exactly the case. The story was more profitable for war

to do with the way the story is often told has to do with the recounting of the relationships between the chaplains and its impact on theological matters. The emphasis on the collegiality of the chaplains and even the way they conducted their ministries, is presented in a way that suggests it is preferable to minimize the differences among religions, rather than admitting them; that acknowledging real disagreements is in some way negative, or divisive, or combative. Consider, for example, the following account by Dan Kurzman:

> Roy Summers, one of these men [rescued due to the efforts of the chaplains], recounted, 'When I got off guard duty I went down to the chapel. I didn't know which chaplain would be there. But the Catholic Chaplain Washington was there and I enjoyed his service very much, although I'm Protestant. I would have listened to any of them.' And Roy listened to a troubling, if heartfelt plea: 'All of you know the Lord's Prayer,' the priest said. 'Go and sin it, say it, whatever. It'll help you.' A soldier later commented on the priest's advice: 'That's the only time that I ever saw that he brought his religion in. The rest of the time he was just a man who wanted to take care of other men. I would imagine that would make him a very, very good priest, because people could get with him.'[30]

While it must be admitted that some disagreements over religion, especially theology can become combative, and that throughout the history of humanity, many wars have been waged in the name of religion (though a careful assessment of most of these will reveal that political, economic and ethnic factors were always at play as well), we should not suppose that all disagreements over theology will lead to strife.

My concern, though, is that the story can be used to present a sterilized religion for the American public; some form of an ideal of how religions *should* get along not in spite of their differences, but rather by virtually eliminating or perhaps ignoring them. Consider, for example, the description of the chaplains' experience at the Harvard Chaplain School, where they received their initial chaplaincy training. A particularly influential event was a speech presented by the commandant in which he challenged the new chaplains to strengthen their religious commitments *to whatever faith they hold*:

---

bond sales with the mythic nature it took on than it most likely would have been with the truth.

30. Kurzman, 114–15.

> The colonel's talk awakened in George [Fox] some painful memo-
> ries, since after that war [WWI) he had abandoned Catholicism,
> seeking to shed every sign of his past in embracing a completely
> new identity. But now, at Harvard, it didn't seem to matter much
> which house of prayer one attended. . . . Now the practitioners
> of many religions were thrust together, six to a room furnished
> with two-tier bunks, in a dormitory called Perkins Hall. They ate
> together, studied together, marched together, drilled together, and
> even prayed together.[31]

When I attended chaplain's school, I had a similar experience. All of
the chaplains and chaplain candidates were housed in the same building,
though we had personal quarters. We had per diem, so we didn't eat in the
chow hall, but we still found time to eat with one another. Sometimes we
would go out to eat and sometimes we would invite others to our rooms for
a meal of microwaved cuisine. It was enjoyable to get together with people
of faith and discuss our different beliefs. I especially remember one night
when our whole class went out to Red Lobster together. It was interesting to just observe how different we really were. The Lutherans, Catholics,
Presbyterians, some of the Methodists, and the Rabbi all got drinks at the
bar, while myself and the other Baptists, along with the various Charismatics
(Church of God, Cleveland; Assemblies of God, Four-Square Gospel) and
the Seventh Day Adventists chose to not drink. It was humorous to watch
one guy in particular, a seminary student with the Church of God, Cleveland,
who was always wound up. I thought he would explode when one of our
Lutheran friends sat down at our table with a beer and offered him a sip! He
was a really good guy, who loved Jesus. Probably the most funny incident
was at the dinner table. Several of us were eating lobster, and we decided
to tease one of the Seventh Day Adventist chaplain candidates—he always
had a smile on his face. He seemed curious about the taste, and we picked
up on this, so we started moaning in ecstasy as we ate and went on and on
about how good it was. He asked me what it tastes like. As I described the
sweet taste of the meat, I could tell his curiosity was growing. Several of us
then offered some to him in a joking fashion, "Go ahead, have just a little
taste. We won't tell. . . . We'll be your friend." Of course, he refused, and
we all laughed together. We wouldn't have given him some anyway, if not
because we agree with his view, but because we wouldn't want to jeopardize
his position or ours, and we wouldn't want to serve as a source of conflict,
especially over a joke.

31. Ibid., 16.

Sometimes our differences were not a matter of joking, though. My second or third day at the school, Rabbi Fields, who sat beside me in class, turned to me and asked if I thought he is going to Hell. There had been a relatively recent controversy in the media over the proselytization of Jews by Southern Baptists and this was evidently fresh on his mind. I was a little taken aback at first, but then I told him, "Well, that depends."

"On what?" he asked.

"Let me ask you a couple of questions first." He agreed, and then I said, "Do you believe Jesus is the Messiah of God; the one the prophets predicted would come and deliver God's people?"

He looked at me, chuckled, and said, "No."

"Do you believe Jesus is the unique Son of God, who has come to take away the sins of the world?"

"No."

"Do you believe Jesus was God incarnate, God in flesh, and have you placed your faith in him as your personal Lord and Savior?"

At this, Rabbi Fields looked at me in horror and exclaimed, "No! Absolutely not!"

I replied, "Then yes, I believe you are going to Hell."

He was aghast; he couldn't believe that I would make such a statement: "How can you say that?! The Jews are the People of God! Your Bible even says so!"

I responded by pointing out that there are several passages in both the Old and New Testaments that make it clear that each and every Jewish person will not be saved. The prophets constantly warned the people of Israel against this very attitude. For example, Isaiah told the people that God hates their new moon festivals and their feasts; that their worship of Him was tainted because they assumed performing the letter of the Law was sufficient for salvation. By contrast, he tells them to be cleansed of sin and then they may come to the LORD and worship in a proper fashion:

> Bring your worthless offerings no longer, incense is an abomination to Me, new moon and Sabbath, the calling of assemblies—I cannot endure iniquity and the solemn assembly. I hate your new moon festivals and your appointed feasts, they have become a burden to Me; I am weary of bearing them. So when you spread out your hands in prayer, I will hide My eyes from you; yes, even though you multiply prayers, I will not listen. Your hands are covered with blood. Wash yourselves, make yourselves clean; remove

> the evil of your deeds from My sight. Cease to do evil, learn to do
> good; seek justice, reprove the ruthless, defend the orphan, plead
> for the widow. 'Come now, let us reason together,' says the LORD,
> 'Though your sins are as scarlet, they will be as white as snow;
> though they are red like crimson, they will be like wood. If you
> consent and obey, you will eat the best of the land; but if you refuse
> and rebel, you will be devoured by the sword.' Truly the mouth of
> the LORD has spoken. (Isa 1.13–20, NASB)

Amos makes a similar point regarding the value of sacrifices. The
point, of course, is that the mere fact of offering sacrifices is not enough.
The mere fact of being Jewish is not enough. Instead, a change of heart is
what is needed:

> Alas, you who are longing for the day of the LORD, for what pur-
> pose will the day of the LORD be to you? It will be darkness and
> not light; as when a man flees from a lion and a bear meets him,
> or goes home, leans his hand against the wall and a snake bites
> him. Will not the day of the LORD be darkness instead of light,
> even gloom with no brightness in it? I hate, I reject your festivals,
> nor do I delight in your solemn assemblies. Even though you offer
> up to Me burnt offerings and your grain offerings, I will not ac-
> cept them; and I will not even look at the peace offerings of your
> fatlings. Take away from Me the noise of your songs; I will not
> even listen to the sound of your harps. But let justice roll down
> like waters and righteousness like an ever-flowing stream. (Amos
> 5.18–24, NASB)

I then explained to my Rabbi friend that in the New Testament, John
the Baptist (a Jewish apocalyptic preacher) said to those who came out to
hear his preaching in the Judean wilderness, "Do not think to yourselves,
'We have Abraham as our Father,' for I tell you, God can raise up children
for Abraham from these rocks!" (Matt 3.9; Luke 3.8). I also noted that
Jesus himself claimed that he is the Way, the Truth, and the Life, and that
no one can get to the Father, except by him (John 14.6). Similarly, the
Apostle Peter, who was himself a Jew, said that there is no other name
given by which men can be saved (Acts 4.12).

Our conversation quickly became a class-wide argument. Many of
the Christian chaplains disagreed with me; one told me that I have "cave-
man" theology, presumably because I am not as enlightened as he. I was
disturbed by this, not because he made me doubt my own position, far
from it, but because there were so many Christian chaplains who have lit-

tle regard for the exclusivity of the gospel claims. However, I was pleased to see that many also agreed with me, claiming that salvation through Christ is clearly the simple meaning of the Gospel. If we don't hold on to that, then we don't have anything left. As the Apostle Paul says, if Christ is not raised, then we are still in our sins and are to be pitied more than all men (1 Cor 17–19)!

We had chapel every day at 1000 hours. There was a Catholic chapel, a Protestant chapel, a Jewish chapel, and a Lutheran/Episcopal chapel. Rabbi Fields invited our class to attend Jewish chapel for a special service in which he would explain the significance of each portion of the service. Most of us attended out of curiosity and a sense of solidarity and support for our classmate. The service was indeed, both informative and interesting. Similarly, Rabbi Fields came to one of the Protestant services during the three months of training. It was the service I spoke in. I was surprised to see him, but I think he understood that what I said that first day, while offensive to him at the time, was simply a matter of my personal conviction. He came to realize that it was not out of malice or hatred that I said what I did, but rather out of love. He later told me that he respected my conviction and integrity. The point of this is to show that, while my experience was similar to that described of the chaplains above (in particular Rabbi Goode and Reverend Fox), I would never say that it seemed that *it did not matter which house of prayer one attended.* It did, and it does! I suspect that Rabbi Fields would agree with this point. After all, he remains a Jewish chaplain and holds to his convictions. In fact, he recently had a conversation with him while attending some training for chaplains at Fort Sam Houston. He complained that some Protestant chaplains are trying to sell themselves as Messianic Jewish Rabbis and that this causes confusion for Jewish soldiers and skews the numbers of Jewish chaplains in the military. He and I agreed that it is somewhat misleading for a Messianic Jewish chaplain to wear the tablets as his symbol rather than a cross. I have even stronger convictions than he does, as I believe this violates Paul's intent in his condemnation of the Judaizers in his letter to the Galatians and elsewhere.[32] Nevertheless, the important point here is

---

32. This is assuming, of course, that the individual was a convert to Judaism after Christianity. I would not make the same argument for those who were already trained rabbis and then converted to Christianity. Someone who was brought up Jewish, converted to Christianity, and then attended a Christian seminary (or Hebrew Union University for that matter) presents a somewhat more difficult problem. I myself and

that Rabbi Fields does see a difference among the religions, and it really does matter what one believes. To deny this is to deny the very basis of our faiths!

Similarly, I still stand by my conviction that salvation is found nowhere except in Christ. By this, I mean that an individual cannot be saved unless he places his personal faith in Jesus Christ, trusting him for forgiveness of sins, and believing that he is the unique Son of God, God incarnate (in the flesh), and that he died on the cross to pay the penalty for our sins because we could not live up to the divine standard of perfection. If a person does not place his personal faith in Jesus Christ, then his own sins condemn him. This means that those non-Christian faiths do not lead their followers to God, the true God who is Triune in nature, but rather, they turn them away from Him. We must retain this distinctive feature of our faith, if it is to remain true to its history and its nature. Christianity simply *is* exclusivistic in its claims regarding salvation.

Unfortunately, most renditions of the story of the four chaplains typically fail to include any discussion of differences in theology. Perhaps the most striking example of the attempted homogenization of faith in the four chaplain's story can be seen in the way their end is described. The solidarity of the four chaplains is depicted as a unity not just in selfless love of others or in a sense of honor or duty that led them to take care of the soldiers entrusted to them before caring for themselves, and not even just in a commitment to their individual religions, but rather as a unity of faith. The story is often told in such a way that the audience is led to think that the preferred stance toward different religions is cooperation to the extent that differences are meaningless and of little consequence. Consider, for example, the following excerpt from a version of the story written for children:

> ... So the Four Chaplains stood on the heaving deck, with their arms linked—each without a life jacket. Violent squalls confused the last moments of the S.S. Dorchester—flares on the bridge showed the huge waves dashing over it ... And somewhere in the seething ocean perhaps four men were cheating death, supported by the chaplains' gifts.
>
> Frigid waters reached to their knees as the Four Chaplains stood together, their lips moving in prayer, each in the tradition of his

inclined to say he should wear the cross so that it is clear which religion he represents).

faith, but the God to whom they prayed was One. A wave swept over the ship and then again but—though the ship rose to breast a third wave—it was useless. The Dorchester fought to right herself, failed, and plunged below the surface.[33]

The emphasis on the unity of the object of prayers (same God) suggests in a subtle way that the tradition within which the prayers were given is inconsequential. When this aspect of the four chaplains story is upheld, many evangelicals feel uncomfortable. We believe that the aspect of the story to be held up for emulation is the self-sacrifice and the love of others. But to take that and turn the story into a lesson about how religious differences are inconsequential or should not be emphasized or perhaps even allowed is to miss the point of these men's sacrifice. It seems to me, then, that the story can be used as a symbol of heroism and self-sacrifice; of love of others more than self, or it can be used as a symbol of religious pluralism; of the removal of faith distinctions. Some may see this as a false dichotomy; some may wish to argue that the story is both. However, there are good reasons for concern that the second can, and almost always will, overshadow the first. The use of the story as a symbol of religious pluralism unwittingly detracts from its value in several ways.

First, it detracts from the importance and value of the story of what the men actually did—they gave their lives for others. The citation of the Distinguished Service Cross awarded to each man begins with the following sentence: "For extraordinary heroism in connection with military operations against an enemy of the United States."[34] At the dedication of the national memorial to the sacrifice of the men, President Harry S. Truman correctly noted the significance of their bravery, but then moved to tie it to faith, ultimately claiming that the real lesson is not heroism, but obedience to God. At the opening of his speech, he declared, "This Chapel commemorates something more than an act of bravery or courage. It commemorates a great act of faith in God."[35] Later, he tied that idea with the concept of loving others: "Those four chaplains actually carried

33. Margaret E. Sangster, "Saga of The Four Chaplains" in *The Chapel of Four Chaplains: A Sanctuary of Brotherhood*, ed. Walter H. White (Philadelphia: Chapel of Four Chaplains, 1979), 58–59.

34. *The Chapel of Four Chaplains: A Sanctuary of Brotherhood*, 26.

35. President Harry S. Truman, *Speech Dedicating the Chapel of Four Chaplains*, Philadelphia, PA, February 3, 1951, recorded in *The Chapel of Four Chaplains: A sanctuary of Brotherhood*, 16.

out the moral code which we are all supposed to live by. They obeyed the divine commandment that men should love one another. They really did live up to that moral standard that declares: 'Greater love hath no man than this, that a man lay down his life for his friends.' (The quotation is from St. John, 15th Chapter, 13th verse). They were not afraid of death because they knew that the word of God is stronger than death. Their belief, their faith, in His word enabled them to conquer death."[36]

Second, it can serve to turn off chaplains of evangelical or sectarian persuasions. As already noted, it is not uncommon for evangelicals to feel uncomfortable about the story of the four chaplains, to even feel a sense of resentment, because of the suggestion that religious beliefs are secondary or inconsequential. Yet evangelicals believe that salvation is exclusively gained by grace through faith in the shed blood of Christ on the cross and his subsequent resurrection from the dead. Some younger chaplains from evangelical denominations have confided in me that, when they first heard the story of the four chaplains, they were ready to quit the chaplaincy. They were at that point, not for fear that they may have to make a similar sacrifice, but rather for fear that they were in the wrong profession because they themselves did not think the religious telling of the story to be helpful.

Finally, this use of the story devalues the men themselves, who felt called of God to serve soldiers according to their own faith traditions. Father Washington, while able to work with those of other faiths, still believed in transubstantiation and that God's grace is given in the administration of the sacraments. Similarly, Chaplain Poling was still a man of evangelical faith; he believed in the exclusivity of the gospel and the necessity of faith in Christ for salvation. The point, then, is this: while the men were friends and worked together to help raise troop morale, they still held to their distinctive beliefs, and to tell their story in order to remove those distinctions (except to show that they were different without strife), or to diminish their value is to detract from the meaning of their sacrifices insofar as they ultimately died for their faith(s). They were there because they believed God called them to minister according to their respective faiths.

This attempt to diminish or ignore religious differences in religions is, at its most basic level, a manifestation of theological liberalism. It

36. Ibid.

envisages a commonality among religions where emphasis is placed on feeling instead of knowledge or belief. It is motivated by an affirmation of a common experience of the Other (most often described as God) as the key to religious truth.

GOVERNMENT RELIGION

Thus far, we have seen that evangelicals have had something of a self-identity as a persecuted people since their beginnings, and concluded that this may have contributed to both Klingenschmitt's and the wider evangelical community's readiness to believe in systematic persecution of evangelicals. In addition, the charge that the ideal chaplain is one who is liberal in leanings can be sustained from an examination of the way the four chaplains story has been passed on. But what of Klingenschmitt's claim that there really is a government-sponsored religion that is imposed upon military chaplains? Can such a charge really stand up to scrutiny? It may at some level, even if not as obvious as he states. Many candidates for the government sponsored religion have been proposed in addition to Klingenschmitt's claim of Unitarian Universalism. For example, Noonan argues that the United States government, through its Establishment Clause jurisprudence, has in effect made military service, paying taxes, and the judiciary sacred.[37] While other, more viable candidates exist, per-

37. See John T. Noonan, *The Lustre of Our Country: The American Experience of Religious Freedom* (Berkeley: University of California Press, 1998), 216–31. Drawing upon sociologist of religion Emile Durkheim's claim that some shared sacred beliefs and/or practices are necessary for any social body, Noonan argues that there are aspects of American government that function as a state religion. Specifically, he points to taxation, military manpower, and the judiciary. In order to make his case, he offers examples in which the interests of each were elevated above some of the most cherished rights/freedoms of our country. For example, the obligation to pay taxes trumps freedom of religion and the tax exempt status of religious organizations is granted as a sort of gracious act of the government. By way of example, Noonan points to the Amish and Bob Jones University cases. In 1980, the Old Order Amish challenged Social Security and lost. While the government can extend grace to some lesser religious groups and allow them to opt out of taxes, it is not seen as a religious right. Bob Jones University was denied tax exempt status because of some of its racist policies regarding interracial dating. According to Noonan, in the Bob Jones case, community consensus was elevated to religious status and allowed to outweigh the religious views of school administrators (which supposedly formed the basis of the policies). In each of these cases and other like them, the government makes a judgment on religious organizations and beliefs.

Similar judgments are involved in certain cases regarding exemption from military service. Some groups have been granted exemptions, while others have not (e.g.,

haps the most serious and plausible candidate for the title, "Government-sponsored Religion" is *ceremonial deism*, since it actually serves as the legal basis for the constitutionality of instances where religion and government mix.

In the previous chapter, the concept of *ceremonial deism* was introduced and cited as the legal basis for the Constitutionality of many instances of religion in the public square. It was noted that many legal scholars have challenged ceremonial deism because of its religious overtones. If it is religious but stands approved by the U.S. government, then it may very well fit the bill as government-sponsored religion. Therefore, a theological analysis of ceremonial deism is in order.

Ceremonial Deism and Civil Religion

The relationship between ceremonial deism and civil religion is unclear. Robert Bellah is often credited with articulating the concept of an American Civil Religion and developing its themes. In his landmark article, he suggested that there is a religious dimension to American civil/political life that is separate from the Judeo-Christian ideals of the coun-

---

Jehovah's Witnesses were denied exemption), even if the request was on religious grounds. Some atheists have been granted exemptions from service, but in the process, Secularism was defined by the courts as a religion. Thus, government was making one of its roles that of defining religion. In fact, whenever an individual claims conscientious objector status, the representative of the government—the commander—must make judgments regarding the sincerity and legitimacy of claimed religious beliefs. According to Noonan, these considerations, along with the military's ability to override the First Amendment—Establishment in the case of the Chaplaincy, and Free Exercise in the case of its management of personnel (e.g., Goldman case)—lead to the conclusion that military service is itself sacred.

These issues also point to the sacred nature of the judiciary, as it is permitted to sit in judgment of religion. The courts have taken on three sacred functions: (1) recognize particular religions, levy taxes, and allow public worship (i.e., define/determine legitimate religion); (2) adjudicate disputes within religious organizations (e.g., settle a property dispute when a congregation splits); and (3) provide theological commentary on religious practices. The third claim rests on discussions surrounding ceremonial deism later in this chapter.

It should be clear that Noonan does not really demonstrate the sacredness of taxation, military service, or the judiciary as competitors or a competitor to legitimate religion or that they comprise something of an established religion in the United States. Rather, what he does show is that freedom of religion is not absolute, even in the U.S. As noted in the previous chapter, though, neither is Separation of Church and State. The two clauses of the First Amendment are ideals meant to prevent abuse from a variety of sectors. Held in tension, they are perhaps the best humanly possible.

try's founding.[38] The fact that Bellah refers to the ceremonial use of civil religion might lead some to conclude that the two are to be equated, that Bellah's *civil religion* just is Rostow's *ceremonial deism*, but that would be a mistake, at least if Bellah and Rostow are allowed to define their own ideas and concepts. In point of fact, Bellah actually raises the question of the function of religious references in the political arena and rejects the view that they have only ceremonial significance. Instead, he argues, American civil religion has theological and religious content, a claim explicitly denied by Rostow and other proponents of ceremonial deism.

Part of what distinguishes the two is their very ontology. According to Bellah, there is an objective existence to civil religion; it is not just an idea or an interpretive scheme. It is a sort of religious devotion to the ideals of liberty, freedom, equality, etc., and a belief that America is the country which (by divine appointment) embodies those ideals. Bellah writes,

> It is that abstract faith, those abstract propositions to which we are dedicated, that is the heart and soul of the civil religion; but we can, of course, never forget the historical circumstances in which those words [of Washington and Lincoln] originated—a revolutionary war and a war to decide whether this nation would be slave or free. While there are many other embellishments, symbols, traditions and interpretations that have become, more or less securely, part of the American civil religion, I think we already have before us the fundamental form of its faith.[39]

As Bellah conceives of it, then, American civil religion should not be confused with religion in general on the one hand, or with mere patriotic God-talk on the other.[40] While not Christian, it is both religious and specific. For example, it has typically included a belief in God who is active in history and has guided the founding of the United States as the New Israel. The United States became enshrined as a pseudo-religious ideal to which other nations and peoples could aspire. This aspect of American Civil Religion can be seen in Lincoln's Gettysburg Address, where he argued

38. Robert N. Bellah, "Civil Religion in America" *Daedalus*, 96:1 (Winter, 1967):1.

39. Robert N. Bellah, "Response to the Panel on Civil Religion" *Sociological Analysis* 37:2 (1976): 153.

40. Bellah identifies religion in general with a general civil religion which, he argues, was present in the minds of the founding fathers alongside the special civil religion here defined. See Robert N. Bellah, "Civil Religion and the American Future" *Religious Education* 71:3 (May-June 1976): 237.

that the Union must be preserved, not merely for the sake of the country, but for its idea for the rest of the world and ultimately, for humanity.[41]

Nevertheless, some have argued that ceremonial deism and civil religion are really just two sides of the same coin, viewed from different standpoints. Ceremonial deism is a legal term, while civil religion is a sociological analysis, but both represent a way of understanding the same phenomenon in this country, namely the role religious belief has played in the American political consciousness, and the religious nature of our shared values and our view of our nation's role in the world.

Problems with Ceremonial Deism

Problems with Ceremonial Deism and its first-cousin, Civil Religion, abound. Even Robert Bellah, the champion of American Civil Religion, questioned its usefulness as a category because of its vagueness. As Murray contends, "The language of civil religion can be used to inform, motivate, and inspire, but it can also be used to pander, manipulate, control, and deceive. It can represent the best of the national character, but it can also degenerate into egoism, chauvinism, and hubris."[42] Criticisms tend to fall into one of two categories and generally come from two competing worldviews: Secularists tend to argue that they are a violation of the Establishment Clause because they are too religious, and religious conservatives (among others) tend to argue that they are too ambiguous and detract from the content of the religious language and symbols they use.

Theologically speaking, what may be of greatest concern is not the thought that, in the government use of ceremonial deism, Deism—the seventeenth century English movement—has become the unofficial official religion of the United States, but rather that ceremonial deism is patently irreligious! That is, the way ceremonial deism is described makes a mockery of legitimate religious belief. Recall Justice Blackmun's dissenting opinion in *Lynch v. Donnelly*. There, he noted that if the ceremonial deism argument holds, the crèche seems to have devolved to the status of a secular symbol for a secular holiday. This, of course, is an offense to the

---

41. Bellah writes, "The phrases of Jefferson constantly echo in Lincoln's speeches. His task was, first of all, to save the Union—not for America alone but for the meaning of America to the whole world so unforgettably etched in the last phrase of the Gettysburg Address." Bellah, "Civil Religion in America," 9.

42. Bruce T. Murray, *Religious Liberty in America, The First Amendment in Historical and Contemporary Perspective* (Amherst: University of Massachusetts Press, 2008), 70.

meaning of the nativity scene. Similarly, Justice O'Connor's own words defending ceremonial deism betray its questionable (at best) theological assessment of prayers offered at government-sponsored events: they are neither invoking the aid or blessing of God nor instilling a sense of penitence, worship, or piety in the gathered crowd and are, in effect, not *real* prayers! While O'Connor seems to think that the reasonable (and informed) observer would view such invocations and benedictions as mere solemnizations of the occasions at which they are given, this is hard to believe. Nevertheless, ceremonial deism currently stands as the reasoning behind many religious functions in the public arena, including chaplain-led prayers at official military events.

Evangelical Responses

The implications of this fact for evangelical chaplains and more broadly, for Christianity in the public square are many. First, it means that the legal basis for public prayers is that they are viewed as having a secular purpose. It also means that some may claim that the prayers are meaningless as far as religious value goes, and that their real value lies in their ability to add solemnity to an event or to commemorate the religious heritage of our nation. This, it should be remembered, is a *legal*, not theological, analysis. We should take care to avoid confusion between the legal basis for certain actions and the theological content of those actions. That is, just because ceremonial deism serves as the basis for declaring something Constitutional, it does not follow that the action *really is* devoid of theological meaning.

Consider a contemporary example: "God bless you"—Here we have an example of God-talk that, to many in our society, is meaningless with respect to theological content. When most say it, even Christians, they do not mean to convey a special blessing upon the recipient. Nevertheless, it would be wrong to conclude, then, that the statement *must* be meaningless, for the sincere believer may, indeed, mean to convey something more than mere polite response to a sneeze, and in so doing, may indeed invoke the blessing of God upon the other. Similarly, a prayer offered for an outgoing commander at a change of command ceremony may be allowed legally because it adds solemnity to the occasion, but may also actually function to intercede for that individual such that, he is blessed by God in a way that he would not have been had the prayer not been offered.

Perhaps the greater part of wisdom here is silence. If the Courts wish to preserve a function like public prayer because it has historical roots, this is not to say that historical commemoration is all the prayer means for the one praying or for those in attendance.

Second, it may mean that chaplains and others asked to give prayers at government-sponsored events may be asked to give nonsectarian prayers. That is, it may be the case that we will be asked to offer prayers that do not end with "in Jesus' name." If that occurs, the evangelical (and other Christian) chaplain will be faced with three choices: refrain from offering prayers at secular events, fight for the right to pray faith-specific prayers, or offer prayers that do not end "in Jesus' name." A brief examination of the theological implications and practical considerations of each follows.

If the chaplain decides that he would rather avoid controversy altogether by simply not praying, he should realize that he may be missing out on valuable opportunities for ministry. First, as noted above, prayer actually accomplishes something; it is an activity that is revealed in Scripture as making a difference. For the chaplain to refrain from praying is to reduce his sphere of influence into the spiritual realm. Second, sometimes prayers at secular events give the chaplain exposure to all the employees of the organization (or soldiers/sailors/airmen in the unit), as well as visitors in attendance. To refuse to offer prayers at these events is to miss an opportunity for visibility. Last, it may be the case that the individual in charge of the event will ask someone else to offer a prayer, and if this occurs, members of the unit/organization may wonder why the chaplain refuses to lead in prayer. This could send the wrong impression about the chaplain's love and commitment to the persons in the unit.

If the chaplain chooses to fight for the right to pray "in Jesus' name" in the face of direct orders to refrain from doing so, he certainly has biblical warrant and something of a precedent. It is not a stretch to view the prohibition of teaching in Jesus' name placed upon the apostles by the Jewish leaders as analogous. The words of the Apostles Peter and John seem particularly applicable: "Whether it is right in the sight of God to give heed to you rather than to God, you be the judge; for we cannot stop speaking about what we have seen and heard" (Acts 4:18–20). Still, those who choose to fight ought to at least consider their reasons for fighting.

For some, the basic reason for fighting may be (surprisingly) sin. It may be that his own pride, or desire to be right, or need to be on top is driving him to resist. It may be that he is just contrary in personality. If any of these reasons serve as the basis for such resistance, then to fight is sin, for it is more a manifestation of pride than of righteous indignation.

Others may view the structure of prayers as a non-negotiable; they may believe that prayers must be offered with the formulaic expression, "in Jesus' name" in order to be legitimate Christian prayers. Some have even suggested that prayers to God do not count if they do not end in this way. It seems to me that this position is based on a rather wooden reading of Jesus' exhortation to ask in his name and it borders on sacramental theology. The phrase, "in Jesus' name" almost functions like an incantation, rather than an expression of a relationship. The phrase (i.e., "Whatever you ask in my name, will be given") occurs six times, all in the farewell discourse of John's Gospel. The first two times occur following Philip's request for Jesus to show the Father to the disciples (14:13–14), and are meant to convey unity within the Trinitarian relations. Jesus' response is to emphasize the unity of Father and Son. In fact, in verse 13, the prayer is directed at the Father, but in verse 14, it appears to be directed to Christ. Thus, their interchangeability is the focus here, just as Jesus had mentioned in answering Philip's request: "Anyone who has seen me has seen the Father" (John 14:9). Later in the same chapter, the promised coming of the Holy Spirit points to the unity of the Godhead. The *Paraclete* will come in Christ's name (14:26) and will teach the disciples all things and remind them of what Christ said.

The next reference to asking in Christ's name is found in John 15 when Jesus teaches about the love he has for the disciples and the love they should have for one another. They are to remain in Christ as a condition for answered prayer (15:7). In doing so, they will bear much fruit (15:8). The disciples are to love one another and to be obedient to Christ (15:12, 14). As a result of this combination of love, obedience and unity, the disciples will bear lasting fruit and it is at this point that the Father will give whatever is asked in Christ's name (15:16). Thus, in chapter 15, asking in Christ's name is inextricably linked to union with Christ and a consequent bearing of fruit. The prayers that are answered positively are those requests that flow out of such a close communion with Christ such that we could argue that asking in his name must be out of such a context with a view to bearing fruit (which seems to be obedience to his commands grounded in love).

The next three references are found in chapter 16. Jesus tells the disciples somewhat cryptically that they will soon not see him for a little while and will grieve and will then rejoice when they see him again. This is an obvious allusion to his crucifixion and subsequent resurrection and all that those events entail—vicarious, substitutionary sacrificial death, propitiation of the Father's wrath, the expiatory nature of his death, and the forgiveness that comes, the conquering of death through life, etc. It is at this point that Jesus makes the rather startling claim that in *that* day, the disciples will no longer ask him anything, but will ask the Father directly in his name and their requests will be granted (16:23–24). This appears to be a reference to the mediatorial work of Christ in that his death made the way to the Father clear (cf. Hebrews). This leads to the sixth reference to prayers in Jesus' name, in which Jesus clarifies that he will not ask the Father on behalf of the disciples, but rather their prayers in his name go directly to the Father because the Father loves Christ's disciples (16:26–27). Thus, all three references to payers in Jesus' name in John 16 are meant to convey the direct relationship with the Father believers can have as a result of the mediatorial work of Christ. Believers do not have to go the Son *instead* of the Father, but rather can go directly to the Father through the Son because of his sacrifice on their behalf.

This rather brief examination of the biblical references to prayers offered in Jesus' name reveals that the emphasis in those passages is on unity within the Godhead and unity among the disciples. To pray "in Jesus' name" is not so much to use that particular phrase, as it is to offer prayers that are heartfelt and sincere as born out in one's actions and life, to offer prayers that are a direct outflow of one's faith in Christ, and to offer prayers that are humble and do not seek to place God in a position of obligation. As Morris writes, "Whatever the disciples ask in his name Christ will do. This does not mean simply using the name as a formula. It means that prayer is to be in accordance with all that that name stands for. It is prayer proceeding from faith in Christ, prayer that gives expression to oneness with Christ, prayer that seeks to glorify Christ. And that purpose of it all is the glory of God, a glory that is 'in the Son.'"[43]

My point here, is not to argue against ending prayers with the phrase, "in Jesus' name," and it is certainly not to condemn my brothers (and sisters) in Christ who feel their faith is under attack. It is, however, to express concern at the way the discussion over this issue is playing out in the public eye. I fear that the emphasis the phrase "in Jesus' name" is getting from

43. Leon Morris, *The Gospel According to John*, rev. ed. *New International Commentary on the New Testament* (Grand Rapids: Eerdmans, 1995), 574.

some evangelical theologians may send mixed theological messages. The insistence by some evangelicals who have written on this topic to say "in Jesus' name" in prayers sounds virtually indistinguishable from modern-day modalism. It is my concern that laypersons privy to the debate may fail to distinguish the particular concerns of orthodox evangelicals who fear pressure from State or liberal leadership to compromise their faith, from the theological concerns of Oneness Pentecostals (e.g., T.D. Jakes) who deny the doctrine of the Trinity. The discussion over praying "in Jesus' name" has failed to address this important facet. However, there is clearly room for discussion here, as there is admittedly great importance place upon the name of Jesus throughout the New Testament, as upon the name of God throughout the Scriptures.[44]

Others will be inclined to fight because they believe ceremonial deism *really is* a competitor (and thus false) religion to Christianity. This position has merit, but it may lead to some unsavory conclusions. Those who fight for this reason ought to be cognizant of the implications of doing so, and be willing to pay the price.

Ceremonial Deism as Competitor to Christianity

As the concept of ceremonial deism takes root in the popular culture with its antipathy toward religion and its embracement of spirituality, there is cause for concern. Already ceremonial deist websites are being operated which claim the following monikers for ceremonial deism: "the only religion blessed by the Supreme Court" and "The official religion of the United States."[45] The seriousness with which the groups operate the sites seem to vary, but at their heart, they point to the undermining of sacred faith that takes place with the acceptance of ceremonial deism as a valid concept. Consider the following:

---

44. From Jesus' exhortation to welcome children in his name (Mt. 18:5; Mk. 9:37; Lk. 9:48), to gather in his name (Mt. 18:20), to his warnings that others will come in his name to deceive (Mt. 24:5; Mk. 9:39; 13:6; Lk. 21:8), to his command to make disciples in his name (Mt. 28), to Paul's proclamation that his name is above every name in Heaven, Earth and under the Earth such that every knee will bow at its hearing (Php.2:10f.). A significant amount of literature devoted to understanding the references to prayers in Jesus' name in John 14–16 exists. Virtually all evangelical scholars agree that Jesus was not offering his name as a sort of magical formula to be used for personal power or gain.

45. www.ceremonialdeists.com and www.ceremonialdeism.com, accessed March 4, 2009.

We suspect that most ceremonial deists are atheists but atheism is not required. There will probably be a lot of agnostics too, as well as people who just go along with the rituals of the religion of their childhood because they find it comforting. We accept anyone—including people of faith—who enjoys a bit of tradition as long as they don't take it too seriously. You can think of us as the Unitarians of atheism.[46]

The problem this raises for theists generally and evangelical Christians specifically is that it suggests that the constitutionally-allowable prayers and religious-sounding mottos encapsulated by ceremonial deism are really devoid of theological content. Thus, followers of ceremonial deism can proclaim as the center of their belief system, "We believe in God. Ritually, not literally," and claim that religious traditions (presumably in the United States, Judeo-Christian traditions) provide structure to life and society, even though they are based in belief systems characterized as "silly."[47] Similarly, others have identified the deity of ceremonial deism as "Providence" *in contradistinction to* the deity of Christianity, Judaism, Islam, or other so-called *great religions*.[48] Our concern is not so much that prayers at civic events, statements made at the beginning of the court, national and state mottos, etc., are void of theological content and are not directed at or heard by the One True God by virtue of the declaration made by proponents of ceremonial deism, but rather that our acceptance of ceremonial deism and its secular revisioning of religious statements and acts may communicate something about our faith that we do not wish to communicate; namely, that it is not important. That is, by accepting the legal reasoning of ceremonial deism, evangelicals may be hurting our witness to the culture by detracting from the seriousness of our faith. Ultimately, of course, we should be concerned with how ceremonial deism may detract from the glory of God.

If one does choose to fight against ceremonial deism, he ought to consider how that fight may result. It seems to me that two possibilities exist. First, it may move the Court to do away with public prayers

46. www.ceremonialdeists.com/content/view/13/34, accessed March 4, 2009.

47. Ibid.

48. www.ceremonialdeism.com, accessed March 4, 2009. The website claims, "Christianity? Bah! Judaism? Bah! And forget Islam and Hinduism and Buddhism and the cult of Cthulhu. Our deity is Providence. The Capital City of Rhode Island is even named for our national God."

and acknowledgements of religion altogether. That is, in challenging the constitutionality of forced pluralistic prayers (for example), evangelicals are in actuality undercutting the legal basis for those very same public prayers. Since, as we have seen, that basis is to be found in the view that the prayers have no theological content, when we argue that they do, in fact, have theological content, we undermine the legal basis. We are, in effect, asking the Court to recognize the religious nature of our prayers when the nonreligious nature of those prayers (in the eyes of the Court) is the only reason they are allowed in the first place.

Some evangelicals may contend that prayer should be removed from the public sphere if that prayer is mandated as nonsectarian. This may be a valid point and at least theologically, it has much to commend it. After all, the prophets seem to constantly chastise the leadership of ancient Israel and Judah (as well as the people) for compromising the faith. Nevertheless, it is important that we at least acknowledge that this approach would be a shift in evangelical thought and political activism, as it has been something of a standard in fundamentalist and evangelical preaching/teaching to blame many of the country's ills on the removal of prayer from public schools in 1962.[49] We should also note that many evangelicals have lobbied for generic *moments of silence* in public schools as a replacement for those former prayers, but this is hardly distinguishable from the generic prayers being seen as liberal compromise here.

Second, the choice to fight could result in an overturning of the constitutionality of ceremonial deism. This would allow for public prayers, not on the basis of ceremonial deism, but rather on the basis of pluralism. According to Delahunty, the only other Constitutional option is that of what he calls "Pluralist Polity."[50] By this, he means an approach which permits prayers of any kind, but also requires that, over time, the prayers reflect a sufficient variety of religious voices and perspectives to dispel any appearance that the legislature is favoring any particular form of religious belief. Put plainly, it may mean that Buddhist priests, Muslim imams, Jewish rabbis, Hindu priests, etc. must all be given an opportunity to lead in prayer in whatever setting is considered. This, though, also seems to be

49. See, for example, Gary Bergel "Banning Prayer in Public Schools Has Led to America's Demise" http://www.forerunner.com/forerunner/X0098_Ban_on_school_prayer.html, accessed March 25, 2009.

50. Robert J. Delahunty, "'Varied Carols': Legislative Prayer in a Pluralist Polity" *Creighton Law Review* 40:3 (April 2007): 517–68.

a failed suggestion for evangelicals, if reactions to Rajan Zed's prayer to the Hindu gods at the opening of the U.S. Senate is any indication.

Of course, there is one other alternative not yet mentioned: one could argue against separation of Church and State. One could make the case that, while American Civil Religion was not to be seen as a competitor to Christianity, it has since so become and we have all, in one sense or another, bowed the knee to the god of religious liberty. On such an argument, one could suggest that faithfulness to the One True God requires that we abandon the American experiment and acknowledge the Lordship of God over our nation with an established religion.[51] However, it seems to me that we have good political, historical, and theological reasons for rejecting this move, and all involve a fear that the religion established by the government would not be friendly to our theological position(s).

So it seems that it may be best to not fight and be willing, if asked, to offer a nonsectarian prayer at government-sponsored events. I must confess that it is relatively easy for me to make this suggestion since I, even in the confines of my own home, offer prayers "in Your name" already. However, as already noted, there is good reason to think that the offering of prayers by a Christian chaplain at mandatory events can have a positive effect, even if the prayer does not end with the formulaic expression, "in Jesus' name." Still, there may be concern over *compromising* in this way. In fact, some may have concern that we are betraying the heritage of religious purity handed us by the early Christians. Some may fear that we are denigrating the sacrifice of the brave men and women of old, who died as martyrs because they refused to burn incense to the genius of the emperor. Some may see in my suggesting to capitulate on events prayers as analogous to burning incense to the genius of the emperor. But there are some important differences. The early Christians refused to burn incense to the genius of the emperor because they recognized the act as a commitment of religious devotion to a competitor to the One True God. If ceremonial deism required a rejection of the biblical revelation or a rejection of the Lord, or if it required religious devotion to the State, then it would be similar, but it does not. So capitulating here is not selling out

51. In fact, many evangelical seem to think that not only *should* Christianity be the established religion, but that it *was* the established religion, and so attempt to use historical citation to argue for a return to that establishment. It would be more correct to argue that each state had its own ideas regarding state-sponsored religion.

to a false god. It is allowing the legal recourses in place to justify some religious activity in the public arena.

Ultimately, the answer to the question of praying in Jesus' name and to the broader question of whether Christians should accept the *ceremonial deism* interpretation of Establishment Clause jurisprudence is a matter between the chaplain and God. In my mind, there is some cost to pay in accepting it, but the risk associated with fighting it may be too great. I would rather have the opportunity to be visible, to conduct a public ministry, and most importantly, to pray in order to make a difference, than to fight an almost guaranteed losing battle.

CONCLUSION

One of the most difficult issues evangelicals face in chaplaincy ministry—military or otherwise—is how to minister effectively in a pluralistic environment. In chapter one, we introduced some of the concerns/issues that are unique to chaplaincy, the primary concern relating to pressure to please one's commander/boss. In this chapter, we have discussed how certain theological commitments that are contrary to historic evangelicalism seem to fit well with the military environment and other forms of institutional chaplaincy. In our examination of the remarkable story of the four chaplains, we saw that it is sometimes used to promote a theology which diminishes denominational or faith-group distinctives, the suggestion being that chaplains can minister to persons of all faith groups as long as they keep their references general enough. While it is true that evangelical chaplains agree that they should seek to minister to all soldiers, no matter what their faith, they disagree that the way to do so is to shy away from their own distinctive faith commitments or to suggest that other faiths are equally valid or true. Thus, there is a real practical issue of how one can minister to those of other faiths while remaining true to his own beliefs. This issue, of course, is not new to the chaplaincy, as evangelicals have struggled with it for many years.

While systematic persecution of evangelicals is not occurring within the military chaplaincy *en toto*, it is clear that there is a preference for more liberal theology among chaplains, largely due to the fact that those from more liberal traditions do not tend to have the same reservations about how they can/ought to work with others of faith groups different from their own. Yet evangelicals can maintain their theological commitments and be successful in chaplaincy ministry if they determine ahead of time how they will conduct ministry in a pluralistic environment. Such ministry requires sensitivity, but not compromise. Perhaps the most interesting aspect of these issues, though, is found in the fact that many evangelicals are, indeed, moving more toward a liberal theology as a matter of course for many of the same reasons Schleiermacher did—dynamic, emotionally charged worship. A change is taking place within evangelicalism; one that has ominous implications for the future of the movement. It is driven by an adoption of postmodern philosophy along with a concern for authentic spirituality. It is to these topics that we turn in the next chapter.

5

"Perform or Provide"

Pluralism, Postmodernism, Ethics, and Worship in the Military

INTRODUCTION

WHILE I WAS PREPARING for deployment to Kosovo at Fort Hood, the installation chaplain asked all of the chaplains to read a book entitled, *The Faith of the American Soldier*. The point of the book is to examine trends in religious attitudes, belief and practice among the soldiers of the American forces in today's climate. The author, Stephen Mansfield, argues that, contrary to appearances, the current generation of soldiers, those who come from the so-called, "Generation X," really do have faith and really do care about truth and the spiritual realm. He points out, though, that the religion of the soldiers is largely pragmatic and experience-based. It is also small-group focused; even sometimes individualistic, but rarely traditional. The other characteristic of the popular piety of the soldiers that emerges from the study is that it has an emphasis on ritual, but little emphasis on theology or truth in an absolute sense. Mansfield suggests that chaplains, who have traditionally served as the spiritual voice in the military, are not allowed to speak to the religious nature of our fight and that this inability has stifled their ability to be spiritual leaders. There are several troubling issues with Mansfield's work, some due to the nature of the observations being made and the implications those observations have upon the state of religion in our country, and others due to the erroneous assumptions/perceptions regarding the nature of chaplaincy in the United States military that it perpetuates.

First, there are problems with the individualistic, pragmatic religion described by Mansfield. In many cases, this sort of spirituality is shallow, self-centered, and unable to sustain an individual through crisis or life. For example, in his discussion of the importance of rituals to many soldiers, Mansfield cites the actions of Kathleen Burk, and physician's assistant at Camp Seitz who describes herself as agnostic, but sometimes prays the Hail Mary when a friend is wounded. He quotes her as saying, "You hang on to what you're taught. Sometimes the words come when you don't intend it. You'll use anything that works, even if you're embarrassed by it later."[1] While Burk's honesty is to be commended and her approach is probably reflective of a great number of soldiers (and civilians for that matter), there are still several causes for concern, the least of which is not the lack of faith it projects. A prayer that is voiced in a time of distress which is denied or rejected in a time of calm is far from the kind of saving faith that Jesus spoke of when he challenged the rich young ruler to sell all of his possessions and follow him. Such prayers are much closer to pagan ritual than to Christian faith; they are similar to the ancient work of magic, in which priests and priestesses sought to control the deity figure by means of idols. In addition to the lack of faith they evince, there are other problems. The most obvious problem with spirituality based on pragmatism has to be with its tentativeness; when something fails to work, it is then discarded. Mansfield gave several more examples of how soldiers were incorporating a variety of rituals, practices, and beliefs into their personal pieties. In many cases, a blend of evangelical free, Catholic, and even secular or pagan beliefs emerged. We may be tempted to chalk this picking and choosing of religious practice, ritual, or faith up to the infiltration of American consumerism into the Church, a sort of "have it your way" religion, but it may also be indicative of a larger cultural and philosophical shift in thinking among younger generations.

Second, there are problems with Mansfield's assessment of the predicament of military chaplains with respect to having a prophetic or moral voice. It is simply erroneous to claim that chaplains cannot speak to the propriety of the wars we wage. As Mansfield puts it in describing the inconsistencies of chaplains, "They wear the uniform but cannot carry a

---

1. Mansfield, *Faith of the American Soldier*, 63.

weapon. They receive a check from the state to do the work of the church in a society deathly afraid of the mixture of church and state. They can preach God's will for the individual soul but may not preach God's will for the war. They are ordained by a single religious denomination to preach its truth but as chaplains must tend every possible religious persuasion."[2] Mansfield even tells the story of a young soldier seeking assurance of the affirmation of God for his actions in combat and a chaplain who says he cannot give that assurance! In fact, the chaplain is reported as saying, "Our government is officially nonreligious, and so are our armed forces. We do not fight holy wars. We do not view our enemies in religious terms. I can tell you that you fight for a great nation, though, and that God is with you if you turn your heart to Him."[3] Understandably, the soldier, James Gault, is not comforted because, as Mansfield points out, he needs a moral compass with which to interpret his past actions and to guide his future decisions. The chaplain was little help in meeting that need. While it may be true that some chaplains do not think they can speak to the virtue of a given conflict, there is nothing in the Army regulations that prevents chaplains from doing so. There is no regulation that says we cannot say that our enemies are the enemies of God. In fact, the American armed forces have a long tradition of saying just that. In addition, lawmakers from the Founders have traditionally viewed the rise and development of this country in religious terms; as blessed, ordained, and guided by God. Chaplains should speak to the morality of any given conflict!

The turn toward individualistic piety devoid of chaplain leadership is due to a number of reasons, one being the lack of prophetic voice on the part of many chaplains. The basis of this lack is a matter of contention. It may be the case that some chaplains feel intimidated by command-ers or others in the chain of command who do not want them to make waves (as noted in chapter one), it may be the case that some are simply misinformed regarding their ability/right to address such issues, but it is also just as likely that there are too many chaplains who have bought into a postmodern worldview which precludes them from seeing the world in terms of good and evil, or which prevents them from having any certainty about any claims they wish to make, be they pragmatic, epistemological, theological, philosophical, metaphysical, or axiological (e.g., moral). This

2. Ibid., 80.
3. Ibid., 4–5.

is a real danger and could ultimately lead to the downfall of the chaplaincy, our military, and our country.

POSTMODERNISM

We hear it all the time—we live in a *postmodern age*. It is often simply taken as a given; mentioned as a matter of fact. I hear pastors refer to our postmodern culture, there is postmodern art, postmodern architecture, postmodern literature, postmodern haircuts . . . but it is not clear that most who use the term really know what postmodernism is. So to what does "postmodern" refer? In some ways, it is exceedingly difficult to say, since the word virtually defies definition. After all, to define something is to claim some sort of knowledge of what it is, some level of certainty regarding your understanding of it; and such a claim is expressly at odds with the spirit of postmodernism and smacks of modernity; that which postmodernism rejects. Consider, for example, the words of Jacques Derrida, who applied the principles of postmodernism to words, meaning, and literature in what he referred to as *deconstruction*: "All sentences of the type, 'deconstruction is X' or 'deconstruction is not X,' a priori, miss the point, which is to say that they are at least false. As you know, one of the principle things at stake in what is called in my texts 'deconstruction', is precisely the delimiting of ontology and above all of the third-person present indicative: S is P."[4] The point, of course, is that Derrida hoped to demonstrate that words cannot fully encapsulate the totality of that to which they refer, that their ability to signify something tangible is limited, that they do not have meaning in themselves, and ultimately, that they are given meaning by the reader/hearer. Thus, deconstruction cannot be defined.

Yet, in order to speak of something, some measure of agreement regarding what it is must be present. Derrida could not disagree too strongly, for after all, he himself attempted to communicate something of what deconstruction is by raising the issue and coining the term. He attempted to define deconstruction by writing about it, and he obviously does not leave the meaning of his words entirely in the hands of his readers, for he rejects the understanding of his writings which claims to understand what he means and to have the ability to explain it.[5]

4. Derrida, "Letter," 3.

5. This, of course, is somewhat contradictory and illustrates the self-defeating or self-refuting nature of relativism in general, of which deconstruction is arguably an

Postmodernism is best conceived in opposition to modernity. As the name indicates, it is perceived by its adherents as a rejection—a moving beyond—the philosophical positions and attitudes associated with modernity. Modernity is typically characterized as an era of confidence in the ability of humanity—the ability to move towards peace, racial and ethnic harmony, to eradicate most sicknesses, to come to a knowledge of the universe—in a word, to "progress." Perhaps the most common way of speaking of modernity has to do with its approach to epistemology and its confidence in man's ability to attain objectivity in the pursuit of knowledge. Rene Descartes' foundationalist approach to knowledge epitomizes the modernist ethos; it includes radical doubt of tradition and authority and elevation of individual autonomy, followed by a supposed indisputable acknowledgment of fact (foundation), and then a tightly constructed rational argument to other beliefs. The knowledge gained through this rationalistic approach is beyond dispute, for it either inheres in the individual naturally, or is entailed by truths known innately. While Descartes' rationalism is most often placed in opposition to the empiricism of John Locke, since one assumes innate knowledge and the other assumes that the mind is a blank slate (*tabula rasa*) at birth and that knowledge comes via the senses, both are typically viewed as expressions of the modernist notion that the individual, through his own powers (either reason or the senses), can attain objective knowledge; can come to know what is really there.

The optimistic view of humanity found in modernity has an impact in a variety of endeavors. In the hard sciences, it manifests itself in the still-ongoing project of developing a unified theory of everything, the goal being a theory which has predictive capability regarding the way all things function. In the conclusion to his text on astronomy and astrophysics, Stephen Hawking noted that the discovery of such a theory will enable man to know not just physical, but also metaphysical truth: "However, if we do discover a complete theory, it should in time be understandable in broad principle by everyone, not just a few scientists. Then we shall all, philosophers, scientists, and just ordinary people, be able to take part in the discussion of the question of why it is that we and the universe exist. If we find the answer to that, it would be the ultimate triumph of human reason—for then we would know the mind of God."[6] Hawking's lofty

---

instantiation.

6. Hawking, *Brief History of Time*, 175.

goal captures well modern man's confidence in his ability to gain knowledge and progress in it; Hawking essentially asserts that man can attain to omniscience! Much of the hard sciences are premised on the notion that there is objective truth, that impartial observations can be made and recorded, and that data, unlike statistics, cannot be manipulated. In the social sciences, the optimism is somewhat different, but still a confidence in humanity's ability to know. In historical studies, it manifests itself as belief that the past can be discovered; that our understanding of the past is dependent upon our uncovering of the facts of what happened and that, through a scientific-like process, those facts may be evaluated and reconstructed, giving knowledge of what actually happened and why. In the study of literature, it manifests itself as an assumption that words have meaning and that that meaning can be ascertained through a variety of interpretive methods. Perhaps the most common approach to a modernist hermeneutic has been that of Ed Hirsch, who argued that the meaning of a text is to be found in the author's intention; what the original writer meant to communicate with the words he chose is just what the document means.[7] Such an approach has characterized much biblical exegesis as well as critical examination of the text. The task of the interpreter, in this case, is to determine what the author meant through a variety of means including historical investigation, cultural awareness, linguistic analysis, etc. At its heart, this approach assumes that there is only one meaning of a text; that which the author meant to convey. The reader/hearer does not contribute to meaning, but rather discovers it.

By contrast, postmodernism is characterized by a skepticism regarding man's ability to come to such knowledge of the universe and meaning, at the very least. Individuals, it is argued, simply do not have the ability to view an object or an event from all possible vantage points in order to have comprehensive knowledge, and this is what is required in order to claim knowledge of the objective truth. Many postmoderns take the skepticism further, beyond epistemology and into metaphysics. Not only are we unable to attain knowledge because of a limited perspective, but there is no objective truth to be known. Put more properly, many postmodern thinkers have argued that truth itself is dependent on the individual and that there can be many truths regarding events, objects, or words. Many competing interpretations of an event may all be true. Many ideas regard-

7. Hirsch, *Validity in Interpretation*.

ing the use or value of an object may all be true. Many understandings of the meaning and implications of a speech or writing may be equally valid and true. While modernity still seems to hold sway in the natural sciences, there have been some inroads of postmodern ideas, largely due to acknowledgment of problems associated with overconfidence in the scientific arena. Genuine indeterminacy at the quantum level and below, effects of the uncertainty principle associated with laboratory experimentation, and relativity theory have all led to a questioning of the deterministic assumptions and objectivity which underlay traditional scientific processes. Still, without the assumption of a certain measure of constancy, scientific experimentation would cease. Predictability requires an assumption that the future will behave like the past, even if that assumption cannot be based on incontrovertible laws. And so, science moves forward on generally modernist premises. In the social sciences, though, postmodernism has flourished.

In history courses, it has manifested itself in a questioning of all historical narratives, as in the mantra, "the winners write the history," which is meant to suggest that the history we have inherited is flawed, skewed, and distorted to favor the position of those in power. In the study of literature and writings, it has manifested itself in a reader-centered approach to interpretation; words are viewed as means to an end for the reader, not as symbols meant to communicate objective truth. That is, the meaning of a given text is not found in the intent of the author who penned it or even in the words with which it is composed, but rather in the meaning it has for the individual reader. Underlying this approach is a philosophy of language which questions the possibility of communication ever taking place, since words have different meanings to individuals: "black" for me might not be the same as "black" for you and therefore, when I describe something as "black," you understand it through your interpretive lens, while I mean it in light of mine. As Wittgenstein put it, "If a lion could talk, we could not understand him."[8] This approach to meaning and interpretation has serious implications for biblical hermeneutics and preaching. The text comes to mean whatever the individual reader takes it to mean. The sermon means whatever the individual congregant takes it

---

8. Wittgenstein, *Philosophical Investigations*, 223. It must be admitted that Wittgenstein did not mean to suggest complete relativity in words, but only that the socially-constructed language games of lions would presumably be very different from those of humans and therefore, understanding would be limited, perhaps severely so.

to mean. This is not to say that it means whatever he/she *wants* it to mean, but rather that its meaning is found in how the hearer(s) take and apply it. Of course, this approach has already made its way into evangelical Bible studies; we often share what the biblical text means *to us*, and we are loathe to correct erroneous interpretations, for fear that we may hurt feelings or worse, undermine spiritual journeys. However, such an individualistic approach to Bible study can be dangerous to both individual spirituality and ironically, to the church. This approach encourages personal devotion almost to the exclusion of corporate worship; it suggests that the life of faith is primarily about one's personal walk with Christ separated out from the community context of Church life. This individual focus may actually feed the sinful nature, which is most often manifest in one's exaltation of himself as Lord. To be fair and somewhat paradoxically, while postmoderns place meaning in the hands of the interpreter, they rarely encourage such an individualized life or spirituality. In fact, they see such an approach to be reflective of a modernist ideology.

In order to more clearly visualize the difference between modernity and postmodernity, consider two television shows, one from the height of modernity, the other from the birth of postmodernity. One of my favorite television shows has been *Star Trek: The Next Generation.* Evangelical theologian Stanley Grenz, who was well known for his interest in the implications of postmodernism for evangelicalism, used this series in comparison with its forerunner, the original *Star Trek*, to highlight some of the differences between modernity and postmodernity. Comparing Mr. Spock, the Vulcan crewman who epitomized modernity's assertion that knowledge is located in rational thought, with Data, the android second officer on *Next Gernration's* Enterprise, Grenz writes, "In a sense, Data is a more fully realized version of the rational thinker than Spock, capable of superhuman intellectual feats. Nevertheless, despite his seemingly perfect intellect, he is not the transcendent human ideal that Spock embodies, because he is a machine. Unlike Spock, he desires not only to understand what it means to be human, but in fact to become human."[9] The fact that Data wishes to become human encapsulates the postmodern idea that perspective can be just as important to truth as the supposed *facts*. Data's ability to process facts and information does not complete him as an individual; something intangible is missing. The goal of life,

9. Grenz, *Primer*, 9.

what the Greeks referred to as the *telos*, is not necessarily just knowledge attainment, and it is in fact, different for each individual. Other comparisons between the two series are also illustrative. For example, in many cases, the moral of episodes of *The Next Generation* is that man's quest for knowledge is an ongoing one, in which the goal has less to do with the gathering and processing of data and information by exploring strange new worlds, as it seemed to be in the original series, and more to do with the experience of interacting with those other worlds and cultures. While original series episodes often included a sense of moral outrage at some of the policies and actions of the cultures encountered by the Enterprise crew, any outrage expressed by characters in *the Next Generation* is normally discredited as imperialistic or hubristic. The Prime Directive, a rule followed by *Next Generation* characters in which they are forbidden from interfering with the normal development of alien cultures, epitomizes the postmodern ethos that all perspectives are equally valid. While it is true that Jean-Luc Picard, the *Next Generation* captain, does, on occasion violate the Directive and justifies his actions, it is normally in order to save lives, but never to impose his own ideals/morality upon others. To do so, it is implied, would be the greatest of evils.

So the spirit of the current age is one of questioning and skepticism. There is a questioning of man's ability to arrive at truth, to have certainty regarding his beliefs, especially those in the metaphysical realm. This questioning and skepticism leads to doubts about religious claims— claims regarding revelation, claims regarding salvation, claims regarding morality, claims regarding eternal truth. Evangelical chaplains should be aware of the impact that this questioning has on Christian ministry, particularly as it impacts military ministry.

PLURALISM

One of the most controversial issues within military chaplaincy has been the proper approach to ministry in a pluralistic environment. The term, "pluralism" is thrown around the chaplaincy and its training programs, often with little care or clarity. This has made evangelical chaplains and chaplain candidates uneasy at times. For example, when I first attended initial chaplain training at Fort Monmouth, New Jersey, our class leader said that "we celebrate pluralism." Many of us were unsure of his meaning; did it mean that the chaplaincy leadership is happy that there are many religions represented in the U. S. military? Did it mean that he himself was happy that many religions were represented? Did it mean that he was happy that several Christian denominations were represented? These questions, of course, provoke further inquiries: In celebrating pluralism, is the chaplaincy communicating that all religions really are the same? What theological issues are at stake? For evangelicals, the very truth of the Gospel seems to be (at stake), and it is comments like these that lead to evangelical reluctance to enter chaplaincy ministry. The confusion stems from the various ways that the term, "pluralism" can be used. In the prevailing culture, it is typically used to refer to the fact of numerous cultural, religious, racial, and ethnic backgrounds represented in our society. In this usage, we may say that the military culture is pluralistic. We may also say that military chaplaincy is a pluralistic ministry, insofar as chaplains must minister (perform or provide) to persons from various backgrounds. In theological circles, though, it is most often associated with a particular approach to understanding the relationship between the various extant religions.

There are several approaches to understanding the relationships between different religions and their respective claims to salvation. They are most easily divided into four categories, with each involving a range of belief or diversity of expression: Universalism, Pluralism, Inclusivism, and Exclusivism. Each will be discussed, if only briefly, followed by an evaluation.

Universalism

Universalism is simply the claim that all persons are saved; that none will ultimately be condemned by God. The assumption is that all persons are made in the image of God and loved by Him, and that these two facts preclude the condemnation of anyone. Many universalists reject the reality of Hell and argue that it is an outdated tool which served a purpose in the past to try to gain obedience in cultures which were unstable and in their infancies. Its theological basis is typically found in a sociological approach to religion which sees all religions as having a common origin (e.g., in man's attempt to understand death). All religions are seen as true because they are expressions of an original primordial faith.

There are numerous problems with universalism. The argument that all religions have a common origin is both historically and sociologically naïve. More problematic than this, though, is the relativistic and self-contradictory nature of its claims. For universalism to be true, all religions must be true, but since most religions include some form of condemnation of other faiths, no religions can be true. Similarly, if universalism is true, all moral claims of religion must be true; yet, since there are competing moral claims, no moral claims can be true as well. In fact, the issue of morality is where much of the discussion takes place. Christians are accused of being judgmental, of attempting to force their morals on others, while universalists see themselves as being open, allowing persons to express themselves as they desire. Yet, the universalist critique of absolutist morality is itself absolutist. Similarly, for universalism to be true, all beliefs must be justified; all adherents of all faiths must be viewed as having warrant for their beliefs, but because there are competing beliefs, no beliefs may be justified. All of this is to say that universalism is, at its heart, self-contradictory. This can be seen most clearly in the universalist critique of exclusivism. Universalsists criticize exclusivists for being harsh, judgmental, unloving, closed-minded, and the like, but this just is an expression of exclusivism. That is, the universalist critique of exclusivism is itself exclusivistic. Universalists commit the very crime they accuse exclusivists of committing: thinking they are right and others are wrong.

Pluralism

The pluralist position on the relationship among religions is the belief that all religions basically point in the same direction; that each religion can lead to salvation or some end state which is, in essence, the same as the Christian idea of salvation (e.g., Nirvana in Buddhism). This view is to be distinguished from universalism in that it does not necessarily claim that all persons will be saved, though certainly some pluralists would be hard pressed to identify anyone worthy of damnation. Rather, it is the claim that all religions can lead to a form of salvation, or peace. One of the most well known defenders of this view is John Hick, professor of philosophy at Claremont School of Theology. He claims that while the conceptions of salvation among various religions are different, they describe the same process: "These are different experiences, formed by very different conceptualities and integral to very different religious totalities. But they are all forms of the same fundamental human transformation from self-centeredness to a recentering in the ultimately Real as variously thought and experienced within the different ways of being human that constitute the great religious cultures of the earth."[10]

The basis for Hick's claim is found in his observation of the world's religions and their adherents, and in his reflection upon the traditional Christian claim that salvation is only found in personal faith in Christ. According to Hick, the soteriological power of any given tradition can only be measured by the morality of the human actions produced by the tradition. He points out that all religions have produced good and evil in roughly the same amounts. He notes that if Christianity were *exclusively* true, we should expect Christians, on average, to be more virtuous than adherents of other religions. That is, we would expect Christians to be more loving, joyous, peaceful, patient, kind, good, faithful, gentle, and self-controlled (Gal 5:22). This, however, does not seem to be the case. Christians fare no better than Muslims, Buddhists, Hindus and Jews in these categories. It should be noted that Hick does not accuse Christians of being *less virtuous*, but rather makes the lesser claim that "it is not possible to establish the moral superiority of the adherents of any one of the great traditions over the rest."[11] Hick also complains that the traditional Christian view, which condemns all non-Christians as eternally damned, is inconsistent with the biblical portrait of God as all-loving Father.[12] This portrait, he believes, is based on a metaphysical truth, namely that God exists, is all-loving, and that love necessarily implies an allowance for error regarding His nature among persons to be saved.

Pluralism, as it is typically conceived, suffers from a number of deficiencies. Perhaps its greatest problem is a lack of consistency. One area in which it is inconsistent has to do with its basis as a system of thought. It is distinguished from universalism in its allowance, at least conceptually, that some persons may be condemned. The basis for this claim is difficult to locate, for in its assertion that persons may be saved via their own faith positions, pluralism rejects revelational claims, and in so doing, divorces itself from objective morals with which to judge the actions of persons. For example, when Hick rejects the exclusivistic claims of Christianity (e.g., Jesus' claim that persons cannot come to the Father apart from

10. Hick, "A Pluralist View," 44.

11. Ibid. It is interesting to note that while Hick uses this lack of disparity as evidence of his claim that all religions are manifestations of divine truth with one being no more true than another, Sam Harris uses it to condemn all religion. See Harris, *Letter*.

12. See Hick, *Death and Eternal Life*, ch. 13.

him; John 14:6), he undermines the authority for his belief that God is an all-loving Father. He also undermines the basis for his belief that, for example, rape or murder is objectively evil. He may claim that God has revealed this to be the case, not through an inerrant, inspired text (e.g., the Bible), but through the common acknowledgment of all persons and/or all religions. The difficulty here is that some religions allowed and even required some practices thought reprehensible in other religions contemporary with them. For example, the worship of Molech included child sacrifice while the Hebrew faith condemned such practice as abominable, worthy of capital punishment. The point here is clear: without revelation, there is no clear basis upon which eternal judgment may be allowed; and with revelation, some religions are excluded as salvific.

Inclusivism

The inclusivist position on the relationships among religions has been variously conceived. Clark Pinnock explains his own approach: "Inclusivism believes that, because God is present in the whole world (premise), God's grace is also at work in some way among all people, possibly even in the sphere of religious life (inference)."[13] Catholic theologians have contributed a significant amount of work in this area. For instance, Karl Rahner has spoken of non-Christian adherents of faith as "anonymous Christians," and Yves Congar has referred to *degrees* of membership in the Church.[14] Although Pinnock's approach is a little more open, inclusivism generally maintains that salvation comes only through Christ. That is, it avoids the pluralist notion that non-Christian religions are or can be salvific in themselves. Instead, worship in non-Christian religions is viewed as being directed toward Christ, even if the adherent does not know or intend it to be so directed. In explaining this feature, Pinnock points to C. S. Lewis' *Chronicles of Narnia*: "I was open to hear him say that he could detect God's presence among other faiths and that he believed people could be saved in other religions because God was at work among them. His view was wonderfully summed up for me in that incident in *The Last Battle*, the last volume of the Narnia cycle, where the pagan soldier Emeth learns to his surprise that Aslan regards his worship of Tash as directed

---

13. Pinnock, "An Inclusivist View," 98.

14. See Rahner, *Ecclesiology*, 282; and Congar, *Wide World My Parish*, 101–04.

to himself."[15] Thus, according to inclusivism, true faith can be found in a false religion—the sincere Muslim or the sincere Jew may be saved as a result of his faith being accepted by God as directed toward Christ, even if he expressly rejects worship of Christ.

It should be noted, though, that inclusivism is neither universalism nor pluralism. Truth is not equally present in all religions (pluralism), and some religions may even lead to condemnation (contra-universalism). The inclusivist maintains that Jesus is the criterion of truth; the *interpretive lens* through which religious claims and beliefs are evaluated. However, inclusivism does allow for salvation outside of expressed, personal faith in Jesus as Lord and Savior. The perceived strengths of this approach are in its acknowledgement of the sanctity and sincerity of non-Christians and their religions, its minimization of the idea that God plays favorites, its emphasis on God's grace (especially for those individuals who did not have a fair chance at accepting Christianity), and its commitment to the supremacy of the gospel and of Christ.

Inclusivism is perhaps the most popular position among conservative Christians, next to exclusivism. It is growing in popularity among some evangelical groups, but it is not without its problems. Apart from its unbiblical basis, it has at least five related problems. First, it does not seem to take faith seriously. If faith in the true religion is not necessary, then the whole concept of faith is weakened. After all, faith has to do with not mere belief (though that is certainly a component), but with wholesale devotion of oneself; trust. It includes intellectual, emotional, and spiritual abandonment to God. If the object of faith does not really matter, then the content of faith seems less important as well. Second, motivation for missions is lessened on an inclusivist reading of the gospel. It seems ludicrous to inform others of their error and risk condemning them to Hell if, in their ignorance, they will be saved. If, for example, Buddhists are saved through the activities of Buddhism because it is all they know, it makes no sense to tell them about Jesus and thereby condemn them. A good inclusivist may argue that truly faithful Buddhists, the kind that would be saved if they died in ignorance of Christ, just would accept Christ if given the opportunity, but history has not born that out. Thus, if ignorance really is bliss (and salvific), it seems that the most loving thing to do is preserve that ignorance. Third, inclusivism is patronizing. It does

15. Pinnock, 107.

not take the religious claims of the "untrue" (notice I did not say, "false") religions seriously. It does not allow them to stand on their own religious claims. Buddhists reject the notion that their devotion to Buddha is really devotion to Jesus, and that rejection should be taken seriously. Fourth, inclusivism offers no criterion by which to determine the true religion. No reason is ever given as to why one should not be a Muslim inclusivist or a Buddhist inclusivist as opposed to a Christian inclusivist. That is, on the same basis as Christian inclusivism, a Muslim could argue that devotion to Jesus or devotion to Buddha is accepted by Allah as directed at himself; no argument is given for the superiority of Christianity (or any other religion for that matter). Inclusivism is just asserted as a truth. Fifth, inclusivism is, at its heart, self-contradictory, for it claims that Christianity is the one true religion, but then undercuts the exclusivist claims of the faith (or at a minimum, does not take them seriously).

Exclusivism or Particularism

The exclusivist position is the claim that salvation can only be found in Christ. That is, it is the belief that only people who place their trust in Jesus as Lord and Savior will receive eternal life. This belief is based primarily upon Scripture passages that either imply or explicitly state that only Christians will be saved (e.g., John 14:6; Acts 4:12; Rom 1:16; 1 Cor 15:20–23, etc.), and on the Old Testament rejection of the religions of the Ancient Near East.

This position seems to be stronger than the other two because it takes the conflicting claims of various religions seriously, and it offers a more viable interpretation of those passages of Scripture which refer to religions other than that of the Hebrew people. The people who inhabited the land of Canaan worshiped god(s), but they were not spared. Worship of Dagon was not considered to be the same as worship of YHVH. Worship of Baal was not thought to be no different from worship of YHVH. Worship of Molech was certainly not equated with worship of YHVH. In a similar fashion and unlike the inclusivist position, the exclusivist position does not ascribe worship of Allah or Krishna as worship of Christ. Most Muslims would be horrified at the thought of such an understanding of their faith! Unlike the universalist or pluralist position, it allows the prohibitions against worship other than that prescribed by the sacred text to stand, along with their accompanying judgments. It holds in tension the biblical portraits of God as Loving Father and Terrible Judge. Thus, this position, though it is often accused of being imperialistic, judgmental, and condescending, actually preserves the integrity of all the religions under consideration, and is therefore, the most respectful of the non-Christian religions. I would prefer that someone disagree with me rather than mischaracterize or alter my position in an effort to force agreement.

TRUTH

The dangerous aspect of postmodern thought, that which many evangelicals have railed against, is its attack upon truth; its claim that truth not only comes in many forms or can be discovered/represented in a variety of ways—these claims may or may not be sustained, depending upon what one means by them—but also that truth *cannot* be known because it is not something that inheres in objects or propositions and because all perspectives are tainted. Instead, terms are given meaning by those who use them. As noted, while most postmoderns are satisfied with making an epistemological point—that one cannot be certain he has arrived at truth or knowledge, many have moved to the metaphysical claim that there are many truths or that there is no objective truth. This claim, if taken seriously, undermines many of the traditional beliefs of Christianity, from assertions regarding the exclusivity of salvation in Christ, to the advocacy of moral absolutes, to the belief in the unique status of Yahweh as God.

POSTMODERNISM IN EVANGELICALISM.

Some of the ideas of postmodernism have made their way into the evangelical church in what has come to be known as the emergent (or emerging) church movement. Proponents of this movement, like most postmoderns, defy characterization, and even refuse to be called a "movement," preferring the process and personal terminology of "conversation." Whether viewed as a movement or conversation, what is clear is that it is an intentional attempt to rethink Christianity for a postmodern age. As with postmodernism generally, the movement is often identified more with what it is against that what it is for, or as Gibbs and Bolger note, its leaders sometimes focus more on what they are emerging from than looking forward to what they are emerging into, largely because of the dismantling of the old forms as preliminary to building something new.[16] Gibbs and Bolger admit that this dismantling work often comes across as excessive negativity or antipathy toward the church, but argue that it is more properly seen as part of an important process which seeks to remove unnecessary components that are more reflective of culture than of the Church: "Many of us do not know what a postmodern or post-Christendom expression of faith looks like. Perhaps nobody does. But we need to give these leaders space to have this conversation, for this dismantling needs to occur if we are to see the gospel translated for and embodied in twenty-first-century Western culture."[17]

This rethinking does not necessarily mean innovation, though it certainly may. Consider the subtitle of Brian McLaren's book, *A Generous Orthodoxy: Why I am a Missional, Evangelical, Post/Protestant, Liberal/ Conservative, Mystical/Poetic, Biblical, Charismatic/Contemplative, Fundamentalist/Calvinist, Anabaptist/Anglican, Methodist, Catholic, Green, Incarnational, Depressed-yet-Hopeful, Emergent, Unfinished CHRISTIAN.*[18] It captures McLaren's own approach to Christian spirituality and theology which resonates with so many in the so-called "postmodern" generation because of its anti-foundationalist approach. He pulls ideas, beliefs, and practices from a variety of sources he finds helpful in his own understanding of theology, spirituality and worship, without a particularly high level of concern for consistency.

For most *emerging Christians*, there is no requirement for internal consistency in theology, though they may, themselves, have a consistent theology. Such a requirement is viewed as a relic of modernist thinking, and serves as evidence of how modernity has shaped the way most Christians think about their faith. As Kimball puts it, "The Enlightenment assumed that human thinking can solve everything. So when modernism then assumed we could figure out God and systematize our faith, we went astray."[19] Bell compares his own approach in theology to jumping on a trampoline (something fun) and juxtaposes it to the approach of moderns, which he compares to building a brick wall (something arduous). The imagery of the brick wall is meant to depict the modernist foundationalist approach in which all beliefs are intertwined, with core beliefs

---

16. Gibbs and Bolger, *Emerging Churches*, 28.

17. Ibid., 29.

18. McLaren, *A Generous Orthodoxy*.

19. Kimball, *Emerging Church*, 49.

as a base and others built upon them. Bell criticizes those who follow the brick wall approach, suggesting that God is bigger than any brick wall and "God is bigger than any religion" or worldview.[20] He claims that the demise of one doctrine should not require the demise of others; that each doctrinal belief can stand on its own and can be evaluated and either retained or discarded, devoid of implications for other doctrines. By way of example, he points to the virgin birth. Even though he believes in it, he offers several (questionable) reasons for not accepting it as true, and suggests that it is not essential for being Christian.[21] Even though he, himself, affirms the traditional orthodox doctrines of the faith, he does not appear particularly troubled if others do not.

This lack of concern and the theology it represents is itself troubling. It evinces an anti-systematic approach to theology, and while one may agree with Bell's specific point about the virgin birth (I am not favorably disposed toward it), the implications of his point as a general rule are harmful to faith. After all, if the discarding one belief cannot cause the whole faith system to be in error, then there appear to be no essential or core doctrines which one must affirm in order to be Christian; in order to be saved. Surely this is not the case. Surely Bell does not mean to suggest that belief in the incarnation, for example, is incidental to one's Christianity. Surely he does not mean to imply that one can deny the doctrine of the Trinity and still be saved. Perhaps he does, and this is the problem with such an anti-systematic approach to theology. Some doctrines simply are essential to the faith, if the faith is to be in any meaningful way distinct (e.g., God's existence, Christ's divine essence; God has revealed; salvation by grace through faith, etc.). Some doctrinal beliefs really are mutually constitutive; are inextricably tied together such that, to discard one is to discard both/all (e.g., incarnation and Trinity; divine omnibenevolence and salvation; etc.). Part of the problem here has to do with the conceptions of truth and knowledge adopted on the part of postmodern evangelicals.

Postmodern evangelicals often view truth grounded in rational reflection or abstract thought as cold, and instead embrace a more nuanced view of truth as personal. Erwin McManus, pastor of Los Angeles'

20. Bell, *Velvet Elvis*, 027.
21. Ibid., 026.

postmodern church, *Mosaic*, emphasizes the importance of the personal nature of truth in the Bible:

> It is not enough for us to know or even believe all that is true. It is essential that we know the one who is true. In this sense, the nature of truth is critical. Contemporary philosophy would propose that all truth is subjective. This position embraces relativism and makes the individual the center of reality. Science and modern Christianity would advocate that truth is objective, standing outside of the individual and empirically or rationally provable. The Scriptures give us a different position. Truth is neither relative nor objective. The biblical view is that truth is personal, relational, and subjective.[22]

While the accuracy of McManus's claim that truth in the Bible is not objective could rightly be questioned, his desire to point persons to Christ should not. Webber echoes these same concerns. His Ancient/Future writings have become a favorite among evangelical postmoderns, though many have moved beyond his ideas. In reflecting on his own life, he complains that his move from the jungle, where his parents served as missionaries, to the city parallels a spiritual journey in which awe and wonder of God and His work was replaced by rational reflection: "Everything, even religious experience, I learned, was to be subjected to reason, logic, and observation. Claims to mystery, to wonder, and to the experience of things too deep to explain were looked upon as primitive, anti-intellectual, and weak-minded."[23] By way of example, he points to his Old Testament survey course in university. He was handed a comprehensive set of notes, filled with names, dates, and other facts and expected to regurgitate them on an exam, but he had neither learned the true message of the Old Testament, how God has worked in history, not how to "discern his contemporary presence and power in the world for me and for the peoples of the world."[24] The Bible had been reduced to a somewhat irrelevant *textbook of facts.*

He complains of the same type of experience in his further studies of theology and apologetics—study of the resurrection was reduced to proofs for its historicity rather than an exposition of its significance for the life of faith, a course in the Pentateuch was really an exercise in de-

22. McManus, "Global Intersection," 255–56.
23. Webber, *Canterbury Trail*, pg. #.
24. Ibid., 23.

fending Mosaic authorship rather than a presentation of God's covenantal loving plan for humanity, Systematic Theology seemed like a reduction of the mind of God to discrete propositions, devoid of life. Webber notes, "My experience was simply this: the more certain I became about my ability to defend God's existence and explain his character, the less real he seemed to me. . . . I was drying up spiritually."[25] [Unfortunately, this is the experience of many students attending conservative Christian seminaries, bible colleges and the like.] He eventually converted to the Church of England.

In relating his own journey from the evangelical *status quo* to Episcopalianism, Webber notes, "Why would I, the son of a Baptist minister, become an Episcopalian? Why would I, a graduate of Bob Jones University walk the Canterbury Trail? Why would I, an ordained minister of the Reformed Presbyterian denomination, forsake my orders? Why would I, a professor at a main-line evangelical college [Wheaton], risk misunderstanding and put my career in possible jeopardy to follow my heart?"[26] He sees his own move to Episcopalianism as paradigmatic for the growing number of evangelical Christians drawn to the liturgy of mainline denominations (and presumably, Roman Catholicism and Orthodoxy) and offers his own story as illustrative. He begins by noting his own Christocentric understanding of the core of Christian faith—Jesus Christ is the substance which stands behind every Christian tradition.

Webber claims that he moved to Anglicanism because it more adequately fulfilled six aspects of Christian life for him. In summarizing these aspects, Webber emphasizes that this was a personal issue for him and notes that the decision was primarily motivated by his experience of worship:

> For me, Anglicanism preserves in its worship and sacraments the sense of mystery that rationalistic Christianity of either the liberal or evangelical sort seems to deny. I found myself longing for an experience of worship that went beyond either emotionalism or intellectualism. . . . I also felt a need for visible and tangible symbols that I could touch, feel, and experience with my senses. This need is met in the reality of Christ presented to me through the sacraments.[27]

25. Ibid., 25.
26. Ibid., 11.
27. Ibid., 15.

What is most striking in these comments is that Webber, a long-time theology professor at Wheaton College, a bulwark of evangelicalism, presents his own shift in denominational identification as growing out of his own felt needs. His move from classic Protestant evangelicalism to the sacramentalism of the Anglican Church was driven not by biblical exegesis, but by *feeling*; not by deep theological reflection on the faith, but by a comparison of how the worship experiences impacted his emotional response(s) to God. The correlations to a liberal theological method are obvious. This being said, it should be noted that most emergent church leaders identify more closely with neo-orthodox (e.g., Barth) than with liberal theology.[28] However, just as the students of neo-orthodox luminaries moved back toward feeling-based theology because encounters with the living Christ were too subjective to ground doctrinal formulation, so also second-generation emergent church leaders have moved toward theology based on personal subjectivity.

Emergent Christians are concerned with the personal nature of faith; they fear that evangelicalism has lost its way with an overemphasis on technical theological questions to the detriment of relationship (with Christ and one another). They are also concerned with authenticity in worship and life. They have become disillusioned with the façade that many put on when they walk through the church doors. If anyone is authentic in this world, it ought to be followers of Christ. Emergent Christians also desire to be relevant; to offer the message of hope in Christ in a way that is both biblically accurate and culturally responsible. Each of these concerns are worthy of attention, and while there are many issues within the emergent church movement which are helpful correctives to abuses or errors within evangelical traditionalism, there are some terribly disturbing trends as well. The two most troublesome are movements away from biblical inerrancy and Christian exclusivism. Evangelicals have long identified themselves with these two doctrinal positions, and the minimizing or questioning of them has led some to question the evangelical nature of the emergent church movement (or at least some within it).

28. Mohler has provided a helpful discussion of Barth's contribution to postmodern theological formulation. He argues that, while Barth did criticize liberal theology and its ties to modernity, he can neither be categorized as a pre-modern nor as a post-modern: "In the end, Barth may be best characterized as an *anti-modern modernist.* . . . He deserves full credit for his critique of the prevailing liberal theology. But he is not a postmodern model for evangelical theology. What the postmodernists find most attractive in Barth, the evangelicals may find most dangerous." Mohler, "The Evangelical Tradition," 76.

Doubtless those whose evangelical commitment is questioned do not care, for "evangelical" is just a label of men, but it must be remembered that labels, even those created by man, have meaning attached to them. The term, "Christian" is also a label.

Biblical Inerrancy

The skepticism regarding authority, knowledge, and tradition can be seen in the negative portrayal of formal theological training in the writings of many emergent church leaders. This same skepticism feeds into a questioning of the status of the Bible as itself the written Word of God; as divine revelation.[29] For example, the following quote from William Young's bestseller, *The Shack*, implies that, not only is special revelation still operative, but that the Bible is not, in itself, the revelation:

> In seminary he had been taught that God had completely stopped any overt communication with moderns, preferring to have them only listen to and follow sacred Scripture, properly interpreted, of course. God's voice had been reduced to paper, and even that paper had to be moderated and deciphered by the proper authorities and intellects. It seemed that direct communication with God was something exclusively for the ancients and uncivilized, while educated Westerners' access to God was mediated and controlled by the intelligentsia. Nobody wanted God in a box, just a book. Especially an expensive one bound in leather with gilt edges, or was that guilt edges?[30]

The sarcasm here cannot be denied. More importantly, though, neither can the allure nor the dangerous nature of the point. There is something enticing about the claim that God's voice cannot be "reduced to paper," for it keeps open the possibility that we can have a direct encounter with God, something like what Mack, the book's hero, experiences. There is something compelling about the suggestion that anyone, no matter how little formal training he may have, can know God and His will by personal encounter. What self-respecting evangelical would dare deny such a claim? In fact, it is a rather common affirmation in evangelical churches. The conservative Southern Baptist church with which I identified early in my Christian walk used a baptismal formula which appropriated this

29. For a more detailed discussion of this issue, see Beale, *Erosion of Inerrancy*.

30. Young, *Shack*, 65–66.

language: Candidates for baptism were not asked to demonstrate their knowledge of Christology or Soteriology, but were rather asked if they had had an experience with Jesus and if they would follow him for the rest of their lives. Upon confirmation of their experience, they were baptized. There is also something attractive about the skepticism of authority which runs through the quote. Its attractiveness (at least to Protestant Evangelicals) is probably due in part to its anti-hierarchical tone. After all, the concept of the priesthood of the believer (variously understood) is a hallmark of Reformation theology.

However, though much of what Young says here is indeed to be commended, there is still cause for serious misgivings. First, the claim that evangelical bibliology reduces God to a book is just silly. No evangelical makes such a claim. To suggest as much is misleading at best. Rather, evangelicals simply assert that the words of Scripture are direct revelation of God; that the words are themselves, revelatory and not merely a means to an experience of God. This, however, is not to say that they are exhaustive, or that everything that can be known about God is revealed in Scripture. In fact, the Apostle John seemingly addresses just such an understanding at the end of his Gospel, in which he makes it clear that his record of Jesus' teachings and actions are selective. Evangelicals do, however, claim that Scriptural revelation is sufficient for faith and practice. Neither the doctrine of the sufficiency of Scripture nor the concept of the cessation of direct revelation (to which some evangelicals subscribe) requires comprehensiveness of the revelation in Scripture.[31] Second, most evangelicals do not deny *direct communication* with God for modern believers. In point of fact, most evangelicals believe God speaks to them all the time, through His Word and the illuminating work of the Holy Spirit. Evangelicals typically affirm more than mere direct communication; they affirm direct *communion* with God through the indwelling of the Holy Spirit. The only thing some evangelicals deny is that new special revelation has been given post-canonization. Third, evangelicals have historically affirmed the perspicuity of Scripture; that it is clear, so clear that all persons can read and understand it for themselves.[32] Again, here the

31. In point of fact, the rationalistic theology against which so many emergent thinkers rail, requires a denial of comprehensiveness of revelation. Consider the following simple logic: If God is infinite, then He cannot be completely revealed in a finite book, for that would require infinity to be contained by finitude, which is clearly impossible.

32. Some may prefer to add the caveat, ". . . all persons who have the Holy Spirit."

reformed roots of evangelical movement speak loudly to the claim. The commitment to perspicuity can be seen in the long-standing heritage of the evangelical movement to translation of the Scriptures into the *lingua franka*, and to personal devotion and Bible study. Evangelicals have long encouraged average laypersons to read the Scriptures for themselves and to test the claims of the ordained clergy. It may be that Young has in mind some evangelical preaching which overemphasizes the importance of the original Hebrew and Greek, which can suggest that formal training is needed to understand the Bible, but this can hardly be viewed as some sort of concerted effort on the part of evangelical leadership to control biblical interpretation, on par with the Catholic Church's historical attempts to keep the Scriptures out of the hands of the untrained. Fourth, the suggestion that there can be direct communication of the sort Young seems to advocate, special revelation, may undermine biblical authority in the life of the believer. Some of the revelations that Young's hero, Mack, received certainly seem to question clear teachings of Scripture.

Many evangelical postmoderns think that the traditional evangelical doctrine of inerrancy improperly seeks to limit God, conceptualize God, or rationalize the faith. Some have expressed concern that evangelicals have replaced allegiance to Christ with allegiance to the doctrine; have supplanted biblical faith with an unbiblical word. As McLaren puts it,

> Interestingly, when Scripture talks about itself, it doesn't use the language we often use in our explanations of its value. For modern Western Christians, words like *authority, inerrancy, infallibility, revelation, objective, absolute,* and *literal* are crucial. Many churches or denominations won't allow people to become members unless they use these words in their description of Scripture. . . . Hardly anyone notices the irony of resorting to the authority of extrabiblical words and concepts to justify one's belief in the Bible's ultimate authority.[33]

Similarly, Raschke argues that the doctrine of inerrancy places too much emphasis upon what man can come to know from the Bible and thereby shifts focus to man's interpretation. He even compares the evangelical notion of inerrancy with ancient Gnosticism, claiming that among inerrantists, faith becomes equated with a mental-state and not a heart-state; an affirmation of discrete propositions of doctrine and not a rela-

---

33. McLaren, 182–83.

tionship. According to Raschke, evangelicals have often viewed the work of interpretation as somehow confirming inerrancy: "Inerrantists . . . have on the whole discounted the classical confidence that the truths of God's promise and redemption do not require certification by any means or tests other than *sola fide*. For Paul, Augustine, and Luther, what God said was true because God said it, and meant what he said."[34] This, of course, is exactly what evangelicals have argued about the nature of Scripture: because it is God's Word, it is true.

Raschke implies that proponents of inerrancy do not allow for disagreement in doctrine or biblical interpretation. For example, he states that inerrancy "denies all intellectual and semantic heterogeneity for the sake of universal rigor."[35] Two sentences later, he identifies this heterogeneity in the Reformers with Luther's and Zwingli's disagreement over the meaning of the Eucharist, thus suggesting that inerrantists cannot tolerate such disagreement. Nothing can be further from the truth, as the various denominational positions represented within the Evangelical Theological Society makes clear (there are, in fact, members of the Lutheran and Reformed movements represented). Raschke then moves to claim that inerrancy is actually a form of idolatry; bibliolatry "inasmuch as it cannot see beyond the logical lattice of the text to encounter the One who is ever calling us into his Kingdom and before his throne."[36] This is a tired accusation leveled at inerrantists which is devoid of substance. No inerrantist has ever suggested worshipping the Bible.[37] As already noted, inerrancy does nothing to diminish the personal nature of one's relationship with God. On the contrary, the spiritual progeny of inerrantists have long preserved the notion of quiet times and personal relationship with God against the attacks of historical criticism which call into question the truth of the stories upon which that relationship is built.

---

34. Raschke, *Next Reformation*, 129.

35. Ibid., 131.

36. Ibid., 135.

37. I can see how some may be suspicious of the Bible Pledge practices in some churches, but it should be noted that it is no more worship than the Pledge of Allegiance to the American Flag (and arguably more appropriate).

Exclusivism

A number of emergent church leaders are also moving away from claims regarding the necessity of faith in Christ for salvation. To be fair, most do not opt for universalism, pluralism, or inclusivism, but rather deny the certainty with which we proclaim personal faith in Christ as the only basis for salvation and condemnation. Nevertheless, as the movement continues to develop, changes are taking place, and newer leaders are pushing the movement further from its evangelical roots. There is a grow-ing tendency toward pluralism and inclusivism. For example, consider the following discussion between a man and Jesus from *The Shack*:

> Again Jesus stopped. 'Those who love me come from every system that exists. They were Buddhists or Mormons, Baptists or Muslims, Democrats, Republicans and many who don't vote or are not part of any Sunday morning or religious institutions. I have followers who were murderers and many who were self-righteous. Some are bankers and bookies, Americans and Iraqis, Jews and Palestinians. I have no desire to make them Christian, but I do want to join them in their transformation into sons and daughters of my Papa, into my brothers and sisters, into my Beloved.' 'Does that mean,' asked Mack, 'that all roads will lead to you?' 'Not at all,' smiled Jesus as he reached for the door handle to the shop. 'Most roads don't lead anywhere. What it does mean is that I will travel any road to find you.'[38]

Some evangelical leaders are concerned that this trend could lead toward full-blown universalism within the church. Perhaps a more care-ful interpretation will see it as tending toward pluralism or inclusivism. Nevertheless, both of these approaches, as noted earlier, have serious problems. The idea of Jesus *traveling any road* to find a sinner may sound like an allusion to a modern rendition of the parable of the lost sheep (Luke 15:4–7). Both include Jesus searching out his followers, finding those who are not already "in the fold." However, in Young's story, *roads* are clearly meant to refer to different religions, and so the suggestion is that Jesus will use any religion which works to bring persons to him; to personal faith in Christ. Jesus referred to roads as well, and he did affirm that most roads do not lead to salvation (though he did identify their destination—destruction, a clear reference to Hell), but he also noted that only a narrow road leads to life (Matt 7:12–14). This seems at odds with the words of Young's Jesus quoted above.

38. Young, 182.

Conclusion

Many emergent church leaders view the movement as continuing the great tradition of the Reformers. For example, in the forward to McLaren's, *Generous Orthodoxy*, Tickle compares the work of emergent leaders with that of Luther: "But I am sure of two things: The emerging church has the potential of being to North American Christianity what Reformation Protestantism was to European Christianity. And I am sure that the generous orthodoxy defined in the following pages is our 95 theses. Both are strong statements, strongly stated and, believe me, not lightly taken in so public a forum as this. All I can add to them in defense is the far simpler statement: here I stand."[39] Raschke argues that postmodernity has actually given evangelicals the opportunity to reclaim the reformation slogans, *sola fide* and *sola scriptura*, by turning away from rationalism and toward fideism. However, the significant differences (e.g., scope, goals, and foci) between the two movements raise serious doubts about such a connection. Carson quite nicely highlights those differences and calls the connection into question:

> What drove the Reformation was the conviction, among all its leaders, that the Roman Catholic Church had departed from Scripture and had introduced theology and practices that were inimical to genuine Christian faith. In other words, they wanted things to change, not because they perceived that new developments had taken place in the culture so that the church was called to adapt its approach to the new cultural profile, but because they perceived that new theology and practices had developed in the church that contravened Scripture, and therefore that things needed to be reformed by the Word of God. By contrast, although the emerging church movement challenges, on biblical grounds, some of the beliefs and practices of evangelicalism, by and large it insists it is preserving traditional confessionalism but changing the emphases because the culture has changed, and so inevitably those who are culturally sensitive see things in a fresh perspective. In other words, at the heart of the emerging reformation lies a perception of a major change in culture.[40]

That is, the Protestant Reformation was driven by a concern that the church had departed from Scripture, while the emergent reformation is

---

39. Tickle, "Forward," 12.
40. Carson, *Becoming Conversant*, 42.

driven by a concern that the church has not adapted to the culture. The question that evangelicals need to ask is, "Should the church adapt to the culture, or should it transform the culture?"[41]

POSTMODERN WORSHIP

Many have come to identify postmodernity and postmodern worship with worship that is not traditional; that is different from what the norm has been. In fact, one of the most disturbing trends among Gen-X and Gen-Y worshippers is the individualized worship and the lack of need for communal worship. Soldiers are increasingly relying on streaming sermons from home and downloads for their personal worship time, and are substituting it for corporate worship altogether. After all, if Christianity is really about the individual and Jesus, there seems to be no need for others! Many within the culture have turned away from the Church as an institution, and have instead sought personal encounter with God. This attitude is reflective of the postmodern culture, though it cannot be said to reflect the views of most involved in the emergent church movement, who tend to emphasize the importance of community. This internal inconsistency has been the cause of rancor among some emergent leaders. Raschke points out that postmodern ministry is deeper than a mere rejection of standard ministry forms. He writes, "Postmodern ministry is a meaningless construct if it signifies little more than featuring youthful worship leaders with earnings and nose piercings who wear baggy pants on stage and dim the lights in the fellowship hall in order to replicate a coffeehouse ambience. That is simply one more up-to-date, flamboyant example of the Christ of culture. Postmodern ministry is the mobilization of the ragamuffin spirit that demands certainty in neither its concepts, its commitments, nor the outcome of its conversations."[42] Similarly, Kimball expresses distress at the shallow understanding of emergent ministry. It seems that many pastors view it as just the latest church-growth fad; the next generation of seeker-sensitive services: ". . . I get e-mails all the time from pastors telling me they know they need to do something and are planning on starting a radically different 'postmodern service,' but all

---

41. I suspect that many emergent leaders would see this as a false dichotomy; that adapting to the culture in order to reach the culture is a precursor to transforming the culture. However, if historical study has taught us anything, it is that more often than not, when the Church adapts to the culture, it rarely has a transforming effect on the culture.

42. Raschke, 174.

they talk about is changing the style of what they're doing, which misses the point and meaning of postmodernism. . . . The discussion in Christian circles does need to go beyond just using the word postmodern. It needs to go beyond candles and cool worship music. It is not about surface things that we generally describe as postmodern."[43]

There are several points of import here. First, the rejection of traditional church and its forms among postmoderns has begun to manifest itself in a rejection of the accepted postmodern forms. That is, some within the postmodern generation, in turning to individualized worship, are following the emergent church's advice to reject authority by rejecting the emergent church's authoritative declaration that corporate worship is essential. Second, the fact that emergent leaders see corporate worship as essential for spiritual life should not be lost on evangelical chaplains. We need to emphasize the value of the corporate experience and the connectedness that only takes place in the embodied experience of worship together. Third, the effort to speak to the culture must not allow the culture to dictate or alter the message. Even Raschke recognizes this danger. Fourth, and most importantly, the preaching of God's Word should remain central in worship led by evangelical chaplains.

During my last deployment, some of the younger soldiers desired to start a coffee house styled worship service on Friday nights. The lights were turned down, tables were set up with candles in the middle, and soldiers were encouraged to wear their PT uniforms. One enthusiastic congregant even volunteered to buy each attendee a macchiato from the base coffee shop. A rock band played several contemporary Christian songs, and we sang a variety of praise choruses. The chaplains took turns bringing the message. After a few weeks, the soldiers who requested the service sat down with the chaplains and informed us that our messages were too focused on the Bible, and asked if we could cut down on the doctrine and exegesis; if we could consider even doing without a message some weeks. I refused, as there was something wrong about consciously omitting the teaching of the Bible from a worship service. The hearts of the men were in the right place—getting more lost folks to come in and stay—but I determined that my job as a chaplain is to give the congregant what they need; not necessarily what they want. Our goal should be to

43. Kimball, 47.

help people come to a point where they want what they need, but that is not always possible; there just may be some people that we lose.

Evangelical chaplains should not just seek to utilize the tools that the younger generation of soldiers is using. While it may be tempting to upload sermons onto Facebook or create webpages for chapel in order to reach those who will not come to a worship experience, such a move may be counterproductive, both for the chaplain's effectiveness and for the individual soldier's spiritual development. Corporate worship centered on the ministry of the Word is necessary for spiritual vitality.

EVANGELISM

Evangelicals are becoming increasingly concerned that an essential aspect of their spirituality—the ability to evangelize—will be banned in institutional chaplaincy. It has long been frowned upon by non-evangelical chaplains and leaders. Consider the following quote from a textbook on chaplain ministry by Paget and McCormack, two moderate Southern Baptists: "Because Americans enjoy the right to the free exercise of religion, proselytizing—intentionally trying to convert someone to one's personal religious faith or belief system—is highly unethical."[44] This is unfortunate wording. Most evangelicals would find this statement to be, at least taken in isolation, *unethical*. After all, to purposely avoid the attempt to win converts to Christianity is to allow those persons to go to Hell, and that is tragic! To be fair, Paget and McCormack do suggest that chaplains could share their faith in a way that is, in their words, "respectful." Nevertheless, even as they refuse universalism, they note that chaplains "help people find meaning and purpose in their existence," even if they view the sacred as "the transcendent, family, nature, or community."[45] The stance they take, then, is understandably confusing to ministerial students. It appears that their point has to do with the rights of those non-Christian patients who feel accosted by well-meaning, but perhaps overly enthusiastic Christian volunteers who wish to make converts of every person in the shortest amount of time possible. Certainly, there is some room for valid concern here.

It reminds me of a situation I found myself in not long ago at a hospital where I was attending a short course in medical ministry. Just prior

44. McCormack and Paget, *Work of the Chaplain*, 16.
45. Ibid., 17.

to sending us out on pastoral visits, the instructor endeavored to tell us students that our primary function here was not to share our faith with the patients and that our goal as chaplains should not be to win converts for our respective faiths. Being one of the senior persons in the class, I felt compelled to respond, since I took issue with those claims. It became clear to all that there was a measure of misunderstanding between us, for when I said it was my goal, the instructor (always a gracious man) simply smiled and moved on, noting that he knew I was only joking. When I corrected him, everything stopped and he asked me to clarify. It quickly became clear that we were talking past one another; referring to two aspects of chaplaincy ministry.

My concern had to do with the odious suggestion that a Christian can embark on meaningful ministry without seeking to lead people to either a deeper relationship with God through Christ, or an initial salvation decision/experience. For most evangelicals, this is the bottom line: the most important function of ministry is leading souls to peace with God through faith in the crucified and risen Christ. If this end goal is not kept in mind, the chaplain may find that he has contributed little to the kingdom of God. While I suspected that our instructor himself was an evangelical with similar concerns, I also felt that his choice of presentation, one which is rather common in chaplaincy training, was poor because it ran counter to evangelical (and biblical) commitments. His concern had to do with the lack of sensitivity, respect, tact, etc., with which some evangelicals broach the subject of salvation and forgiveness. Apparently there had been a relatively recent incident at the hospital, in which a ministry volunteer had blind-sided a chaplain during a pastoral visit and virtually accosted a patient with the gospel. The patient was both offended and outraged, and the work of the whole chaplaincy team was undermined as a result. While the zeal of the volunteer is to be commended, his confrontational approach is not, especially given the fact that he had received training regarding this very issue. Similarly, though, while concerns of the instructor were certainly valid, his method of communicating them were not, especially since there were younger, more impressionable students present and since his own beliefs did not concur with his statements.

Thus, this may seem like common sense, but it ought to be said: Christian chaplains have a responsibility before Christ to hone their interpersonal and communication skills so that they may communicate the gospel in such a way that their ministry will be received. This is not to say that everyone will accept Christ as a result, and some will surely find the content to be offensive, as the Apostle Paul makes clear (1 Cor 1:23; Gal 5:11). However, there is a difference between the content being offensive and the presentation being offensive. We should endeavor to keep the offense of the content (of the cross) while removing the offense of the presentation (at least when dealing with non-Christians).

So the question must be answered: Is it appropriate for evangelicals to proselytize in a pluralistic culture? The answer that used to be given was that one can evangelize those with no stated faith group, but cannot seek to convert those of another religion, or even denomination. However, in recent years the premise of that approach, namely that there can be such a thing as "no religious preference" has rightfully been called into question. Atheists have long complained of the lack of equity associated with this policy, since it allowed chaplains to try to convert them, but protected Jehovah's Witnesses, Jews, Muslims, Buddhists, etc., from being the targets of proselytizing efforts. It seems to me that those complaints are justified, at least from a legal standpoint, if nothing else, though a good philosophical case could also be made—if Freedom of Religion is an ideal or right, then atheists' right to not believe should be protected just as anyone else's right to believe as he wishes is protected.

Nevertheless, all of this is not to say that evangelicals in the military, even chaplains, cannot share their faith with others. The idea that Christian chaplains cannot share their faith is perhaps the most widespread misconception regarding the chaplaincy. This misconception has probably taken root for a variety of reasons: DoD policy against proselytizing, certain religious literature (e.g., Chick tracts) being banned from use on military installations, particularly restrictive readings of the DoD policy by mainline and liberal chaplaincy leaders, to name a few. While it is true that chaplains cannot go door-to-door on base, *Evangelism Explosion* outline in mind and *Four Spiritual Laws* tracts at the ready, they can still practice evangelism, if they are creative, considerate, and sensitive to the leading of the Holy Spirit throughout the work. Of course, these requirements are those which any evangelical leader would embrace, and this fact leads to the important point here—chaplaincy is really not particularly restrictive with respect to evangelism. The restrictions in place are not much different from those that most persons place upon themselves when sharing their faith in the first place.

Perhaps some examples of how I have shared my faith within the context of military chaplaincy ministry will make the point more clear. Each year prior to our Annual Training, I would prepare a small devotional guide with Scripture passages and devotional thoughts for each day of the two-week (normally) period. They were small enough to fit into a front pocket on the battle dress uniform, and designed to address typical issues that arise during AT: flaring tempers within squads or sections, weather problems in the field, irritation with eating Meals, Ready to Eat (MREs), etc. It was my philosophy that if the devotional was brief, relevant to the specific issues soldiers face, and small enough to carry without being a burden, soldiers would read them when bored (e.g., when on guard duty). At the end of the devotional, I would write a brief plan of salvation with an invitation to pray or talk to the chaplain. As I would make my rounds visiting with soldiers, I would take out a devotional guide, extend it toward the individuals, and ask them if they would like a copy of the devotional guide I wrote especially for our unit. On most occasions, soldiers would take the guides, place them in their pockets, and that would be the end of it at that time. However, throughout the course of the "summer camp," as it is sometimes called, individuals would come up to me and comment on particularly relevant ideas or devotions in the guide. Some even came to ask more about salvation.

My practice of making and handing out devotionals, though, has raised some concerns with supervisory chaplains, who felt it bordered on violating DoD policy on proselytizing. My response is simple: it does not because I take care to ensure that those to whom I offer the devotionals are Christian. I make a point of checking my unit's religious makeup in order to find out, as far as possible, the religious preferences of the soldiers within the battalion I serve. Most soldiers identify with some form of Christianity and so, even if they are not currently practicing, I am well within my rights to offer Christian devotions to them. If I find soldiers of a non-Christian religion or specifically atheist, then I simply do not offer them a devotional or provide a separate, tailor-made devotional to those persons. For example, I served a unit that had two Jewish soldiers in the headquarters, one who was messianic, and one who was not. I decided that I would make Jewish versions of my devotional for them, using passages from the Old Testament and replacing the invitation to salvation with the Shema. I gave the messianic soldier copies of both the Christian and Jewish devotionals, and the non-messianic soldier a copy of the Jewish devotional. The Jewish soldier was astounded that I had taken the time to prepare a devotional for him. He said, "You are the first chaplain to care about me." I told him that I did. Interestingly, he then asked for a copy of the Christian devotional as well, and I did not refuse him. It seems to me that my demonstration of love for him led to his request. He did not accept Christ as messiah and savior, but had many talks about the issue throughout my time with that unit. Evangelism, as will be shown in the next chapter, should not be construed as something we do, separate from our personal interactions with others. Rather, it is a natural outflow of our love for the Lord and our love for others. As we engage others in personal relationships, we naturally talk about the things that are important to us, and when non-Christians see the sincerity of our love for them, they respond positively.

The above example may raise some concerns about pluralism. Was I, in preparing a Jewish devotional, sending a mixed signal regarding the salvific nature of a non-Christian religion? Was I not suggesting that Truth can be found in both Christianity and Judaism? Was I not compromising my Christian witness and integrity by preparing such a document? These are valid questions that deserve some attention. The short answer is that I do not think I compromised my belief in the exclusivity of Christianity because I would only make such a devotional for Judaism; I could not do the same for a Muslim or Buddhist soldier because I do not accept their sacred writings as Holy. That is, I could make a devotional for Judaism because the Jewish Scriptures are Christian Scriptures. In fact, many of the days' devotions were identical in the two guides (Jewish and Christian) because the Christian guide included devotions from the Old Testament. If I had had a Muslim soldier (for example) in that unit, I would have sought him out and asked if there is any devotional material I can order for him. That would be my way of treating him equally without compromising my own faith.

I have also shared my faith with soldiers as I have visited with them. In counseling, it comes naturally, though I ensure the individual coming for counseling is receptive to my approach (see chapter seven). In the day-to-day visitation of the ministry of presence, it comes as a result of open conversation. Once soldiers know what a chaplain is and does, the subject of spirituality seems to naturally enter the conversations. For example, I was visiting with some soldiers out in the field, and one took me aside and asked what denomination I serve. Once I told him that I am Southern Baptist, he seemed somewhat disappointed. When I asked for an explanation, he proceeded to tell me that he was Wiccan and that I probably think he is going to Hell. Without denying it, I asked what it is they believe. He began to explain Wicca to me, as best he could, and a conversation ensued. When he explained the Wiccan concern for the environment, I explained the Christian concept of dominion and care for the Creation, but also explained the hostility between man and creation as a result of the Fall. As the conversation progressed and as we met over the next couple of weeks, I was able to share the gospel with him (and he was able to share his faith with me). The dialogue was real, not contrived, and respectful. He did not convert, but he told me that he appreciated my respect of him, but also my honesty in telling him of my opposition to his views. The point here is that evangelical chaplains need not shy away from sharing their faith or from taking a strong stand against false belief. They need only do so in a way that is respectful of others' rights to disagree and in a way that clearly communicates the love they have for others in Christ.

ETHICS IN THE MILITARY

One of the more disturbing ways that we can see the influence of post-modernism on the military is found in the instruction in ethics. Before deploying to Iraq, soldiers are required to sit through a briefing on ethics, which is no longer taught by the chaplain. Instead, it is now taught by the Judge Advocate General (JAG; lawyer). Tongue-in-cheek references to the woe passages aside, this shift signals an alarming change in the way military leadership, soldiers and perhaps even the wider culture view morality, It is no longer a matter of what is right and wrong or good and evil, but rather about what is legal. In a perfect world, of course, the legal system just would reflect morality; those actions deemed "bad" would be illegal, and those actions deemed "good" would be legal, and consequently, those individuals who perform bad actions would be penalized or punished in a perfect justice system, while those who do not perform bad actions would not. However, this is hardly the case, and is rather an ideal to which we strive. Nevertheless, the point is that, even in an ideal system, legality is a function of morality, and not the other way around. That is, the good is not defined by what is legal, but what is legal is defined by the good (or what is illegal is defined by the evil or what is not good).

Having the JAG teach ethics suggests that the military is not really concerned about whether actions are proper or right, but rather with which actions one can get away with while not incurring liability. This, in itself, should serve as a cause for concern, for, as many postmoderns are want to point out, "The winners write the history," and sometimes, "Might makes right." Both of these somewhat crass slogans point to an underlying and disconcerting truth regarding relativistic or perspectival ethics: morality becomes a function of power. If the postmodern view of ethics is correct, then if the Nazis had defeated the Allies, the extermination camps would have been morally justified! It is not a far leap from this to justification of the use of excess force or torture by American military when we are the most powerful.

Having lawyers teach ethics (rather than chaplains) also seems to be a subtle acceptance of the postmodern view that "good" and "bad" (and other measures of morality) are culturally defined and are not absolute. Since laws are culturally determined and are temporary, insofar as they may be altered, repealed, or reinterpreted, ethics based on legality are also culturally dependent and contingent. This approach to ethics is problematic for a number of reasons. First, it has the relationship between ethics and law backwards. Laws should be an expression of moral truths applied to life. This approach has a long history in Western culture and philosophy. For example, when Socrates was in his death row cell and his friend, Crito, came to try to talk him into escaping, he refused. In his refusal, Socrates claimed that, even though he had been wrongly condemned, to escape would be tantamount to a rejection of justice and an embrace of lawlessness. His unjust conviction was not an offense of the law, but rather of men, but his offense, were he to follow Crito's well-intentioned advice, would be against Law itself. It would be better to die and uphold justice than to escape and undermine it. After all, his whole life had been based on the pursuit of truth and justice. His refusal, though, was not born out of mere stubbornness, a sort of dogged determination to live a consistent life, even to the point of death. Rather, Socrates saw something more fundamental behind Law; namely, it is a reflection of the very nature of God. Socrates told Crito that he could hear Law speaking to him: "Listen, then, Socrates, to us who have brought you up. Think not of life and children first, and of justice afterwards, but of justice first, and of justice afterwards, but of justice first, that you may be justified before the princes of the world below."[46] After intimating that these words continue to ring in his ears, drowning out all other exhortations, he requested that his friend let him follow "the intimations of the will of God." The implications here are clear. The law is not a mere pragmatic construction of man, molded to suit the needs of the season, but is rather a reflection of the nature, mind, and will of God. It is good for Good's sake. Law is supposed to flow naturally out of the Good; it does not define the Good. Second, it leads to a relativistic approach to ethics and is based on questionable philosophical presuppositions. In order to see why, a more detailed examination of the argument must be undertaken.

CULTURAL RELATIVISM

One of the most often used arguments for a relativistic approach to ethics is some form of the diversity of cultures argument. Different people from different cultures have different values because they have encountered different situations, have had different needs that had to be met, were brought up with different values, and may be at a different stage in their development as a culture. These facts, along with the fact that our words and ideas have different meanings because meaning itself is developed over time through values, lead to the conclusions that members of one culture *ought not* [should not] criticize the beliefs and/or practices of another culture *and* that members of one culture *cannot* criticize the beliefs and/or practices of another culture because they may not even be *speaking the same language*; may not mean the same thing even if using the same words. It is not a far leap from belief that ethics are relative to cultures, to belief that ethics are relative to persons, i.e., relativist ethics.

So, put simply, cultural relativism is the belief that, given the fact that there are different moral beliefs and practices among different cultures, no objective moral truths exist. In a simple argument form,

(1) Different cultures have different standards of conduct and/or different beliefs about the morality of given actions.

(2) Beliefs about the morality of given actions and standards of conduct are culturally conditioned or created [from (1)].

(3) Therefore, there are no universal moral truths.

46. Plato, *Crito*, 484.

Christian ethicists and philosophers have rightly questioned this line of thinking at a variety of points. Of course, the simple argument presented above does not address all of the complexities and nuances of cultural relativism, and other forms of cultural approaches to moral relativism could be presented, but even a cursory reading of the argument reveals some problems with its flow. For example, and most obviously, the move from (2) to (3) is hardly compelling. Nevertheless, the argument could be developed more fully, and gaps such as those could be filled. What is most important are the basic claims of cultural relativism. Each will be briefly examined and evaluated, largely following the analysis of Arthur Holmes.

Diversity Thesis

The diversity of cultures argument is grounded in two basic theses: the *diversity thesis*, and the *dependency thesis*. The diversity thesis is best characterized as the claim that different people from different cultures have different values and standards of conduct. At its most basic, this is a factual anthropological statement. By this, I mean that the nature of the statement is *factual* as opposed to *evaluative*, not that it is necessarily true. Many anthropologists have observed differences in values and practices among different people groups. Yet, the accuracy of the diversity thesis has been called into question, at least insofar as it is used to make the claim that there is diversity of morality and value at such a fundamental level that *no* absolutes may be affirmed.

It is clear that there are *some* similarities between cultures; there are some human characteristics that seem to transcend culture and society. Anthropologist Clyde Kluckhohn has noted that almost every culture sees incest as morally unacceptable and that all cultures view murder within the group as an offense.[47] Arthur Holmes points out that, additionally, common human needs lead to at least *some* shared values: health, life, economic sufficiency [I would instead refer to material needs met], marriage and family. I would even add personal worth/honor and community as two other common human values. The point, of course, is that these basic similarities are not accidental, but instead point to universal characteristics of human cultures and societies.

---

47. Kluckhohn, "Ethical Relativity," 663–77.

As Holmes notes, differences in *actions* do not necessarily mean differences in *values*. In fact, similar values can serve as motivators for different actions in different contexts:

> The diversity thesis further fails to distinguish diversity in particular moral practices from diversity in the principles implicit in such concerns. Practices, like moral rules, are guided by more general concerns. Thus, how societies define property rights and how they punish wrongdoers can vary greatly, but they may still be equally concerned about both conserving property and punishing offenders, and equally concerned about an ordered society. Diversity seems to be more widespread in specific application than in principle.[48]

This can even be true *within* societies and cultures. Consider our own society. There are very different beliefs about how to properly administer justice—some people believe in appropriateness of the use of capital punishment, for example, while others disagree with its use. Yet both groups have argued for the value of *justice*. And both may even present their cases for/against capital punishment *on the basis* of a respect for human life! So the diversity of belief is not at a most basic level of values, but instead at the level of *application* or *protection* of the values to/from particular instances or situations. So, it is far from clear that the diversity thesis, one of the claims upon which the truth of cultural relativism hinges, is true in the first instance. It may *appear* to be true, but upon further investigation, it could very well be mistaken.

Dependency Thesis

The second thesis in which cultural relativism is grounded is the dependency thesis, the claim that moral beliefs and values are culturally derived/conditioned. Anthropologists have long claimed (or assumed) that valuations within societies are birthed within those societies; that mores are reflective of the wider cultural context within which they developed. Consider the following quotation from anthropologist William Sumner:

> It is of the first importance to notice that, from the first acts by which men try to satisfy needs, each act stands by itself, and looks no further than the immediate satisfaction. From recurrent needs arise habits for the individual and customs for the group, but these

---

48. Holmes, *Ethics*, 17.

results are consequences which were never conscious, and never
foreseen or intended. . . . a higher stage of mental development
must be reached, before they can be used as a basis from which
to deduce rules for meeting, in the future, problems whose pressure can be foreseen. The folkways, therefore, are not creations
of human purpose and wit. They are like products of natural
forces which men unconsciously set in operation. . . . which are
handed down by tradition and admit f one exception or variation,
yet change to meet new conditions, still within the same limited
methods, and without rational reflection or purpose.[49]

There are several items worth noting (or implications) of/in Sumner's
quote here. First, Sumner is here arguing that cultural norms are unconscious creations of man's need. A need arises, a man discovers a way to
meet that need and, as others of his societal group also meet the same
need by the same means, over time, the activity used to meet the need
becomes a social convention and eventually a moral norm (with an underlying sense of obligation or duty). Second, though, Sumner does allow
that, before a practice becomes a rule or social convention, the members
of the society must reach a more enlightened stage of cognitive development. This, of course, will be important for our evaluation of cultural
relativism as a thesis. Third, there is an underlying commitment to some
form of determinism in Sumner's claim. He describes the development of
the folkways as similar to *natural forces* which impose themselves upon
the people/culture who cannot have, or at least *do not* have any rational
response to them. Related to this is the fourth point, which is that Sumner
argues that beliefs are developed at a prereflective level. Beliefs are not
the product of reflection, thought, or rational argumentation, but instead
develop at an unconscious level. At a popular level, these ideas tend to
express themselves (or are expressed) as outrage at the suggestion that
the beliefs of some cultures or some persons within a culture, could be in
error, for, so the argument goes, they cannot help what they believe—it is
how they were brought up!

As before (with the diversity thesis), the dependency thesis has been
criticized at a variety of levels and for a variety of reasons. We will consider
three. First, the major thrust of the dependency thesis has been to argue
that all beliefs are so constructed; that they are culturally conditioned.
This, of course, means that even the dependency thesis itself is culturally

49. Sumner, *Folkways*, 23.

conditioned/created. There may be other cultures which have developed beliefs contrary to the dependency thesis, which believe that beliefs do not arise like natural forces as men meet needs but instead are developed through rational thought, and that belief would have to be seen as equally valid by the proponent of cultural relativism. If the response were to say that, because *that* belief was developed through culture and therefore, is not necessarily correct, then so the dependency thesis would also need to come under suspicion.

Second, if *all* beliefs are a *natural product* of culture and are not the result of rational reflection upon life and morality, then there would never arise persons who would radically question the social norms. The fact that there are individuals who question social conventions means that not all beliefs are wholly dependent upon culture. Holmes states the problem well:

> Independent critical reflection breaks the monopoly of cultural determinants. Yet if not all moral beliefs are culturally determined, but some are formed by critical and rational activity, then not all beliefs are as culturally relative as was claimed. If the dependency thesis is pared down to size, relativism does not follow; and if relativism does not follow, then we may ask the truth-question about moral beliefs after all.[50]

Third, we should at least question the assertion that every moral belief is what it is due to a deterministic force that causes men to believe what they do and there is nothing they could do [or believe] otherwise. In other words, for the dependency thesis to work, we must believe that no one is able to break free in any sense from cultural barriers and rationally reflect on the truth of his values/moral beliefs. He writes, "It is hard to believe that even primitive cultures never engage in reflective self-scrutiny, or that their reflection in no way affects behavior patterns. Certainly in developed cultures such reflection occurs in legislatures, educational institutions, churches and the media; and certainly such activities have affected patterns of moral behavior."[51]

---

50. Holmes, 19.

51. Ibid.

Conclusion

So, it seems that at the end of the day, both the diversity thesis and the dependency thesis are at least questionable. This, along with the detrimental effects of adopting a relativistic stance on ethics, should give evangelicals who are enamored with postmodern ideas pause. However, the problems with the diversity and dependency theses are only the beginning of an informed critique. Other problems with the basic claims of cultural relativism exist as well: 1) argument does not follow (differences do not necessitate relativism), 2) impractical to the point of absurdity, and 3) evinces an attitude of hubris (ethnocentrism/elitism).

First, the very structure of the argument for cultural relativism is weak. In the basic argument, as already noted, the move from (2) to (3) cannot be sustained. Put simply, even if the claim that there is a great deal of variance at the most fundamental level of values among peoples of different cultures were granted, it does not follow that there are no moral absolutes; that there is no fact of the matter regarding how one *ought* to act in any given situation. Even if it were granted that *all* beliefs are culturally conditioned, situated and created, it does not follow that there is no right or wrong. The origin of a belief does not, in most cases, say anything about its truthfulness or its ability to have truth value.[52] This, of course, is the primary problem with the argument for relativism from cultural differences.

Second, cultural relativism is impractical at the level of experience and therefore, cannot consistently be held. We live in a global age. Persons from diverse political, social and religious backgrounds can and must engage one another on a regular basis. There must be shared norms of behavior and practice in order to conduct business and communicate. Thus, while some level of diversity is acknowledged, there must also be a greater level of homogeneity in values. For example, there must be agreement on the value of honesty in dealings. Otherwise, international commerce and trade would come to a standstill.

There is also an impracticality with the suggestion that cultural differences in values mean that both views are equally valid. When cultures come into contact with one another, beliefs which are inconsistent

---

52. Of course, if a belief has its origin in God, it will be true; if a belief has its origin in Satan, it will have some form of insidious motive, though properly speaking, it still could be *true*.

necessarily clash, but if cultural relativism were true, then no people or government could have a basis upon which it could legitimately influence another people or government. For example, no moral objection could be offered for the Nazi holocaust or the attacks of 9/11. Indeed, no objection could be offered for any activity whatsoever, including some form of imperialism or tyranny. After all, a militaristic culture who attacks and subjugates other peoples would just be acting in accordance with its norms and culture. . . . Most proponents of cultural relativism would be hard pressed to admit that all actions of all governments and peoples throughout the history of time were morally justified in their actions, no matter what they were. So, I would maintain, that no one *really* believes in cultural relativism. Now, if no one really believes in cultural relativism (which is a descriptive term), by its own criteria for truth (that at least *some* people believe it), then it is false by its own admission.[53]

Third, one of the charges often leveled against opponents of cultural relativism is that they [we] are ethnocentrist; that we believe our own beliefs are true *just because* our own culture has so conditioned us; we believe it to be best, and we are somehow blind to that fact. In addition, the charge of elitism is often included here, the claim being that we [particularly in the West] are elitist, or in some sense hubristic. This criticism seems wrongheaded, at least with respect to Christians, for a variety of reasons, the most obvious being that few Christians defend the beliefs of American culture wholeheartedly. Rather, many evangelical Christians are the leaders in criticizing what has come to be American culture.

Nevertheless, this objection also turns in on the cultural relativist; Sumner's claims are, in a certain way, ethnocentric as well. He claims that members of any socially definable group must reach a more enlightened stage of cognitive development before norms can be established for actions in response to differing situations. The obvious implication of this claim is that there are some cultures that are less enlightened than others—the more rules, it would follow, the more enlightened. But even if this principle of a correlation between the number of rules and the level of enlightenment were not admitted [it can be questioned], the very idea of levels of enlightenment smacks of ethnocentrism. Presumably Sumner would see himself as more enlightened than others, surely more so than those who reject his thesis. So, the criticism of those who hold to moral absolutes fails

53. Notice here that I am suggesting that, underlying the claims of cultural relativism is the presupposition, "If something is believed by at least one culture, then it is true."

because the very basis for the dependency thesis is ethnocentristic at its very heart as well, not to mention that the proponents of cultural relativism are ethnocentristic in their advocacy of cultural relativism.

Thus, there are good reasons for rejecting the diversity of cultures argument and the resulting conclusion that ethics are relative. Nevertheless, the argument presented thus far has not undermined the general ideas behind postmodernism. Chaplains have long served as the sort of moral conscience of the command, yet, as noted in the introduction to this chapter, there is a trend among some chaplains who have become convinced of the claims of postmodernism to refrain from making moral judgments at all (in the example given, a refusal to proclaim the war just or unjust) due to their limited epistemological perspective. This sort of reluctance places military chaplains in a precarious position, for as they attempt to point persons to God, they simultaneously undermine their own certainty regarding religious claims. If we can't know whether a given action is right or wrong because truth and morality are perspectival, then it appears that we cannot know whether God exists, His Word is true, or the claims He makes upon us are binding. Chaplains would do well to heed to the words of Duke University ethicist/philosopher Alasdair MacIntyre: "Theologians [chaplains] still owe it to the rest of us to explain why we should not treat their discipline as we do astrology or phrenology."[54] One would think that the increased focus on practical application would at least yield moral teachings that address real human problems. Unfortunately, the mixture of praxis and relativity has instead produced confusion. In order to illustrate the problem, Mitchell describes an incident at a conference on genetic engineering in which physicians and scientists asked questions about the proper use of the technology. When a theologian addressed the audience, presumably in order to present a systematic and well-thought-out response, the result was anything but! Instead, he offered little in the way of moral certitude. Reflecting on his own frustration, Mitchell writes,

> It was upsetting, not because of expecting easy resolutions to exceedingly difficult problems. Human genetic engineering presents incredibly tough questions. It was upsetting to witness that theology once again had been seen to be at best irrelevant, at worst, harmful. Rather than answering questions or, at least, helping clinicians to focus on better questions, theological distillation

54. MacIntyre, "Theology, Ethics and the Ethics of Medicine and Health Care," 443.

produced moral ambiguity. Is that all there is? [New Paragraph in quote] How many times will clinicians and policy-makers dip for answers in the once-teaming waters of theological discourse, only to draw up the dust of the earth?[55]

CONCLUSION

Chaplaincy is in a crisis, and the loss of moral voice is deadly to the corps. An acceptance of postmodern ideology will inevitably and naturally lead to a loss of that voice. Evangelical chaplains have at their disposal several avenues of response. The first and most obvious is engagement with individuals. It is in the personal interaction of discipleship that chaplains can help soldiers/sailors/airmen see the bankrupt nature of postmodern ideology and its disastrous effects on American society.

55. Mitchell, "Is That All There Is?" 268.

6

"A New Kind of War"

*Evangelicals, the Global War on Terror,
and the Changing Face of Military Chaplaincy*

*There is no neutral ground—no neutral ground—in the fight between
civilization and terror, because there is no neutral ground between
good and evil, freedom and slavery, and life and death. . . .
The war on terror is not a figure of speech.
It is an inescapable calling of our generation.
The terrorists are offended not merely
by our policies—they are offended
by our existence as free nations.*

—PRESIDENT GEORGE W. BUSH,
MARCH 19, 2004.

INTRODUCTION

AS NOTED EARLIER, RECENT legal cases regarding evangelicals in the military chaplaincy have raised questions about the appropriateness of evangelical service in that role. The military fosters a culture of inclusivism and tolerance, and the issues that are being raised in court cases have long been discussed in the official military training for chaplaincy. Yet, the questioning of [the appropriateness of] evangelical involvement in military chaplaincy has recently been given new impetus due to the Global War on

Terror. While the traditional role of chaplains, and it is still the primary role, has been to provide religious support to the soldiers of an assigned unit, a new role or duty has evolved in the contemporary use of the military in Military Operations Other Than War (MOOTW); that is, in Peacekeeping and Peace Enforcement Operations and Nation Building. MOOTW have expanded the role of chaplains to include liaison duties with local religious leaders.[1] These duties specifically have raised some interesting questions regarding the role of evangelicals in military chaplaincy.

The army regulation which covers chaplaincy issues (AR 165-1, *Chaplain Activities in the United States Army*) is virtually silent on the question of the chaplain's role outside of religious coverage. However, the primary field manual for chaplain activities (FM 1-05, formerly FM 16-1, *Religious Support*) does attempt to address the chaplain's role in civil military operations. Specifically, it states that chaplains will support the commander through advisement by "relations with indigenous religious leaders when directed by the commander."[2] It further states that chaplains will not directly participate in negotiations or mediations "as sole participant," and will not participate in "human intelligence (HUMINT) collection and/or target acquisition."[3] The manual cites Title X of the U.S. Code as the legal justification for these prohibitions.

One other source of information for the chaplain's role in MOOTW is the field manual covering those issues (FM 3-07.31, *Peace Operations*), though it is vague to the point of irrelevance. It notes that chaplains "have a key and unique role in PO [Peace Operations]."[4] It further explains, "Most of these complex contingencies have significant religious issues. The chaplain can assist the commander by serving as a liaison, with CA [Civil Affairs] and intelligence representatives, to local religious leaders, NGOs [Non-Governmental Organizations], and international organizations."[5]

---

1. The importance of the chaplain's role in these operations was the focus of a recent issue of *The Army Chaplaincy*, the professional journal of the Army's unit ministry teams. See Adams, "Chaplains as Liaisons"; Griffin, "RLL and the Emerging Role"; and Houck, "U. S. Army Chaplaincy's involvement."

2. FM 1-05 (April 2003), *Religious Support*, Appendix A "Religious Support in Civil Military Operations," A-1:A-1.

3. Ibid.

4. FM 3-07.31, *Peace Operations*, II-9.b.

5. Ibid.

Numerous questions arise as the chaplain considers his role in MOOTW and how he can function within such an environment. Some of the questions are specific to evangelical chaplains, while some cut across religious and denominational lines. There appear to be four areas of concern for chaplains with respect to their role(s) in MOOTW. There are legal questions, philosophical questions, theologico-ethical questions, and evangelism questions. Each set of questions will be addressed, if only briefly, by means of logical argumentation and reflection on personal experience as a chaplain in the United States Army serving overseas in the Global War on Terror, primarily during the KFOR7 (Kosovo) mission.

LEGAL QUESTIONS

Two legal items/documents must be considered in determining the legality of liaison responsibilities for chaplains deployed for MOOTW: United States Code, Title 10, and the Geneva Conventions. Title 10 of the U.S. Code sets forth legal requirements and constraints for the structure, function, and use of the United States military. It is the governing law for U.S. military operations. However, it does not offer much in the way of specific guidance with respect to the limits and constraints placed upon chaplain activities. Essentially, it offers up a statutory base for the existence of army chaplaincy by establishing a Chief of Chaplains and a chaplaincy branch.[6]

Chaplains have a unique role and status under the Geneva conventions. While they are still considered soldiers of a member states military, they are accorded the status of noncombatant. This status allows chaplains certain privileges and protections. Among such privileges is protection from being considered a prisoner of war. In Conventions I and III, chaplains are singled out for protection. Those who are captured may not be considered prisoners of war and may be detained only if their services

---

6. 10 U.S.C.A. §3073 provides that there are chaplains in the Army and that they include: (1) the Chief of Chaplains; (2) commissioned officers of the Regular Army appointed as chaplains; and (3) other officers of the Army appointed as chaplains in the Army. 10 U.S.C.A. §3064 establishes chaplains as a "special branch" to which regular army officers may be appointed, but not assigned. See also §3036 on duties of the Chief of Chaplains, and §3547 on the chaplains requirement to perform some religious services. It is interesting to note that the statute names Sunday as the appropriate day of worship, which is, in itself, sectarian.

are needed by prisoners.[7] Detained chaplains are to be afforded the opportunity to minister to prisoners of war and are given additional rights for sending out correspondence to their clerical associations.

Convention 1 briefly states the kinds of activities chaplains may not engage in; specifically, it states that chaplains may not participate directly in hostilities. The question that must be asked is whether or not gathering intelligence is a violation of this provision. It seems that the writers of Army doctrine generally and of chaplaincy doctrine specifically, have viewed it as just such a violation, but it is not clear that such activity is, at its heart, a direct participation in hostilities, especially when hostilities have supposedly ceased within a military unit's area of operations. Peace Enforcement and Peacekeeping Operations are both based on an assumption that a peace of some sort exists; this is in contrast to, for example, Peace Making Operations or the prosecution of war by Combat Operations or Full Spectrum Operations. Thus, there are some underlying philosophical questions that need to be addressed if a chaplain is to know his proper role within a military engaged in MOOTW.

PHILOSOPHICAL QUESTIONS

There is, at the very beginning, a seemingly philosophical dilemma regarding how one can function as a liaison without gathering intelligence, for it seems that, as one serves as a liaison between a commander and members of the local populace, as he converses with his counterpart(s) in the local area, information will be exchanged. Invariably, some information of concern to U.S. interests or to the U.S. military operations will be given during the course of a conversation or a series of conversations with local personnel, religious or otherwise. What the chaplain is to do with such information and whether gaining such information is a violation of the stated prohibition is far from clear. What is needed is a definition of Intelligence Gathering so that chaplains can have a clear understanding of their duties and responsibilities and so they can accurately advise their commanders on their proper roles and uses in MOOTW.

Consider the following definition of Intelligence Gathering:

> (IG1): Intelligence gathering is the act of acquiring new information regarding a military unit's area of operations.

7. Convention I, Article 28, Convention III, Article 33.

If (IG1) is correct, then the prohibition against gathering intelligence seems to be an absolute prohibition on gaining any new information whatsoever, but this is impossible if the chaplain is to take on the new role as liaison to local religious leaders. For example, every time a soldier, whether a chaplain, infantryman or any other job-skill, goes "outside the wire" [leaves the confines of the military base], he is obligated, for purposes of force protection, to gather information about the surroundings. He is obliged to look for any signs that indicate the safety of the soldiers and others who live on the base may be in jeopardy. In fact, the Army field manual which covers issues related to intelligence confirms this claim.[8] To suggest that one should go outside the base to meet with persons in the local populace, but refrain from gathering information is to suggest that the individual ignore standard military procedure regarding force protection. It makes no sense, tactically speaking. In addition, it is not even reasonable. In order to abide by a prohibition against intelligence gathering as defined by (IG1), the chaplain would have to take drastic measures to prevent the acquisition of new information. He would have to ride to the meeting location blindfolded, he would need to prevent himself from seeing those to whom he speaks and to prevent himself from hearing those with whom he is to meet, but this is to incapacitate him in his ability to function as a liaison [and it sounds ridiculous at best]! So at its very heart, (IG1) is flawed because it would be impossible to avoid. This virtual impossibility seems to be tied to the *general* nature of the information and/or knowledge gained, so perhaps a greater level of specificity could alleviate this problem. Consider the following two definitions of Intelligence Gathering:

> (IG2): Intelligence gathering is the act of acquiring sensitive or classified information regarding a military unit's area of operations.

---

8. In the discussion of "Full Spectrum Operations," the field manual states, "Every soldier in the command is responsible for detecting and reporting enemy activities, dispositions, and capabilities. This task is critical because the environment we operate in is characterized by violence, uncertainty, complexity, and asymmetric methods by the threat. The increased situational awareness that soldiers develop through personal contact and observation is a critical element of that unit's ability to more fully understand the OE [Operational Environment]." FM 2-0, *Intelligence*, "Full Spectrum Operations," 3-3:3-2.

(IG3): Intelligence gathering is the act of acquiring information
that directly impacts the success or failure of a military unit's current or future operations.

Both (IG2) and (IG3) seem to have some merit; they delineate the
kind of information that chaplains should not be acquiring and so remove the initial implausibility of (IG1). The field manual for military intelligence does make a distinction between merely *gathering information*
and *collecting intelligence.*[9] However, (IG2) still seems to place a requirement upon the chaplain that he may well be unable to meet. Sometimes
the chaplain has no control over the information he is given during the
course of his meetings with local religious leaders. By way of example,
and without giving away too much information so as to compromise the
sensitivity of the information, I was involved in a meeting with an imam
who, just as we were departing, suggested that Salifist Muslims were operating in the American sector and causing trouble in the mosques. He
proceeded to tell me of an incident in which he was blindfolded, taken
outside the city, and beaten over the head because he had told the radicals
that they were not welcome in his mosque. He then moved to implicate
another imam in the area as having ties to radical groups from the Middle
East. Presumably the information I was given would meet the definition of
intelligence offered in (IG2) and so by receiving it, I would have violated
the prohibition against intelligence gathering [as defined by (IG2)], even
though I had little or no control over my acquisition of the information.

(IG3) has some of the same weaknesses as (IG1) and (IG2) in that
it, as well, does not seem to be avoidable, at least in certain situations. In
addition, it suffers from a further weakness in that it suggests that one
[specifically, the chaplain] can *know* what sorts of information will be
helpful in the success of a given unit's mission. That is, while educated
guesses can be made with regard to the usefulness of information to mission success, we cannot *know*, in the proper sense of the term, which information will serve as the deciding factor in mission success.[10] So (IG3)
fails as well.

9. Ibid. It specifically states that while all soldiers are required to gather information,
not all soldiers should seek to gather intelligence. However, it does nothing to clarify the
difference between the two actions.

10. It is the responsibility of the commander, in consultation with his higher headquarters and security section, to determine which information is needed for mission
planning and what information is most likely to contribute to mission success. But even

It should be noted that up to this point, the proposed definitions have been limited to activities without regard to intention or use. As has already been made clear, there is an unreasonable expectation in a prohibition against an activity that one only has limited control over. Thus, the prohibition against gathering intelligence must have in view a definition of intelligence gathering that includes a greater level of responsibility for the chaplain, which seems to be dependent upon either the *use* of the gathered information or the *intention* of the action being prohibited. Consider the following definition, which gets at use of the (even perhaps unintended) new information gained by the chaplain:

> (IG4): Intelligence gathering is the combination of the acts of acquiring sensitive or classified information regarding a military unit's area of operations, and of passing that information on to the unit's intelligence section and/or command.

(IG4) has the strength of placing the responsibility for intelligence gathering upon the chaplain; he has the ability to control whether or not he shares the information he gains with his unit's intelligence officer or commander. Under (IG4), if he refuses to share any sensitive or classified information, then he does not violate the requirement, even if he has gained the knowledge (which we have seen can be acquired unintentionally). This avoids the problem of prohibiting an activity of which the individual has limited control.

Yet, (IG4) is not without its problems. The most glaring problem is that it raises serious ethical issues/problems for the chaplain. Is the expectation that the chaplain will withhold critical information from his chain of command, even if it could potentially save the lives of American soldiers, simply out of obedience to a regulation? This does not seem to be the intention of the prohibition. In fact, it could be argued that the chaplain is *obligated* to share such information with the command. Another problem with (IG4) is that it changes the nature of the prohibition. Under (IG4) intelligence *gathering* as is typically understood is acceptable, but the *sharing* of the intelligence is deemed inappropriate, but if *that* were the intention of the prohibition, we would expect the regulation to state that chaplains are prohibited from *sharing* sensitive and classified information

---

the commander does not *know* what information will aid current operations. Of course, knowledge of which future operations will be conducted in not even possible, much less which information is needed for future mission success.

gained during the course of functioning as a liaison with local religious leaders for the military commander. So, consider the following:

> (IG5): Intelligence gathering is the activity of meeting with persons in the community or the observation of the community for the purpose of acquiring new information about a military unit's area of operations.

(IG5) has merit because it places the control over violating or not violating the prohibition in the hands of the chaplain. Certainly the chaplain himself has the ability to determine his own intentions with regard to his meetings with persons in the community. However, one must ask if mere information about an area can be defined as "intelligence." There may be times when the chaplain wants to gather information about the area so that he knows where he is going the following week for a meeting. There was more than one occasion in which, while my assistant and I were out in the community, we conducted a "recon" of another area so that our upcoming meetings would go smoothly. This does not seem to be the sort of activity that the prohibition has in mind. In fact, it is seen as a wise use of time. So a proper definition must include both elements, something like:

> (IG6): Intelligence gathering is the activity of meeting with persons in the community or the observation of the community for the purpose of acquiring new information which has been identified by the military unit's intelligence section as vital to mission success.

(IG6) has additional merit because it more narrowly identifies the *kind* of information that chaplains are prohibited from gathering. It seems to get at the intention of the prohibition placed upon chaplains. An analogy can be drawn between chaplains and medical personnel, who are also categorized by the Geneva Conventions as noncombatants. A similar prohibition exists for them (medical personnel): "While medical personnel cannot be assigned ISR [Intelligence, Surveillance, and Reconnaissance] tasks due to their Geneva Conventions category status, medical personnel who gain information through casual observation of activities in plain view while discharging their humanitarian duties will report the information to their supporting intelligence element."[11]

---

11. Ibid.

Here, the noncombatant is required to report any information gathered through *casual observation* of activities *in plain view*, which were noticed while he was going about his *normal daily tasks*. All of these qualifications make it clear that there should be no effort on the part of the noncombatant (in this case, medical personnel) to gain new information that could be construed as intelligence. Here is where the analogy to chaplains breaks down, for chaplains serve as the staff officers who advise the commander with regard to the religious climate of the unit's area of operations and information gathered about religion from activity outside the wire can aid the chaplain in that role. Medical personnel have no analogous function.[12]

Since the chaplaincy field manual specifically prohibits HUMINT, a closer examination of what the field manual for intelligence says about it may clarify the meaning of the prohibition. One of the key elements identified in HUMINT is that the information gathered is "to satisfy the commander's intelligence requirements and cross-cue other intelligence disciplines."[13] Elsewhere, it is even more clear that HUMINT is a task-oriented intelligence-gathering activity: "The HUMINT force is focused on and dedicated to the collection of data and information relevant to the commander's PIRs [Priority Intelligence Requirements] and IRs [Intelligence Requirements]."[14]

So it seems that (IG6) is an accurate description of the kind of activity that chaplains are prohibited from engaging in. When conducting bilateral meetings (BILATS), chaplains just are going to gather some information, but they must be careful to resist the temptation to seek out information which answers the Commander's Priority Intelligence Requirements (PIRs) or Commanders Critical Information Requirements (CCIRs).

---

12. The role of the chaplain as advisor is particularly critical for MOOTW/Stability Operations, as FM 2-0 makes clear: "The commander requires the appropriate intelligence and IPB product in order to determine how best to influence the threat, political and information dimensions of the operational environment, and enhance regional stability. The identification and analysis of characteristics of the terrain and weather, politics, infrastructure, health status, civilian press, attitudes, and culture of the local populace and all possible threats are important in conducting stability operations. A lack of knowledge concerning local politics, customs, and culture could lead to US actions which attack inappropriate targets or which may offend or cause mistrust among the local population." Ibid., "Stability Operations," 3-9: 3-3.

13. Ibid., "Human Intelligence," 6-1:6-0.

14. Ibid., "Human Intelligence," 6-12: 6-4.

While the chaplain will surely be aware of the issues and concerns of the command, he must remember that he is not an Intelligence, Surveillance, and Reconnaissance (ISR) asset. His intention in conducting BILATS is at issue here. Additionally, he cannot be tasked by the unit's intelligence officer (G2/S2) or even commander to get specific information, and he cannot be part of the targeting process. He *can* provide information about the religious culture/environment which may help focus intelligence and information targeting and he is obligated to share any relevant information received while conducting BILATs. These constraints seem to accurately reflect the intent of the military requirements.

THEOLOGICO-ETHICAL QUESTIONS

The Global War on Terror has largely been conducted in countries where the dominant religion is Islam. Consequently, U. S. military chaplains are increasingly being asked to serve as liaisons with Islamic religious leaders. My own experience overseas included regular meetings with both Orthodox priests and Muslim imams, including the Head Imam of the region. While no specific stated goal for the meetings was given, the intent of the commander (and the training we received prior to deployment) was for the chaplain to foster good relations with the religious community within which the U.S. military is operating. Such good relations are thought to aid the overall effort of "winning hearts and minds" of the people of the region/area/country.

Yet some evangelical chaplains have been reluctant to participate in such liaison operations, not out of fear for their own safety (though surely force protection and personal safety is an ongoing concern, especially for operations in Iraq and Afghanistan), but out of a concern for their theological commitments.

The complex operational environment in MOOTW creates or raises some questions of an ethical concern. The changing role of the chaplain presents some of these problems in a unique way. For example, suppose that a unit has gained some intelligence which indicates an attack upon a U.S. convoy is imminent, and suppose that there is good reason to believe that the imam at the local mosque has information or access to information that could help the Americans prevent the attack. The question that needs to be raised is whether or not the chaplain can or should use the "good relationship" he has fostered with the imam in order to gain the necessary information to protect his soldiers.

Of course, if no clear definition of intelligence gathering can be given, or if the feasibility of the prohibition against intelligence gathering can be shown to be nonexistent, then the chaplain *could*, and perhaps *should* seek to use his position as liaison with local religious leaders to gain the information needed to save American lives. Suppose, though, a clear definition *can* be given; that, as I have argued, something like (IG6) is true; then the question must be asked if it is better to obey the regulation, risk the loss of American soldiers, and feel the guilt of believing something could have been done to prevent the loss, or to disobey the regulation, perhaps face court martial, but potentially save the lives of the soldiers. Similar questions have long been the fare of heated debate and spirited conversation at the uniformed services' chaplains' schools. For example, an analogy can be drawn between this question and the question of whether or not a chaplain should take up arms to defend the lives of his soldiers in the heat of battle. The Global War on Terror has provided the occasion for many younger (or at least, more recently commissioned) chaplains to question the orders of the Chiefs of Chaplains expressly denying chaplains the choice of bearing arms. For example, a large number of army chaplains serving in, or recently returned from Iraq and Afghanistan petitioned the Army Chief of Chaplains to rescind the long-standing order. The Chief responded by reiterating, in no uncertain terms, the policy which states that army chaplains will not bear arms in any circumstance.[15] Recently, the new Army Chief of Chaplains, Chaplain (MG) Douglas Carver, reaffirmed the long-standing prohibition against bearing arms. Interestingly, he clarified the prohibition to include training in arms, even for fun.[16]

Admittedly, the analogy breaks down somewhat, for in this case, there is no legal question, at least with respect to the United States Code and the Geneva Conventions—no prohibition against chaplains bearing arms exists in either document. While some defenders of the policy have attempted to do so by suggesting that the chaplain's status as noncombatant would be forfeited if he were to utilize or even carry a weapon,

15. Hicks, Memorandum to MACOM chaplains. See also, "The U.S. Army Chief of Chaplains Newsletter (August 2004), Department of the Army, Washington, D.C.

16. Carver, "Memorandum: Chief of Chaplains Policy: Chaplains as Non-Combatants" 22 April 2008.

such claims simply cannot be sustained. It is well known that military medical personnel (e.g., doctors and nurses) are considered noncombatants by the Geneva Conventions, but they are not only *allowed* to bear arms, but are *required* to both bear arms and evince proficiency with such [by qualifying annually or semi-annually]. In fact, it is even suggested that they are *morally obligated* to use their weapons to defend the lives of their patients in the event that hostiles are nearby and they are reasonably sure that their intent is to do harm to the patients. Yet, the comparison to medical personnel is not exact. It seems that the reasons for the Chiefs of Chaplains to deny chaplains the right to bear arms has to do more with the perception of a religious leader bearing arms than it does with any legal status of chaplains serving in the military.[17] There is not time here to discuss the propriety of such a position, though it certainly could be both defended and disputed; the point to be seen is that while many chaplains officially agree to stand by the Chief's orders, most seem unsure of how they would respond if placed in a situation where they are the only individuals left to stave off an attack by the enemy, especially an enemy that does not respect the guidelines presented in the Geneva Conventions.[18]

17. It is clear that negative press coverage of chaplains bearing arms during the conflict in Vietnam had some impact, but it seems that there is more of a religious position being proffered in the prohibition than is normally admitted. There is a religiously-motivated precedent of an unarmed clergy of sorts, accompanying military operations. In medieval England and France, clergy who traveled with the armies and ministered to the soldiers were prohibited from carrying swords. Yet, this prohibition did not seem to be based on the idea that bearing arms of any kind is unbecoming of a man of the cloth, but rather on a somewhat literal reading of Jesus words to Peter, "Those who live by the sword, die by the sword" (Matt 26:52). Notice that Jesus said nothing about the mace. It is interesting to note that there were reports of clergy riding into battle carrying a mace. I suppose one was allowed to bash in his enemies skulls "in Thy mercy," but was prohibited from "giving him a flesh wound" by cutting off his arms, legs, or head.

18. After the beheadings of several Americans and other foreign workers captured by so-called "insurgents" in the Iraq conflict, my wife made me promise that I would never allow myself to be taken prisoner alive. I agreed to her request. Whatever I would have to do to prevent my wife and daughter and mother and father and friends from seeing me beheaded on video, I would do. Of course, this promise does not entail taking up arms, but it does, in certain situations, certainly leave it as an option. I think that any chaplain who is honest with himself and others would have to admit to a measure of uncertainty with regard to how he would react in such a situation. While it may be difficult for some to imagine that an individual who chose to do so in a situation where he felt that he had no other recourse except to take up arms in violation of a direct order could be court-martialed, I suspect that the only reprieve would be if the individual could prove beyond all doubt that he was the only individual capable of defending a group of soldiers, that

Of course, inherent in both of these questions—bearing arms in certain situations, and gathering intelligence in order to save the lives of friendlies—is the nature of obedience chaplains should offer to the orders given him by those in military authority over them. For example, one definition of military obedience that could be offered is the following:

> (MO1): Chaplains should never violate direct or indirect orders, Army Regulations, or the prescriptions set forth in Field Manuals, Department of the Army Pamphlets, or other official publications for military operations.

This is the most strict interpretation of how chaplains (and other soldiers) should behave. It is surely the most common view of how the military operates and has a sort of common-sense air to it. However, it is flawed from the very start, for U. S. soldiers are trained to ignore or disobey *some* orders in certain circumstances. While the military is strongly deontological in its orientation—commanders need to know that their orders will be obeyed without question within the context of the battlefield—it should be noted that soldiers are trained to evaluate all orders given.

One of the lessons of modern warfare has been that the "just following orders" defense is no defense at all. It did not work for the German war criminals at the Nuremberg trials, and it did not work for SPC Charles Graner and PVT Lynndie England in the Abu Ghraib scandal in Iraq. U.S. soldiers are instructed to only obey *lawful* orders by superiors. While it must be admitted that little or no training is provided to soldiers for *how* to evaluate the legality of any given order, the point that is important for purposes of this discussion is that allowance is made for discrimination on the part of the individual soldier.[19]

A more nuanced definition of military obedience should be offered that takes into account the allowance for disobedience in light of a concern for the law of war. Perhaps something like the following gets more at the concern:

---

the intent of the enemy fighters was to kill all persons captured or found. Even then, technically speaking, the command could chose to discipline the chaplain for ignoring a legal order.

19. Soldiers are typically given a one- or two-hour briefing on the law of war, with primary emphasis given to rules of engagement.

(MO2): Chaplains should never violate direct or indirect orders, Army Regulations, or the prescriptions set forth in Field Manuals, Department of the Army Pamphlets, or other official publications for military operations, except when obedience to such would be an express violation of the laws of war.

(MO2) certainly corrects the deficiencies that were so obvious in (MO1), in that they take into account the specific legal agreement of all member nations to the Geneva Conventions that their governments will not prosecute members of their militaries who, out of concern for human rights and the law of war, disobey any orders by their superiors which would cause them to break the law, and the general acknowledgment of all civilized governments that protection of human rights should override military expediency.

However, (MO2) is still too restrictive, especially for limiting the ability of chaplains to deny orders given by commanders and/or superior officers. That is, chaplains need to have the freedom to refuse orders beyond those that are express violations of the law of war without fear of reprisal. Consider the following scenario: Suppose a commander of an infantry unit is Roman Catholic and wishes to have his soldiers blessed before they go into combat and he calls upon his chaplain, who is neo-evangelical, to do so. The chaplain does not believe in the activity of "blessing," and offers to pray for the soldiers or to get a priest to do the blessing, but the commander insists on a blessing from the unit chaplain. In this case, the military allows the chaplain to refuse for at least two reasons: first, to conduct a blessing upon all the soldiers going into combat is to violate the religious rights of all who are not Catholic; but second, the chaplain may refuse because he cannot be forced to do anything which is a violation of his own faith tradition and/or commitments. So even if in the scenario, the commander asked the chaplain to bless the Catholic soldiers of the unit who were about to go into combat, the chaplain could (and *should)* refuse to follow the order. So (MO2) needs to be revised to reflect this allowance and obligation.

(MO3): Chaplains should never violate direct or indirect orders, Army Regulations, or the prescriptions set forth in Field Manuals, Department of the Army Pamphlets, or other official publications for military operations, except when obedience to such would be an express violation of the laws of war, or when obedience would require the chaplain to act in ways contrary to his own faith tradition.

The protection of the chaplain against being forced to act in ways contrary to his own faith tradition has been under scrutiny as of late. Some cases are very clear, as in the example given, but some are not so clear.[20] The growing number of evangelical chaplains who come from non-confessional backgrounds have pushed the interpretation of this protection to seemingly include personal beliefs. That is, in the past, if a question of fidelity to one's faith tradition came up, there were confessions or manuals that could be consulted in order to settle the dispute (e.g., official Roman Catholic dogma as found in encyclicals, papal bulls, and *ex cathedra* pronouncements, United Methodist Book of Discipline, etc.), but chaplains from faith groups that are less doctrinally defined are increasingly appealing to personal religious conviction for authority to disobey orders. That is, the *discernment* allowed on the part of the chaplain with regard to obedience to orders arguably includes an appeal to *personal conscience*. Thus, some have proposed something akin to the following for a definition of proper military obedience for chaplains:

> (MO4): Chaplains should never violate direct or indirect orders, Army Regulations, or the prescriptions set forth in Field Manuals, Department of the Army Pamphlets, or other official publications for military operations, except when obedience to such would be an express violation of the laws of war, or when obedience would require the chaplain to act in ways contrary to his own faith tradition or violate his personal religious convictions and/ or conscience.

(MO4) has the strength of protecting those chaplains from faith traditions that are less clearly defined doctrinally or that have wide variances in practices and beliefs, from having to perform actions that could/would create a crisis of conscience, without fear of reprisal. Of course, (MO4) could be refined to exclude the appeal to conscience, while retaining the appeal to personal religious convictions. This revision could protect

---

20. Loveland discusses issues similar in nature to the issues discussed here. Specifically, she describes the issue, during Operation Desert Storm, of chaplains removing their crosses in order to avoid offending host country Saudi Arabia. Most chaplains complied and evangelical endorsing agents agreed because it was not a comprehensive order; it was restrictive. See Loveland, *American Evangelicals*, ch. 20, "Maintaining the Sectarian Ideal," 296-322.

against fears of rampant disobedience by chaplains on personal grounds; of too subjective criteria for allowable disobedience. While an appeal to personal religious convictions may appear to be extremely subjective and no different from an appeal to personal conscience, it is not so, for proof could still be required for both the religious basis of the belief and the fact that the individual actually holds the belief. In fact, just such proof is required of soldiers who wish to claim Conscientious Objector status after joining the military.[21]

So perhaps (MO4) should be modified to look more like

> (MO5): Chaplains should never violate direct or indirect orders, Army Regulations, or the prescriptions set forth in Field Manuals, Department of the Army Pamphlets, or other official publications for military operations, except when obedience to such would be an express violation of the laws of war, or when obedience would require the chaplain to act in ways contrary to his own faith tradition or violate his personal religious convictions.

(MO5) seems to have all of the strengths of (MO4), while reducing some of the concerns of military commanders of too subjective a criterion for obedience among chaplains. Armed (no pun intended) with our new definition of military obedience, we are now in a position to evaluate whether chaplains can reasonably argue that they may, for operational purposes, violate the prescriptions of the regulation which state that chaplains shall not gather intelligence, even if the chaplain is the only person able to gain information needed to protect the lives of American soldiers.[22]

---

21. Soldiers must apply for Conscientious Objector status to their commanders. An investigation is then undertaken in order to determine if the applicant's opposition to war is genuine, general, and religious in nature. Just because the individual *claims* to hold to a particular belief on religious grounds, he is not automatically thought to be telling the truth. Various criteria are used for evaluating the veracity of the individual's claim, which are, admittedly, somewhat subjective. Typical in such an investigation is an interview with a chaplain who offers an opinion to the commander regarding the religious nature of the individual's objection to war.

22. Of course, it is difficult to imagine any such scenario. After all, most imams who are willing to meet with Christian chaplains are open-minded enough to allow soldiers other than the chaplain into their mosque, or would be willing to meet with other military leaders (e.g., the commander, executive officer, or even an intelligence officer). We may be able to imagine the local religious leader asking for the presence of the chaplain at the meeting, but it is hard to imagine him refusing to speak to anyone except the chaplain. If he holds the chaplain in such high regard, we should expect him to trust the chaplain's

So, if a chaplain wishes to have the right to bear arms or to gather intelligence, he would need to argue that to obey the prohibitions would require him to act in ways contrary to his own faith tradition or personal religious convictions. He would also have to demonstrate that his violation of the regulation (or any order for that matter) was in the best interests of the military itself, as the courts typically give deference to the military with regard to its judgments about what is necessary for order and discipline. In addition, he would potentially have to prove this to a military court-martial. This could prove exceedingly difficult, especially with regard to the bearing of arms.[23] In most cases with regard to intelligence gathering, chaplains should seek to convince the local religious leader to speak with another officer, perhaps his commander or intelligence officer. If the religious leader refuses, then the chaplain must make

recommendation to talk with the other officer and pass the information on to him.

23. If he attempted to take the case to civilian court, he would most likely lose. As noted in chapter three, civilian courts tend to favor the military, even denying military members rights that would otherwise have been granted to a civilian plaintiff. In the landmark case, *Goldman v. Weinberger*, the court gave deference to the military. The majority opinion stated, "We have repeatedly held that 'the military is, by necessity, a specialized society separate from civilian society.' Parker v. Levy, 417 U.S. 733, 743 (1974). . . . Our review of military regulations challenged on First Amendment grounds is far more deferential than constitutional review of similar laws or regulations designed for civilian society. The military need not encourage debate or tolerate protest to the extent that such tolerance is required of the civilian state by the First Amendment; to accomplish its mission the military must foster instinctive obedience, unity, commitment, and esprit de corps." *Goldman v. Weinberger*, 475 U.S., 503 (1986), cited in Benjamin, "Justice, Justice Shall You Pursue," 8. Benjamin summarizes the implications of this case: "Goldman gives the military unfettered discretion to restrict religious practice, at least by a military member. The Court, in deference to Congress and the military, will accept any rational argument that the needs of morale, discipline, or uniformity trump a service member's desire to practice religion." Ibid., 9. It is worth noting, though, that the Departments of Defense and the Army have both since prepared documents which offer commanders guidance for accommodating religious practices of soldiers serving within their commands. If a commander has to decide whether or not to accommodate a particular person's request for special consideration on religious grounds, he must first determine the level of sincerity of the individual, for requests for accommodation of practices are not limited to the mandatory tenets of a particular religion, but may be "required by individual conscience or personal piety." DA-PAM 600-75, *Accommodation of Religious Practices*. It should also be noted that the appeal to personal piety and individual conscience is not absolute; the individual still needs permission from the commander. Thus, the chaplain could find such an appeal to have few sympathetic jurors in a court-martial hearing. As Benjamin notes, "Neither free speech, nor free exercise rights override the commander's obligation to maintain good order and discipline and to effectuate army equal opportunity values." Benjamin, 18, n. 140.

a decision regarding his conscience. The chaplain may be able to offer a good ethical basis for disobeying the prohibition (e.g., the principle of preservation of life over following of human rules/laws), but it is doubtful that he will be able to offer a compelling legal defense.

EVANGELISTIC CONCERNS

Some chaplains may have concerns over their evangelical witness. Two concerns may be raised here: first, there may be concern for the soldiers to whom the chaplain ministers, and second, there may be frustration with the prohibition of evangelistic activity with respect to the local religious leaders. While both issues have a legitimate basis in an evangelical commitment to the gospel and winning souls, neither should be detrimental to participation by evangelicals in military chaplaincy.

The first concern seems to be rooted in a fear that, by merely fostering good relations with local religious leaders, particularly those from a non-Christian tradition, chaplains may send a message that all religions are the same, and this could confuse some soldiers who may be moving toward a faith commitment to Christ. So, the chaplain is concerned that his liaison activity with local religious leaders may be destructive of the faith development of those for whom he is spiritually responsible: the soldiers of his unit.

While such a concern is admirable, it is ultimately unfounded for several reasons. Most importantly, the majority of soldiers have no knowledge of the content of the chaplain's meetings with the local religious leaders and could only assume what may or may not be discussed. In fact, many soldiers do not even know that the chaplain is meeting with religious leaders in the community. Those few that do have knowledge of the content of the meetings (chaplain's assistant along with, perhaps, a security detail) could have any fears or concerns allayed by the chaplain if he felt the need to do so. The fear is also unfounded because those soldiers who would think about the issue enough to warrant concern over the role of the chaplain, are more likely than not to be regular participants in worship services. Chaplains have ample opportunity to make their personal convictions clear to all who believe. The evangelistic concerns of the chaplain can/*should* be communicated to all in attendance at chapel services [e.g., have an altar call], and so, there should be no confusion regarding either the chaplain's or the Bible's stance on issues related to soteriological inclusivism, pluralism and/or universalism. Other reasons can be given, but the two provided are sufficient to remove this most basic concern.

A related issue to the first concern is that the chaplain may fear that some of his soldiers who are "weaker brethren" could stumble by judging his actions; they may assume that he is theologically liberal or compromising and thus, sin by judging the heart of a brother (1 Cor 8:7–11). Similarly, some soldiers who are new Christians may make the same assumption about the chaplain and as a result, refrain from participating in chapel activities. These "babes in Christ" may then miss out on the experience of many blessings and growth due to the chaplain's positive meetings with local religious leaders.

Two brief responses should make it clear that this situation should not be a cause of concern to evangelical chaplains. First, as already noted, most soldiers are unaware that the meetings are even taking place, not to mention the positive nature of the meetings or the goal of the meetings to be to foster good relations. Very few are privy to the content of the meetings, so wild assumptions would have to be made by anyone who would judge the actions of the chaplain. These assumptions would have to be so sweeping and devoid of factual content or basis, that they should be of little concern to the chaplain; assumptions based on little or no information cannot be prevented. In order to do so, one would have to ensure that no one ever has any basis, perceived or factual, for assuming anything other than the truth, but this is not a reasonable expectation!

Second, the application of the Apostle Paul's discussion of meat sacrificed to idols is hermeneutically flawed. While Paul does note that he would neither eat nor drink if it would cause a brother to stumble (1 Cor 8:13), the application of this principle to mere meetings with non-Christian leaders is questionable at best. Paul's concern was related to *participation* in activity that could be construed as non-Christian worship or that could be construed as devotion to non-Christian deities or as other pagan religious commitments. In fact, he was concerned that such activity would not lead others to judge him, but to think that the worship of pagan gods is acceptable for Christians. If a chaplain were to participate in a worship service at a mosque, or were being told to participate (with non-Christian religious leaders) in a ceremony which could be thought religious in nature, then the argument could stand, but to apply the principle here seems to widen the applicability so much as to lead to inactivity outside the confines of the church or the wider evangelical culture.[24] Surely evangelicals do not wish to so limit their activities! Jesus was called a drunkard and a glutton because he did not so limit his own activities. He was not concerned about those who judged him because of the company he kept. In fact, he condemned them for their hardness of heart!

The second concern—frustration over the chaplain's inability to share the gospel with local religious leaders—is also without warrant. At least two reasons can be given for why there should be little concern by evangelical chaplains over the prohibition. First, the limitation imposed against attempts at proselytizing local religious leaders is nothing new. The same limitations exist for proselytizing soldiers within the unit to which the chaplain is assigned. Limitations upon evangelistic activity by all chaplains have long been a part of military chaplaincy doctrine.[25] Chaplains are not allowed to proselytize soldiers who have a stated faith commitment, but they are allowed to evangelize those who have no professed faith.[26] These constraints and allowances are in all of the armed ser-

24. As a side note, I was invited by an imam to attend and even participate in a Friday worship service at a mosque. I thanked him, but noted that it probably would not be appropriate for several reasons. My own religious convictions were primary, but even if I were invited to participate in a Baptist church service, it would not be appropriate, for it could be perceived as favoritism in the eyes of the local populace. This could, in turn, cause harm to the U.S. mission. It is best, as a general rule, to avoid participation in local religious services and thereby avoid the appearance of favoritism or the U.S. military having a religious agenda/component as part of its operational objectives.

25. While the prohibition against proselytizing is seen as a protection of the rights of the soldiers, it is generally accepted that proselytizing activities of chaplains constitute a violation of the Establishment Clause. See chapter three for more details.

26. For example, Brigadier General Cecil Richardson, Air Force Deputy Chief of Chaplains told the New York Times (July 12, 2005), "We will not proselytize, but we reserve the right to evangelize the unchurched." While this has been the accepted practice among the services' chaplaincy, it is far from clear that such allowances will continue. The right to refrain from religious belief has been defended more vigorously of late. Military Judge Advocate Major Michael Benjamin sees little difference between proselytizing a person with a stated faith and proselytizing a person with no stated faith: "Military leaders (including chaplains) should not take an overly *proactive* approach to garnering attendees for religious events. In essence, the command should be *reactive*—responding to the free exercise needs of soldiers, without pushing them into religious activities. . . . Military chaplains, in particular, must be cautious. Clearly, military chaplains should not attempt to proselytize soldiers. One reason chaplains 'hold rank without command' is to eliminate the formal authority of chaplains to coerce religious participation." Benjamin, 16. A similar position has been argued by the Secular Coalition for America, which claims that the mere act of witnessing, that the nature of proselytizing, is a violation

vices, and as noted in a previous chapter, seek to strike a balance between the Free Exercise and Establishment clauses of the U. S. Constitution.[27] Soldiers of all recognized faiths have the right to believe what they wish and to practice their faiths without fear of harassment, intimidation, or discrimination. Recent complaints have suggested that some of these protections were being violated or ignored by senior leadership at the United States Air Force Academy in Colorado Springs. In this case, evangelicals in positions of power were apparently encouraging proselytizing activities among the student body, offering specifically Christian prayers

---

of the Establishment Clause of the Constitution: "If the chaplain actively promotes his/her religion to soldiers of other faiths or what some of these chaplains have referred to as 'the unchurched,' or the chaplain sees his/her position as a government paid mission to convert, this would not meet the requirements of the Establishment Clause." www.secular.org/issues/militar/?view=summary.

Perhaps what is most disturbing about this trend is that, for example, Benjamin sees nothing wrong with a peer attempting to proselytize his co-workers, as long as it does not affect mission readiness or capability. Such evaluations are ultimately the call of the unit's commander. So what seems to be the tendency, at least as far as the law goes, is that leaders (which includes chaplains), especially chaplains, are prohibited from proselytizing, while others are free to exercise their desire to proselytize.

27. Such a balance has been difficult to maintain, and has been the cause of much consternation on both sides of the issue. Some have argued that the mere allowance of a chaplaincy paid by tax dollars is a violation of the Establishment Clause. For a discussion of this issue, see Weber, "The First Amendment and Military Chaplaincy"; see also Kaplan, "Military Mirrors," 1210–36.

The military chaplaincy has typically seen the outcome of the Second Circuit Court case of *Katcoff v. Marsh* as defending its viability. In that case, two Harvard Law students challenged the constitutionality of a taxpayer funded chaplaincy. The court ruled that, on the surface, the existence of the chaplaincy does violate the Establishment Clause, but then noted that the establishment clause must be interpreted in a way that accommodates "other equally valid provisions of the Constitution, including the Free Exercise Clause [and Congress' War Power Clauses] when they are implicated." 755. F2d 233 (2nd Cir. 1985). As Benjamin notes, "The best defense of the chaplaincy, and of any religious program in the military, is that it preserves a soldier's right to freely exercise his religion. In the absence of government funded chaplains, soldiers would be stymied from practicing religion in situations made necessary by military service. The Free Exercise Clause 'obligates Congress, upon creating an Army, to make religion available to soldiers who have been moved by the Army to areas of the world where religion of their own denominations is not available to them.' Further, the Army needs chaplains to accompany soldiers to places where civilian clergy do no go—field training exercises and actual combat. Conceivably, if the Army did not have chaplains it would be violating both the Establishment Clause and the Free Exercise Clause by *inhibiting* religion. Thus, the Free Exercise Clause carves out a limited exception to the Establishment Clause prohibition." Benjamin, 3–4.

at mandatory-attendance events, and suggesting mandatory attendance at church for students or sports players.[28] All chaplains are aware of the constraints and agree to work within them prior to commissioning as a chaplain, so if any given chaplain has a theological problem with the limitations placed upon evangelistic activity in the military, he should not accept a commission in the first place.

Second, the prohibition against seeking to proselytize does not preclude the chaplain from sharing his faith, as long as it is done in a way that is respectful of the other person(s). In fact, it seems only natural that, in the context of friendly discussions among clergy, theological views will be shared and explained. My own experience confirms this suspicion. As I continued to meet with the Head Imam in the American sector (of Kosovo) and we became more comfortable with one another, we began having more in-depth conversations about our beliefs. In fact, the second time I met with him, he informed me that he knows what Orthodox and Catholic Christians believe, but he was interested to know what Protestants believe. He was, essentially, asking me to share the gospel with him! On another occasion, he told me that Muslims believe in Jesus as well. I noted that I was aware they believe Jesus was a prophet, but he corrected me. He said that they believe Jesus was the greatest prophet and that he was savior of the world! This, of course, was intriguing to me and led to an exchange about the meaning of "Savior," with him explaining that it is a reference to Jesus' miracles of physical healing, and I explaining that we believe his death was substitutionary, expiatory, and propitious. I did not ask if he wanted to accept Christ as his Lord and Savior, but I was able to explain the gospel in as clear a way as possible, and without violating military protocol. The free exchange of ideas was part of the relationship we had. Of course, a certain amount of trust and rapport must be developed before such exchange can take place. It is up to the chaplain to discern when the time is appropriate. The point here, though, is that it is not a violation of military regulations and if done right, can actually enhance the effort and fulfill the intent of BILATs with local religious leaders.

Two additional concerns stem out of the discussion of evangelism and meetings with local religious leaders in a military unit's area of operations. The first has to do with the value of meetings in which soul-winning

---

28. For a rather detailed discussion of the legal issues involved, see Cook, "Service Before Self?" 1–26.

is not the goal, while the second has to do with the possible results if/ when the gospel is shared within the context of those meetings.

Some evangelicals may question the value of meetings, or any other chaplaincy work/activities for that matter, in which the stated goal or focus is not in winning souls. Some may argue that all effort should move toward the redemption of the lost, and the value of any work is to be found in results which include the changed spiritual states of some persons. After all, everything Jesus did, at least once his ministry years (proper) began, revolved around calling sinners to repentance. The only things that will remain at the *eschaton* are the souls that were changed as a result of our efforts.[29]

At the heart of the objection, there seems to be an untenable assumption that just every activity one undertakes ought to have the stated goal of winning souls, but this is unreasonable, impractical, and unrealistic (though it will preach!). It is true that evangelicals should always look for opportunities to share the good news of Jesus Christ and that all of our activities should be done with a view to bringing glory and honor to Christ, but this is not to say that every single activity one undertakes is or should be for the stated goal of winning souls. After all, while there is a desire to honor Christ with honesty, it does not seem that evangelicals fill out their federal income tax forms for the expressed purpose of winning souls! And there is a whole host of other sorts of activities that most evangelicals would say we *ought* to participate in that do not have soul-winning as their stated goal (e.g., brushing our teeth, flushing toilets, etc.), so the objection fails from the start for its unreasonable basis.

Beyond this failure, it seems clear enough that there is at least *operational value* in chaplaincy bilateral meetings as part of MOOTW. Two examples should suffice to demonstrate this point, though others could surely be given. Robinson tells of the work of Chaplain (LTC) John Worster, who deployed to Kirkuk, Iraq, with the 116th Brigade Combat Team of the Idaho National Guard in 2004. The area is well known by Americans for much of the violence that has occurred, but what is less well known is the religious diversity of the community, which is made up of Shiite and Sunni Muslims, Syrian, Assyrian, and Chaldean Catholics, as well as Presbyterian Christians. Chaplain Worster helped form the

---

29. This is obviously a bit simplistic, but it does appear to get at the heart of the basic objection. It should be noted, though, that this does not seem to be the case. Revelation 21–22 seem to make clear that there will be much that endures beyond the souls of men.

Kirkuk Religious Unity Council, which was composed of leaders from all of these communities. The council met weekly to discuss ways of cooperating in order to present a united effort for peace in the area. Robinson summarizes: "These local religious leaders expressed their deep gratitude to CH Worster for his work in bringing them together. At meetings, all of them greeted him with the traditional cheek-to-cheek embrace so common in that culture. CH Worster even offered a 'Making Your Voice Heard' media-training event. Here, the local imams, sheiks, and Christian pastors were trained in how to use print and broadcast media to promote safe and secure elections. 'We would not be here today,' one imam rose to say, 'if it were not for CH Worster.'"[30]

The second example comes from my own experience in Kosovo. While the American sector has historically seen the least amount of violence since the NATO/UN occupation, U.S. forces still remain vigilant in order to guard against an escalation in hostilities among the local populace as took place in March of 2004, when a series of riots throughout the province resulted in 19 deaths, over 900 injuries, and at least 30 churches burned or damaged, along with almost 1,000 homes. Growing frustration at the lethargy of the United Nations and the final status negotiations contributed to already existing ethnic tensions which erupted when a story broke which claimed that some ethnic Albanians boys were chased into a river by some ethnic Serbian men with dogs. Three of the boys drowned, though it was later discovered that the boys had lied; they were simply playing too close to the river and fell in.

During the rotation of KFOR 7 (my rotation), final status talks had slowed and the people were beginning to feel frustrated with the process. A political demonstration was scheduled in the largest city in the American sector by one of the more radical Albanian political groups in Kosovo. The leadership of our forces was concerned that the demonstration could turn violent, so I was asked to meet with all of the imams in town to ask if they would emphasize to their congregations a desire for *peaceful* political activity. We were careful to let them know that we did not wish them to

---

30. Robinson, "In Service of God and Country," 33. Of course, there are force protection issues whenever a recurring meeting is planned and attended by U.S. military members. Some may even question the wisdom of having a regularly scheduled meeting outside the safety of the U.S. military base, which I assume is how these meetings took place. However, such issues can be addressed through a variety of measures which I am confident CH Worster and his unit accounted for and implemented.

dissuade their people from demonstrating as it is a part of a democratic society (or at least the right to demonstrate is such). I called the Head Imam and told him what I would like to do, and he was able to get three of the five imams to a scheduled meeting with me and another chaplain. He also offered to draft a letter from the Islamic Council which would be read in all of the mosques the next day (Friday, the primary day of worship). I took him up on his offer, but still tried to meet the other two imams face-to-face, which was the desire of my commander. I was only able to meet one of the imams before the scheduled demonstration, but the other imam told me, after the fact, that he read a letter by the Islamic Council which encouraged his congregants, if they were going to participate in the demonstration, to do so peacefully. This was a success on our part. Incidentally, the demonstration took place without incident.

In both of the above examples, the chaplain's relationship(s) with the local religious leaders added to the military's mission of providing a safe and secure environment for all people within the unit's area of operations. In both cases, there is operational value derived from the chaplain's new role as liaison to the religious community within that AO. But it would be a mistake to suggest that the only value to be found in this activity is of an operational sort; there is also a spiritual value to the efforts.

The chaplain's role as liaison to local religious leaders does have a spiritual value as well. Jesus said, "Blessed are the peace-makers," and it seems evident that this activity contributes to the peace of the communities involved. As noted in chapter one, Harvey Cox and Gordon Zahn have both argued that the military environment is at odds with the work of the ministry.[31] To be fair, they were most concerned with the use of military chaplains to "bless off" on just any operation or use of force that a commander may wish to prosecute. Their concerns had more to do with the crossed purposes of the military and the ministry, and they argued that the chaplain will be less likely to have a prophetic voice, but will instead look more like a court minister who places a divine stamp of approval on whatever the king wishes to do. Cox's assessment is certainly accurate historically speaking, in that there have been many military chaplains who have done so, but it is not necessarily so and there have been many who have challenged their leadership.[32]

31. Cox, ed. *Military Chaplains*. Zahn, "Sociological Impressions." See also, Zahn, *The Military Chaplaincy*.

32. For example, Chaplain (CPT) Carl Creswell was told of the My Lai massacre by a

Zahn also implies that the very natures of the military and ministry are at odds; that one cannot be a good member of both. The Bible makes it abundantly clear that he is mistaken, though the reason David was prevented from building the Temple should not be ignored. In addition, though, I would argue that chaplaincy activity outside the wire is increasingly allowing chaplains to play a significant role in the peacemaking and peacekeeping operations so prevalent in MOOTW, and peacemaking/peacekeeping are surely not at odds with Christian ministry.

The last concern I would like to address has to do with the possibility of a local religious leader converting to Christianity as a result of his bilateral meetings with an evangelical chaplain. Most of us would hail this as a positive outcome, spiritually speaking, but we would have to be oblivious to the political realm to not recognize it as a public relations disaster. An ever-present fear among military leaders during the Global War on Terror has been that the perception of American military operations in the Middle East (and elsewhere) as a *Crusade* would prevail. This concern is also relevant for military operations in the Balkans, especially Muslim-dominated Kosovo.

At one point during my rotation there, a group of Arab journalists, to include *Al Jazeera*, came to see how a Muslim-dominated society functioned peacefully with American troop presence. In addition to observing the day to day life of the people in society, the journalists wished to visit a mosque and speak with an imam. It fell on my shoulders to line up a meeting, and so I called the imam who had been beaten by radical Islamists; I reasoned that he would give *Al Jazeera* a negative interpretation of terrorist activities in the Middle East. When we all arrived at the mosque, not only was that imam there, but also the Head Imam, who had studied theology in Saudi Arabia. He began speaking with the reporters in Arabic and eventually invited them into the main worship area of the mosque for prayers. Only a few of the reporters wished to pray, while others waited outside, and still others took photographs of those praying. I went into the mosque as well, though the other soldiers waited outside.

---

helicopter pilot, WO1 Hugh Thompson, and he reported the atrocities to chaplain above him, CH (LTC) Francis Lewis, though he did little with the information. This example serves as both proof that chaplains can speak out, and as proof that they do not. One chaplain went to his superiors, while the other (the senior chaplain in this case) did not follow through with the investigation and reporting. See Peers, *My Lai Inquiry* and "Report of the Department of the Army Review of the Preliminary Investigations into the My Lai Incident."

One of the reporters informed the Head Imam that American soldiers are not allowed in the mosques in the Middle East, but Mullah Agim [the Head Imam] responded, "This is not the Middle East! I am honored that my friend, Chaplain Laing, would come into our mosque." This, of course, can serve as further evidence that the bilateral meetings have operational value. It is hard to imagine purchasing a better public relations statement for *Al Jazeera* [and other Arab news agencies] to hear than those words from an influential, middle-eastern trained imam!

However, the important point of the story is really found in what happened inside the mosque. As the imams and some reporters were praying, I stood at the back of the mosque, out of the way. One of the reporters tried to take a photograph of me standing and watching them pray, and I could tell that it could be used for negative publicity, as if American soldiers are even occupying the mosques in Kosovo, disrupting worship services, so I looked downward in order to prevent the picture being so construed.

So, how are evangelical chaplains to respond to the possibility of a local religious leader converting to the faith? It seems to me that we cannot see it as a negative, no matter what the public relations fallout may be. We ought to pray for all lost souls and utilize all opportunities to share the gospel as outlined above. Great care should be taken to avoid the perception that the chaplain is there as a missionary to the local populace and he should never attempt to force the discussion. Yet, when the subject comes up, we should not shy away from it or apologize for our beliefs about Christ and salvation. A good balance requires wisdom, discernment, grace, and a prayerful attitude. We should recognize that our evangelistic activities, though, could create serious problems for ourselves, those within whose command we function, and the United States military as well. The perception of the U.S. military as operating a Christian Crusade is a powerful motivator for some radical *jihadists*. The conversion of an imam to Christianity because of meetings with a U.S. military chaplain would only add to the perception, and would most likely result is widespread demonstrations, violence, and condemnation. The fallout from such evangelistic activity could include, but is not limited to: court-martial of the chaplain, increased violence directed against American military and civilians in the area of operations as well as throughout the world, or even a breakdown in international peace relations. The chaplain who chooses to lead a local religious leader to the Lord must be aware of these costs and be willing to accept at least some of the responsibility for the results. Nevertheless, my admission here should not be surprising or cause for alarm. After all, local Muslim religious leaders would also, if honest, be happy to see a Christian chaplain convert to Islam. So just as it is natural for religious leaders to talk theology when they meet, so also it is natural for each to view his own position as true and therefore, ultimately desire the conversion of the other.

While I have argued that evangelical chaplains cannot claim that obedience to the prohibitions on chaplains bearing arms and gathering intelligence requires a violation of their religious commitments, personal or corporate, obedience to an absolute prohibition against leading someone to the LORD would constitute just such a violation, as long as the individual made the choice on his own without coercion or pressure from without.[33] At the end of the day, it seems that if a local religious leader wishes to accept Jesus as LORD, the evangelical chaplain should not discourage him from doing so, and trust in the providence of God to bring good from whatever fallout there may be. This could be seen as terribly controversial, but as noted above, it should not so be.

CONCLUSION

In this chapter, I have attempted to answer some of the complex questions that have arisen due to the chaplain's new role within the military's mission in the Global War on Terror, primarily as liaison to local religious leaders. I have attempted to define which activities the chaplain can undertake, and which activities he should avoid. Chaplains can and should report any sensitive information gained in the context of bilateral meetings with local religious leaders, but should not attend those meetings with the goal of gaining any specific information relative to the military unit's mission, especially the intelligence requirements identified by the command. I have also attempted to alleviate concerns over the prohibitions placed on chaplains in sharing their faith with their counterparts

---

33. By saying that the individual made the choice on his own, I do not mean to suggest that the decision is a human work or based on human effort, devoid of the work of the Holy Spirit. Instead, what I mean to communicate is that the military chaplain did not coerce or bring political, economic, or military pressure to bear on the individual's decision. In fact, the chaplain should make no effort to elicit a faith response from the individual. Similarly, though, I am arguing that the chaplain should not refuse to allow the person to accept Christ, or try to talk the person out of it.

in the local populace, and have offered some guidelines for doing so in keeping with the military's intent. I have also warned that doing so with success could prove damaging to U. S. interests, military effectiveness, and the safety of U. S. soldiers and civilians, in addition to the chaplain's career. These may be risks worth taking, as the spread of the gospel is an important aspect of evangelical faith, and love of neighbor compels us to share the good news of Jesus Christ. Still, wisdom and clear direction from the Holy Spirit is vital in the endeavor. In fact, it could be a matter of national security. The evangelical chaplain or soldier should be aware of the dangers and use tact, grace, and respect in his interactions with those of other faiths. When he does so, the love of Christ shines through.

7

"With All Your Heart, Soul, Mind, and Strength"

Evangelical Chaplains, Pastoral Counseling and Psychology

*Moreover, love itself, which binds men together in the bond of unity, would
have no means of pouring soul into soul, and, as it were, mingling them
one with another, if men never learnt anything from their fellow-men.*

—AUGUSTINE,
ON CHRISTIAN DOCTRINE.

INTRODUCTION

CHAPLAINS *HAVE TO COUNSEL*. In fact, one of the oft-surprising features of chaplaincy ministry for those beginning their careers is just
how much counseling can be involved.[1] As a military chaplain deployed
overseas, I was sometimes overwhelmed with the counseling load. I
found that approximately one-half to two-thirds of my time was spent
counseling soldiers for a variety of issues and that my experience was not
uncommon. Marriage/relationship problems and depression are the most
common issues that affect soldiers' ability to focus on the mission, though
a whole range of issues can manifest itself over the course of deployment.
For most units, redeployment adds substance abuse among some soldiers

1. Soldiers turn to chaplains for a variety of reasons, from a fear of stigma associated
with seeing a mental health professional, to preferring faith-based counseling. There is
a trend among Americans in general to seek out faith-based counseling over secular
psychology. See Paul and Arnin, "With God as My Shrink," 62–68.

to this volatile mix. Thus, the work of counseling can provide challenges to military chaplains.

I have often claimed that my own spiritual gift is that of teaching (hence, my chosen profession) and have long felt inadequate in the counselor's role.[2] It is understandable, then, that I have also found it somewhat of a relief when those in supervisory roles above me in the "chaplaincy chain" have advised that we refer hard counseling cases to the "professionals." That advice/permission has allowed me to refrain from seeing myself as a failure when I feel uncomfortable with a counseling issue or when the situation stretches my abilities beyond my comfort level. Yet, an increasing number of evangelical chaplains are reluctant to refer counselees, even the hard cases, to mental health professionals. This should be no surprise, as some proponents of a particular approach to Christian counseling have argued that counseling is properly understood as the purview of the minister as he is empowered by the Holy Spirit, not of the secular health professional. In fact, Powlison advises that Christians should never refer (for counseling) unless the psychiatrist or psychologist is committed to biblical counseling.[3] Likewise, Adams suggests that referring persons to psychiatrists or psychologists is a shirking of ministerial responsibility; it is something those chaplains/ministers will have to answer for before the Lord.[4] If Powlison and Adams are correct, then attitudes like mine and advice like that which I was given are erroneous and perhaps sinful. This should give us pause in too quickly referring our counseling cases. The arguments over referring are part of a larger dispute within conservative Christian circles over the nature of pastoral counseling.

2. Nauta argues that, in actuality, most ministers are ill-prepared for the counseling roles they must take on when actually ministering to others (as opposed to talking theology in the classroom). Nauta, "Not Practicing Theology," 197–205.

3. He admits he would refer for other, medical diagnoses or for intelligence testing, but maintains that in most cases, a medical doctor (non-mental health), policeman, or pastor can best address the relevant concerns. He notes that, between these three, "you should be able to do what can be done humanly," and concludes, "Psychologists' success with so-called schizophrenics is not noteworthy." Powlison, "Queries & Controversies," 65. The advice given is in reference to a situation in which a wife exhibits signs of schizophrenia and runs down the street screaming hysterically.

4. Adams, Competent to Counsel, xii.

THE CONTROVERSY OVER COUNSELING
IN EVANGELICALISM

There has, in relatively recent years, arisen a controversy within evangelical circles regarding the nature of Christian counseling. The bulk of the dispute has to do with the relationship between specifically Christian counseling and secular approaches to understanding the human psyche. That is, there is much debate over the value of psychology training for pastoral counseling and even for any other counseling that purports to be Christian. Proponents of what has come to be known as *nouthetic counseling* have argued that secular theories and approaches to understanding and curing the human psyche are faulty, and have therefore questioned both the value of secular counseling training for Christian counselors and the value of secular counseling itself.[5]

Jay Adams is the person most often credited with founding the nouthetic approach to counseling, though he prefers to see his role as reviving the proper biblical perspective on human interaction and instruction. The name for this method is derived from the Greek word, *nouthesis*, variously translated as admonish, teach, or counsel. According to Adams, it is particularly characteristic of the Apostle Paul's ministry, and includes three elements which distinguish it from traditional counseling theory: 1) a call for change in the individual counseled, 2) verbal instruction and/ or correction, and 3) a goal of growth in holiness for the individual. Thus, nouthetic counseling focuses on *what* the individual does or is doing rather than on *why*, and then seeks to offer advice or direction for future activity which will bring about healing and restoration. An underlying assumption to this approach is that, generally speaking, the individual's emotional difficulties are rooted in faulty or even sinful actions, thoughts, or perspectives. Adams writes, "Nouthetic confrontation, then, necessarily suggests first of all that there is something wrong with the person to be confronted nouthetically. . . . The fundamental purpose of nouthetic confrontation, then, *is to effect personality and behavioral change*."[6] The idea is that the counselor's job is to help the counselee see how his depression is born out of his own sinful actions/attitudes or how a proper faith perspective can address the issue/problem in a way that he has not

5. For a sociological analysis of the divide between proponents of Christian Psychology and Nouthetic Counselors, see Beck, "Value Tensions," 107–16.

6. Adams, 45.

conceived. In fact, Adams does not approve of the language of *emotional problems* because he believes it to be misleading. The problem is not with the person's emotions, as if they have somehow malfunctioned. Rather, the problem is behavioral and therefore, solutions which alter his emotional state only address symptoms: "People feel bad because of bad behavior; feelings flow from actions."[7] Adams' point, then, is that emotional distress is the result of sinful behavior, while emotional peace comes from good behavior grounded in Christian faith: "A good conscience, according to Peter, depends upon good behavior. Good lives come from good deeds; good consciences come from good behavior. . . . Visceral discomfort is a God-structured means of telling human beings that they have violated their standards."[8]

There can be no doubt that Adams' theory is influential among evangelical counselors, pastors, and educators. The rise in interest in nouthetic counseling among evangelicals can be seen in membership statistics for the National Association of Nouthetic Counselors (NANC). At its inception in 1974, it had one member and by 1977–1978, it had five and eight respectively. By 1990, the organization had grown to 48 members, and by 2000, it had 204. In February, 2008, the membership was at over 600. As impressive as these numbers are, they do not tell it all, for there are many more pastors and laypersons who have been through the NANC's certified-counselor program (and others like it) who are not members of NANC. The point, then, is that there has been an increasing interest in the topic and the popularity of biblical counseling has grown exponentially in the years since Adams and others first began talking about it. In fact, Adams sees the growth, despite a lack of financial and administrative support and promotion, as evidence of the movement's divine origin: "That this thing took off in the first place, and is now taking off in a new and fresh way, is unbelievable to me. I was just thinking back to pushing the little desk in and out of the closet and the telephone in the drawer. There has been no money, power, position or anything else in it. If this movement of God's people was not of God, it would have died long ago."[9]

7. Ibid., 93.

8. Ibid., 94.

9. Powlison, "25 Years of Biblical Counseling," 13. The reference to the little desk and phone in the drawer are to the beginnings of the Christian Counseling and Education Foundation (CCEF), when it was run one day per week out of a couple of rooms in the church Bettler served as pastor. Ibid., 9. See also Bettler, "CCEF: The Beginning," 45–51.

Not all Christian counselors and educators have agreed with the nouthetic approach or its arguments. Some, typically known as Integrationists, have sought to blend Christian theology with secular psychology training and methods.[10] They typically argue that truths of secular psychology discovered by non-Christians are instances of common grace; that God enabled men like Rogers, Freud, and others, to discover some truths about the human psyche by means of His grace which extends to all. Some of the most well-known are James Dobson of *Focus on the Family*, Larry Crabb, and Gary Collins.[11] The controversy over the value of psychology for Christian counseling has made its way into theological education. Many seminaries have sought an integrationist approach to the study and practice of theology and psychology by offering counseling and psychology programs that lead to professional credentialing. For example, Fuller Theological Seminary in Pasadena, CA, offers two doctoral degrees in psychology (Ph.D. and Psy.D.) and was the first seminary to offer programs of study accredited by the American Psychological Association (APA). While some may question the evangelical commitment of Fuller Seminary, none would so question Biola University, whose Rosemead School of Psychology offers comparable APA-accredited programs of study.

However, a number of seminaries are moving away from such a psychology-based focus to a biblical counseling emphasis. The motivations behind the move to the nouthetic approach are complex and involve pragmatic/missional as well as theological concerns.[12] The pragmatic or definitional concerns have to do with the nature of theological education, the vocational goals of seminary graduates, and fiduciary responsibility of school administrators. In recent years, some of the nation's largest seminaries have had to re-evaluate the programs they offer in light of the stated missions/goals of the schools and increasing budget shortfalls. Particularly in times of financial crises, every dollar's contribution to the mission of the school must be evident. When push comes to shove, most evangelical seminary administrators will argue that their schools are in business, first and foremost, to prepare individuals for local church min-

10. Day takes a Christological approach to integration. Day, "Incarnational Christian Psychology," 535–44. See also Strong, "Christian Counseling: A Synthesis," 589–92.

11. Collins' text on Chrsitian Counseling has been widely-used in evangelical seminary classrooms. Collins, *Christian Counseling*.

12. Here I use the word, "missional" to refer to the institutions understanding of its basic mission and not in the sense used by many within the emergent church movement.

istry or foreign missions service. While there are certainly other worthy areas of ministry, these are the two which serve as the bread and butter of theological education. Thus, while evangelical leaders readily admit that earlier aversions to social ministries were an overreaction to perceived connections to liberal theology like that of Rauschenbusch or Matthews, social ministry programs in evangelical seminaries have nevertheless come under increasing scrutiny of late. For example, in 1995, the Southern Baptist Theological Seminary in Louisville, Kentucky, sold its W. O. Carver School of Social Work in part due to unacceptable requirements by the secular accrediting agency for the Master's in Social Work degree, but also in part to questions of the appropriateness of such a school at a seminary. To some trustees and administrators, it seemed more appropriate for a Christian college or university setting, since it was designed to prepare persons for work outside of the local church and traditional ministerial positions.[13] Similar concerns exist today with credentialed counseling programs as well. Seminaries, so the argument goes, are in the business of preparing persons to be pastors, not psychologists or psychiatrists, and there is certainly some truth to that claim. Thus, there is a trend in evangelical ministerial schools to move toward a biblical counseling emphasis and away from a mental health approach to pastoral care.[14] The theological concerns with the mental health approach to pastoral counseling have to do with the secular (or even ungodly) basis of psychological theories which undergird the practice of psychology and with the sufficiency of Scripture.

Secular Psychology

One concern of many biblical counseling advocates is that secular psychology is less science and more secular religion.[15] As Powlison says,

13. Some may take issue with this claim, but hiring records of graduates of the program reveal that the majority went to work outside of the church, often in secular settings. This is not to critique such employment; in fact, it is desired that Christians should work in the secular arena and make an impact there, but it is to say that programs which lead to such employment, on the whole, fall outside of the seminary's goal. Of course, chaplaincy could be described in this way, but the ministerial nature of chaplaincy (as opposed to, for example, social work) precludes such an objection.

14. A short but helpful article on the topic as it relates to Southern Baptist seminaries was published in a relatively recent issue of *Christian Century*. Winfrey, "Southern Baptists Reject 'Pastoral Counseling,'" 24–27.

15. Vitz, *Psychology as Religion*. See also Rieff, *Triumph of the Therapeutic*. It should be noted that Rieff does not make the claim that psychology is a religion, but rather that

"Modern psychotherapy is simply the attempt to do face-to-face pastoral work in service to different gods, different ideals, different diagnoses, a different gospel."[16] At first glance, such a charge may seem to be an over-statement, and perhaps it is, but there are good reasons for not dismissing it out of hand. First, even some from within the guild have questioned the scientific status of psychiatry, psychology, and their diagnoses.[17] Szasz, no friend of nouthetic counseling, has for years expressed doubts about the scientific status of psychiatric diagnoses. He was silenced/censored within the psychiatric community, but his work was well received among ethicists, philosophers, psychologists, and sociologists.[18] Second, there can be no doubt that psychotherapy typically encourages a sort of self-focus that is at odds with Christianity's emphasis on self-denial. As Boyd writes, "I view the psychotherapy emphasis on the 'self' as encouraging patients to be more successful in pursuing their self-centered goals, i.e., it promotes the old Adam approach according to which we live in bondage to the flesh."[19] Adams concurs, condemning the popular Rogerian system (de-

---

it functions, along with entertainment, in our society in a way that religion (Christianity in particular) historically has functioned prior to the secular age.

16. Powlison, "Biblical Counseling," 213.

17. Then again, it may not be an overstatement. The history of mental health professions are rife with philosophical speculation and metaphysical commitments. For a particularly engaging account of the question of the scientific status of psychology and its dependence upon ancient philosophy, see Robinson, "Lecture 1: Defining the Subject" and "Lecture 2: Ancient Foundations."

18. Szasz, Professor Emeritus of Psychiatry at the State University of New York, has authored several books and articles questioning the scientific status and its use to control others: Szasz, *The Myth of Mental Illness*; Szasz, *Psychiatry: The Science of Lies*; Szasz, *The Manufacture of Madness*; Szasz, *Coercion as Cure*; Szasz, ed. *The Medicalization of Everyday Life*. See also Schaler, ed. *Szasz Under Fire*. Szasz argues that psychiatry gains power from its perceived scientific status and that that power is sometimes abused (e.g., when persons diagnosed with "mental illness" are hospitalized against their wills for their own good; Szasz sees this as no different from criminal incarceration, but with greater societal consequences). He fears that the power of psychiatry will eventually be used in service of the state: "The more the state empowers doctors, the more physicians will strengthen the state (by authenticating political preferences as health values), and the more the resulting union of medicine and the state will enfeeble the individual (by depriving him of the right to reject interventions classified as therapeutic). If that is the kind of society we want, that is the kind we shall get—and deserve." Szasz, "Mental Illness is Still a Myth," 39.

19. Boyd, "An Insider's Effort," 27. Boyd recounts his own spiritual and professional journey as he sought to understand the soul. He was disappointed by many liberal Christians who did not see the relevance of faith or the Bible for mental health and sur-

veloped by Carl Rogers) because of its client-based discovery approach: "The Rogerian system confirms sinful man's belief that he is autonomous and has no need of God. Conservatives must reject Rogerian counseling on the basis of its humanistic presuppositions alone. It begins with man and it ends with man. Man is his own solution to his problems."[20] Of course, Adams is no more friendly to Freudian, Jungian, or any other secular theories which he sees as suggesting the answer to man's problems are to be found within himself. Third, the resistance within the guild for self-examination and criticism also could be legitimately viewed as bordering on a sort of religious fervor. As noted above, even critics within the secular mental health mainstream (like Szasz) who dare to question the status quo are silenced and/or censored, virtually without a hearing. Such aversion to re-evaluation is more characteristic of religious fundamentalism or political extremism than of legitimate scientific investigation.

Another argument that some proponents of nouthetic counseling make against psychology is that it is not helpful. Some, like Adams, argue that psychotherapy and psychoanalysis have not had good track records of healing and that many of the clinical tests touting their effectiveness are flawed.[21] In fact, even some psychologists have admitted that psychology has not, in itself, been as effective at healing as once supposed. Consider the following quotation from Paul Vitz, professor of Psychology (Emeritus) at New York University, as he reflected upon the humbling of psychology in recent years: ". . . many of the leading enthusiasts for psychology and psychotherapy in the '60s and '70s soon learned what the majority of psychologists have now recognized: that although psychotherapy is helpful, it rarely provides life-transforming insight or happiness. As a result, many psychologists themselves moved off into spirituality and religious experience as a more successful form of healing . . ."[22] Others argue that the erroneous assumptions which serve as the basis for secular psychological

---

prised by secularists who discounted his claims of the efficacy of faith in the healing process. Richard Ganz had a similar experience working at a state mental hospital. When he brought his faith into the counseling sessions and saw success with some patients, he was given the choice to leave his faith at the door, or be fired. He chose the latter and entered into a life-long journey and struggle with integrating his Christian faith with his training in psychology. Ganz, "Confession of a Psychological Heretic," 18–22.

20. Adams, 82.

21. See, for example, Adams, 1–10.

22. Vitz, "Psychology in Recovery," 20.

theories lead them to seek the wrong information or misguide those in need of help. For example, Powlison questions the value of attempting to identify the origins of destructive behavior in one's personal history because it is wrongheaded and it provides no aid in determining how to deal with the problem:

> The fact that a pattern of craving became established many years before—even that it was forged in a particular context, perhaps influenced by bad models or by experiences of being sinned against—only describes what happened and when. The past does not explain why. For example, past rejections do not cause a craving to be accepted by others, any more than current rejections cause that craving. A person who was always accepted by significant others can be just as mastered by the lust for acceptance![23]

He argues that the search is wrongheaded because destructive behavior originates in the sinful nature of the individual, not in an event, and that it is unhelpful to locate the origin because doing so really offers no answer regarding how to change. There are good reasons for both accepting and rejecting Powlison's arguments here. On the one hand, Powlison's basic point that sinful activity originates in the heart of the individual and is not the result of determinative forces outside his control is surely correct, and therefore, the basic answer to the person's problem is faith in Christ, not understanding how the circumstances influenced him to make the wrong decision. On the other hand, Powlison's argument appears to commit him to the erroneous notion that the past event is virtually unrelated to the sin, yet the Apostle Paul seems to argue just the opposite. He suggests that an event can serve as the origin of destructive behavior because if it weren't for the event, that particular natural, God-given desire would not have transformed into destructive behavior. As the Apostle Paul puts it, "Yet if it had not been for the law, I would not have known sin. I would not have known what it is to covet if the law had not said, 'You shall not covet.' But sin, seizing an opportunity through the commandment, produced in me all kinds of covetousness. Apart from the law, sin lies dead." (Rom 7:7b–9). For Paul, the occasion of hearing the law against coveting became the impetus for transforming his natural ability to desire into an unholy covetousness. Thus, the occasion did not create sin, as the sinful nature was there already, but it did serve as the ori-

---

23. Powlison, "The Sufficiency of Scripture to Diagnose," 9.

gin of that particular sinful activity in his life. So locating the originating event of a particular sinful activity may be more helpful than Powlison allows, for it may give the individual some insight into his own spiritual state or weaknesses so that he can address them in an appropriate manner (e.g., prayer, accountability partner, avoidance, etc.).

Sufficiency of Scripture

The most popular theological argument against the use of psychology in a Christian counseling program and, by extension, against Christian endorsement or referral to psychologists, has been based on the principle of the sufficiency of Scripture. Mack's arguments are representative. He begins by first admitting his own suspicion that those who make use of psychology do not believe in the sufficiency of Scripture, but instead see it as deficient in some ways. Relying heavily upon John MacArthur, he goes on to assert that those who believe psychotherapy can help with emotional or mental problems effectively deny both the lordship of Christ and the doctrine of total depravity. These are serious charges, something of which no Christian, evangelical, conservative or liberal, would wish to be guilty! His argument needs to be examined in more detail.

Mack's argument for the sufficiency of Scripture in counseling and his subsequent rejection of Christian use of the findings/teachings of secular psychology is threefold. First, he points to the finitude of man and argues that it necessarily calls into question the adequacy and accuracy of his knowledge. In order to illustrate his point, he makes use of the somewhat tired story of the group of blind men unsuccessfully attempting to ascertain the nature of an elephant. He writes, "Their knowledge of what an elephant was like was restricted and even erroneous because of the limitations of their experience and perception. And so it is and always must be with finite mortal man when it comes to the matter of discerning absolute truth apart from revelation from the living God, who knows all things and sees the whole picture clearly and perfectly."[24] Thus, Mack concludes that any humanly-discovered or developed theory (like those of psychology) must be erroneous. But is Mack's conclusion warranted? It is not, and for several important reasons, it must be rejected.

First, his assertion that finitude necessarily implies error is simply false. Consider mathematical truths (e.g., "1+1=2") or the fundamental

24. Mack, "The Sufficiency of Scripture," 72.

laws of logic (e.g., principle of identity; principle of non-contradiction; principle of excluded middle). They were discovered by pagans, but are nevertheless true. Perhaps Mack could argue that they were discovered by means of general revelation or more properly, by means of common grace, but this is the very argument made by integrationists regarding the truths of secular psychology which most nouthetic counseling proponents reject! Similarly, as we will see, Mack seems disinclined to allow non-Christian discovery of truth in any form. It is true that all knowledge gained by human intellect is provisional or tentative, but as I often note to my theology students, even doctrine falls into this category! An evangelical doctrine of revelation views Scripture as Revelation but rejects Doctrine as Revelation (the Catholic perspective). Thus, we affirm that the biblical text is inerrant while admitting that the doctrines derived from that text are not, but this is not to say they are therefore in error. Quite the contrary, I believe the doctrines of the Trinity, two-natures of Christ, etc., are all correct, though not inerrant in the technical theological sense. Ultimately, this is due to the fact that Scripture is inspired by God, but doctrine and tradition are not; or more properly, the authors of Scripture were inspired, while the developers of doctrine and tradition were not. The important point here, though, is that a humanly-constructed idea can still be true.

Second, Mack's implied "levels of truth" is incoherent. He seems to suggest that there are different levels of truth or different kinds of truths when he refers to an "absolute truth," but truth is a property that a proposition either has or does not have. It is not *partially* true or *absolutely* true. We use these phrases colloquially, but a moment's reflection will reveal that they simply do not make sense. A statement of a factual nature is either true or false. It is correct to designate the truth of a statement as either contingent or necessary, but that is a different matter. What Mack seems to have in mind is a sort of distinction of truthfulness, similar to the idea, "God's truth" versus "man's truth," but this is nonsense. Truth is truth, period.

Third, as has already been hinted, Mack's line of reasoning is not only erroneous, it is dangerous to evangelical commitments, for it is identical to arguments proffered against the doctrine of biblical inerrancy by liberal and neo-orthodox scholars. For example, Karl Barth argued that identifying the Bible with the Word of God was tantamount to a supplanting and rejection of the living Word of God, Jesus Christ. He saw such accolades (i.e., inerrancy) as idolatrous because the Bible was written by fallible men: ". . . the prophets and apostles as such, even in their office, even in their function as witnesses, even in the act of writing down their witness, were real, historical men as we are, and therefore sinful in their action, and capable and actually guilty of error in their spoken and written word."[25] He continued to argue that the sinfulness and fallibility of the human authors of Scripture make it a fallible product, but that complete accuracy is not necessary:

> To the bold postulate, that if their word is to be the Word of God they must be inerrant in every word, we oppose the even bolder assertion, that according to the scriptural witness about man, which applies to them too, they can be at faulty in any word, and have been at faulty in every word, and yet according to the same scriptural witness, being justified and sanctified by grace alone, they have still spoken the Word of God in their fallible and erring human word.[26]

Evangelical and fundamentalist scholars have continually demonstrated the faulty logic underlying the rejection.[27]

Fourth, taken at face value, Mack's assertion should lead the Christian to doubt a whole host of truths he holds dear, for man's (finite) intellect is used in the hermeneutical and theological task. As indicated above, Protestants have continually rejected the notion that doctrine or tradition is inspired. If divine inspiration is a requirement for truthfulness, then our doctrines must be rejected. Similarly, it is doubtful that Mack would claim inspiration along the lines of the biblical authors for himself, MacArthur, Adams, Powlison, or other biblical counseling proponents in their biblical interpretation. Thus, Mack's argument is self-defeating, for the biblical principles for counseling which Mack upholds as correct are influenced by man's finite intellect. Under Mack's interpretation, though, we ought to question those principles. Of course, this is not what he means to say and therefore, this particular argument must be rejected.

The second aspect of Mack's argument against the incorporation of secular psychology is related to the doctrine of total depravity. According to Mack, the noetic effects of the Fall make unredeemed man's insights and interpretations of human behavior erroneous, distorted, and self-

---

25. Barth, *Doctrine of the Word of God*, §19.2.4, 529.

26. Ibid., 529–30.

27. For example, see Lewis, "Human Authorship Scripture," 229–64.

seeking: "Scripture teaches that the minds of unredeemed men have been adversely affected by sin and, as a result, even if they observe something accurately, they are likely to interpret it wrongly."[28] Mack goes on to correctly note that Scripture serves as the standard for evaluating truth, but he takes this to mean that we "are not able to ascertain truth apart from Divine revelation."[29] This seems to be an odd statement, for the reasons already given. To be fair, Mack is here specifically addressing the understanding of man and his problems, but his arguments are presented in such a sweeping manner that he appears to believe they apply to all knowledge. In fact, later in the same article, Mack (drawing upon Richard Pratt) even rejects the notion that non-Christians can arrive at truth.[30] Nevertheless, the important point for our purposes is his claim that secular psychological theories were developed by persons whose motives were improper. Thus, the theories themselves are flawed because of a flawed goal and philosophical basis. This claim has an initial theological attractiveness that cannot easily be dismissed, especially since the issues at stake have a spiritual aspect to them. The comparison above related to mathematics and logic, but psychology is different; it has to do with the care of the soul, and this seems to be the real concern of nouthetic counselors. Thus, this argument merits further consideration.

The claim is that the Fall so adversely affected the way unredeemed man thinks that he is incapable of pure or holy motives; that all of his thoughts, ideas, schemes, etc., serve his own selfish, sinful purposes. At their base, those purposes are an exaltation of self over God. Thus, unredeemed man's attempts to understand human problems and his prescriptions for fixing them have as their basis the lordship of self. Secular

---

28. Mack, 75.

29. Ibid., 75.

30. Mack seems to argue that, since the goal of the knowledge-attainment (of non-Christians) is not God-honoring or selfless, the knowledge gained is somehow tainted and therefore, false. For example, Mack writes, "Extrabiblical statements that seem to reflect biblical truth must be regarded as false because, as Richard Pratt states, 'They are not the result of voluntary obedience to God's revelation. . . .'" Ibid., 76. It is difficult to see how one could take this, at least broadly construed, seriously, since many facts have been discovered for spurious or selfish means. In fact, much scientific progress has been made with a view to serving mammon. There is no connection between the truth of a finding and the motivation for discovering it; rather, there may be a connection between the methods chosen for discovery or the interpretation of the findings, and it may be the case that selfishness or greed or a secular worldview will lead a scientist into error, but it is not necessarily the case.

psychology simply has a false goal and basis, and therefore ends with erroneous conclusions and methods. Johnson, an integrationist, is sympathetic to this argument, and admits that most integrationists have ignored the antithesis of Christian and secular worldviews as they manifest themselves in this area. He also candidly admits that many integrationists have failed to think deeply about the theological implications of the positions they take and calls upon Christian counselors to find "greater intellectual independence from modernity and greater interpretive sophistication" in order to truly integrate theology and counseling theory.[31]

Still, Johnson also correctly points out that an over-emphasis on antithesis to the detriment of creation grace (common grace) can lead to problems as well. In fact, he argues that ignoring creation grace (as nouthetic counselors tend to) denies glory to God because non-Christians will not glorify Him for the truths they discover by common grace: "This is perhaps the most important reason why Christians in psychology and counseling should be eager to discover the genuine truth and goodness available in non-Christian psychology: to claim it for the God to whom it belongs and rejoice in him for his remarkable goodness and wisdom."[32] Additionally, Johnson warns against the tendency of some who over-emphasize antithesis to become judgmental or to cause strife within the church. He advises that Christians within the counseling field expend less energy fighting one another over these issues and instead focus on their own struggles with sinful attitudes and motivations.[33]

Third, Mack argues that the Bible clearly states that God has given us everything we need for living and godliness, and moves to examine three passages of Scripture. He first turns to Psalm 19:7–11, and argues that the text makes claims for the Bible that no one would make for the ideas of man. He points out that the passage describes the Bible as perfect, sure, containing right precepts, authoritative, clean, enduring, and providing

31. Johnson, *Foundations for Soul Care*, 106. Johnson faults the training Christian psychologists have received; they have been given either one course in theology with little attention to how it integrates with practice, or they have received no theological training at all! He writes, "What has dogged the integration movement over the past forty years is the fact that psychology education in American requires the mastery of complex modern psychology texts and offers little to no help training people how to read them *as Christians*, with one's worldview highly salient, so the texts can be interpreted in light of the antithesis [noetic effects of the Fall], for example." Ibid., 103.

32. Ibid., 115.

33. Ibid., 116.

insight, and then concludes: "Believing as I do in the inspiration and inerrancy and authority of the Scriptures, Ps 19:7–11 settles the sufficiency issue for me. If words mean anything, how could I come to any other conclusion?"[34] Mack then turns to 2 Timothy 3:14–17 to argue for the "total adequacy of God's Word," and outlines the claims of Paul for the text: holy, unique, powerful, and inspired.[35] He highlights the utility of Scripture for reproof and correction, noting, ". . . it is the instrument the Holy Spirit uses to point us in the right direction and correct our sinful thoughts, motives, feelings, actions, and speech."[36] He then points out that, according to verse 17, the Holy Spirit uses Scripture to equip believers to do everything he wants them to do, concluding that those desires include understanding people, their problems, and how to resolve them. Turning to the Apostle Peter's second epistle (God has given Christians all they need for life and godliness; 2 Pet 1:3–10), Mack points to the new life we have in Christ and the new nature we receive in Christ, and argues that they necessarily imply our sufficiency in Christ. Mack takes this to mean that Christians receive a new nature with new desires, dispositions, interests, etc., and thereby have the capacity to overcome the sinful nature which leads to emotional or mental problems, and grow in faith, knowledge, self-control, perseverance, etc.: "Peter declared that these divine resources become ours through the true knowledge of God and of Jesus our Lord and through the medium of His precious and magnificent promises (2 Pet 1:2–4). In other words, the repository of the *everything* we need for life and godliness is found in our glorious and excellent God and His precious and magnificent word (2 Pet 1:2–4)."[37] Mack concludes that, because the Bible clearly teaches its own sufficiency two things follow: first, those who deny it (with respect to counseling) actually deny inerrancy and second, secular psychology has nothing to offer.

This argument is a favorite of nouthetic counseling proponents because it appears so obvious and intuitive. After all, what Bible-believing Christian would wish to deny the sufficiency of Scripture? Still, a further investigation will reveal several problems with this line of argument. The most glaring is that most proponents do not really construct an *argument*

---

34. Mack, 78.

35. Ibid., 79.

36. Ibid., 80.

37. Ibid., 81.

for their position, but instead assume that all reasonable readers of the biblical text (who are not blinded by the power of sin) will just agree with their interpretation and applications of the text to the question of the appropriateness of Christian use of findings from secular psychology, psychiatry, and other mental/behavior health fields. Take, for example, John MacArthur who, in an article discussing Psalm 19 and the sufficiency of Scripture, makes a similar point to that of Mack [that those who go outside of Scripture for knowledge of the soul are denying the sufficiency of God's Word]. While MacArthur admits that verse 1–6 discuss natural revelation, he maintains that verses 7–9 address special revelation and its sufficiency, and it is here where he focuses. Commenting on verse 7 ("The law of the Lord is perfect, restoring the soul"), MacArthur claims that it refers to the teaching of the Bible regarding creed character, and conduct, in contrast to "the imperfect, flawed reasonings and instructions of men."[38] It is unclear where MacArthur (and Mack) finds such a contrast, for it is not in the text. Rather, the flow of the Psalm is from general revelation's proclamation of the glory, majesty, power and work of God (vss. 1–6), to special revelation's perfection, righteousness, value, and usefulness (vss. 7–11), to the specific request of the psalmist for divine protection from, and strength to overcome, his own sinful proclivities (vss. 12–14). There is no mention of the thought processes of humans in the psalm. It could be argued, and is likely the case, that there is a direct connection between one's procurement/reception of the divine protection/enablement to conquer sin and his facility with God's Word. However, this is not the sort of contrast to which MacArthur refers. Thus, it appears that he has inserted a contrast into the psalm which is not present in order to make a point about the weakness of human reason and insight. Unfortunately, the rest of his explication of the psalm follows this approach. While it may be too strong to charge MacArthur with eisegesis, the point is that his argument certainly goes beyond the words (and arguably, the intent) of the passage.[39]

38. MacArthur, "Biblical Counseling," 12. Powlison commits some of the same errors. While his article begins with a brief discussion of 2 Timothy 3:15–17, he quickly moves away from discussion of the text and the sufficiency of Scripture, to a critique of secular psychology's anthropology. Powlison, "The Sufficiency of Scripture to Diagnose," 2–14.

39. To suggest that MacArthur has gone beyond the intent of the passage is to make *some* claim regarding our knowledge of what the psalmist meant to communicate. Obviously, there are limits to our knowledge an it is *possible* that as the psalmist contemplated the richness and glory of God's revelation, he set up a contrast with human ideas and knowledge in his own mind. The problem is, we cannot know, and there is no

So the point of Psalm 19 is not to undermine or denigrate human thought, human-discovered ideas or truths, or anything of the sort, but rather to proclaim the glory of God, His Word, and its usefulness and value in our lives, particularly with respect to the constant struggle with sin. God's holy Word has a sanctifying power, both in the way it reveals sin to us and in the way it transforms our hearts' desires.[40] These truths, though, do nothing to call into question Christian use of truths discovered by psychology, psychiatry, and other mental health professions, assuming there are some truths to be found.

MacArthur makes the same error in his discussion of Second Timothy 3:16: after stating that the verse addresses both inspiration and sufficiency and quoting it, he simply assumes that it settles the question in favor of nouthetic counseling and against psychology. He writes, "There is no spiritual need that is not met in Scripture. There is no necessary resource that is not supplied there. No right teaching, reproof, correction, or training with regard to spiritual matters is possible apart from the all-sufficient Word of God. Let's not let that great reality be swept away by the fads and clamoring of an ungodly age."[41] To be fair, MacArthur seems to be concerned with a whole range of trends and activities he sees in churches, many of which are admittedly disturbing to say the least. His basic complaint is that pastors and churches seem to be turning to the secular world and secular wisdom for answers to questions of a spiritual and ecclesiological nature. In addition to his concerns about the use of psychology in pastoral counseling, he also expresses frustration at the importing of business models into church administration (in preference to developing a biblical doctrine of the Church). Thus, his complaint seems to be the superseding of Scriptural truth with secular ideology.

Thus, while MacArthur expresses doubts about the value of psychology and psychotherapy and has serious concern about the worldview underpinning the study of psychology, his real complaint seems to be that Christian counseling or psychology is really no different from its secular counterparts.[42] But MacArthur's criticisms do not seem fair to those

---

indication in the text that he did so.

40. It should go without saying that these ministries are conducted in conjunction with the ministry of the Holy Spirit in one's life.

41. MacArthur, 12.

42. While MacArthur points out that psychology theory is based upon "atheistic and evolutionary presuppositions," and that this should give Christians pause in consider-

Integrationists who do seek to honor God's Word and who acknowledge the deleterious effects of sin upon human emotional and psychological development. Similarly, his proclamation that the Bible is sufficient for addressing all spiritual matters does not necessarily undercut the value of training in psychology for counseling effectiveness. There are many integrationists who do not deny the sufficiency of the Bible, but nevertheless also argue that if truth (regarding spiritual or psychological care) can be found elsewhere, it should be utilized. The Bible is a test for exclusion—that is, if something discovered by natural means conflicts with biblical truth, then it should be rejected—but it is not a test for inclusion (i.e., if the Bible does not address it, then it must be wrong or erroneous).

Here is the problem: the Bible often addresses the broad issue without specifically identifying how one moves beyond it. All Christian counselors agree that the Bible presents salvation in Christ as the beginning point for healing and that the sanctifying work of the Holy Spirit moves persons toward emotional/psychological healing, but most of us also admit that there are some practical steps we can take in dealing with temptations that are not always addressed specifically in the Bible. Integrationists argue that sometimes there is not a single answer to a complex problem, because humans are complex creatures with a variety of factors influencing behavior and psychology can be helpful in identifying those factors. For example, Brister argues that psychology can be useful to theology, particularly with respect to empirical research related to personality development and human relations. He writes,

> Pyschology's services to Christian caregivers are being increasingly recognized, investigated, and verified. Personality scientists have developed varied instruments for data measurement and testing, and for exploring the development neuroses, and growth of personality. . . . Studies are being conducted in areas of mutual interest to theology and psychology, such as: faith development, value formation, gender issues, vocational concerns, parenting, guilt and forgiveness, prejudice, spirituality, aging, and grief work.

---

ing it veracity and value, he makes it clear that many who claim to engage in Christian counseling do nothing of the sort: "The sad truth is 'Christian' psychology offers nothing distinctively Christian . . . the psychology that has taken evangelicalism by storm is nothing more than Freudianism disguised with spiritual imagery or re-packaged with sprinklings of Christian terminology." Ibid., 13. MacArthur goes on to point out that some Christian counselors have even admitted that their approach to counseling is not different from that of secular psychologists.

Christian ministers will be wise to observe these distinctions and varied resources when referring to theories of personality.[43]

An example may be instructive. Consider a person with a problem with drunkenness. Clearly, the Bible states that such a disposition is sinful, but it does not give clear guidance for how to avoid it. Of course, one option (advocated in my own denomination) is abstinence (Prov 31), but this is not *the* biblical answer, for there are times when alcohol consumption is recommended (Num 15:7, 10; Deut 14:23; 1 Tim 5:23). Laying aside discussion of the relative strength of alcohol consumed in the Ancient Near East, the point here is that the best approach for avoidance of drunkenness will depend on the individual. If alcoholism can be proven to have genetic roots, then persons with a genetic makeup that predisposes them to alcoholism would do well to avoid alcohol altogether. Others, though, may not have such a physical predisposition, and other factors are at play with their problem. Training in psychology and personality development may help a counselor to identify the underlying desires, fears, dispositions, etc., which contribute to an individual's proclivity toward this particular sin. Just saying, "Don't do it!," while correct, is not as helpful as guiding the individual to see why he drinks as he does.

Nevertheless, nouthetic counseling advocates may argue that the very processes of these studies are defective since the models which undergird them are anti-Christian. This, however, is exceedingly difficult to prove, as none have explained what a *Christian* scientific method looks like; e.g., how a Christian examination of personality development will differ from a secular examination of personality development. It seems that the differences are found in the interpretation of the data, not the collection of the data themselves. Thus, it seems that Christians should support psychological study and engage their secular counterparts on the significance of the findings.

Criticisms of Nouthetic Counseling

Other criticisms of nouthetic counseling have been offered. Some integrationists have criticized nouthetic counseling for its approach, fearing that it may lead to unhealthy relationships in the church. Clinebell argues that it "encourages authoritarian advice giving" on the part of pastors and counselors, which can "increase counselees' dependency and block spiri-

43. Brister, *Pastoral Care*, 64.

tual maturity."[44] He also complains that the nouthetic approach stifles the work of the Holy Spirit in the counselee's life because he is not trained to hear the voice of God and discern His will for himself, but is instead confronted with his own supposed sins and then pushed "by the use of scripture, to conform to a legalistic and literalistic understanding of the teachings of the Bible."[45] While Clinebell's critique has some merit with regard to the way nouthetic counseling *can* be utilized, it is largely based on a caricature of the approach. For example, he charges Adams with "moral reductionism" which sees "all psychological problems to sin and irresponsible living." This, of course, is an oversimplification of Adams' position, which does claim that many problems are the result of personal sin, but also claims that some are the result of sin's entry into the world (i.e., the Fall). Still, Clinebell's concerns are not completely without merit (especially with regard to the application of the nouthetic approach), and those chaplains who use it should be aware of these dangers, but there is also no necessary connection between following a nouthetic approach and experiencing the problems cited. Self-awareness and care on the part of the chaplain is in order.

Carter has criticized the nouthetic emphasis on actions, charging that it denies fundamental aspects of the human person, that it stems from a deficient view of the image of God, and ironically, that it does not take sin or the Fall seriously. He first complains that Adams' approach virtually ignores the inner or emotional component of man; that it does not take the biblical concepts of soul, spirit, and heart seriously, at least with respect to how they impact one's emotional life: "In contrast to Adams' external behavioral orientation, Jesus focuses on the heart and makes this inner aspect fundamental."[46] In response, Ganz has charged that it is Carter's anthropology which is defective because it suggests a dualism in which inner (emotional, psychological) and outer (actions) are disparate as if studying the emotional component will yield information different from a study of actions. He argues that nouthetic counselors do not deny the heart, but believe that actions are reflective of the heart. In addition, Ganz avers that beginning with the heart, rather than actions, is not helpful because only God can know the heart, and it is deceitful. He further

44. Clinebell, *Basic Types of Pastoral Care*, 127.

45. Ibid., 127.

46. Carter, "Adams' Theory," 152.

argues that Jesus' interest in the heart is always tied to commandment keeping; that Jesus connected the heart condition to outward actions.[47] It seem here that the differences are related more to method or emphasis than actual disagreement on theological grounds. Both nouthetic counselors and integrationists agree that actions follow the emotional and psychological state. The disagreement seems to be over where to begin the healing process and over the counselors primary function—listen, or teach/direct.

Carter argues that Adams' view of the *imago dei* seems to be overly concerned with dominion. The external focus of Adams' counseling theory leads him to see man's fundamental problem as conflict with the environment. This criticism may be justified, as reformed theology, especially when combined with a postmillennial eschatology, can tend to highlight the rulership aspect of the *imago dei,* while de-emphasizing the relational and representative aspects.[48] Nevertheless, to be fair, Adams is not concerned with developing a complete anthropology, but rather is merely addressing specific issues as they relate to his primary concern— the Christian minister's right, ability, and obligation to provide biblically informed and based counseling.

Carter also sees the nouthetic emphasis on activity as problematic for a healthy hamartiology. Surprisingly, he argues that Adams denies the sinful nature and holds to a Pelagian anthropology. By this, he seems to mean that Adams' focus on changing activity leaves the impression that counselees need only *decide* to change their activities to be in conformity with God's Word: "The whole of Adams' emphasis is that all man needs to do is reorganize his bad habits by changing his mind (with the aid of the Spirit to effect this change); man's sinful nature and any of its psychological consequences are not discussed as sources of problems and neither is

---

47. Ganz, "Nouthetic Counseling Defended," 199–201. Carter wrote a response to Ganz's article. In it, he clarifies some of his earlier points, and lays out some further criticisms of Adams and Ganz. See Carter, "A Reply to Ganz," 206–216. One argument that seems to have some substance is that nouthetic proponents have not used their biblical model for personality theory. Some have attempted to remedy this deficiency with mixed success. See Hindson, "Toward a Christian Theory of Personality," 11–31.

48. This overemphasis is most evident in the Reconstructionist movement as epitomized in the writings of Chilton, Rushdoony, North, and Bahnsen. See for example, Chilton, *Paradise Restored;* Rushdoony, *Institutes of Biblical Law;* North, *Theonomy;* Bahnsen, *By This Standard.*

the New Testament concept of *flesh* with its connections to sin."[49] Carter has surely overstated the case in referring to Adams' theory as *Pelagian*, as it is clearly more comfortable in Reformed circles than not. Adams (and most other nouthetic counselors) has repeatedly highlighted man's inability in and of himself, to do good and overcome his destructive sinful activity. The beginning and basis of healing is salvation in Christ and the consequent work of the Holy Spirit. However, Carter has touched on one important consideration—the question of complete psychological healing in this life.

Protestant theologians have long struggled with the question of the relationship between sanctification and the sinful nature after regeneration, but prior to glorification. Generally speaking, those from the reformed traditions have emphasized man's inability to do good and have tended to focus on the struggle with sin in this life, even for Christians. Those from the Wesleyan and Pentecostal traditions have emphasized the sanctifying work and indwelling of the Holy Spirit and have tended to focus on the victory Christians presently have in Christ. Both groups, of course, acknowledge the truth of both concepts, as they can be found in the writings of the Apostle Paul; he seems to express frustration at his own failings in action, but at the same time speaks of the perfection we have through faith in Christ and the power we have in the Spirit. Consider his words in his letter to the Galatians. In chapter five, he chastises those who believe salvation can be obtained through obedience to the Torah and goes on to note their inability to follow all of the law. He then admonishes the Galatian Christians to live by the Spirit so that they "will not gratify the desires of the sinful nature" (5:16). Yet, he then suggests that they will not be able to live by the Spirit, because the Spirit and the sinful nature "are in conflict with one another" so that they "do not do what you [they] want" (5:17). Nevertheless, he again encourages his readers to "keep in step with the Spirit" (5:25) so they will bear the fruit of the Spirit, avoid the acts of the sinful nature, and fulfill the law by loving their neighbors. Whether Paul sees this as a real possibility or simply an unattainable goal to be nevertheless strived for, is unclear. The point here, of course, is not to settle the question of Paul's commitment to perfectionism or sanctification prior to glorification, but rather to point out that nouthetic counseling, which is generally rooted in reformed theology, seems to have

49. Carter, "Adams' Theory," 150.

a greater emphasis on sanctification than most reformed movements. There are times when reading nouthetic counseling literature that I have thought I was reading something from a charismatic group. This emphasis may be seen as a strength or a weakness, depending on the theological position of the reader.

Conclusion

What does all this mean? Certainly, there are good reasons to question some of the claims of nouthetic counselors. The sufficiency of Scripture argument, while seemingly strong, does not really undermine the use of extra-biblical material and is therefore, unpersuasive. Similarly, the claims by nouthetic counselors that psychology and psychiatry have perpetrated abuses and are based in secular, ungodly philosophy can be sustained, but it does not follow that all information which comes from these areas of study is false. The integrationist claim that common grace can lead even secular theorists to find truth is both reasonable and theologically valid; psychology and psychiatry may (and probably do) include truth and Christians should make use of it. While the loving thing to do in some cases is to confront others with their error, this is not always the case, though it is hard to tell if any proponents of nouthetic counseling would agree. Clearly, there are some legitimate concerns with the way the nouthetic approach can be abused. However, the nouthetic counseling movement has also made some significant contributions to Christian counseling.

First and most importantly, the biblical counseling movement has heralded the importance of theological reflection and biblical exegesis on the part of Christian counselors. Being a counselor who happens to be Christian is not enough. Rather, Christian counselors should think theologically and biblically, and allow their personal relationships with God to impact the counseling endeavor. They should train themselves to view their work and analysis through a biblical worldview.

Second, not only should Christian counselors think theologically and biblically, but they should evaluate the claims and processes they use for theological fidelity and truth. This involves not only scrutinizing overt claims or ideas, but also tracing implications of philosophies and theories in order to identify the theology and worldview underlying them. If any are found to necessarily conflict with biblical truth, they should be jettisoned.

Third, the biblical counseling movement reinvigorated pastors and laypersons for the work of Christian counseling. It has helped reverse the trend of a perceived need for professional help for all counseling services, and has emboldened local parish pastors to provide care for the soul. This was the basic point of Adams' *Competent to Counsel*, and the return of Christian advice and counseling to the purview of the local church is to be applauded and welcomed.

Fourth, biblical counseling has made it clear that it may be appropriate, at times, to direct the individual counselee in action. There are times when it is proper to admonish him, or to chastise, confront, or challenge him, particularly if there is unconfessed sin in his life. Christian counselors have too long shied away from this responsibility. The call of the nouthetic approach is a call to biblical accountability relationships within the church.

Fifth, the nouthetic approach has caused many in the Christian counseling community to rethink personal responsibility and emotional problems. In a culture which teaches its citizens to blame others for their own problems, the nouthetic approach offers a clarion call to accept responsibility for one's own mistakes and sins. Such an acceptance and recognition stands at the heart of the gospel, for saving faith requires recognition of one's own guilt and culpability for sin. It is only upon this recognition and acknowledgement that one can truly accept the forgiveness that comes through God's grace by means of Christ's substitutionary death on the cross. Saving faith requires admission and confession of one's personal sin.

All of this should lead Christian chaplains to feel free to refer some of the tough cases to the combat stress control team. Some persons seem literally incapable of listening or responding to the counseling that chaplains are equipped to provide. Even Adams admits this. As noted at the beginning of the chapter, I have found it somewhat of a relief to have that option, but I have been blessed to have Christians (who I came to know as faithful followers) serving as the mental health professionals for our unit. However, it should also lead Christian chaplains to take care, lest they refer too quickly. The Christian chaplain has a duty and obligation to care for the souls of those personnel entrusted (by God) to him, and he ought to do everything within his power to help the afflicted to find peace in Christ. The examination of the controversy in Christian counseling should have a sobering effect on all Christian chaplains; we have a responsibility with regard to counseling, and we should make sure that we only refer when we feel the individual would truly be better off—better off emotionally, psychologically, and most importantly, spiritually.

CRITICAL INCIDENT STRESS MANAGEMENT

Critical Incident Stress Management (hereafter CISM) is an approach to psychological intervention following a traumatic event. The developers of this program are Jeffrey T. Mitchell and George Everly, who saw a need to address the psychological responses of emergency workers following extraordinarily traumatic events. CISM is meant to serve as a total approach to emergency mental health after a crisis situation. Consider the following definition: "CISM is a comprehensive crisis intervention system consisting of multiple crisis intervention components which functionally span the entire temporal spectrum of a crisis. CISM interventions range from the pre-crisis phase through the acute crisis phase, and into the post-crisis phase. CISM is also considered comprehensive in that it consists of interventions which may be applied to individuals, small functional groups, large groups, families, organizations, and even entire communities."[50] The CISM toolbox includes a variety of interventions which may be used at various stages of healing/response following a traumatic event: Defusing (immediately following the event; very short meeting with those involved); Demobilizations (at the event site for emergency workers; to calm down and receive information); Crisis Management Briefings (public; to put out information and manage perceptions in community); Debriefings (after some time, with target groups at various levels of engagement; longer meeting and more in-depth than Defusing), etc. While it does deal with psychological issues, proponents are clear that CISM should not be confused with psychotherapy or as a replacement for in-depth, one-on-one counseling with a mental health professional.[51]

The Army has found CISM to be a great tool and, working with Mitchell, Everly, and the International Critical Incident Stress Foundation (ICISF), developed its own pared-down version known as Trained Crisis Responder (TCR) training. All chaplains are encouraged to become

50. Flanney and Everly, "Crisis Intervention: A Review," 121.

51. See, for example, Everly, "Emergency Mental Health," 3–7. In the article, Everly provides a helpful table juxtaposing crisis intervention and psychotherapy on nine key items: context, timing, location, duration, provider's role, strategic foci, temporal focus, patient expectation, and goals.

certified in TCR or CISM I and CISM II training.[52] Thus, there is a sense in which chaplains who are theologically opposed to psychology have no choice but to get this sort of training. However, as already noted, CISM is not psychotherapy and much of the training involves simple techniques for guiding discussion. Nevertheless, there are issues associated with the implementation of CISM that chaplains ought to consider prior to its use.

One of the pragmatic difficulties of utilizing CISM in the military is associated with the vague nature of definitions for critical incidents. For example, Flannery and Everly see a critical incident as "any stressor event that has the potential to lead to a crisis response in many individuals. More specifically, the critical incident may be thought of as the stimulus that sets the stage for the crisis response."[53] Similarly, Everly and Mitchell define it as "an event which is outside the usual range of experience and challenges one's ability to cope. . . . [It] has the potential to lead to a crisis by overwhelming one's usual psychological defenses and coping mechanisms."[54] These representative definitions show that identifying exactly what a critical incident is and which events count as such can be terribly difficult and somewhat subjective. This difficulty is exacerbated by the combat environment, where seemingly every event is (or at least has the potential to be) a critical incident. Commanders are increasingly being trained to call upon chaplains to intervene after members of their units experience traumatic events such as helicopter crashes, automobile accidents, IED incidents, enemy attacks or even combat deaths. There is a danger here, though, in that the vague nature of critical incidents can lead to an overuse of CISM. This can reduce its effectiveness, waste valuable resources, or even impede the soldiers' natural psychological healing.

In order to guard against this problem, chaplains ought to establish policies and guidelines with unit commanders regarding when defusing or debriefings should be required and when other forms of counseling or care can be requested. Everly has addressed the general issue of premature crisis intervention and suggests two strategies for prevention: (1) clear delineation of what a crisis is for the particular persons involved

52. It is important to note that TCR courses are not only for chaplains, as soldiers from a variety of MOSs are encouraged to attend in order for units to have more resources to respond to a traumatic event. See Everly et. al., *National Guard TCR Course,* esp. v-vi.

53. Flannery and Everly, 119.

54. Everly and Mitchell, "The Debriefing 'Controversy,'" 212.

in the incident, and (2) recognition that crisis intervention (specifically CISM) is not a rigid step-by-step process, but involves some measure of psychological evaluation by the mental health worker or chaplain. That is, while a CISM team may be mobilized by the occurrence of a potentially traumatizing event, that team is not obligated to use CISM: ". . . the direct implementation of crisis intervention tactics is predicated upon evidence of human distress and/or dysfunction, not merely the occurrence of an event (critical incident). . . . not everyone exposed to a traumatic event develops PTSD."[55] For example, it could be SOP [Standing Operating Procedure] that any group involved in an enemy attack (direct combat, sniper, IED, etc.) the first 30 days in country, or which has a casualty any time during the tour, will participate in a defusing and debriefing. After that, it may be wise to mobilize a CISM team every time an enemy attack occurs, but the CISM facilitator (e.g., chaplain) will determine if any emergency mental health intervention is needed. The policies and procedures will need to be tailored to the unit and the operational tempo that it experiences during deployment.

Criticisms of CISM

While the Army has enthusiastically embraced CISM for use with soldiers and as a tool for chaplains and commanders to increase combat effectiveness, it is not without its critics. Some opponents of CISM question whether it really differs from its progenitor, Critical Incident Stress Debriefing which, as noted earlier, has been incorporated into CISM as one aspect or part. For example, Devilly and Cotton charge that even Everly and Mitchell cannot distinguish the two, pointing out that in articles touting the effectiveness of CISM, they cite studies in which only CISD is utilized. They also complain of confusion over terminology in the literature and demand clarification.[56] In response, Mitchell admits that in the early years of CISM's development, there was confusion over

---

55. Everly, "Five Principles of Crisis Intervention," 2.

56. Devilly and Cotton, "Psychological Debriefing," 144–50. Devilly and Cotton further question the sincerity of Everly's and Mitchell's claim that CISD was never meant to function as a stand-alone treatment, but was designed to be part of a larger, broader-based crisis intervention care approach: "It is difficult to see how this can be the case since the term CISM did not even enter the debriefing lexicon until the mid-1990s and CISD was advocated as a method for mitigating the effects of trauma back in the early 1980s." Ibid., 145.

terminology because CISD was frequently used as both a generic term for what was later to develop into CISM, and a specific term for the debriefing process that he and Everly advocate as a part of a larger traumatic intervention program.[57] The important point, though, is that a broad, far-reaching program which includes group discussion and debriefing was always a part of their treatment plan, even though it was called Critical Incident Stress Debriefing.[58] Lack of clarity is not the only critique of CISM. In fact, there are four main complaints leveled against it: (1) It is unnecessary; (2) It has not been proven to be valuable; (3) It may actually cause harm rather than bring healing; and (4) It has a questionable ethical practices associated with it. Each of these will be commented on, if only briefly.

First, some critics argue that immediate intervention is not necessary for most people; that CISM or similar emergency mental health interventions do not really help persons heal emotionally after a traumatizing event. It seems that all agree that most persons exposed to a traumatic event experience some of a broad array of emotional and/or psychological responses in the weeks following the event. Numbness, dissociative amnesia, avoidance behavior, insomnia, irritability, desensitization, and reduced awareness of one's environment are just some examples of such responses.[59] However, there is also ample evidence to suggest that most people who exhibit some signs of post-traumatic stress disorder heal over time; that there is a natural flow from initial protective responses to reduced PTSD symptoms, to emotional and psychological recovery in victims.[60] At least one controlled random study of soldiers returning from

57. Mitchell, "Response to Devilly and Cotton," 25. Mitchell accepts much of the blame for the confusion, but notes that corrections have appeared in CISM workbooks and in the scholarly literature on the subject since 1998. He also maintains that the change in terminology was not engendered due to, as Devilly and Cotton argue, mounting evidence against the effectiveness of CISD. Instead, he claims that the idea of an overall, far-reaching program which included group intervention at various stages was in the ideas presented from the very beginning. For another detailed response to Devilly and Cotton, see Robinson, "Counterbalancing Misrepresentations," 29–34.

58. Richards, "Critical Incident Stress Debriefing Versus Critical Incident Stress Management," 351–62.

59. See, for example, Cardena and Spiegel, "Dissociative Reactions," 474–78; Sloan, "Post-traumatic Stress in Survivors," 211–19.

60. See Bryant, "Acute Stress Disorder," 15–34. Studies of victims of violent crimes, those most likely to develop PTSD, show that healing comes naturally over time. In one study, 94% of rape victims displayed symptoms of PTSD within two weeks of the assault, but the rate dropped to 47% by the eleventh week. Rothbaum, et. al., "Post-traumatic

a Peacekeeping mission in Kosovo seemed to reveal that CISD is not appreciably more helpful in preventing PTSD symptoms than allowing persons involved in traumatic events to manage their own emotional care. However, the authors of the study also note that those soldiers involved in CISD rated it as highly helpful to them personally, and that it did not seem to lead to any adverse effects.[61] If it is the case that emotional healing following a traumatic event comes naturally, then the effectiveness, value, and necessity of immediate intervention (e.g., CISM) is called into question, or as Fawzy and Gray have suggested, it at least demands that some controlled studies on the effectiveness of CISM (versus a lack of intervention) be conducted. "Given that nearly all survivors exposed to a PTE experience significant distress acutely, followed by dramatic symptom reductions over time, suggests that the use of control groups in debriefing studies is absolutely essential."[62] This leads to another criticism of Critical Incident Stress Management: its lack of validation for its efficacy.

Second, some critics of CISM charge that it has never been proven to be of value and that the literature in support of CISM is flawed. For example, Fawzy and Gray note that it is difficult to find any controlled studies of the effectiveness of CISM. In fact, they could only locate one article supporting the efficacy of CISM, a meta-analysis presented by a group of researchers who included one of the co-founders of ICISF.[63] While Fawzy and Gray do not mean to suggest corruption or deception on the part of the researchers, they do claim that more broadly recognized and

---

Stress Disorder in Rape Victims," 455–75. In another study, Rothbaum, Riggs, and Foa found that within four months of an assault, 21% of women and no men exhibited signs of PTSD, even though within three weeks of the assault, 70% of the women and 50% of the men had been so diagnosed. Riggs, Rothbaum, and Foa, "Post-traumatic Stress in Victims of Non-Sexual Assault," 201–14. Studies of New Yorkers following the attacks of September 11 suggest the same process. Galea, et.al., "Psychological Sequela," 982–87. See also Galea, et.al., "Trends of Probably Post-Traumatic Stress Disorder in New York City," 514–24.

61. Adler, et.al., "Randomized Trial of Debriefing Provided to U.S. Peacekeepers," 253–63.

62. Fawzy and Gray, "From CISD to CISM: Same Song Different Verse?" 34. They write, "Given the compelling evidence from RCTs that debriefings are at best inert, debriefing proponents must address the issues empirically rather than advancing more poorly controlled studies in support of their claims." Ibid., 35.

63. Everly, Flannery, and Eyler, "CISM: A Statistical Review," 171–82. Of the eight studies included in the meta-analysis, six were conducted by directors of the ICISF and two were published by the ICISF journal.

conducted studies are still needed in order to establish the value of CISM.[64] Another significant problem with the meta-analysis is that the interventions used were not consistently applied, some debriefings taking place long after the stressing event and others virtually immediately following. While this methodology poses difficulty for evaluating the efficacy of the belated interventions, it is most disturbing because it seems to reveal questionable research practices on the part of proponents of CISM, who rejected negative studies for similar inconsistencies. As Fawzy and Gray put it, this "seems to demonstrate an inconsistency and selectivity in choosing supportive studies (and evidentiary criteria) on the pat of CISM supporters."[65]

Proponents of CISM do not deny that randomized controlled trials have not been conducted (at least not a substantial number) in order to test its effectiveness as a treatment or intervention. However, they have also questioned the requirement for and appropriateness of such trials for CISM. For example, Robinson argues that randomized controlled trials work well in medical settings where various factors may be isolated and evaluated, but that they will not work with interventions for traumatic events because a sort of prescience would be needed if the persons involved were to be evaluated prior to the event (thereby establishing criteria for the normal psychological/emotional range of each persons involved).[66] After the incident, half would then go through a CISM program, while the others would not. Each would then be evaluated as to his return to normalcy for him. As Robinson notes, it is doubtful that these conditions could be met. Robinson is surely correct with regard to traumatic events in the civilian sector (e.g., automobile accident, fire, or even criminal acts of violence), but there is good reason to think that they could be met for an evaluation of CISM with military personnel deploying to combat zones, since such foreknowledge of a traumatic event is not necessary. All deploying soldiers could receive an initial evaluation prior to leaving the mobilization platform and then, as traumatic events hap-

---

64. They also point out the obvious fact that the most ardent supporters of any given approach (in this case, CISM) are likely to unintentionally sway the data analysis to favor their own position. Fawzy and Gray, 36. Boudreaux and McCabe agree, noting that more independent studies of CISM as a whole are needed to establish its effectiveness. Boudreaux and McCabe, "Interventions and Effectiveness," 1095–97.

65. Ibid., 37.

66. Robinson, 33.

pen, some soldiers could be exposed to CISM-styled interventions while others would not.

However, such an approach, at least according to some CISM advocates, raises ethical questions. The most common ethical objection to the use of randomized controlled studies of the effectiveness of CISM has to do with the morality of withholding treatment from traumatized persons for the sake of an experiment. However, as Freedman has pointed out, all social scientists agree that ethical clinical research assumes a state of genuine uncertainty (known as clinical equipoise) about the effectiveness of the methods or treatments evaluated (if one treatment is acknowledged superior by the scientific community, then the trial should not be conducted).[67] The important point here, though, is that the superiority must be generally accepted among experts in the field and this typically requires more than one uncontrolled pilot experiment. Fawzy and Gray argue that refusal to test CISM because of such concerns is based more on what Freedman refers to as "theoretical equipoise" rather than clinical equipoise, because the refusal assumes that CISM is effective without ever having tested it. This is problematic because it begs the question of the value of CISM and disallows any questioning of that value. This stifles the scientific process and can reinforce a potentially negative or destructive activity.[68]

Third, some opponents of CISM have argued that immediate care following a traumatic event can impede psychological healing and return to normalcy. Satel and Sommers cite three possible negative effects of debriefing. Each will be considered with its relationship to military effectiveness and the role of the chaplain in crisis counseling. First, there is some evidence that constantly reviewing events and feelings associated with a traumatic event can undermine the individual's natural coping mecha-

---

67. Freedman, "Equipoise and Ethics," 141–45.

68. Regarding theoretical equipoise, Fawzy and Gray write, ". . . any bias or hunch would be grounds for either disregarding the use of a control group of [sic] discontinuing an investigation. Thus, the very reason for a clinical trial—substantive disagreement among a community of clinicians and scholars—takes a back seat to the subjective intuition of a single individual. Only a controlled clinical trail is capable of resolving legitimate disagreement of the clinical community. A controlled trial should be conducted even if the experimenter believes in the superiority of one of the interventions relative to the alternatives, provided that other learned colleagues are in disagreement. Fawzy and Gray, 35. See also Gray, Litz, and Olson, "Methodological and Ethical Issues," 179–98; and Weijer, Shapiro, and Glass, "Clinical Equipoise and Not the Uncertainty Principle," 756–57.

nism. For example, one study concluded that debriefing can actually be harmful to victims by causing them to relive the traumatic event too soon after its occurrence.[69] That is, a healthy measure of denial is actually a good thing! This, of course, is a staple of military training; in order to get sane individuals to place themselves in harm's way, military trainers have to instill a sense of invincibility in the minds of soldiers. Many soldiers, especially those who enlist in combat arms specialties, seem to already have personalities which tend toward such self-perceptions and so, it seems unlikely that an occasional defusing or debriefing following a particularly traumatic event will appreciably undermine such coping mechanisms in these particular persons.[70] Second, Satel and Sommers suggest that intervention by professionals may interfere with communication between victims and their friends or family because the victim may believe he is already healed and does not need to discuss his feelings, or because friends/family may believe he is treated and perceive themselves as "in the way." This would deprive those involved in traumatic events of their best support systems.[71] This concern is unfounded for several reasons, most notably due to the fact that CISM facilitators make a point of encouraging victims to utilize their typical support networks. In addition, the military context already deprives soldiers of their family as support and thereby encourages "battle buddy" support structures. Traumatic events in combat zones are likely to involve teams, squads, or platoons which already include battle buddy systems in their makeup. Thus, the other individuals involved in the debriefing sessions just are the persons most soldiers are closest to, and it seems that getting the group to talk about the event in a structured format will encourage further discussion outside the group.

69. Van Emmerik, et.al., "Single Session Debriefing," 766–71. Mitchell has responded to the charges in the article by noting the flawed approach of the study. According to Mitchell, it includes confusion of crisis intervention with psychotherapy and counseling, critical analyses of single-session debriefings applied to CISM, confusion of a variety of interventions with CISD, and outdated material and data. Mitchell, "It Is Neither New Nor News."

70. It is important to note that the studies cited by Satel and Sommers were conducted on civilians in unforeseen traumatic events (e.g., automobile accidents), quite different from the situation discussed here. Some studies conducted on soldiers have suggested that the more early interventions, the less likely it is that unhealthy psychological reactions will develop. See, for example, Solomon, Shklar, and Mikulincer, "Frontline Treatment," 2309–14.

71. Satel and Sommers, "Mental Health Crisis that Wasn't."

Third, Satel and Sommers argue that sometimes immediate emotional or mental health intervention can "prime victims to interpret otherwise normal reactions as pathological or as the beginning stages of PTSD."[72] It is true that some persons who receive counseling (no matter what the form, clinical, pastoral, etc.) do take it as an opportunity to see themselves as having a mental problem when they do not, but this is not a problem restricted to CISM or other immediate traumatic interventions. In fact, it seems that those who are disposed to such self-perceptions are likely to seek out chaplains or mental health professions on their own anyway.[73]

While there are some good reasons to doubt such a conclusion—common sense suggests that individuals already do relive the event and that the debriefing does not *occasion* such recollection—the concern of the conscientious chaplain is the spiritual and emotional well-being of the soldier, and so a measure of caution is in order here. Chaplains trained in CISM or TCR often wish to help (and perhaps demonstrate their own relevance) and lurch at the chance to utilize their newly found skills, but an ethical response to traumatic events in the unit requires some restraint and self-evaluation. The chaplain must examine his own reasons and/or desires to conduct defusing, debriefings, or the like, and evaluate his own readiness to deal with the issues involved. Similarly, the chaplain must also have the ability to determine (as best as humanly possible) the ability of the individual soldiers to cope with a debriefing session. The last thing he wants to do is cause more harm. Thus, wisdom and discernment should dictate the use of CISM by the chaplain.

Fourth, some critics have raised ethical concerns with CISM and the way it is marketed and used. Everly and Mitchell have been very effective in creating a specialty niche for their training program, so effective that CISM certification is virtually required for entry into disaster areas as a first responder, mental health worker, or chaplain. As Satel and Sommers note, after the Oklahoma City bombing incident, trained professional psychologists and psychiatrists, many experts in trauma counseling, were turned away because they did not have credentials from ICISF, while amateurs were admitted with their CISM certificates. Satel and Sommers have also expressed concern over the money thrown at emergency mental

72. Ibid.

73. In a related problem, some soldiers who do not wish to serve attempt to be diagnosed with mental health problems so their duties will be restricted. Chaplains need to be careful in order to avoid encouraging or validating such behavior.

health programs following the September 11th attacks. In fact, millions of federal dollars, in addition to those from private charitable organizations, were spent to provide counseling services to New Yorkers in the subsequent months and years, though there was only a minor increase in persons seeking help.[74] Both complaints have some legitimacy. The first is problematic because it creates a sort of monopoly on crisis intervention and could prevent the best care to the injured. Of course, while this is a concern, it is doubtful that chaplains can do anything about it and even if they could, it is unclear they should, for it seems to be outside the purview of the chaplaincy and instead that of local, state, and federal disaster response agencies. Still, chaplains could use their influence with administrators in those agencies to prevent hard-line rules about the need for one particular certification and encourage an agency-approval process that may include CISM training, but could allow for other training as well. The problem here, of course, is that standardization of credentialing makes for a streamlined vetting process, something of value to governmental agencies. This is the basis for the educational requirements of governmental chaplains. Some means of verifying care-giver training, qualifications, and experience is advisable and this seems adequate. The second is problematic because it raises questions about the motives behind the actions of those involved in emergency mental health. While fraud, waste, and abuse of tax dollars is certainly a concern of all citizens, it is unlikely that chaplains will appreciably effect the situation and like the previous issue, it is unclear that they should seek to do so (in their capacity as chaplains). At the end of the day, it seems that Everly, Mitchell, and others involved in CISM really believe their work to be of help and are not simply seeking financial gain.

Post-Traumatic Stress Disorder

The increased emphasis on CISM and other counseling training within the chaplaincy is a direct result of mental instability among veterans returning from combat. Some studies have found that as much as 70% of soldiers returning from Iraq and Afghanistan suffer from post-traumatic stress disorder or at least exhibit symptoms. Many evangelicals are skeptical of these findings and doubt the legitimacy of the diagnosis. Still, chaplains, especially those who tend to take a hard line on a nouthetic approach and

---

74. Satel and Sommers.

disregard psychology, psychotherapy, psychiatry, and pharmacological treatments for emotional problems should be aware of studies to the contrary and the arguments advanced in support of them. Most mental health professionals accept the claim that there is such a thing as post-traumatic stress disorder and that medications are an efficient treatment.[75] Reducing levels of serotonin, among other neurotransmitters, is the most common approach to managing the symptoms of PTSD—depression, intrusion and avoidance, nightmares, flashbacks, hyperarousal, numbness, anxiety, and the like.[76] Nevertheless, it is also widely held that psychotherapeutic interventions, like various forms of counseling, are beneficial "in addressing the range of social, interpersonal, and occupational problems associated with chronic PTSD."[77]

Stewart and Wrobel recently analyzed the published findings of approximately 25 studies on the effectiveness of either pharmacological or psychotherapeutic approaches to treating PTSD in combat veterans. While they acknowledge several limitations to their study, they found that pharmacotherapeutic approaches led to a faster decrease in PTSD symptoms.[78] This led them to the somewhat disturbing conclusion that current Department of Veterans Affairs advice which states that pharmacological intervention should be reserved for those sufferers of PTSD who have not responded positively to counseling is wrong, and to instead advocate pharmacological treatment as an initial step, at least in some cases.[79] At the end of the day, they recommend that more studies regard-

75. Cyr and Farrar, "Treatments for Posttraumatic Stress Disorder," 366–76.

76. See, for example, Lesch and Merschdorf, "Impulsivity, Agression, and Serotonin,"581–604; McEwen, "Neurobiology of Stress," 172–89; Albucher and Lizerbon, "Psychopahrmacological Treatment in PTSD," 355–67; Marmar, Neylan, and Schoenfeld, "New Directions in Pharmacotherapy," 259–70.

77. Stewart and Wrobel, "Evaluation of the Efficacy of Pharmacotherapy," 461. Stewart and Wrobel cite several articles in support of this contention. See, for example, Breslau, "Outcomes," 55–59; Kessler, "Burden to Individual and Society," 4–12; Ruzek, Young, and Walser, "Group Treatment," 53–67. See also Young and Blake, eds., *Group Treatments.*

78. Limitations of the study include (but are not limited to) the fact that some results used came from examinations of Vietnam-era vets, persons who had suffered symptoms far longer than other vets (e.g., Desert Storm, Enduring Freedom, Iraqi Freedom, etc.) and some participants in the studies were either taking multiple medications or on medication while receiving psychotherapeutic treatment.

79. To be fair, Stewart and Wrobel do note that there are some vets who seem unable, because of PTSD symptom intrusion, to tolerate conventional psychotherapeutic

ing the effectiveness of combined treatment methods be conducted, since the incidence of PTSD in returning veterans from Iraq and Afghanistan is sure to rise, especially due to the fact of multiple tours for most.[80]

The prevalence of PTSD in the current military context affords chaplains several opportunities for ministry. First, they have increased visibility in the units because of concern about mental health and spiritual problems by commanders. Second, they have more opportunities for one-on-one counseling with soldiers/sailors/airmen involved in traumatic events. Use of CISM by the chaplain can open the door for some service members, who would not otherwise do so, to seek out the chaplain. Third, it encourages chaplains and military mental health professionals to work more closely together. Chaplains ought to make their concerns about medicinal treatment for stress known to the psychologists/psychiatrists working with their units. It has been my experience that most mental health professionals do not want to simply prescribe drugs for every emotional difficulty, but feel somewhat constrained by the environment; a combat theater is no place for in-depth psychotherapy. Most also see value of the chaplain's counseling service because they acknowledge the importance of spiritual care.[81] Thus, the chaplain should not view the mental health professional as the enemy, but rather as a colleague. He can help the doctor here by first listening to him and talking to him about these issues, but also by partnering with him to bring healing to the soldier. There may not always be agreement on the best approach to treatment, and there may be times when the mental health worker decides to prescribe anti-depressants, but a good working relationship between the two can minimize the use of drug treatments.

---

interventions without first receiving medication. Stewart and Wrobel, 466.

80. Ibid., 467. At least one study has suggested that collaborative care models reduce symptoms of PTSD. Engel, et. al., "RESPECT-Mil," 935–40. Similarly, Platman recommends further study of pharmacotherapy along with counseling for sufferers of PTSD. Platman, "Psychopharmacology and Posttraumatic Stress Disorder," 151–55.

81. A growing number of mental health professionals are not only acknowledging the value of chaplains, but actually advocating referral to chaplains. Galek, et.al, "Referrals to Chaplains," 363–77.

Conclusion

It seems clear that further studies on the effectiveness and value of CISM, especially with respect to its use in a military environment, are in order.[82] Nevertheless, it also seems clear that soldiers find it helpful and it can be a useful tool for both commanders and chaplains. The ethical concerns associated with CISM are minimal and should not impede chaplain use of the program. Concerns with secular psychological theory ought not impede chaplain use of its methods. Chaplains, especially those deployed to a combat environment, should be sure to open dialogue with combat stress control team members and work closely with military health professionals in order to ensure service members get the best care available, and not necessarily a quick fix. The chaplain, as the ethical voice of the command, can have a positive impact on this issue if he remains engaged with the parties involved.

OTHER ISSUES OF CONCERN OR INTEREST

Suicide Prevention

One area of training related to counseling and mental health in which chaplains have historically been active is the military suicide prevention program. There is a natural connection between spiritual care and suicide prevention, and so chaplains are most often tasked with conducting the annual training on the subject, in addition to specialized training for deployments or other occasions for which an emphasis on the topic is deemed necessary or appropriate. There has been an upsurge in suicides within the armed services in recent years, ostensibly due to post-traumatic stress reactions to the wars in Iraq and Afghanistan. In fact, in February 2009, the number of soldier deaths in Iraq due to enemy actions was surpassed by the number of suicides, and the Department of Defense mandated a stand-down for all military units (at least CONUS) with mandatory suicide awareness and prevention training. Suicide is rightly a real concern for military leadership and so there is a desire for some standardization of training to ensure that all personnel get the same information. In order to facilitate that effort, the U.S. Army Center for Health Promotion and Preventive Medicine, along with input from the Office of the Chief of Chaplains, developed the ACE

---

82. Some studies have suggested its value. Deahl, et. al., "Psychological Sequelae Following the Gulf War," 60–65.

suicide intervention program, the latest in a long line of such programs. The program is designed to be simple and easy to remember, and has a degree of flexibility not found in many of its predecessors.

Part of the curriculum includes the dissemination of information about counseling services, particularly from mental health professionals. Some chaplains may object to teaching this portion of the class based on their objections to psychology and/or psychiatry. After all, to put out the information could be seen as an endorsement and is therefore, tantamount to a referral. It seems to me, though, that the advantages of teaching the class far outweigh the possible confusion or ethical concern with being perceived as recommending secular mental health services, the previous discussion notwithstanding. The suicide prevention class affords the chaplain the opportunity to stand before soldiers in the unit that may never darken the chapel door. It has a flexibility that allows the chaplain to address spiritual issues related to combat stress and depression, and is an entrée for the chaplain to demonstrate his ability to communicate effectively and with compassion. It is one of the chaplain's rare opportunities to make himself known to the unit members on a personal level. If they see that he cares, that he is knowledgeable, that he is professional, that he is not afraid to deal with difficult issues, that he is a person of spiritual depth, that he is personable, then they may be more likely to come to him when in distress. If the chaplain does not conduct the training because of concerns over a perceived endorsement of mental health professions, then it will most likely be taught by someone with a more secular take on the issue; possibly even a mental health professional who is not a Christian. In that case, the evangelical will have abandoned his platform to a secularist. Thus, while there are some legitimate concerns on the part of the psychology/psychiatry skeptic for conducting the suicide prevention training, there are much more compelling reasons for viewing the class as a great opportunity to enhance the chaplain's ministry capabilities within the unit of assignment.

Clinical Pastoral Education

Clinical Pastoral Education (CPE) is a hospital-based pastoral ministry training program in which students typically attend lectures, participate in peer-group interactions, and minister to patients as chaplaincy students under the mentorship of a CPE supervisor. Most hospitals which have CPE programs offer both full-time residency and part-time (one- or two-day per week) extended unit options for the training. A small stipend is usually available for CPE residents, while extended unit service is typically unpaid. Most seminaries and divinity schools accept CPE units for Master's-level credit, and some even require it as part of their Master of Divinity programs. The content of the lectures can vary from program to program, but normally include topics in theology, counseling, and medicine. Most full-time hospital chaplaincy positions require a minimum of four units of CPE, the equivalent of one-year of residency, and some hospitals even require their volunteer chaplains to have some exposure to CPE. Military chaplaincy is no different. Clinical Pastoral Education is quickly becoming a virtual requirement for advancement within the chaplaincy ranks, and is strongly recommended for those who wish to enter active duty, especially among overrepresented denominational groups (e.g., evangelicals). However, many evangelicals have expressed concern over the theological underpinnings of the CPE movement.

The history of CPE reveals a number of tensions which helped shape the movement as it now exists. CPE developed out of an atmosphere of dissatisfaction with the theological education of the early twentieth century, which seemed distant from the actual practice of ministry. Theology students and educators both sensed a need for a practical training aspect to seminary. Richard Cabot, a physician, heart disease researcher, and professor of medicine at Harvard University, recommended that ministerial students get a year of clinical study in their theological training. He envisioned a program in which seminarians put their theology into practice where it is needed most—in relationship to others (in need), and he specifically rejected the notion that this training was medical, psychological, or sociological in nature.[83] Of course, Cabot's is a noble and desirable goal, one which no evangelical theological educator could take issue.

However, all were not agreed on the nature of the deficiency in theological education and the best approach to fixing it. Some saw the problems in theological education not only related to a lack of praxis, but also to a disconnect between intellectual belief (theology as abstract propositional knowledge) and emotional life. Hall argues that Clinical Pastoral Education sought to address this deficiency with a clinical ap-

83. Cabot, "A Plea for a Clinical Year," 1–22.

proach to theology which presupposes the primacy of emotions in theological development:

> Clinical theology seeks to understand traditional theological concepts as they relate to human experience. It requires being open to one's feelings and emotions, and to the emotions of those to whom one ministers, and seeking the meaning of those emotions and their relationship to theological concepts. It sees any belief in the codification of religious doctrine in a final form as likely being due to human arrogance and pride. It is open to the possibility that understanding specific human experience, in a particular cultural context, may bring a revision and a new approximation of theological truth. . . . The CPE Movement is the story of searching for a conceptual and experiential theological understanding as a basis for pastoral care and counseling.[84]

As noted earlier, the primacy of emotions in theological development and thought suggests a preference for theological liberalism. Thornton even admits that liberalism was a constituent part of the growth of CPE as a movement: "Theological liberalism prepared the way for the initial acceptance of clinical pastoral education in seminaries such as Chicago Theological Seminary, the University of Chicago Divinity School, Union, Yale, and the major schools of Boston."[85]

That CPE has liberal theology as its basis cannot be doubted. Consider the words of Anton Boisen, widely considered the father of clinical pastoral education, as he reflected on how theological education would change as a result of CPE-type models: "What is involved is a thoroughgoing shift of attention and a new method of attack and then, in the end, a new authority, grounded not in tradition but in experience. . . . The attention will be shifted from the past to the present; from books to the raw material of life. Experience will no longer be fitted to the system but system to experience."[86] Many of the early developers of CPE agreed with this approach: Hellen Dunbar, Carroll Wise, and Seward Hiltner, to name a few; but all did not, including Cabot and his followers. Hall, reflecting on the contributions of Cabot and Boisen, writes, "Cabot emphasized the need for supervised experience in the application of theology in pastoral care. Boisen emphasized the need to study theology by seeking to understand

84. Hall, *Head and Heart*, xv.

85. Thornton, *Professional Education for Ministry*.

86. Boisen, "Challenge to Our Seminaries," 11–12.

the religious experiences of persons. In many ways, Cabot's approach was a logical extension of the theological school curriculum, while Boisen's approach represented a change in the method of theological inquiry."[87]

These differences in approach to training manifested themselves as differences in emphases and practice as well. Early in the development of CPE, there was disagreement and even tension over the role of psychoanalysis and mental health in the program. Some, represented by the Boston-based Institute of Pastoral Care (New England group), preferred an intellectual approach to faith with a view to practical application. This group was associated with Cabot. Others, represented by the New York-based Council for Clinical Training, focused on an experiential approach to theology and emotional/psychological insights as the goal of clinical visits. The New England group took a more conservative stance and was more closely associated with theological schools, seeing its role primarily in the preparation of clergy for parish ministry. The New York group encouraged theology students (as well as medical and law students) to undergo psychoanalysis in order to understand themselves better. The idea was that one cannot understand others until he understands himself, and he cannot help others until he has such understanding. Its leaders conceived of its role more broadly, serving society as a whole.

The second and third generation leaders attempted to bring the two together. Hiltner specifically argued for integration of theory and method and believed a complete CPE program would teach both.[88] Still, tensions and division remained. In fact, Hall views the history of CPE as the struggle of these two emphases, but argues that both were necessary to the development of a holistic pastoral theology. While this may be the case, Hall also admits that some of the newer, more progressive ideas led to problems. Commenting on some of the problems associated with the New York group, he writes,

> As is often true in radical changes, the newer view at times led to extremes. A number of supervisors changed vocation and became psychologists or, as ministers, put psychological understanding above theological understanding. In the process of becoming aware of repressed emotions, some supervisors had periods of rebellion against the conventions of society. This was a concern of theological school and church officials. Although the radical

87. Hall, 13.

88. Hiltner, *Pastoral Counseling*, 244.

innovations of the New York group provided valuable new understanding of human beings, the innovations needed the balance of
the more conservative New England group's viewpoint.[89]

Concerns over the loyalty of CPE supervisors to the faith are
common and not confined to the New York group or area or the era
of the beginnings of CPE. In fact, they are so common that Thornton
was surprised that, when working with the Institute of Religion of the
Texas Medical Center in Houston in 1958, the hospitals seemed more
concerned about theology than the theological schools were: "One of
the amusing ironies of that situation was to discover that some of our
seminary committee members were more anxious to have proof of our
clinical competence than of our theological sophistication, while many of
our medical colleagues distrusted us for fear that we would abandon our
religious identity."[90] Thornton describes a situation in which he served on
a committee preparing a constitution and bylaws for the newly formed
Association for Clinical Pastoral Education. Debate arose over the wording of the preamble's purpose statement. Some were concerned that too
much emphasis on theology and not enough emphasis on clinical work
was present. In the end, all references to the Church and its mission were
removed and the statement simply read, "The general purpose of this
Association is to facilitate clinical pastoral education." Thornton sees this
process as reflective of the tension between theological and medical concerns present in CPE.[91] For evangelicals, though, it may simply confirm
suspicions that CPE is dominated by politically-correct liberals who are
more concerned with helping people find wholeness in whichever ways
suit them, rather than with serving the Lord and seeing souls saved and
healed by the power of the risen Christ.

Concerns over theological depth and fidelity led some denominational groups to institute their own training programs and organizations.
For example, Louis Sieck, president of Concordia Theological Seminary
helped form the Lutheran Advisory Council on Pastoral Care in order
to provide oversight for CPE training that was consistent with Lutheran,
particularly Missouri Synod, theology.[92] Similarly, Wayne Oates, of the

89. Hall, 43.
90. Thornton, 12.
91. Ibid.
92. Hall, 70.

Southern Baptist Theological Seminary in Louisville, Kentucky, helped form the Southern Baptist Association for Clinical Pastoral Education in 1967. Still, most denominational CPE organizations eventually merged with or worked closely with the major national organizations because of logistical and organizational difficulties.

The characteristic feature of CPE, as it is currently practiced, is the *verbatim* group exercise, in which word-for-word write-ups of the CPE student's interactions with patients are analyzed and discussed by his peers and CPE supervisor. The goal of these analyses is primarily self-examination on the part of the student in an effort to determine if his practice aligns with his theology. Many students find that their default responses to stressful or uncomfortable situations are born out of love for self rather than love for others. The process of self-examination can help reveal this so that steps may be taken to remedy the situation. For example, if a student offers a prayer when there is a lull in the conversation, his peers may ask why he chose to do so at that time. Upon further investigation, it may be discovered that he is uncomfortable with silence and offering a prayer serves as a means of alleviating his own feelings of awkwardness, rather than to lift the patient up before the throne of grace.[93] This peer-directed introspection does not see oneself as the remedy, and in fact, does not prescribe a fix to any problems which may arise. Rather, it only seeks to help one find areas that may need improvement or need to be addressed. Russell Dicks, the man chiefly responsible for developing this method of inquiry, describes it as a means of growth: "When we reproduce in writing a contact, an interview, a working relationship, we do not merely record it, we rethink it and so develop its meaning . . . It is a check upon one's work; it is a clarifying and developing process . . . It is a new creation of ideas which reveals lack in what we have done. . . . It is self-criticism. It is self-evaluation. It is preparation for self-improvement."[94]

In a Christian theology, we may say that this process identifies attitudes or actions that need to be brought into captivity to Christ. It seems to me that all those involved in pastoral ministry, evangelicals,

---

93. In point of fact, this is a rather common response/finding among CPE students. Many of us tend to use prayer as a way of filling in the blank space or as a means of transitioning out of the hospital visit in order to go to another room. Some self-awareness of this tendency can help the minister to more effectively use prayer for what it is intended and not for his own purposes.

94. Cabot and Dicks, *The Art of Ministering*, 244–48.

non-evangelicals, clergy, laypersons, pastors, chaplains, Christian social workers, and the like, can benefit from participation in a close-knit group centered on such activity. The noetic effects of the Fall can blind us to our own selfish motivations in action, even in ministry. The verbatim group activities associated with CPE can serve as a pastoral care accountability group of sorts; it can be a tool in shaping our Christian character and our theology of ministry.

Thus, even though some CPE programs appear antagonistic to evangelical theological sensibilities, and even though there seems to be a preference for liberal theology in the philosophy which undergirds the way CPE has developed, there are still good reasons for evangelicals to enroll in CPE programs. It takes wisdom to sift through the materials in order to determine what is of value, but the payoff in both the experience of working in a clinical environment, with a variety of patients and their families, and in the aid with self-examination far outweighs any liabilities which one may perceive to inhere in the system or process. Still, there are other issues related to CPE which may prove disturbing to evangelicals.

In the conclusion to his history of CPE, King sets forth a common understanding of the ideal for CPE: "May CPE and its participants experience an environment of respect and openness as well as the courage needed to trust the process of taking meaningful risks and being open to transformation."[95] On the surface, this ideal seems innocuous and rather noble, but many conservative Christians have expressed concern over the vague nature of expressions of this sort, and have been suspicious that it is meant to leave open the possibility of genuine spiritual transformation from self-discovery or worse, non-Christian faith. They have been suspicious that the ideal prefers those who hold to a weak or watered-down theology; it smacks of criticism of those who hold to strong theological positions and are critical of some ideas opposed to their own (e.g., differing religious or moral positions). These suspicions are not without warrant and in fact, King seems to imply that spiritual growth can and should come from the interplay of various perspectives in the CPE program. Earlier in the same paragraph, he celebrated the pluralistic nature of modern CPE programs: "CPE has a rich history and a future full of potential. . . . In the 1920s, who could have foreseen the tapestry of diversity that has been coming together in CPE—ethnic, religious/spiritual,

95. King, *Trust the Process*, 157.

gender, organizational, philosophical, sexual orientation?"[96] For evangelicals, the diversities mentioned are not on par with one another, yet their listing together here suggests that those within the CPE community view them as such. Clearly, diversity of sexual orientation cannot (at least in an evangelical theology) be viewed with the same positive affirmations as ethnic diversity. Similarly, religious diversity may be of value when it is within the Christian tradition, but most evangelicals would bristle at the suggestion that, for example, paganism (Wicca) has something to teach us about authentic spirituality, but this may very well be the position leaders of many CPE programs take. How are evangelical chaplains who wish to get the clinical experience associated with CPE to respond? How should those evangelicals who feel called to ministries which require CPE (e.g., hospital chaplaincy) proceed? It seems to me that there are a few options, some more viable than others.

First, evangelicals could simply eschew professional credentialing and form their own *pastoral care to patients* training programs at evangelical seminaries, or develop hospital visit mentoring programs with pastors and allow the training to take place out of the local church. There are strengths and weaknesses to this approach. One strength is that it does not subject seminary students (some of whom are still impressionable) to the influence of false teachers; it keeps the theological education of ministerial students under the authority of the evangelical denomination or institution. Another strength, at least with respect to the second option, is that it restores responsibility for ministerial training, arguably a facet of discipleship, to the local church. A mentoring program like that envisaged here allows the local pastor to develop a pastoral care team with a philosophy of ministry consistent with his own, and this can lead to greater unity within the local body of believers.

Even though there are some obvious advantages to this option, it also has some distinct disadvantages. While it is hoped that pastors are mentoring ministerial students who are members of their churches (even if they attend seminary), it is unclear that such a program, at least in most cases, could provide the kind of educational experience that one gets by taking units of CPE through a hospital program. Most pastors do not have time to devote to pastoral care students that is comparable to a CPE supervisor. Perhaps a mega-church could have a pastoral ministry supervisor run-

96. Ibid.

ning a department, but most churches simply do not have the resources to create such an elaborate program. It is also unlikely that local pastors and their trainees will be given the kind of access to patients, doctors, hospital facilities, and medical records/information that is afforded students in a traditional CPE program. Another issue has to do with pastoral turnover; many evangelical churches have dismal records on pastoral retention. If a pastor trains persons to provide ministry consistent with his model and then he leaves, there is no guarantee that the next pastor's philosophy and methodology will fit with the training received. This leads to another deficiency with both incarnations of this option: a lack of standardization. This was a problem which dogged CPE itself in the early years until the various groups involved in clinical training came together and settled on some standards of training and care. If evangelicals go out on their own, a pastoral care student at one school may not receive training comparable to a student at another school. While this is almost always the case with any educational endeavor, this issue is particularly problematic here, at least with respect to the ministry prospects for seminary students. As noted earlier, many chaplaincy positions are requiring several units of CPE, and it is doubtful that programs such as those described here would be accepted as substitutes.

Second, evangelicals could develop their own, alternate CPE-styled programs in local hospitals. Evangelical denominational leaders and educators could seek partnerships with hospitals to provide alternate pastoral care programs in the hospital settings. They could also develop their own pastoral care associations and eventually, credentialing standards. At first glance, this option may seem unreasonable or too idyllic. After all, just getting evangelicals to agree to work together is an unenviable (and often thankless) task in itself! Let's face it—many conservative Christian groups are reluctant to even refer to themselves as "evangelicals," let alone work with others who so designate themselves. As noted in a previous chapter, the term is becoming increasingly unclear as those who refer to themselves as evangelicals leave traditional evangelical beliefs behind. Still, it seems that enough persons and groups identify with the concerns (if not the term) to create something of a consensus regarding how a biblical pastoral care to patients program might look and be structured. With the emergence of large, national healthcare systems, development of an alternate program may be more feasible than initially thought, at least if evangelicals can convince system administrators of the potential loss of pastoral care providers if they refuse to work with the evangelical alternative. In order to accomplish this, evangelicals would first need to have a professional organization already in place, something that has yet to develop. The organization would need to have a character that is both theologically conservative, but also receptive to scientific inquiry, research, and findings, if it were to be taken seriously by the medical community as a whole. Herein lies the greatest difficulty in this option. In addition, even if evangelicals endeavored to put support and organizational structures into place, it seems that at least twenty years would be needed to develop into a serious contender for healthcare system attention/recognition. It should also be remembered that some conservative denominations already tried to start their own groups, but eventually merged with the existing groups in order to benefit from the resources they provided. Nevertheless, none of the difficulties already mentioned are insurmountable, but they are substantial. In the meantime, evangelicals who need the kind of clinical experience provided by CPE will need to enroll in programs and learn to glean the valuable insights from the dross.

The third, and I believe most viable option, is for evangelicals to influence the shape of CPE from within. By this, I do not mean to suggest a full-scale assault in an attempt to take over, but I do mean to develop CPE supervisors who are theologically conservative and who are sympathetic to evangelical beliefs of CPE residents. Of course, some have already done so and others are continuing to do so even now, but it is also the case that many evangelicals who have enrolled in CPE programs have been met with hostility and rancor for their beliefs, and the majority of CPE supervisors are from mainline denominations. There will surely be instances of discrimination and some evangelicals may find roadblocks to their advancement, but it is doubtful that such difficulties will be (are) systemic, institutional, or widespread. Just as the history of CPE reveals diversity of philosophy regarding the nature of clinical training needed and the intended recipients of that training, so also there is/will be diversity of receptivity to decidedly evangelical residents among hospital administrators and chaplaincy supervisors. Evangelical chaplains within CPE training programs should be prepared to meet some resistance as they hold fast to their beliefs, but should not *expect* it. If we can persevere, we can help train others in the important work of caring for the sick, dying and grieving.

As with other issues discussed in this book, it seems that wisdom is needed here. Evangelicals should not seek out martyrdom; the earliest Christian leaders advised against doing so, but also prescribed limits to the extent one should go in order to avoid it. The wise evangelical will conduct research before applying for residency to any given CPE program. Each program has its own personality and theological emphases; some are more conservative than others, and a little bit of research can prevent a lot of grief in the long run. It is just as much the responsibility of the applicant to ensure a good fit as it is of the program administrators. At the end of the day, those evangelicals who wish to get CPE training and experience must evaluate their own spiritual maturity, ability to cope with challenges to their faith, and facility in dealing with others with whom they disagree, and determine if a given program is right for them. If they are able to hold on to their beliefs in the face of opposition and grow through challenges, then CPE may be right for them.

While there are some potential dangers, they need not preclude involvement by evangelicals. On a practical level, those enrolled in CPE ought to recognize those dangers and mitigate them by meeting regularly with a pastoral colleague or mentor who can serve as a sort of theological accountability partner. It is preferable that this individual be outside of the clinical community in order to preserve a level of objectivity in the discussion. If unacceptable shifts in theology are perceived, the evangelical should be prepared to take steps to protect his own spiritual well-being. Such steps could take a variety of forms, from simple involvement in discipleship groups at church, to something more drastic, even removal from the CPE program. This may require a revisioning of one's ministry calling, but the spiritual health of the ministerial student is paramount if he is to be effective for the Lord. While it may appear that much of this projects a negative outlook on CPE, it is not intended to do so. CPE can be a rewarding experience for one's own spiritual development and for his concept and practice of ministry. As alluded to earlier, the benefits of participating in a CPE program are incalculable and the potential dangers can be minimized for most. Thus, it is advisable that most evangelicals called to chaplaincy ministry enroll in a CPE program. If one is unsure of his own ability to remain true to his faith, he can participate in an extended unit on a sort of trial basis. From there, he can determine if continued participation is advisable for him. At the end of the day, the goal is growth in Christ and expansion of one's ministry focus and abilities.

CPE can help many in these areas if, as with anything, they are discerning and sensitive to the work of the Holy Spirit in their lives and through the training.

Counseling Non-Christians

Chaplains are often faced with the prospect of counseling persons of different faiths from their own. This is due to a variety of reasons; sometimes because of unit isolation and the availability of other religious at the time of crisis, sometimes due to personal interaction between the chaplain and the individual. However they arise, situations like this can present something of a challenge to evangelical chaplains for reasons similar to those already mentioned in chapter five. Evangelicals want to witness to all non-Christians, but they must also adhere to DOD regulations and guidance which specifically prohibits chaplains from trying to convert those of other faiths.

On a pragmatic level, this is really not that difficult of an issue. When someone comes to me for counseling, I immediately ask about their faith background and the faith tradition with which he most closely identifies. If it is non-Christian, I offer to try to find a chaplain or religious from his own faith background. It has been my experience that most persons are not picky by the time they actually come in for counseling. As one Catholic soldier once put it to me, "I know you're not a priest, but you're the closest thing to it right now; and besides, I like you." If the individual turns down my offer or I am unable to secure a minister from his own faith tradition, I then make sure that the potential counselee knows that I am a Christian and that my faith will not only influence, but will actually guide my counseling method and agenda. If at that point the individual still wants to talk to me, I make sure he understands that I am going to offer advice from the standpoint of my own faith and that I am not there to help him (and in many cases, am incapable of helping him) think about his own faith. I see this first and foremost as a matter of integrity; it is truth in advertising. It also serves as a protective measure. No one can accuse me of taking advantage of my position or of the individual's vulnerable state. This approach allows me to follow DOD and DA guidelines and policies, while still retaining my evangelistic zeal. Interestingly, it has been my experience that most persons assume that the chaplain is closer to God than they are, and consequently, wish to receive counseling, even if the chaplain is of a different faith or tradition.

I will witness to the individual, as I believe that wholeness can only come through Christ. I will encourage him to read the Bible daily, to pray for divine guidance, and to purpose to submit himself to the will of God. If he chooses to accept Christ as his Savior, I will happily lead him to do so. Nevertheless, any conversion must be arrived at through a genuine work of the Holy Spirit in the individual's life. If I were to manipulate the discussion, coerce the individual, or otherwise force my faith upon the person, the resulting confession would be suspect at best. This, though, is not anything particularly special about chaplaincy, but rather is simple common sense in ministry and evangelism.

Privileged Communication

One of the areas of on-going confusion within the chaplaincy is the nature and extent of confidentiality that the chaplain enjoys or is obligated to in the counseling role. The training and guidance chaplains have received over the years has varied. In recent years, the Army Office of the Chief of Chaplains has attempted to standardize the chaplaincy's handling of this topic by issuing guidance to the effect that, all chaplains have privileged communication, similar to the Catholic priest confidentiality protocol. In addition to simplicity, the underlying idea is that the typical soldier does not know the difference between Roman Catholic, Anglican, Lutheran, Southern Baptist, etc., chaplains and expects that all chaplains perform the same duties. He may therefore come to a Protestant chaplain and wish to confess something and should be afforded the opportunity. In addition, it is argued, the individual soldier may not have access to clergy of his own faith background (the very legal justification for the chaplaincy, as noted in chapter three) and must therefore rely on the chaplain who is in his area of operations. This could mean (and very often does) that a Roman Catholic soldier may come to a Protestant chaplain and wish to confess his sins. According to the Chief's guidance, Protestant Army chaplains ought to allow the individual to confess and ought to protect that confession, no matter what it contains. This is problematic for several reasons.

First, it may not be legal, and while the Office of the Chief of Chaplains has promised to stick by any chaplains who hold to confidentiality, even under threat of declaration of contempt of court, many evangelical chaplains are skeptical of the protection/legal aid they would receive if they ignored a court order to divulge information they obtained during the course of a counseling session. Many states have laws that require counselors to report incidents of abuse (e.g., child abuse, abuse or neglect of the elderly, counselor abuse of a client, etc.) and failure to do so can result in criminal prosecution. Some advocates of the Chief's policy have suggested that the federal jurisdiction of the Army overrules any singular state's laws, but this claim has not been tested in the court system, and it seems unwise to become a test case. For reservist and national guard chaplains, the issue becomes even more confusing, as questions of military status and jurisdiction are even more complex.

Second, there is good reason to have concerns over what such a policy and/or procedure may communicate about chaplaincy, the individual chaplain, or his theology. Confession and absolution are Catholic doctrines practiced by few Protestants; specifically rejected because they are at odds with the Protestant emphases on justification by faith alone and priesthood of the believer. Therefore, if a Protestant evangelical chaplain practices confidentiality in his counseling ministry, he may send mixed theological signals. For example, it may appear that he is pronouncing forgiveness, which undermines the gospel as evangelicals understand it.[97] It may lead to confusion over the nature of the chaplain. For example, it could be interpreted as communicating that all chaplains are the same, or that chaplains are required to perform services for denominations not his own. It also may undermine the individual chaplain's integrity or witness. For example, it could come across in a way that leads soldiers and parishioners to conclude that the chaplain is a hired servant, rather than a free man (as discussed in chapter one). It also may challenge the chaplain's own ethics, for it requires him to protect even confession of illegal activity, including abuse. Many evangelicals believe it is their duty to report such activities to the authorities, even if the counselee confessed to the chaplain as a religious expression, and to fail to do so is to, in effect, endorse, approve, or enable the activity. All of these problems offer good reasons for rejecting the practice of assuming privileged communication in all cases. The old advice of informing the individual that any confes-

---

97. I have in mind here a distinction between the Catholic practice of *pronouncing* forgiveness (as tied to absolution) and *declaring* forgiveness in Christ. Some of this distinction is also related to the practice of penance. However, it seems that such theological subtleties are lost on most.

sion of felony activity (or at least child or spousal abuse, or murder) may be divulged seems best.

CONCLUSION

Chaplains cannot avoid the role of counselor and should not seek to do so. However, there are a number of concerns related to this ministry that evangelicals in chaplaincy should consider. In this chapter, the controversy over counseling within evangelical circles was summarized. Arguments for and against nouthetic counseling were presented, and it was concluded that, while there are some valid theological concerns with the mental health professions, chaplains can still develop a good relationship with combat stress control teams and refer difficult cases while still keeping in touch with the individual counselee. Chaplains should also take every opportunity to teach and discuss issues related to spiritual care: appropriate use of CISM or TCR, along with suicide prevention training, may alleviate some of the stressors of the combat environment and could open more doors for spiritual counseling. In their counseling ministries, chaplains should operate with full-disclosure of their faith commitments to counselees, and with consistency with their own belief systems, thus protecting their spiritual authority and integrity. In this way, chaplains can help bring spiritual and emotional peace to those who sacrifice of themselves in service of our county.

8

"Preach the Word"

A Charge to Evangelicals in Chaplaincy

But Christ is not speaking of that here; for something more is required,
namely, that no rival or supplementary doctrine be introduced,
nor another word be taught than Christ has taught.

—MARTIN LUTHER

THIS STUDY HAS REVEALED that there are a number of important theological issues with which evangelicals interested in chaplaincy ministry must wrestle. It has also revealed that there is an inherent institutional pressure for chaplains to be more ecumenical, less exclusivistic, and to tend toward a more liberal theology. However, it has also been argued that evangelicals can continue to serve in this vital ministry without sacrificing fidelity to their own Christian commitments, if they are creative and understand their own limits. As I have contemplated how to conclude this work, I became convinced that a mere summary of the contents and conclusions of the various chapters would be inadequate. Instead, an exhortation to evangelical chaplains seemed most appropriate, and there is none better than that which Paul gives to Timothy in his second letter, chapter four, where he charges Timothy with the ministry of the Word:

> I solemnly charge you in the presence of God and of Christ Jesus,
> who is to judge the living and the dead, and by His appearing and

His kingdom: preach the word; be ready in season and out of season; reprove, rebuke, exhort, with great patience and instruction. For the time will come when they will not endure sound doctrine; but wanting to have their ears tickled, they will accumulate for themselves teachers in accordance to their own desires, and will turn away their ears from the truth and will turn aside to myths. But you, be sober in all things, endure hardship, do the work of an evangelist, fulfill your ministry. (2 Tim 4:1–5)

In this passage, there are at least three assumptions alluded to which undergird the charge. First, Paul's charge is given within the context of the community of faith. It is given in, Paul says, "the presence of God and of Christ Jesus" (vs. 1). This may be seen as an appropriation of divine authority for the charge; that while the words are Paul's, the charge itself is God's. This seems to fit well with the spirit of the immediately preceding verses, which speak of divine inspiration, but such a reading could come across somewhat negatively, as a sort of veiled threat. On this reading, Paul could be seen as accusing Timothy or warning him that if he does not preach, he will get zapped! This seems unlikely, given the close relationship of Paul and Timothy, and Paul's confidence in Timothy's faith. There is another reading of this reference which also fits with the context. It may be an articulation of the relationship out of which the charge flows. Timothy's relationship with God is through Christ Jesus. Similarly, Timothy's relationship with Paul is based on their mutual submission to Christ. Timothy's relationship with God is one forged in the fires of faith; there is fellowship between the Father and Son, and that fellowship is the model for fellowship among believers, just as Jesus prayed (John 17:20–24). On this reading, the charge is seen as a positive reminder of the closeness they have with God and one another, and it therefore flows out of a loving discipleship relationship.

Second, Paul alludes to God's position as Judge; to the fact that God will Judge. Here, again, there are two ways of reading the text, one with somewhat negative connotations, and one with positive. It can be read as a reminder that God will condemn those who are not faithful. On this reading, we could see it again as a threat or warning to Timothy: If you are not faithful in preaching, God will judge you! We could also, on this reading, see it as a friendly reminder that, because God will judge, there should be a sense of urgency to ministry; Timothy must preach the Word because the time is short before the End. This seems most likely, given the tone of this section of his letter and Paul's note of Christ's coming (4:1) and the final judgment (4:8), and his later charge to "do the work of an evangelist" (4:5).

Most of us forget what urgency is really like; we often get complacent in our external, as well as our spiritual lives. Just as we get complacent about the dangers of driving on the highway, we also get spiritually complacent, both in our personal walks with God, and also in our evangelistic fervor. We forget or ignore the fact that literally millions of people live and die without hope for eternity because they do not know Jesus. It shouldn't be that way. Christians in the military have a unique opportunity for being reminded of what urgency is like every time they deploy. Every project that has sat unfinished suddenly is a priority. Every moment with family and friends is precious. There is a sense of heightened importance in every encounter; every interaction. There is, at least in the backs of minds, a feeling that the immediate moment may be the last opportunity to converse or interact with this person, and so we seek to make the most of our time. This is the sort of urgency Paul expects Timothy to have with respect to ministering and evangelizing.

It should be noted, though, that there is also a way of reading this reminder which has a positive aspect, and this is tied to the fact that Christians do not have to be fearful of the judgment of God. When reminded of the coming judgment, Christians ought to have both a sense of urgency in their witnessing and a sense of thanksgiving in their salvation. A reminder of God's judgment should produce joy in Christians because of the gracious forgiveness they (we) have in Christ. So there is a sort of joy and peace which come from the fellowship Timothy has with God in Christ Jesus and these ought to form the basis of the preaching which Paul charges.

Third, Paul reminds Timothy that Jesus is coming again to establish his kingdom; a kingdom in which believers will participate. This, again, is a positive for Timothy. So each of these allusions are friendly reminders of the basis upon which Timothy has a message to preach. As Towner writes, "They are strong symbols of promise and power, symbols moreover, of the fulfillment of a power already in effect in his present, that compel him to do and be what God has commissioned (and empowered; 1:6–8; 2:1) him to do and be. The motivational force of these 'promises becoming reality' is certainly to encourage, but also to bind him to his task."[1] Similarly, when evangelical chaplains rise to teach the Word of God, they (we) ought to have those reminders in the forefronts of their (our) minds—the peace, joy, and intimate fellowship with God we have because of Christ's death on the cross, and an urgency to see others come to saving faith because the days are evil and the time is short.

Now we are in a position to look at Paul's charge to Timothy. It is a charge to preach the Word. We take this to mean that Paul is concerned that ministers under his tutelage, those he trains, remain faithful to the text. There is at least a definite and deliberate focus on the text of Scripture, and Paul arguably sees the preaching of the Word as central to responsible Christian ministry. This charge includes a requirement for the message to remain true to the words of Scripture; to teach the meaning of the holy writ. In most cases, this should be an exposition of the passage; a verse-by-verse movement through the text. Unfortunately, this is not always what students in seminary are taught. I am reminded of an encounter I had with a professor of homiletics at a well-known evangelical divinity school. The story is both humorous and tragic (humorously tragic?). I was at a reception for some students, making small talk with folks, and this preaching professor sat down with me, and we began to talk about the usual things—our families, interest, hobbies, etc. Then we moved to talk shop, and I remember sitting there, nodding my head to whatever it was he had been saying, and then I could have sworn he said, "I like to teach my students to break free from the text." I did a double-take and asked for clarification; after all, he could not possibly mean what it sounded like he meant . . . *break free from the text*? But upon further explanation, I became aware of the fact that he did, indeed, mean exactly what he said! I wonder, does that sound anything like what Paul, under the inspiration of the Holy Spirit, charged Timothy to do? Did Paul say, "I solemnly charge you, in the presence of God and of Christ Jesus: Break free from the text!"? Needless to say, I was shocked, irritated, confused, and saddened all at the same time. Evangelicals must be wary of fads in preaching and worship which come and go, and stick to the text of Scripture for guidance. It seems that in our text, Paul makes his desire for a ministry centered on the preaching of the Word known, and he sees the centrality of the Word as necessary for proper Christian ministry. A brief examination of the

---

1. Towner, *Letters to Timothy and Titus*, 599.

development of this theme in Paul's writings to Timothy as background to the charge will make this more clear.

First, the context of the passage within the letter ought to be acknowledged. At the end of chapter three, Paul makes it clear that the life of the faithful should be grounded in the Word—he reminds Timothy of his own Christian heritage and how he has *known the Scriptures* since childhood (3:15). Remaining in the faith is tied to *knowledge of* and *belief in* the Sacred Scriptures (3:14). In every class I teach in seminary, I require my students to read half of the Bible—either the first half (Genesis-Psalms) or the second half (Proverbs-Revelation), and I encourage them to read it through in canonical order. There are many reasons for this requirement, but the most important is quite simple and straightforward: if we are to be people of the Book, we need to *know* the Book, and to know the Book, we need to *read* the Book. I believe that, while much of the training in seminary is important, the most important thing one needs for success in ministry is to be in the Word, for biblical literacy and for the fellowship with God gained in its transforming power. To say this is not to put Scripture in opposition to seminary training; quite the opposite. Rather, it is best to see the relationship as one of reciprocity. Seminary training presupposes biblical literacy and a life in the Word, and seminary training ought to enhance biblical literacy and the life in the Word.

Timothy had learned the Word and had gained *wisdom* (3:15). Paul wants Timothy to be *wise*. In the biblical language, wisdom is not the mere ability to make choices that are profitable or turn out well or the way one wishes. Rather, biblical wisdom is inextricably tied to intimate knowledge of God which manifests itself in obedience. Throughout Proverbs, wisdom is linked to one's personal relationship with God (e.g., Prov 1:7; 2:6; 4:5; 9:10;15:33; 28:11; 30:3). In James, believers are encouraged to ask God for wisdom as the key to enduring persecution and remaining faithful (Jas 1:2–6). Wisdom, born out of an intimate knowledge of God, is what Paul wants for Timothy, and he assumes it in his charge.

The verses immediately preceding the charge are well-known; the exhortation to preach the Word is therefore given in the context of perhaps the best known passage on biblical inspiration and the value of living a life grounded in the Word: all Scripture is breathed-out by God, and because of its divine origin, it is useful (and in this, hear "serves as the basis") for the work of ministry. We often think of the list provided in verse 16 as referring to the value of the Word in the lives of individuals; that it is referring to a perfecting work of the Word in personal devotion, but it is clear from the context that Paul is actually providing Timothy with a formula for successful ministry. Note that its usefulness is for the "man of God", that he may be completely prepared for "every good work" (3:16). Note, also, the nature of the work—the items listed are all associated with ministry: teaching, rebuking, correcting, and training in righteousness. There are, what in our modern conceptions of propriety would be considered both positive and negative actions; rebuking and correcting as somewhat negative, and teaching and training in righteousness as positive. Such a division, though, is foreign to the biblical conception, for the intimacy of fellowship within the Church, coupled with a sincere desire for holiness, lead the individual believers to see all of these activities of ministry to be positive. They are all born out of a love for God and consequently, a love for the parishioner. Each activity is designed to aid and encourage the receiver to grow in godliness. Chaplains ought to look at these activities as a necessary part of their ministry of the Word.

Not only is the exhortation to preach the Word given within the context of perhaps the most famous passage on the biblical text and therefore incorporates its concept of divine inspiration, but it also assumes Paul's view that the Word itself is alive and active. Paul contrasts the state of the Word with his own state; it is not bound (as Paul is in chains), it cannot be held, and it is because of this power of the Gospel, its life-transforming power, that Paul can endure his imprisonment. In chapter two, Paul makes clear his trust in the resurrection and the faithfulness of God exhibited in Christ (2:8–10). Paul knows that the promise of resurrection with Christ is sure because it is in God's Word (2:11ff.). And so the importance and centrality of the Word is again emphasized.

The exhortation also seems to include some of Paul's other exhortations to Timothy regarding the work of ministry. In his previous letter, Paul had told Timothy to teach with authority:

> Prescribe and teach these things. Let no one look down on your youthfulness, but rather in speech, conduct, love, faith and purity, show yourself an example of those who believe. Until I come, give attention to the public reading of Scripture, to exhortation and teaching. Do not neglect the spiritual gift within you, which was bestowed on you through prophetic utterance with the laying on of hands by the presbytery. Take pains with these things; be absorbed in them, so that your progress will be evident to all.

Pay close attention to yourself and to your teaching; persevere in these things, for as you do this you will ensure salvation both for yourself and for those who hear you (1 Tim 4:11–16, NAS).

Timothy should not allow anyone to evaluate his ability to minister on his age or experience, for they are not vitally important. What gives credibility to a ministry is the minster's personal holiness and integrity (in Christ), the ministry's grounding in God's Word, and the Holy Spirit's empowerment of the ministry. Paul tells Timothy to be an example for believers to follow in faith, love, actions and thought. He also reminds Timothy to use his spiritual gift(s) and to be faithful in ministry, using words almost identical to the passage in 2 Timothy: reading, exhortation, teaching (1 Tim 4:13). The main emphasis in this passage is on Timothy's actions and life; he is to be aware of his actions at all times. The souls of those entrusted to his care could very well be at stake (1 Tim 4:16).

So the charge to preach the Word entails a number of things. It entails a life grounded in the Word of God; a life of serious study of that Word. It entails a life of faithfulness; a life of serious application of that Word. It entails a reverence of that Word; a proclamation of the truths contained in that Word; a steadfastness in remaining true to the content of that Word.

Now, the charge and our passage goes further than the exhortation to preach the Word. Paul tells Timothy to be prepared in season and out of season. It may be tempting to develop this imagery more; to talk about how, in the agrarian culture of the Ancient Near East, persons had to make sure they cared for the land at all times so that when planting time came, they could get the most from their crops. Discussion of the various methods used in the region for this work could be included here. I am not sure that such an approach will really lend any aid in understanding the text, at least not any better than taking it at its most straightforward reading—Paul says to always be ready. The concept is a familiar one to all military members. Whenever there is down-time in the training day, non-commissioned officers are supposed to conduct *hip-pocket training*; they are to be ready at all times to give a class to lower-ranked enlisted soldiers.[2] The same idea can apply to chaplaincy ministry.

---

2. The term comes from the idea that they always have their basic soldier skills books with them in their hip-pockets.

Chaplains should always have a sermon at the ready. I learned this lesson the hard way. When I first became a chaplain, I scheduled my religious services for a set time and a set location, and then went out to visit the troops; to engage in a ministry of presence. While visiting a group of soldiers out in the field, one asked if I would conduct a religious service. I was happy to oblige and point out the service times and locations. When he informed me that they would not be able to attend, and asked if I could conduct one right then, I was taken aback. I quickly took out my Bible and began a feverish search for a passage I could easily preach. By the grace of God, the service went well. I suspect that many chaplains have learned this lesson over the years, in much the same way I did. My advice: have a sermon and a couple of funeral messages prepared at all times. It does not require a full-blown sermon, but at least some well-thought-out, appropriate words from the biblical text and some thoughts about the implications and applications of the text.

Interestingly, the positive charge to preach the Word can be seen as placed in opposition to Paul's warnings against becoming involved in godless chatter and arguments, from disputes about the resurrection and second coming (2:16–18), to an unhealthy focus on genealogies (1 Tim 1:3–11). So the exhortation to preach the Word is clearly not an exhortation to look for secrets hidden in the text of Scripture, something for which the Gnostics were famous.

Paul then moves to elucidate what he means by his exhortation to preach: correct/reprove, rebuke, and encourage/exhort (4:2). At first glance, we may think of these items is isolation or removed from the context of Paul's letter to Timothy, and it may be appropriate to do so, once we see to what Paul primarily referred. He seems to be most concerned with doctrinal matters (4:3–4).

It has become somewhat fashionable, even in some evangelical circles, to eschew doctrinal study. Some church leaders have come to view the study of theology as a cold, dead enterprise (as noted in chapter five), something to be contrasted with a living, dynamic spiritual relationship with God. Often times, religion is seen as the villain. For example, Mark Driscoll, in rightly questioning Burke's overemphasis on Jesus' status as religious and moral teacher, writes, "But Jesus stands against religion and morality as enemies of the gospel because, as Martin Luther said, religion and morality are the default mechanisms of the human heart to pursue righteousness apart from him. Therefore, it is essential that Jesus not be

presented in terms of morality or religion because Jesus' mission was not
to establish religion or morality."[3] Consider the words Young puts into the
mouth of Jesus in *The Shack*:

> 'As well-intentioned as it might be, you know that religious ma-
> chinery can chew people up!' . . . 'Like I said, I don't create institu-
> tions; that's an occupation for those who want to play God. So no,
> I'm not too big on religion,' Jesus said a little sarcastically, 'and not
> very fond of politics or economics either.' Jesus' visage darkened
> noticeably. 'And why should I be? They are the man-created trinity
> of terrors that ravages the earth and deceives those I care about.
> What mental turmoil and anxiety does any human face that is not
> related to one of those three?'[4]

While there is certainly room to critique the way in which some
theological study proceeds, it is incorrect to view theology itself as the cul-
prit. In the biblical text, good theology cannot be separated from spiritual
vitality (and vice versa). For Paul, proper theological formulation; correct thought about God, just *should* lead to worship. Put differently, if our
thoughts about God (i.e., our theology) do not lead to worship, then they
are somehow deficient or in error! After all, the more we think about the
meaning of omniscience, omnipotence, omnipresence, and the fact that
the very Being who encapsulates those attributes also loves us, the more
we cannot help but worship! Once, when interviewing for a job at a divinity school, the faculty members asked me what, in addition to the Bible,
I read for my devotional time. After thinking for a moment, I responded,
"Wolfhart Pannenberg." They were taken aback and a little confused. I
continued, "I like to read systematic theology devotionally." They seemed
to think that I had misunderstood the question, for they asked again,
clarifying that they were not asking just what I like to read, but what helps
in my spiritual development. I again said, "Systematic Theology," and
thought to myself, "this is why you need me here." Of course, my point is
not that I think Wolfhart Pannenberg's writing is on par with the Bible or
even that everything he writes is correct [it surely is not!], but rather is to
say that when I read works that make me think deeply about the meaning
of my faith, the Scriptures, and the God in whom that faith rests, I just do
grow closer to God. Here, then, is the value of seminary training. It gives

3. Driscoll, "Response to Burke," 70.

4. Young, *The Shack*, 179.

us the resources for thinking more deeply about our faith and how to put that faith in action in responsible ministry.

CONCLUSION

So it seems clear that the exhortation to preach the Word includes a number of items. First, the instructions to correct, rebuke and encourage have to do with helping congregants to think rightly about God; to ensure that their theology is an accurate representation or articulation of the truths contained in the divine revelation of Scripture.

Second, we must be careful to guard against separating out the exhortation to preach the Word from the life of faith. I have heard sermons on this passage in which so much emphasis was placed on the charge to preach with little or no attention to what it entailed, that one left with the impression that the only thing which is important is the vocalization of the message—there is a virtual disconnect between the man and the message. This sort of bifurcation can have disastrous consequences for the life of the Church. When the holiness of the preacher is seen an unimportant, as long as he can *deliver the goods*, there is a serious problem in the Church. The preacher is reduced to a motivational speaker or a good speech writer. Yet, the history of rhetoric is replete with cries for consistency between speaker and speech, from Socrates' critique of the Sophists, to Cicero's complaints about politicians, and such consistency is nowhere more important than in the preaching of God's Holy Word.

More could be said, but it seems appropriate to end here with Paul's exhortation to Timothy as it applies to all Christian chaplains:

Preach the Word!

Know the Word!

Understand the Word!

Live the Word!

Bibliography

BOOKS

Adams, Jay E. *Competent to Counsel.* Grand Rapids: Baker, 1970.

Bahnsen, Greg. *By This Standard: The Authority of God's Law Today.* Tyler, TX: Institute for Christian Economics, 1985.

Barth, Karl. *The Doctrine of the Word of God, Church Dogmatics I.2.* New York: T & T Clark, 1956.

Beale, Greg K. *The Erosion of Inerrancy in Evangelicalism: Responding to New Challenges to Biblical Authority.* Wheaton: Crossway, 2008.

Bell, Rob. *Velvet Elvis: Repainting the Christian Faith.* Grand Rapids: Zondervan, 2005.

Bergen, Doris L., ed. *The Sword of the Lord: Military Chaplains from the First to the Twenty-First Century.* Notre Dame: Notre Dame, 2001.

Brister, C. W. *Pastoral Care in the Church,* 3rd ed. San Francisco: Harper Collins, 1977.

Budd, Richard M. *Serving Two Masters: The Development of American Military Chaplaincy, 1860–1920.* Lincoln: University of Nebraska, 2002.

Cabot, Richard C. and Russell Dicks, *The Art of Ministering to the Sick.* New York: Macmillan, 1944.

Carroll, J. M. *"The Trail of Blood"... Following the Christians Down Through the Centuries ... or The History of Baptist Churches from the Time of Christ, Their Founder, to the Present Day.* Lexington, KY: Ashland Avenue Baptist Church, 1931; 66th ed., 1992.

Carson, D. A. *Becoming Conversant with the Emerging Church: Understanding a Movement and Its Implications.* Grand Rapids: Zondervan, 2005.

Cash, Lt. Carey H. *A Table in the Presence.* Nashville: Thomas Nelson, 2004.

Chilton, David. *Paradise Restored: A Biblical Theology of Dominion.* Fort Worth, TX: Dominion Press, 1985.

Christian, C.W. *Schleiermacher, Makers of the Modern Theological Mind.* Peabody, MA: Hendrickson, 1979.

Clinebell, Howard. *Basic Types of Pastoral Care & Counseling.* Nashville: Abingdon, 1966, rev. 1984.

Collins, Gary R. *Christian Counseling: A Comprehensive Guide,* rev. ed. Dallas: Word, 1988.

Congar, Yves. *The Wide World My Parish: Salvation and Its Problems.* Baltimore: Helicon, 1961.

Cox, Harvey, ed. *Military Chaplains: From a Religious Military to a Military Religion.* New York: American Report Press, 1971.

Drazin, Israel and Cecil B. Curry. *For God and Country: The History of a Constitutional Challenge to the Army Chaplaincy.* Hoboken, NJ: KTAV Publishing House, 1995.

Everly, George S. Douglas J. Mitchell, Jeffrey T. Mitchell, Diane Myers, and Charles E. Woods. *National Guard Trained Crisis Responder (TCR) Course: Terrorism and Disaster Response.* Ellicott City, MD: International Critical Incident Stress Foundation, 2003.

Ganz, Richard. *Psychobabble: The Failure of Modern Psychology—and the Biblical Alternative* Wheaton: Crossway, 1993.

Garstand, J. and J.B. Garstang, *The Story of Jericho.* 2nd ed. London: Marshall, Morgan, & Scott, 1948.

Gaustad, Edwin S. *Church and State in America.* 2nd ed. New York: Oxford, 2003.

Geisler, Norman L. ed., *Inerrancy.* Grand Rapids: Zondervan, 1980.

Gibbs, Eddie and Ryan K. Bolger. *Emerging Churches: Creating Christian Community in Postmodern Cultures.* Grand Rapids: Baker, 2005.

Grenz, Stanley J. *A Primer on Postmodernism.* Grand Rapids: Eerdmans, 1996.

Hall, Charles E. *Head and Heart: The Story of the Clinical Pastoral Education Movement.* Decatur, GA: Journal of Pastoral Care Publications, 1992.

Hankins, Barry *American Evangelicals: A Contemporary History of a Mainstream Religious Movement.* Lanham, MD :Rowman & Littlefield, 2008.

Harris, Sam. *Letter to a Christian Nation.* New York: Alfred K. Knopf, 2006.

Hawking, Stephen W. *A Brief History of Time: From the Big Bang to Black Holes.* New York: Bantam, 1988.

Hick, John. *Death and Eternal Life.* San Francisco: Harper and Row, 1976.

Hiltner, Seward. *Pastoral Counseling.* Nashville: Abingdon, 1949.

Hirsch, Edward D. *Validity in Interpretation.* New Haven: Yale, 1967.

Holmes, Arthur. *Ethics: Approaching Moral Decisions.* Downers Grove: InterVarsity, 1984.

Holst, Lawrence E., ed. *Hospital Ministry: The Role of the Chaplain Today.* Eugene, OR: Wipf & Stock, 1985.

Hopper, Jeffery *Understanding Modern Theology II.* (Philadelphia: Fortress, 1987.

House, Paul R. *1, 2 Kings, NAC,* vol. 8. Nashville: Broadman & Holman, 1995.

Johnson, Eric L. and Stanton L. Jones, eds., *Psychology & Christianity: Four Views.* Downers Grove: InterVarsity, 2005.

Johnson, Eric. *Foundations for Soul Care.* Downers Grove: InterVarsity, 2007.

Kaiser, Walter. *Toward an Old Testament Ethics.* Grand Rapids: Zondervan, 1983.

Kimball, Dan. *The Emerging Church: Vintage Christianity for New Generations.* Grand Rapids: Zondervan, 2003.

King, Stephen D. W. *Trust the Process: A History of Clinical Pastoral Education as Theological Education.* Lanham, MD: University Press of America, 2007.

Kurzman, Dan. *No Greater Glory: The Four Immortal Chaplains and the Sinking of the Dorchester in World War II.* New York: Random House, 2004.

Lindsay, D. Michael. *Faith in the Halls of Power: How Evangelicals Joined the American Elite.* New York: Oxford, 2007.

Mansfield, Stephen. *The Faith of the American Soldier.* Lake Mary, FL: Charisma House, 2005.

McCormack, Janet R. and Naomi K. Paget. *The Work of the Chaplain.* Valley Forge: Judson, 2006.

McLaren, Brian. *A Generous Orthodoxy: Why I am a Missional, Evangelical, Post/Protestant, Liberal/Conservative, Mystical/Poetic, Biblical, charismatic/Contemplative, Fundamentalist/Calvinist, Anabaptist/Anglican, Methodist, Catholic, Green, Incar-*

national, *Depressed-yet-Hopeful, Emergent, Unfinished Christian.* Grand Rapids: Zondervan, 2004.

Morris, Leon. *The Gospel According to John,* rev. ed. *New International Commentary on the New Testament.* Grand Rapids: Eerdmans, 1995.

Murray, Bruce T. *Religious Liberty in America, The First Amendment in Historical and Contemporary Perspective.* Amherst: University of Massachusetts Press, 2008.

Noll, Mark. *Turning Points: Decisive Moments in the History of Christianity.* Grand Rapids: Baker, 1997.

Noonan, John T. *The Lustre of Our Country: The American Experience of Religious Freedom.* Berkeley: University of California Press, 1998.

North, Gary. *Theonomy: An Informed Response.* Tyler, TX: Institute for Christian Economics, 1991.

Paget, Naomi K. and Janet R. McCormack. *The Work of the Chaplain.* Valley Forge: Judson, 2006.

Peers, W. R. *The My Lai Inquiry.* New York: W. W. Norton & Co, 1979.

Plato. *Crito.* in B. Jowett, trans. *The Republic and Other Works.* Garden City, NY: Dophin Books, 1960.

Rahner, Karl. *Ecclesiology, Theological Investigations.* vol. 9, trans. David Bourke. New York: Seabury, 1976.

Raschke, Carl. *The Next Reformation: Why Evangelicals Must Embrace Postmodernity.* Grand Rapids: Baker, 2004.

Ravitch, Frank S. *Masters of Illusion: The Supreme Court and the Religion Clauses.* New York: NYU Press, 2007.

Reimer, Sam and Samuel Harold Reimer. *Evangelicals and the Continental Divide: The Conservative Protestant Subculture in Canada and the United States.* Montreal: McGill-Queen's University Press, 2003.

Rieff, Philip. *The Triumph of the Therapeutic: Uses of Faith After Freud.* Chicago: University of Chicago Press, 1987.

Rushdooney, Rousas J. *The Institutes of Biblical Law.* Phillipsburg, NJ: Presbyterian & Reformed, 1973.

Sakkelion, J. ed., *Forty-eight Letters of Theodoret of Cyrrhus.* Athens, 1885.

Schaler, Jeffrey, ed. *Szasz Under Fire: The Psychiatric Abolitionist Faces His Critics.* Chicago: Open Court, 2004.

Schleiermacher, Friedrich. *On Religion: Addresses in Response to Its Cultured Critics,* trans. by Terrence N. Tice. Richmond, VA: John Knox Press, 1969.

Sozomen. *Ecclesiastical History.* rev. Chester D. Hartranft, in *Nicene and Post-Nicene Fathers, Second Series,* vol. 2, ed. Philip Schaff and Henry Wace. Christian Literature Publishing Company, 1892; repr. Peabody, MA: Hendrickson, 1994.

Sulpitius Severus. *Life of Saint Martin (ch. III).* ed. Alexander Roberts in *Nicene and Post-Nicene Fathers, Second Series,* vol 11, ed. Philip Schaff and Henry Wace. Christian Literature Publishing Company, 1894; repr. Peabody, MA: Hendrickson, 1994.

Sumner, William. *Folkways* (1906); reprinted in John Ladd, ed. *Ethical Relativism.* Belmont, CA: Wadsworth, 1973.

Szasz, Thomas. *Coercion as Cure: A Critical History of Psychiatry.* Edison, NJ: Transaction Publishers, 2007.

———. *Psychiatry: The Science of Lies.* Syracuse: Syracuse University Press, 2008.

———. *The Manufacture of Madness: A Comparative Study of the Inquisition and the Mental Health Movement.* Syracuse: Syracuse University Press, 1997.

——. *The Myth of Mental Illness.* San Francisco: Harper, 1960, rev. 1984.

——, ed. *The Medicalization of Everyday Life: Selected Essays.* Syracuse: Syracuse University Press, 2007.

Theodoret, *Epistula* 2. ed. and trans. Yvan Azema. *Sources Chretiennes* 40; Paris: Cerf, 1955.

Thornton, Edward. *Professional Education for Ministry: A History of Clinical Pastoral Education.* Nashville: Abingdon, 1970.

Towner, Philip H. *The Letters to Timothy and Titus. NICNT.* Grand Rapids: Eerdmans, 2006.

Vitz, Paul C. *Psychology as Religion: The Cult of Self Worship.* Grand Rapids: Eerdmans, 1994.

Wales, Ken and David Poling, *Sea of Glory.* Nashville: Broadman & Holman, 2001.

Webber, Robert. *Evangelicals on the Canterbury Trail: Why Evangelicals Are Attracted to the Liturgical Church.* Harrisburg, PA: Morehouse, 1989.

White, Walter H., ed. *The Chapel of Four Chaplains: A Sanctuary of Brotherhood.* Philadelphia: Chapel of Four Chaplains, 1979.

Wilson, Robert R. *Prophecy and Society in Ancient Israel.* Philadelphia: Fortress, 1980.

Wittgenstein, Ludwig. *Philosophical Investigations.* 3rd ed. trans. G. E. M. Anscombe. Upper Saddle River: Prentice Hall, 1958.

Young, Bruce H. and Dudley D. Blake, eds. *Group Treatments for Post-Traumatic Stress Disorder.* Philadelphia: Brunner/Mazel, 1999.

Young, William P. *The Shack.* Los Angeles: Windblown Media, 2007.

Zahn, Gordon. *The Military Chaplaincy: A Study of Role Tension in the Royal Air Force.* Toronto: University of Toronto Press, 1969.

ESSAYS/ARTICLES

Adams, George. "Chaplains as Liaisons with Religious Leaders." *The Army Chaplaincy* (PB 16–09–1) (Winter-Spring 2009): 40–43.

Adler, Amy B., Brett T. Litz, Carl Andrew Castro, Michael Suvak, Jeffrey L. Thomas, Lolita Burrell, Dennis McGurk, Kathleen M. Wright, and Paul D. Bliese. "A Group Randomized Trial of Critical Incident Stress Debriefing Provided to U.S. Peacekeepers." *Journal of Traumatic Stress* 21:3 (June 2008): 253–63.

Albucher, Ronald C. and I. Lizerbon. "Psychopharmacological Treatment in PTSD: A Critical Review." *Journal of Psychiatric Res* 36 (2002): 355–67.

Angrosino, Michael. "Civil Religion Redux." *Anthropological Quarterly* 75:2 (Spring 2002): 239–67.

Bachrach, David S. "The Medieval Military Chaplain and His Duties." in Doris L. Bergen, ed. *The Sword of the Lord.* Notre Dame: Notre Dame, 2004, 69–88.

Banerjee, Neela. "Proposal on Military Chaplains and Prayer Holds Up Bill." *New York Times* (September 19, 2006).

Beck, James R. "Value Tensions Between Evangelical Christians and Christian Counseling." *Counseling and Values* 41:2 (January 1997): 107–16.

Bellah, Robert N. "Civil Religion and the American Future." *Religious Education* 71:3 (May-June 1976): 235–43.

——. "Civil Religion in America." *Daedalus,* 96:1 (Winter, 1967):1–21.

——. "Response to the Panel on Civil Religion." *Sociological Analysis* 37:2 (1976): 153–59.

Benjamin, Michael J. "Justice, Justice Shall You Pursue: Legal Analysis of Religion Issues in the Army." DA-PAM 27-50-312, *The Army Lawyer* (November 1998):1–18.

Bergen, Doris L. "German Military Chaplains in the Second World War and the Dilemmas of Legitimacy," in Doris L. Bergen, ed. *The Sword of the Lord.* Notre Dame: Notre Dame, 2001, 165–86.

Bergen, Doris L. "Introduction" in Doris L. Bergen, ed. *The Sword of the Lord.* Notre Dame: Notre Dame, 2001, 1–28.

Bettler, John F. "Biblical Counseling: The Next Generation." *Journal of Pastoral Practice* 8:4 (1987): 3–10.

———. "CCEF: The Beginning" *Journal of Pastoral Practice* 9:3 (1988): 45–51.

———. "Counseling and the Doctrine of Sin." *Journal of Biblical Counseling* 13:1 (Fall 1994): 2–4.

Boisen, Anton T. "The Challenge to Our Seminaries." *The Journal of Pastoral Care* 5:1 (Spring 1951): 11–12; repr. from *Christian Work* (January 23, 1926).

Boudreaux, Edwin D. and Bhrett McCabe. "Critical Incident Stress Management: I. Interventions and Effectiveness." *Psychiatric Services* 51:9 (September 2000): 1095–97.

Boyd, Jeffrey H. "An Insider's Effort to Blow Up Psychiatry." *Journal of Biblical Counseling* 15:3 (Spring 1997): 21–31; reprinted from *Trinity Journal* 17 (1996).

Breslau, Naomi. "Outcomes of Posttraumatic Stress Disorder." *Journal of Clinical Psychiatry* 62 (2001): 55–59.

Bryant, Richard A. "Acute Stress Disorder: Course, epidemiology, Assessment, and Treatment." in Brett T. Litz, ed., *Early Intervention for Trauma and Traumatic Loss* (New York: The Guilford Press, 2004), 15–34.

Cabot, Richard Clarke. "A Plea for a Clinical Year in the Course of Theological Study." *Survey Graphic* (September 1925); repr. In Richard C. Cabot, *Borderline Ethics* (New York: Harper and Row, 1926), 1–22.

Cardena, Etzel and David Spiegel, "Dissociative Reactions to the San Francisco Bay Area Earthquake of 1989." *American Journal of Psychiatry* 150:3 (March 1993): 474–78.

Carter, John D. "Adams' Theory of Nouthetic Counseling." *Journal of Psychology and Theology* 3:3 (Summer 1975): 143–55.

———. "Nouthetic Counseling Defended: A Reply to Ganz" *Journal of Psychology and Theology* 4:3 (Summer 1976): 206–16.

Chisolm, Jr., Robert B. "Does God Deceive?" *Bibliotheca Sacra* 155:617 (January-March, 1988): 11–28.

Cloud, Matthew W. "One Nation Under God: Tolerable Acknowledgement of Religion or Unconstitutional Cold War Propaganda Cloaked in American Civil Religion?" *Journal of Church and State* 46:2 (Spring 2004): 311–40.

Cook, Heather "Service Before Self? Evangelicals Flying High at the U.S. Air Force Academy." *Journal of Law and Education* 36:1 (January 2007): 1–26.

Cooperman, Alan. "Military Wrestles with Disharmony Among Chaplains," *Washington Post*, Tuesday, August 30, 2005: A01-03.

Cox, Harvey. "Introduction: The Man of God and the Man of War." in Harvey Cox, ed. *Military Chaplains: From a Religious Military to a Military Religion,* ed. Harvey G. Cox. New York: American Report Press, 1971, v-xii.

Cyr, Monica. and M. K. Farrar, "Treatments for Posttraumatic Stress Disorder." *Annals of Pharmacotherapy* 34:3 (2000): 366–76.

Davis, Derek H. "The Pledge of Allegiance and American Values." *Journal of Church and State* 45:4 (Autumn 2003): 657–68.

———. "Separation, Integration, and Accommodation: Religion and State in America in a Nutshell." *Journal of Church and State* 43:1 (Winter 2001): 5–17.

Day, Richard B. "Incarnational Christian Psychology and Psychotherapy: What Do We Believe and What Do We Do?" *Pastoral Psychology* 54 (2006): 535–44.

Deahl, Martin P., Adrian B. Gillham, Janice Thomas, Margaret M. Searle, and Michael Srinivasan. "Psychological Sequelae Following the Gulf War: Factors Associated with Subsequent Morbidity and the Effectiveness of Psychological Debriefing." *British Journal of Psychiatry* 165 (1994): 60–65.

Delahunty, Robert J. "'Varied Carols': Legislative Prayer in a Pluralist Polity." *Creighton Law Review* 40:3 (April 2007): 517–68.

Derrida, Jacques. "Letter to a Japanese Friend." in David Wood and Robert Bernasconi, eds. *Derrida and Difference.* Northwestern University Press: Evanston, IL: 1988.

Devilly, Grant J. and Peter Cotton, "Psychological Debriefing and the Workplace: Defining a Concept, Controversies and Guidelines for Intervention." *Australian Psychologist* 38:2 (July 2003): 144–50.

Dobosh, Jr., William J. "Coercion in the Ranks: The Establishment Clause Implications of Chaplain-led Prayers at Mandatory Army Events." *Wisconsin Law Review* (2006): 1493–561.

Douglas, Davison M. "Ceremonial Deism." in Paul Findleman, ed. *Encyclopedia of American Civil Liberties.* New York: Routledge, 2006, 1:258.

Driscoll, Mark. "Response to John Burke." in Robert Webber, ed. *Responding to the Beliefs of Emerging Churches: Five Perspectives.* Grand Rapids: Zondervan, 2007, 70–72.

Engel, Charles C. Thomas Oxman, Christopher Yamamoto, Darin Gould, Shelia Barry, Patrice Stewart, Kurt Kroenke, John W. Williams, and Allen J. Dietrich, "RESPECT-Mil: Feasibility of a Systems-Level Collaborative Care Approach to Depression and Post-Traumatic Stress Disorder in Military Primary Care." *Military Medicine* 173:10 (October 2008): 935–40.

Epstein, Steven B. "Rethinking the Constitutionality of Ceremonial Deism." *Columbia Law Review* 96 (1996): 2083–174.

Everly, George S. "Emergency Mental Health: An Overview." *International Journal of Emergency Mental Health* 1 (1999): 3–7.

Everly, George S. "Five Principles of Crisis Intervention: Reducing the Risk of Premature Crisis Intervention." *International Journal of Emergency Mental Health* 2:1 (2000): 1–4.

Everly, George S. and Jeffrey T. Mitchell, "The Debriefing 'Controversy' and Crisis Intervention: A Review of Lexical and Substantive Issues." *International Journal of Emergency Mental Health* 2:4 (2000): 211–25.

Everly, George S., Raymond B. Flannery, and Victoria A. Eyler. "Critical Incident Stress Management (CISM): A Statistical Review of the Literature." *Psychiatric Quorterly* 73:3 (Fall 2002): 171–82.

Fawzy, Tamar I. and Matt J. Gray, "From CISD to CISM: Same Song Different Verse?" *The Scientific Review of Mental Health Practice* 5:2 (2007): 31–43.

Flanney, Raymond B. and George S. Everly, "Crisis Intervention: A Review." *International Journal of Emergency Mental Health* 2:2 (2000): 119–25.

Freedman, Benjamin. "Equipoise and the Ethics of Clinical Research." *The New England Journal of Medicine* 317:3 (July 1987): 141–45.

Galea, Sandro, David Vlahov, Heidi Resnick, Jennifer Ahren, Ezra Susser, Joel Gold, Michael Bucuvalas, and Dean Kilpatrick. "Trends of Probably Post-Traumatic Stress

Disorder in New York City After the September 11 Terrorist Attack." *American Journal of Epidemiology* 158 (2003): 514–24.

Galea, Sandro, Heidi Resnick, Dean Kilpatrick, Michael Bucuvalas, Joel Gold, and David Vlahov, "Psychological Sequelae of the September 11 Terrorist Attack in New York City." *New England Journal of Medicine* 346 (2002): 982–87.

Galek, Kathleen, Kevin J. Flannelly, Harold G. Koenig, and Sarah L. Fogg, "Referrals to Chaplains: The Role of Religion and Spirituality in Healthcare Settings." *Mental Health, Religion & Culture* 10:4 (July 2007): 363–77.

Ganz, Richard "Confession of a Psychological Heretic." *Journal of Biblical Counseling* 13:2 (Winter 1995): 18–22.

———. "Nouthetic Counseling Defended." *Journal of Psychology and Theology* 4:3 (Summer 1976): 199–201.

Gray, Matt J., Brett T. Litz, and A. Randall Olson, "Methodological and Ethical Issues in Early Intervention Research." in Brett T. Litz, ed. *Early Intervention for Trauma and Traumatic Loss.* New York: The Guilford Press, 2004, 179–98.

Griffin, LaMar. "RLL and the Emerging Role for chaplains in shaping Full Spectrum Operations." *The Army Chaplaincy* (PB 16–09–1) (Winter-Spring 2009): 44–48.

Hick, John. "A Pluralist View" in *More Than One Way?: Four Views on Salvation in a Pluralistic World,* ed. Dennis Okholm and Timothy Phillips. Grand Rapids: Zondervan, 1995, 27–92.

Hindson, Ed. "Nouthetic Counseling: Toward a Christian Theory of Personality." *Journal of Pastoral Practice* 3:4 (1979): 11–31.

———. "The Use of Scripture in Nouthetic Counseling." *Journal of Pastoral Practice* 3:2 (1979): 28–39.

Holst, Lawrence E. "The Hospital Chaplain: Between Worlds" in Lawrence E. Holst, ed. *Hospital Ministry: The Role of the Chaplain Today* (Eugene, OR: Wipf & Stock, 1985), 12–27.

Houk, Ira. "The U.S. Army Chaplaincy's involvement in Strategic Religious Engagement." *The Army Chaplaincy* (PB 16–09–1) (Winter-Spring 2009): 49–53.

Kaplan, Julie B. "Military Mirrors on the Wall: Nonestablishment and the Military Chaplaincy." *The Yale Law Journal* 95 (1986): 1210–236.

Kessler, R. C. "Posttraumatic Stress Disorder: The Burden to the Individual and to Society." *Journal of Clinical Psychiatry* 61(2000): 4–12.

Kluckhohn, Clyde. "Ethical Relativity: *Sic et Non.*" *Journal of Philosophy* 52 (1955): 663–77.

Lehmann, Hartmut. "In the Service of Two Kings: Protestant Prussian Military Chaplains, 1713–1918." in Doris L. Bergen, ed., *The Sword of the Lord.* Notre Dame: Notre Dame, 2004, 125–40.

Lesch, Klaus-Peter. and Ursula Merschdorf. "Impulsivity, Agression, and Serotonin: A Molecular Psychobiological Perspective." *Behavioral Science Law* 18 (2000): 581–604.

Lewis, Gordon R. "The Human Authorship of Inspired Scripture." in Norman L. Geisler, ed., *Inerrancy.* Grand Rapids: Zondervan, 1980, 229–64.

MacArthur, John. "Biblical Counseling and Our Sufficiency in Christ." *The Journal of Biblical Counseling* 11:2 (Winter 1993): 10–15.

MacIntyre, Alasdair. "The Theology, Ethics and the Ethics of Medicine and Health Care: Comments on Papers by Novak, Mouw, Roach, Cahill, and Hartt" *The Journal of Medicine and Philosophy* 4 (December 1979): 443.

Mack, Wayne A. "The Sufficiency of Scripture in Counseling." *The Master's Seminary Journal* 9:1 (Spring 1998): 63–84.

Maddigan, Michael M. "The Establishment Clause, Civil Religion, and the Public Church." *California Law Review* 81 (1993): 293–349.

Marmar, Charles R., Thomas C. Neylan, and Frank B. Schoenfeld. "New Directions in the Pharmacotherapy of Posttraumatic Stress Disorder." *Psychiatry Quarterly* 73 (2002): 259–70.

Mathisen, Ralph W. "Emperors, Priests, and Bishops: Military Chaplains in the Roman Empire." in Doris L. Bergen,ed. *The Sword of the Lord*. Notre Dame: Notre Dame, 2004, 29–43.

Mayhue, Richard "False Prophets and the Deceiving Spirit." *Master's Seminary Journal* 4 (1993): 135–63.

McEwen, Bruce S. "The Neurobiology of Stress: From Serendipity to Clinical Relevance." *Brain Res* 886 (2000): 172–89;

McManus, Erwin Raphael. "The Global Intersection." in Leonard Sweet, ed., *The Church in Emerging Culture: Five Perspectives*. Grand Rapids: Zondervan, 2003, 235–63.

McNabb, Darryl. "The Biblical View of Ill Health." *Journal of Pastoral Practice* 3:1 (1979): 67–73.

Mitchell, C. Ben. "Is That All There Is?: Moral Ambiguity in a Postmodern Pluralistic Culture." in David S. Dockery, ed. *The Challenge of Postmodernism: An Evangelical Engagement*. Grand Rapids: Baker, 1995, 267–80.

Mitchell, Jeffrey T. "A Response to the Devilly and Cotton article, 'Psychological Debriefing and the Workplace . . .'" *Australian Psychologist* 39:1 (March 2004): 24–28.

Mohler, R. Albert. "The Integrity of the Evangelical Tradition and the Challenge of the Postmodern Paradigm." in David S. Dockery, ed. *The Challenge of Postmodernism: An Evangelical Engagement*. Grand Rapids: Baker, 1995, 67–88.

Nauta, Reinard. "Not Practicing Theology." *Pastoral Psychology* 50:3 (January 2002): 197–205.

Patrick, Jeremy "Ceremonial Deisms." *The Humanist* 62:1 (Jan/Feb 2002): 42–43.

Paul, Pamela and Marc Arnin. "With God as My Shrink." *Psychology Today* 38:3 (May/June 2005): 62–68.

Pinnock, Clark. "An Inclusivist View" in *More Than One Way?: Four Views on Salvation in a Pluralistic World*, ed. Dennis Okholm and Timothy Phillips. Grand Rapids: Zondervan, 1995, 93–148.

Platman, Stanley R. "Psychopharmacology and Posttraumatic Stress Disorder." *International Journal of Emergency Mental Health* 3 (1999): 151–55.

Powlison, David. "25 Years of Biblical Counseling: An Interview with Jay Adams and John Bettler" *Journal of Biblical Counseling* 12:1 (Fall 1993): 8–13.

———. "Biblical Counseling." in Eric L. Johnson and Stanton L. Jones, eds., *Psychology & Christianity: Four Views* (Downers Grove: InterVarsity, 2005), 196–225.

———. "How Do You Help a 'Psychologized' Counselee?" *Journal of Biblical Counseling* 15:1 (Fall 1996): 2–7.

———. "Queries & Controversies: Do you ever refer people to psychologists or psychiatrists for help?" *Journal of Biblical Counseling* 13:2 (Winter 1995): 64–65.

———. "The Sufficiency of Scripture to Diagnose and Cure Souls." *Journal of Biblical Counseling* (Spring 2005): 2–14.

Richards, David. "A Field Study of Critical Incident Stress Debriefing Versus Critical Incident Stress Management." *Journal of Mental Health* 10:3 (2001): 351–62.

Riggs, David S., Barbara O. Rothbaum, and Edna B. Foa, "A Prospective Examination of Post-traumatic Stress in Victims of Non-Sexual Assault." *Journal of Interpersonal Violence* 10:2 (1995): 201–14.

Roberts, Robert. "Psychology and the Life of the Spirit." *Journal of Biblical Counseling* 15:1 (Fall 1996): 26–31.

Robinson, CH (BG) Lionel D. "In Service of God and Country." *GX: The Guard Experience* 4:2 (March 2007), 33.

Robinson, Robyn "Counterbalancing Misrepresentations of Critical Incident Stress Debriefing and Critical Incident Stress Management." *Australian Psychologist* 39:1 (March 2004): 29–34.

Rothbaum, Barbara O., Edna B. Foa, David S. Riggs, Tamera B. Murdock, and William Walsh, "A Prospective Examination of Post-traumatic Stress Disorder in Rape Victims." *Journal of Traumatic Stress* 5 (1992): 455–75.

Ruzek, Joseph I., Bruce H. Young, and Robyn D. Walser. "Group Treatment of Posttraumatic Stress Disorder and Other Trauma-Related Problems." *Prim Psychiatry* 10 (2003): 53–67.

Sangster, Margaret E. "Saga of The Four Chaplains." in Walter H. White, ed. *The Chapel of Four Chaplains: A Sanctuary of Brotherhood*. Philadelphia: Chapel of Four Chaplains, 1979, 58–59.

Satel, Sally and Christian Hoff Sommers. "The Mental Health Crisis that Wasn't: How the Trauma Industry Exploited 9/11." *Reason: Free Minds and Free Markets* (August/September 2005); accessed online June 20, 2009, at http://www.reason.com/news/show/33116.html.

Sloan, Patrick. "Post-traumatic Stress in Survivors of an Airplane Crash-landing: A Clinical and Exploratory Research Intervention." *Journal of Traumatic Stress* 1:2 (1988): 211–19.

Solomon, Zahava, Rami Shklar, and Mario Mikulincer. "Frontline Treatment of Combat Stress Reaction: A 20-Year Longitudinal Evaluation Study." *American Journal of Psychiatry* 162:12 (December 2005): 2309–14.

Stewart, Cheryl L. and Thomas Wrobel. "Evaluation of the Efficacy of Pharmacotherapy and Psychotherapy in Treatment of Combat-Related Post-Traumatic Stress Disorder: A Meta-Analytic Review of Outcome Studies." *Military Medicine* 174:5 (May 2009): 460–69.

Strong, Stanley R. "Christian Counseling: A Synthesis of Psychological and Christian Concepts." *Personal & Guidance Journal* 58:9 (May 1980): 589–92.

Szasz, Thomas "Mental Illness is Still a Myth." *Journal of Biblical Counseling* 14:1 (Fall 1995): 34–39.

Tickle, Phyllis. "Foreward" in Brian D. McLaren, *A Generous Orthodoxy*. Grand Rapids: Zondervan, 2004.

Truman, President Harry S. *Speech Dedicating the Chapel of Four Chaplains*, Philadelphia, PA, February 3, 1951, recorded in *The Chapel of Four Chaplains: A sanctuary of Brotherhood*, 16.

Van Emmerik, Arnold, Jan Kamphuis, Alexander Hulsbosch, and Paul Emmelkamp, "Single Session Debriefing After Psychological Trauma: A Meta-Analysis." *The Lancet* 360 (2002): 766–71.

Vitz, Paul C. "Psychology in Recovery." *First Things* 151 (March 2005): 17–21.

Walker, Clarence. "Introduction." in J. M. Carroll, *"The Trail of Blood" . . . Following the Christians Down Through the Centuries . . . or The History of Baptist Churches from the Time of Christ, Their Founder, to the Present Day* (Lexington, KY: Ashland Avenue Baptist Church, 1931; 66ᵗʰ ed., 1992),

Weber, Paul J. "The First Amendment and Military Chaplaincy: The Process of Reform" *Journal of Church and State* 22:3 (Autumn 1980): 459–74.

Weijer, Charles, Stanley Shapiro, and Kathleen C. Glass, "Clinical Equipoise and Not the Uncertainty Principle is the Moral Underpinning of the Randomized Clinical Trial." *British Medical Journal* 321 (2000): 756–57.

Welch, Edward T. "What is Biblical Counseling Anyway?" *Journal of Biblical Counseling* 16:1 (1997): 2–6.

Wildhack III, CDR William A. "Navy Chaplains at the Crossroads: Navigating the Intersection of Free Speech, Free Exercise, Establishment, and Equal Protection." *Naval Law Review* 51 (2005): 1–26.

Williams, George H. "The Chaplaincy in the Armed Forces of the United States of America in Historical and Ecclesiastical Perspective." in Harvey Cox, ed. *Military Chaplains: From a Religious Military to a Military Religion.* New York: American Report Press, 1971, 11–58.

Winfrey, David. "Southern Baptists Reject 'Pastoral Counseling' Biblical Therapy." *Christian Century* 124:2 (January 23, 2007): 24–27.

Wood, Brian. "Did the Israelites Conquer Jericho?" *Biblical Archaeology Review* 16:2 (1990): 44–58.

York, Michael. "Civil Religion Aspects of Neo-Paganism." *The Pomegranate* 6:2 (2004): 253–60.

Zahn, Gordon. "Sociological Impressions of the Chaplaincy." in Harvey Cox, ed. *Military Chaplains: From Religious Military to a Military Religion.* New York: American Report Press, 1971, 59–86.

UNPUBLISHED DOCUMENTS/PAPERS

Baptist Faith and Message (2000); Southern Baptist Convention.

David H. Hicks, Memorandum to MACOM chaplains, 04 September 2003, "Chief of Chaplains Policy Concerning Chaplains Bearing Arms," Office of the Chief of Chaplains, Washington, D.C.

Rostow, Eugene. Meiklejohn Lectures on Law (unpublished), Brown University, 1962.

"Talking Paper: Public Prayer in Military Ceremonies and Civic Occasions" Armed Services Chaplains Board.

"The U.S. Army Chief of Chaplains Newsletter (August 2004), Department of the Army, Washington, D.C.

INTERNET SOURCES

Appendix D: "Chaps line-by-line response to CO's Secret Letter of 'Theological' Instruction; Letter of Instruction from CAPT J.M. Carr, Commanding Officer USS ANZIO to LT Gordon Klingenschmitt dated 07Jul04, pgs. 2–3," D17–D18, www.persuade.tv, accessed July 25, 2007.

Appendix H: "The Sermon that God a U.S. Navy Chaplain Fired", H1, www.persuade.tv, accessed January 5, 2008.

Appendix J: "Proof the Naval Chaplain School Director CAPT Chaplain Bert Moore mandates upon all junior chaplains the Unitarian Universalist Theology of Harvard Seminary' 'Totalitarian Pluralism.'" www.persuade.tv, accessed September 14, 2007.

Appendix L: "Two-Star Admiral overrules Chaps' protest, mandates church quotas" L2, www.persuade.tv, accessed October 15, 2007.

Appendix N: "Two-star Admiral directs chaplains to pray 'government-sanitized prayers,'" N1, www.persuade.tv, accessed July 25, 2007.

Appendix S: "Proof the U.S. Naval Chaplain School and Harvard Divinity School are academically dishonest to claim 'Pluralism' is a 'Non-Sectarian' religion (when Pluralism actually promotes 'Unitarian Universalist' theology, a quite sectarian denomination, but cleverly marketed, through deceitful disguise)". www.persuade .tv, accessed September 14, 2007.

Appendix U: "Private emails proving conspiracy between Navy CAPT James Carr and Senior Chaplain Steve Gragg...agreeing to end junior Chaplain Klingenschmitt's career, partly because Klingenschmitt advocated to feed and accommodate a hungry Jewish Sailor," U7, www.persuade.tv, accessed July 25, 2007.

Associated Press, "Federal lawsuits accuse Navy of religious discrimination" http://www .freedomforum.org; AP,

Bergel, Gary. "Banning Prayer in Public Schools Has Led to America's Demise" http: //www.forerunner.com/forerunner/X0098_Ban_on_school_prayer.html, accessed March 25, 2009.

Booker, Lewis T. "Ruling on the Lawfulness of the Order," *United States v. LT Gordon J. Klingenschmitt, CHC, USNR*, Department of the Navy, 31 August 2006, www .persuade.tv, accessed July 25, 2007.

"Chaplain who prayed 'in Jesus' name' convicted" http://WorldNet Daily.com posted September 13, 2006.

Folger, Janet "When grandmas go to jail for witnessing" at http://www.worldnetdaily.com /news/article.asp?ARTICLE_ID=54125; accessed 10 March 2008.

Hamilton, Marci "A Religious Bias Suit by Evangelical Chaplains Against the Navy: The Law Confronts Denominational Diversity" at http://writ.news.findlaw.com /hamilton/20020829.html

http://chaplainreform.com/ChiefsofChaplains.htm, accessed February 18, 2008

http://chaplainreform.com/WhatHappened.htm, accessed February 18, 2008.

http://www.marblechurch.org/Programs/GayLesbian/tabid/95/Default.aspx.

Klingenschmitt, Gordon James. "Hindu chaplain prayers, Christian chaplain told 'go away'" WorldNetDaily, Monday, July 16, 2007, www.worldnetdaily.com/news/article. asp?ARTICLE_ID=56688, accessed January 25, 2008.

———. "Letter from G.J. Klingenschmitt to Commanding Officer, Naval Station Norfolk, 3 Apr 06," www.persuade.tv, accessed July 25, 2007.

Leaming, Jeremy. "Chaplains sue Navy, claiming religious-liberty violations," (04.20.2000), http://www.freedomforum.org

"Navy religious-discrimination lawsuits given class-action status," http://www .freedomforum.org

"Navy surrenders: Chaplain eating: Hunger strike comes to end with OK to pray in uniform in name of Jesus" http://www.WorldNetDaily.com

Ruehe, F. R. "Punitive Letter of Reprimand" from Commander, Navy Region, Mid-Atlantic, To: LT Gordon Klingenschmitt, USN, -0240, dated 3 Jan 07, www.persuade. tv., accessed July 25, 2007.

Stafford, J. M. "Memorandum for Chief of Naval Personnel, RE: Request for Special Selection Board ICO LCDR S.M. Aufderheide, CHC, USN," dated 23 December 1997, accessed via link at http://chaplainreform.com/Promotions.htm, on May 2, 2009.

"Swedish Pastor Sentenced to Month in Prison for Preaching Against Homosexuality" at http://www.lifesitenews.com/ldn/2004/jul/04070505.html; accessed 10 March 2008

United States Army Chaplain Center and School, *History of Chaplaincy,* "Chapter 3: "The Civil War, 1861–1865" www.usachcs.army.mil/history'brief'chapter_3.htm. accessed 23 December 2008.

www.ceremonialdeism.com

www.ceremonialdeists.com

www.secular.org/issues/militar/?view=summary

LEGAL CASES

Adair v. Johnson

Allegheny County v. Greater Pittsburgh ACLU, 492 US 573, 574 (1989).

Anderson v. Laird, 316 F. Supp. 1081, 1090,93 (D.D.C. 1970).

Anderson v. Laird, 466 F. 2d 283 151 U.S. App.D.C. 112 (1972).

Earley v. DiCenso; and *Commissioner of Education of Rhode Island v. DiCenso.*

Elk Grove Unified School District et al v. Newdow et al, 542 U.S. 1, 85 (2003).

Engel v Vitale, 370 U.S. 421, 429 (1962)

Goldman v. Weinberger, 475 U.S. 503, 507 (1986).

Katcoff v. Marsh, 755 F.2d

Larsen v. United States Navy

Larson v Valente, 456 U.S. 228 (1982).

Lemon v. Kurtzman, 403 U.S. 602, 603 (1971).

Lynch v. Donnelly, 465 US 668, 680 (1984).

Marsh v Chambers, 463 US 783, 790 (1983).

Rigdon v. Perry, 962 F. Supp. 150 (D.D.C. 1997).

Santa Fe Independent School District v Doe, 530 U.S. 290 (2000)

Veitch v. England (formerly *Veitch v. Danzig*)

Widmar v. Vincent, 454 U.S. 263 (1981)

GOVERNMENT DOCUMENTS/PUBLICATIONS

Air Force Instruction (AFI) 36–2903. *Dress and Personal Appearance of Air Force Personnel.* 2 August 2006.

Air Force Regulation (AFR) 35–10. Wear and Appearance of the Air Force Uniform. (1980).

Army Regulation (AR) 165–1. *Chaplain Activities in the United States Army.* March 2004.

Department of the Army Pamphlet (DA-PAM) 600–75. *Accommodation of Religious Practices.* January 1986.

Department of Defense Directive (DoDD) 1300.17. *Accommodation of Religious Practices Within the Military Services.* 3 February 1988

Department of Defense Instruction (DoDI) 1334.01. October 2005.

FM (Field Manual) 1–05. *Religious Support.* April 2003.

FM (Field Manual) 2–0. *Intelligence.* May 2004.

FM (Field Manual) 3–07.31. *Peace Operations.* October 2003.
Navy Regulations, NAVPERS 15665I, Chapter One, "General Uniform Regulations" Section 4, "Laws, Directives, U.S. NAVY Regulations Pertaining to Uniforms" 1401.3.b (4) (a).
U. S. Constitution, Amendment I.

AUDIO LECTURES

Robinson, Daniel "Lecture 1: Defining the Subject" and "Lecture 2: Ancient Foundations: Greek Philosophers and Physicians" in *The Great Ideas of Psychology* audio lectures, Chantilly, VA: Teaching Company.

UNPUBLISHED PAPERS

Carver, Douglas "Memorandum: Chief of Chaplains Policy: Chaplains as Non-Combatants" 22 April 2008.
Mitchell, Jeffrey T. "It Is Neither New Nor News" unpublished paper (2002), available from the International Critical Incident Stress Foundation, Ellicott City, MD 21042; www.icisf.org.